THE BIG VOTE

Reconfiguring American Political History

Ronald P. Formisano, Paul Bourke, Donald DeBats,
and
Paula M. Baker, Series Founders

THE BIG VOTE

Gender, Consumer Culture, and the Politics of Exclusion,
1890s–1920s

Liette Gidlow

The Johns Hopkins University Press
Baltimore and London

© 2004 The Johns Hopkins University Press
All rights reserved. Published 2004
Printed in the United States of America on acid-free paper
9 8 7 6 5 4 3 2 1

The Johns Hopkins University Press
2715 North Charles Street
Baltimore, Maryland 21218-4363
www.press.jhu.edu

Library of Congress Cataloging-in-Publication Data

Gidlow, Liette
  The big vote : gender, consumer culture, and the politics of exclusion,
1890s–1920s / Liette Gidlow.
     p.   cm. — (Reconfiguring American political history)
Includes bibliographical references and index.
   ISBN 08018-7864-0 (alk. paper)
   1. Political participation—United States. 2. Voting—United States.
3. Women in politics—United States. I. Title. II. Series.
   JK1764.G43 2004
   324.973′0915—dc22

                                                      2003015033

A catalog record for this book is available from the British Library.

To my partner

CONTENTS

Illustrations follow page 114.

ACKNOWLEDGMENTS

Acknowledgments are a celebration, a celebration of work completed and of the relationships nurtured along the way. I would like to thank the many teachers, colleagues, friends, and family members whose support helped to bring this project to a joyful close.

From our first meeting, Professor Joel Silbey treated me with respect. For his intellectual engagement, his encouragement, his good humor, and his steady attention to his role as chair of my dissertation committee, he has my lasting appreciation.

Mary Beth Norton and Mary Katzenstein each offered important suggestions, criticisms, and support at the dissertation stage and beyond. Though I was not one of his students, Michael Kammen generously funded my first year of graduate study at Cornell with the Newton C. Farr fellowship and welcomed me to his cultural history colloquium. The history department at Cornell generously and consistently funded my work with Mellon fellowships, the Daughters of the American Revolution fellowship, and teaching assistantships. The program at Cornell-in-Washington enabled me to spend a year in the Manuscript Division of the Library of Congress while enjoying the company of pleasant and talented colleagues, especially Linda Johnson and Steve Jackson. The faculty at Ohio State University was the first to offer support for my aspirations. I thank Michael Hogan and James Bartholomew in particular for creating opportunity.

My colleagues in the history department at Bowling Green State University have graciously supported this project in its latter stages. Don

Nieman, Fuji Kawashima, and Peter Way made funds available for research needs and graduate student assistants. All my colleagues made me feel welcome and offered encouragement and advice.

Many institutions generously supported portions of this project. For the Berkshire Conference of Women Historians' Summer Research Fellowship at the Bunting Institute at Harvard University, the Organization of American Historians' Merrill Grant, and grants from the Bentley Historical Library, the Herbert Hoover Presidential Library, the Inter-University Consortium for Political and Social Research at the University of Michigan, the Hagley Museum and Library, the Franklin D. Roosevelt Presidential Library, and the Women's Studies Program at Cornell, I am grateful.

Expert research assistance was provided by the staffs of the libraries and archives mentioned above, as well as those of Olin Library at Cornell; Jerome Library at Bowling Green; the Arthur and Elizabeth Schlesinger Library on the History of Women at the Radcliffe Institutes; the New York Public Library; the American Legion Library in Indianapolis; the Grand Rapids Public Library in Grand Rapids, Michigan; the Alabama Department of Archives and History in Montgomery; the Birmingham, Alabama Public Library; the Savery Library at Talladega College in Talladega, Alabama; the Metropolitan Life Insurance Company Archives; the American Jewish Historical Society at Brandeis University; and the National Archives. Special thanks is due to Gordon Olson, the now-retired city historian of Grand Rapids, who graciously guided an afternoon tour of the city and whose commitment to local history helped build a very fine research collection.

Joel Silbey critiqued the entire manuscript through multiple drafts. Paula Baker's penetrating questions at an early stage helped me reconceptualize the argument much more clearly. Mary Beth Norton and Michael McGerr also offered valuable insights on the manuscript as a whole. To the many others who critiqued portions of the manuscript in its many forms—Leigh Ann Wheeler, Anne Brophy, James Beeby, William Graebner, Eileen McDonagh, the late Robert Wiebe, Lee Quinby, Carol Mason, Ron Formisano, John Shovlin, Clif Hood, Robert Buffington, Eithne Luibheid, Vicki Patraka, and the writing group at Bowling Green's Institute for the Study of Culture and Society—I also express my thanks. Anne Brophy graciously searched out documents for me in the manuscript collections of the Detroit Public Library. Joe Genetin-Pilawa, David Haus, Chizuru Saeki, Erin McKenna, and Sheila Jones provided excellent research assistance. David Hampshire assisted with the illustrations.

The *Journal of American History* has graciously permitted the reprint here of portions of my article, "Delegitimizing Democracy: 'Civic Slackers,' the Cultural Turn, and the Possibilities of Politics," which appeared in the December 2002 issue at pages 922–57.

Martin Schneider expertly copyedited the manuscript. I appreciate the efforts of the staff at the Johns Hopkins University Press, especially Bob Brugger's work acquiring the manuscript, Trevor Lipscombe's editorial oversight, and Melody Herr's administrative expertise. Paula Baker, a series editor for the Press, graciously intervened to keep the project on track.

Friends and family offered insight, encouragement, delightful dinners, and warm hospitality on research trips. My appreciation extends to Marla Crowthers, Ron Gidlow, Jo Anne Gidlow, Leslie Horowitz, Beth Murphy, Joe Murphy, Molly Murphy, Jeanne Mercer Ballard, Paul Beyersdorf, Mike Crane, Leigh Ann Wheeler, Don Nieman, Andy Schocket, Deborah Schocket, Eithne Luibhéid, Cathi Cardwell, Mark Hernandez, Walt Grunden, James Beeby, Judy Sealander, and Jerry Friedman. Getting to know my grandmother, Hazel Gidlow, better was one of the best things about going to graduate school in upstate New York. Even now I'm sure that somehow she knows how much I enjoyed our visits, shopping trips, and adventures in the kitchen. My sisters and I, the "Gidlow girls," still make quite the team. My thanks to Nathalie Gidlow and Dominique Koukol for their ongoing support. Special thanks, too, to Aubrey, David, and Daniel Koukol for helping me remember what's really important. My wonderful parents, Jocelyne Smith and Dick Gidlow, always made me feel like I could.

This book is dedicated to my husband, Adam Sakel, whose intelligence, patience, good company, and good humor have made life even sweeter.

THE BIG VOTE

Introduction
MAKING DOMINANCE

In 1872, *Harper's Weekly,* a middle-class magazine of current events and fiction, celebrated the election season with a line drawing of "Pennsylvania Miners at the Polls" (see fig. 1). Dressed for work, lunch buckets in hand, the miners thronged at the polling place set up for them near the mine shaft, eager to deposit their ballots into the glass globe signaling the party of their choice. The scene celebrated the participation of white working men in the democratic process, and did so despite the labor unrest that wracked Pennsylvania's anthracite fields in these years, including the strike by twenty thousand miners in 1868 and the labor violence of the Irish "Molly Maguires." The election officials dressed to a higher station, but no one seemed to question that these workers belonged at the polls.

Fifty years later, following the victory of woman suffragists and the ratification of the Nineteenth Amendment, middle-class magazines depicted voting very differently. On a 1922 cover of *Collier's Weekly,* another middlebrow magazine of current events and fiction, a man and a woman considered the multiparty Australian ballots before them (see fig. 2). These distinctly upper-middle-class voters dressed well—he in a businessman's respectable coat and hat, she in a fashionable red dress and fox coat. Neither wore a wedding ring, a clear indication that they were not husband and wife. Rather, his age suggested fatherly experience, her youth inexperience, a metaphor, perhaps, for the inexperience of all new women voters in the early years of their enfranchisement. While the woman peeked at the gentleman's ballot, perhaps looking for guidance, the man marked his ballot not for one of the usual parties (also passing up the arm-and-hammer emblem of a workers' party) but for the "Independent League" instead. These voters cast ballots not at the workplace among coworkers or neighbors but in the vacuum of white space, without community or context, seemingly surrounded by nothing at all. In this post-suffrage depiction of civic activity, a woman was present, but the bustling crowds of working men had disappeared. When it came to representing good citizenship in the 1920s, workers, immigrants, and ethnic Americans were out of the picture—literally.

By the 1920s, middle-class and elite whites dominated civic life. As the citizens most likely to turn out at the polls and vote, they certainly dominated the electorate. But more broadly, they dominated the public sphere of discussion and debate. The largest daily newspapers, many popular magazines, and the civic clubs that provided platforms for discussion of the pressing issues of the day routinely, ubiquitously, and sometimes almost exclusively spoke in the voice of middle-class and elite whites. They made the positions of middle-class and elite whites visible; they engaged issues from those perspectives; they assumed those perspectives on the part of readers.

Political cartoons in major daily newspapers, for example, almost always depicted civic exemplars as racially white, ethnically unmarked, and middle- or upper-class in dress, occupation, and demeanor. The restrained and responsible voice of the editorial "we" employed sober respectability to signify middle-class status. Even publications ostensibly geared for multiclass audiences, such as large-circulation daily newspapers, turned to businessmen when they wanted to quote a voice of authority on civic matters. White clubwomen, speaking on issues of education, social welfare, or peace, presented themselves not as representatives of a specific class and race, but rather as disinterested guardians of the public interest.

Certainly a wide range of groups spoke out vigorously on matters of civic concern: African Americans, immigrants, people marked as "ethnic," workers, women, and diverse so-called "others" actively debated and discussed the important issues of the day, often in forums—newspapers, clubs, colleges, taverns—that they created, managed, or owned. But in "the public sphere" in which "mainstream" publications and civic groups dominated the "public" debate, these conversations appeared unmistakably "other"—invisible much of the time to dominant middle-class and elite whites, or, when depicted at all, described as narrow and particular, lacking the qualities of "publicness" and disinterest that the discourse of dominant groups enjoyed. By the 1920s middle-class and elite whites occupied a distinctly privileged place in American civic life: they alone appeared in the public sphere as representative, normative, and able to speak for the whole.

That in the 1920s middle-class and elite whites alone—women now sometimes among them—occupied the heights of civic privilege was remarkable, for in the recent past, the universe of legitimate civic actors differed dramatically. Participation in public discussions and voting by white men of every class and ethnic background had been a hallmark of nineteenth-century politics. For the better part of a hundred years, the practices of formal politics centered around political parties—partisan political cultures and party-centered ways of organizing electoral politics. Parties valued, institutionalized, and indeed insisted that white men with diverse ethnic and class backgrounds participate in public discourse and decision-making. Workers, immigrants, and ethnic Americans participated in partisan debates and rallies and cast ballots with great regularity and fanfare, all sharing in the privileged status that accompanied enfranchisement. In the thirty-one states that permitted alien suffrage, men who were not even citizens shared this privileged status. This was no golden democratic age, for though this regime was highly inclusive by class and ethnicity, for most of the nineteenth century it also was sharply bounded by sex and race and excluded vast numbers of women, African Americans, Native Americans, and Asian immigrants. But how did one system of civic hierarchies give way to another? How did workers, immigrants, and ethnics lose their legitimacy as participants in public discussion and decision-making? How did middle-class and elite whites alone gain it?

This development was all the more remarkable because middle-class and elite whites achieved their position of civic dominance in a new world of nearly universal suffrage, a world in which almost every adult officially enjoyed the status of a legitimate public decision maker. Property requirements for voting had long since been abandoned, and the Fifteenth Amendment in 1870 and the Nineteenth Amendment in 1920 extended the franchise to the two groups most conspicuously excluded from the nineteenth-century electorate. African Americans in the South, disenfranchised by law and violence, at the end of the century possessed this right only on paper, and yet not even disenfranchisement revoked their official status as people entitled to vote, a fact they presented time and again as they struggled for the freedom to put their rights into practice. How, then, did an officially inclusive regime give way in practice to a politics of exclusion?

This study uses an expansive definition of politics to analyze some of the ways in which people who defined themselves as middle class or elite and white worked for and, despite resistance, in meaningful ways achieved, civic dominance in the United States during the early twentieth century. In the 1920s white clubwomen and businessmen succeeded in profoundly remaking the language and organization of politics in ways that gave them a new position of civic privilege over workers and ethnics and reinforced their power over African Americans. They made themselves highly visible in the public sphere of discourse and debate on civic issues and rendered "other" groups invisible. They defined good citizenship as being constituted by their attributes of race, class, and gender and defined poor citizenship as being constituted by the attributes of "others." They defined their own interests as broad and public and those of others as narrow and interested. They redesigned and relocated much of the actual practice of politics from places that welcomed immigrants, ethnics, and workers to places that excluded them along with African Americans and some women. In doing so, they brought to the worlds of politics and civic participation the class stratification that in the nineteenth century had already transformed "walking cities" into class-distinct neighborhoods, workers' "ranks" into classes, and everyman's Shakespeare into "high art." By reshaping public discourse and institutional arrangements, by transforming both the public meanings of citizenship and the organization of political practices, middle-class and elite whites constructed a new civic regime that legitimized, institutionalized, naturalized, and propagated their political participation, their political interests, their civic privilege, their ways of being citizens.

In order to uncover some of the discursive and institutional strategies through which middle-class and elite whites achieved civic dominance, this study examines the "Get-Out-the-Vote" (GOTV) campaigns of the 1920s. At a time when voter turnout in presidential elections had slumped to forty-nine percent—the first time in nearly a century in which a majority of eligible voters failed to cast ballots—an impressive array of community leaders, including clubwomen, businessmen, veterans, ministers, publishers, and others, most of them native born, middle class or upper class, and white, launched extensive advertising and civic education campaigns to reverse that trend and "Make This the Year of the Big Vote."[1] The League of Women Voters inaugurated the GOTV campaigns in 1923; by 1928, more than a thousand groups had joined in with similar campaigns of their own. Among the long list of participants, five groups stood out for their extraordinary commitment of resources: the League of Women Voters (the LWV or "the League"); the National Association of Manufacturers (the NAM), a business lobbying group; the National Civic Federation (the NCF or "the Federation"), the progressive-era organization that worked to build better relations among labor, management, and government; the American Legion, the organization of World War I veterans; and *Collier's Weekly*.

The GOTV campaigns operated on a grand scale and embraced tactics ranging from the sober to the spectacular. The NAM distributed twenty-five million leaflets urging citizens to vote. The Boy Scouts canvassed door to door and bugled on street corners, an effort that Chief Scout Executive James West described as the group's "biggest national undertaking" since its wartime sale of Liberty Bonds. The American Legion coordinated "hundreds" of "community conferences" in cities from Daytona Beach to San Francisco. The Metropolitan Life Insurance Company took out full-page ads in the *Saturday Evening Post* and other popular periodicals. The League in 1928 began to broadcast the "Voters' Campaign Information Service" on the fledgling National Broadcasting Company (NBC) network. GOTV activists generated countless seminars, workshops, badges, and billboard ads. The campaigns took place in forty-seven out of the forty-eight states and boasted among their backers such luminaries as Eleanor Roosevelt, Samuel Gompers, General John J. Pershing, Carrie Chapman Catt, Elihu Root, and every major presidential candidate in 1924 and 1928. Though the GOTV campaigns have largely been overlooked by scholars since, they were an important feature of the contemporary political scene.[2]

The GOTV campaigns took shape at a historical moment when the meanings of citizenship were very much in flux. Enfranchisement had long served as one of the most important markers of civic hierarchy by drawing a sharp line between those who were recognized as legitimate decision makers in the public sphere and those who were not. The passage of the Nineteenth Amendment in 1920 was critical not only because it enfranchised women but because, for the first time, it established practically universal suffrage. Although in practice many people, especially African Americans in the South, still could not exercise their right to vote, the arrival of universal suffrage, even if only on paper, posed an enormous problem for privileged groups. If nearly all people were now formally eligible to vote, did that mean that all people had become civic equals? If the marker for civic hierarchy had disappeared, did civic hierarchy itself disappear as well?

Indeed, in the 1920s battles over civic hierarchies raged on many fronts. The Nineteenth Amendment not only upset civic relationships between the sexes, but also threatened to undermine established civic hierarchies of whites over blacks. Many African American women in the South, especially churchwomen and clubwomen, had worked hard for woman suffrage; when the amendment was ratified, they insisted that it included them. Nervous whites feared that the enfranchisement of southern African American women might open the door to "Negro rule." When after ratification African American women apparently set out in significant numbers to register and vote, it became clear that they intended to use their ballots not only to advance their communities' interests but also to try to reclaim suffrage for African American men.

On other fronts, law enforcement officials during the Red Scare arrested workers and deported immigrants in part on the argument that radicals were not or could not become good Americans. The national origins legislation of 1921 and 1924 strictly limited the number of new immigrants and assured that most newcomers would be "white" northern and western Europeans who could assimilate with ease. Support for eugenics became respectable, offering another solution to the seeming eclipse of middle-class and elite whites by foreign, poor, black, or otherwise "unworthy" residents. Postwar "Americanization" campaigns by churches, service clubs, and businesses tried to mold immigrants into proper citizens, while the resurgent Ku Klux Klan cloaked campaigns of harassment and violence against African Americans, Catholics, and Jews in patriotic and Christian rhetoric. Organized business promoted the open shop and the "American plan" to roll back the gains made by organized labor during the war. In the workplace, in civil society, at the border, and in law, people contended—sometimes violently—over the meanings and boundaries of good citizenship.

In short, in the 1920s, civic hierarchies were anything but settled. In the GOTV campaigns, these issues came to the fore. GOTV activists worried not only about voter turnout but also more broadly about who could be a good citizen and what good citizenship meant. The GOTV campaigns served as one of the key sites through which middle-class and elite whites worked in the 1920s to resolve dilemmas of democracy and difference. They reveal a great deal about how these groups remade the language and organization of politics and established for themselves a new position of civic dominance.

Though the GOTV campaigns have received very little attention to date, rich studies of late nineteenth- and early twentieth-century politics and culture have shed light on the people, organizations, and movements connected to the campaigns and the contexts in which they worked to secure for themselves a place of civic privilege.[3] The story of the making of middle-class and elite white civic dominance is situated at the nexus of three complementary historical narratives: the decline of party politics, the changing meanings of citizenship in the progressive period and in the wake of universal suffrage, and the rise of a consumer society.

GOTV groups worked in the context of a world of weakened political parties. Parties, the institutions that organized political participation by white men of every class and ethnic background, deteriorated significantly after the realignment of the 1890s. The "party period" was replaced by a new regime, the "fourth party system" of the 1890s through the 1920s, in which party organizations outside urban machines deteriorated, class became a more important predictor of voting behavior, party-line voting declined and independent voting rose, African Americans in the South became disenfranchised, workers and ethnics everywhere saw their political participation curbed by new literacy tests and other hurdles to voting, and voter turnout dropped sharply. How, then, was political participation organized in the vacuum left by decaying parties? Whose political participation did the new regime organize and encourage?[4]

Part of the answer lies in the growth of bureaucracies and interest group politics in this period, and yet neither of these factors explains how workers and ethnics lost their claim to civic legitimacy and how middle-class and elite whites alone gained it. Even if bureaucracies took on many of the policymaking and administrative functions once performed by the parties; even if more citizens formed "people's lobbies" and turned to interest groups rather than the ballot box to get things done; even if newly enfranchised women found that voting lacked "leverage" and failed to produce the policy changes they sought, nonetheless voting remained a crucial part of the political system. Voting was much more than an empty ritual; it was also a symbol, perhaps *the* symbol, of legitimacy and inclusion in the civic world, "a certificate of full membership in society." Whatever the limits in this period on voting as a tool for policymaking or political expression, when it came to the matter of a citizen's legitimacy and civic standing, the right to vote remained supremely important.[5]

The advent of nearly universal suffrage helped to create a crisis of meaning for ideas about citizenship. The Nineteenth Amendment has long been recognized as important because it enfranchised women. It was also very important because it introduced in the United States a new era of near-universal suffrage. The distribution of the rights and obligations of citizenship had always demarcated the civic status of various groups along the lines of racial, ethnic, class, and gender difference. Now, if nearly everyone could vote, did that mean that everyone enjoyed equal status as citizens? The fact of widespread nonvoting in the 1920s complicated the matter further still. For the better part of a hundred years, casting a ballot had been the most basic civic duty and a clear requirement for good citizenship. If now *most* citizens did not vote, then what did it mean to be a good citizen? If citizenship was not necessarily about voting, then what was it about, and how could good citizens be differentiated from bad? The GOTV campaigns served as a key site through which middle-class and elite whites worked to recode the meanings and markers of good citizenship. GOTV groups identified civic legitimacy with whiteness and middle-class or elite status, gendered it in specific ways, and equated these attributes with expertise. "Expert citizenship" became the new gold standard of civic virtue, propagated by middle-class and elite whites in and beyond the GOTV campaigns through their dominance of the public sphere of discussion and debate.

Finally, the rise of consumer culture played an important part in the making of middle-class and elite civic dominance. Consumer culture—an array of diverse cultures of consumption in which goods gave "meaning to individuals and their roles in society"—was a central fact of early twentieth-century life. Especially after World War I, the range of goods available to consumers—appliances, automobiles, radios, and more—multiplied dramatically, cheaper production and distribution techniques and rising wages made them accessible to a broader segment of society, and the new "Madison Avenue" employed more sophisticated, "modern" advertising techniques to sell them. In the 1920s, consumer culture reached a new level of maturity.[6]

The GOTV campaigns put the centrality of consumer culture on display. The campaigns made lavish use of spaces, language, and products associated with consumer culture. GOTV activists placed ads in leisure magazines such as the *Saturday Evening Post*. They set up voter registration tables at department stores—in New York, at Bloomingdale's and Lord and Taylor, but also at department stores in Atlanta, Indianapolis, West Virginia, and beyond. They screened trailers at movie theaters, some 220 theaters in Chicago, but also theaters in South Carolina, Missouri, Michigan, and elsewhere. They handed GOTV fliers to customers at banks and beauty salons; insurance salesmen even handed them out in door-to-door house calls. In a wide range of ways, GOTV groups connected the vote message to consumption, political culture to consumer culture.[7]

The connections between political culture and consumer culture, however, extended far beyond the GOTV campaigns. Indeed, in the late nineteenth and early twentieth centuries, political practices broadly began to reflect the rise of a consumer society. When political candidates began to hire public relations professionals to promote their campaigns, when movie theaters began to announce election results between features, when leisure magazines tried to administer programs to end political corruption, when newspapers began to recount political tales in a tabloid style, politics and consumer culture became profoundly intertwined, much more so than scholars to this point have found. Not only did consumer culture sometimes connect people across ethnic and racial lines and give them a basis of shared experience which they used to push together for political change. Not only, in the alternative, did the satisfactions of consumption depoliticize the masses by distracting them with baubles or anaesthetizing them with private satisfactions. Consumer culture also transformed the very places, techniques, language, and rituals with which, and through which, politics was conducted.

This transformation, this "commodification of political culture," extended far beyond the emergence of an "advertised style" of politics.[8] Rather, it constituted a shift in political regimes, a shift away from political parties and toward consumer culture as the basis for organizing and conducting politics. This shift helped to make middle-class and elite whites dominant in civic life, for it relocated political practices from institutions in which workers and ethnics exercised considerable influence to ones in which middle-class and elite whites exerted greater power.

The GOTV campaigns offer an opportunity to rethink, in the context of familiar historical narratives, the connections between political culture, the public sphere, civic dominance, and markers of difference such as gender, class, race, and ethnicity. Here political culture means the language, symbols, values, practices, and institutions that link individuals and communities to a political system and make politics meaningful. From this perspective, power relations are expressed and constituted in many ways—in, for example, political practices and behaviors that enact ideologies; in institutional arrangements that encourage or discourage particular civic values and behaviors; and in discursive politics or "the politics of meaning-making," the effort to "reinterpret, reformulate, rethink, and rewrite the norms and practices of society and the state."[9] The connections and interplay among these ways of exercising power reveal a great deal about how dominance has been organized, articulated, deployed, resisted, negotiated, institutionalized, legitimized, and naturalized.

In this analysis "the public sphere" means a forum for discussing and debating civic matters, a discursive realm as well as the institutions that support it, "a theater for debating and deliberating." Here "*the* public sphere" is comprised of a "multiplicity of publics" that institutionalize and contest power disparities in a society stratified by race, class, ethnicity, and gender. Powerful groups constitute "*a* public" whose views frequently prevail; less powerful groups contest those views, often in "counterpublics" of their own.[10]

In the GOTV campaigns, clubwomen and businessmen who were middle class or elite and white comprised a powerful "public," while less powerful groups—in this case some African Americans, workers, ethnics, and women—contested those views, frequently in "counterpublics" of their own making. In this contest over the meanings of citizenship in the 1920s, the middle-class and elite whites clearly "won," dominating the "mainstream" media of the day and achieving a monopoly of "the realm of appearances." Middle-class and elite whites used their dominance of the public sphere to recode the markers of good citizenship, to broadcast and institutionalize those definitions, and to present themselves as normative and ideal. They constituted, publicized, and naturalized their power in part by commandeering the "public" sphere of discussion and debate, by deploying power in the name of "the public."[11]

The GOTV campaigns point out the pressing need to problematize "public-ness." In this case, "the public sphere" was not very public at all. It was neither widely accessible, nor widely representative, nor broadly inclusive, nor broadly beneficial. In the GOTV campaigns, "the public sphere" served as an arena in which one group wielded power to include some people in civic conversations and the process of decision-making and to exclude others. Dominant groups signified themselves as "public." Surely "public" can mean something other than "dominant" or "exclusive," and surely the meanings of the term have changed over time.

The GOTV campaigns, however, expose the complexity of the term and show how it is saturated with power.

Here civic dominance means the power to frame the terms—the definitions, norms, rules, organization, and parameters—of public debate and political practices. Dominance means being the point of reference, the center, the point around which others organize. Dominance means the latitude to effectively describe oneself as the norm rather than be relegated to mere "group" status. Dominance means being able to stake a credible claim to being public, to stand in for the rest, to be widely representative or broadly beneficial, rather than unrepresentative, particular, or interested. Dominance means having the power to preempt and undercut opposition by achieving the appearance that a matter is settled when it is actually still being deliberated and contested.

Dominance does not mean that there was no opposition, nor that any one group's dominance was permanent. On the contrary, in the 1920s less powerful groups worked vigorously to negotiate, resist, or remake the civic values propagated by middle-class and elite whites. Because the main focus of this study is the GOTV campaigns, this analysis only begins to consider the many ways that less powerful groups formulated ideas about citizenship, created alternative political practices and institutions, and worked to assert their civic legitimacy and create a more inclusive civic regime. Even so, evidence of their resistance is everywhere. It is evident in discussions in "counterpublics" of their own making—in labor newspapers that insisted upon the continuing value of production, not just consumption, for good citizenship; in the churches and clubs through which newly enfranchised African American women in the South asserted their inclusion in the civic order and worked to restore the suffrage rights of black men; and in the loyalty of urban workers, immigrants, and ethnic Americans to the political parties that welcomed their political participation.

Often this resistance took the form of activities well outside the bounds of formal politics. Weaker groups have long contested power relations with a wide range of "weapons" such as crowd actions, foot-dragging, slander, or a popular culture of resistance. No doubt in this period there were many ways of being citizens, many cultures of consumption, many cultures of politics, many ways of deploying power, and many arenas outside the realm of formal politics for resistance and negotiation. We need to know much more about the ways that diverse groups challenged the new civic regime and promoted their interests, shaped the terms of debate, redefined the public sphere, and embraced paths to power beyond electoral politics and the public debate of issues. That power, exercised in other arenas or in other ways, did not, however, negate the importance of their marginalization in discussions of public issues or their compromised status as public decision makers. By losing on this turf, they lost an important way of making their voices heard on issues that deeply affected their daily lives; they saw their civic equality undermined, despite their "official" status as equal voters; and they saw others discredit their legitimacy as public decision makers.

Within and beyond the GOTV campaigns, many political discourses and practices were organized along lines of class, gender, ethnic, and racial difference. Demographic attributes functioned not as independent variables but rather as a complex and shifting matrix of identities in which each helped to constitute and define the others. The GOTV campaigns show that the old arrangement of civic hierarchies that used enfranchisement to signify the privileged civic status of white men had become obsolete in the face of the new enfranchisement of African Americans and women and the changing meanings and markers of class, ethnicity, gender, and race. Civic hierarchies were reordered and civic privilege remade and by the time they were done, a multiclass, multiethnic political world gave way to one in which civic affairs were closely identified with middle-class whites.

This analysis proceeds at two levels, the national and the local. It broadly surveys the GOTV efforts and then closely examines the efforts of the leading organizations. Rather than catalog every GOTV meeting, leaflet, advertisement, and seminar—an impossible task, given the size of the campaigns—this approach identifies the campaigns' scope and scale, demonstrates their considerable reach and influence, and identifies broad patterns and unifying themes.

The study then considers how the GOTV campaigns played out in the context of local political institutions, cultures, and practices. Three cities serve as case studies for the GOTV campaigns: New York City, with its powerful political machine and ethnic politics; Grand Rapids, Michigan, a midwestern manufacturing city with a two-party system and pockets of ethnic and racial diversity; and Birmingham, Alabama, a city in the one-party Democratic "Solid South" where access to the ballot was sharply restricted, especially by race.

At both the national and local levels, records of groups and individuals, including minutes, newsletters, and correspondence, along with the records and correspondence of political parties, establish who participated in the GOTV campaigns and the actions they took. Large-circulation and influential newspapers and magazines also provide evidence of the presence of and reaction to the GOTV campaigns. Additional resources in the case-study cities such as daily and weekly newspapers and the records, correspondence, and publications of unions, clubs, and churches that served communities of workers, African Americans, and immigrant and ethnic Americans help to pinpoint the identity of local participants and provide rich descriptions of their work. Sometimes the absence of evidence in these sources proves as meaningful as its presence elsewhere, for it helps to mark the boundaries and limits of the GOTV campaigns.

In each instance, reception proved a complicated issue. How many people encountered the GOTV campaigns through advertisements, handbills, and seminars? What did they think when they viewed a GOTV slide at a movie theater, scanned an ad in a newspaper, or heard a Boy Scout bugling? Of course it is impossible to know; direct evidence of the reception of the campaigns is rare. In its place, careful attention to the particulars of how the GOTV message was delivered sheds light on what GOTV activists intended and what the people they encountered might have thought. What did it mean, for example, when League ladies set up voter registration tables just inside the main customer entrances at department stores and not in the shopgirls' break rooms? What did it mean when the GOTV campaigns placed their target audiences—movie patrons, magazine readers, insurance customers—in the roles of citizens and consumers at one and the same time?

Turnout numbers serve as a concrete test of the reception of the GOTV campaigns. By this measure, the accomplishments of the GOTV campaigns appear unimpressive indeed: national voter turnout actually dropped slightly in 1924, and increased somewhat in 1928 for reasons that campaign organizers freely admitted had nothing to do with GOTV. Nor did the campaigns fare better in the case-study cities, where turnout remained for the most part unchanged. Only with the New Deal realignment of the 1930s, years after the GOTV campaigns had ended, did voter turnout increase in a substantial and sustained way. GOTV organizers tried to put the best face on the disappointing results—surely, the NAM claimed, the campaigns had "checked the growing apathy of the people in their national elections"—but they could not hide the fact that the campaigns were a flop.[12]

The failure of the GOTV campaigns to boost voter turnout, however, does not make them unimportant. The scale and urgency of the campaigns makes clear that much more was at stake than the size of the active electorate. The GOTV activists worked to accomplish nothing less than a change in the public meanings of enfranchisement and voting and a broad reorganization of the practice of politics to their advantage. On these counts the campaigns were far more successful. In the GOTV campaigns middle-class and elite whites succeeded in making themselves visible, and workers, minorities, and ethnics invisible, in representations of good citizenship in the public sphere. They succeeded in defining their own ways of being citizens as normative and ideal, and used claims of publicness to mask the way that this set of values privileged them and disadvantaged others. Ultimately they succeeded, in the GOTV campaigns and beyond them, in reorganizing many of the practices of politics around aspects of a culture of consumption in which they enjoyed a privileged place.

A few clarifications and caveats are in order. My frequent recourse to the shorthand of "middle-class or elite and white" to refer to members of these diverse groups reflects my effort to un-naturalize their status as normative citizens. Their experiences and interests were not universal but were instead specific to their class and race, and I have labelled them as such to help dispel one of the myths that shrouded their exercise of power.

Next, how can one know what was GOTV work and what was not? Urban machines, interest groups, churches, women's groups, organized labor, and other groups had long worked to turn out voters to elect favored candidates or to pass referenda on reforms ranging from prohibition to charter reform. The GOTV campaigns, by contrast, were characterized by their nonpartisanship and their refusal to promote specific electoral outcomes. At no point did these activists use GOTV work to campaign for any candidate or referendum: they framed their purpose, vaguely but sincerely, only as working to "improve democracy." That they refrained from working to turn out voters for specific candidates or causes does not mean that they believed that GOTV lacked political consequences, but their efforts should not be confused with campaigns to pass suffrage referenda or elect labor-friendly political candidates.

Strict criteria makes it possible to distinguish GOTV activity from other efforts to turn out voters. Examples of GOTV activity analyzed here include only the following: efforts by individuals or groups that explicitly self-identified their work as part of these campaigns; nonpartisan activities promoting voting participation rather than a particular candidate or policy goal by groups that belonged to a national, regional, state, or local organization that had passed a formal resolution in support of GOTV; and efforts that used specific slogans or graphics (such as the tricolor "Vote as you please, but VOTE!" emblem created by the NAM) that were produced by and for the GOTV campaigns. Many ambiguous examples were thus excluded from this study, meaning that the size and scope of the campaigns is estimated conservatively here.

This account of the making of middle-class and elite white civic dominance is also necessarily incomplete. Certainly, many factors contributed to their rise in civic affairs well before the GOTV campaigns came along. Certainly, too, resistance by excluded groups in formal politics, the workplace, the home, the marketplace, and popular culture helped to shape the new regime. This analysis does not trace out the full process of the changes it identifies; rather, it describes their parameters, the "before" of the late nineteenth century and the "after" of the 1920s, and suggests some reasons why they developed as they did. The GOTV campaigns did not singlehandedly invent expert citizenship, consumer citizenship, or the commodification of political culture, but neither did they stand apart from these changes. The GOTV campaigns resulted from these changes, contributed to them, and propagated them further.

Finally, the text is meant to be read in the context of the illustrations. Readers are urged to consult the gallery in the center of the book while reading.

Despite challenges by many different groups, in the early twentieth century middle-class and elite whites in the United States achieved a new position of privilege in civic life. At a time when the meanings and hierarchies of citizenship were fluid and deeply contested, the GOTV activists succeeded in making their political culture "the" political culture by dominating discussions of citizenship in the public sphere, by framing the debate in ways that identified civic virtue with themselves, and by moving political practices to quarters in which they exerted more influence. Did everyone come to see citizenship as they did? No—their values were contested at every turn. Was their status permanent? No—when the Great Depression of the 1930s once again threw civic hierarchies into flux, workers and ethnics regained a considerable measure of legitimacy and power. But did middle-class and elite whites dominate on these issues during this period? Very much so. The workings of the GOTV campaigns reveal some of the ways in which they acquired and wielded their power.

"CIVIC SLACKERS" AND "POLL DODGERS"

Nonvoting and the Construction of Discursive Dominance

"Poo-pooh! *I* never vote!" the man sniffed, lazily re-
clining on pillows, casually puffing a cigar (see fig. 3).
He might look like an upstanding citizen—middle-
aged, upper class, clothed in a smoking jacket and
banker's pinstripes, the very picture of masculine
respectability—but in the wake of a Great War to
"make the world safe for democracy," postwar labor
unrest, race riots, and the Red Scare, this man's civic
apathy made him, in the artist's phrase, "the most
dangerous man in America."

In the cartoons, newspapers, middlebrow magazines, and club meetings that served as platforms in
the 1920s for the discussion of public issues, middle-
class and elite whites voiced deep concerns about
the problem of low voter turnout. Their fears were
well-founded, for in the 1920s voter turnout slipped
below fifty percent for the first time since the expansion of the franchise to virtually all white men
nearly a century before. All kinds of dangers lurked
when good citizens stayed away from the polls.
Their absence could jeopardize prosperity, undermine good government, embolden radicals. Certainly the low participation rate made a mockery of
the sacrifices the nation had just endured during a
long and bloody war to promote democracy abroad.

Buried in these concerns about nonvoting, however, lay a nagging and more profound problem.
For nearly a hundred years, broad suffrage and faithful voting had been at the crux of the definition of
good citizenship. To those denied the franchise, the
right to cast a ballot had been the most sought-after

1

sign of full membership in the civic community. To the enfranchised, casting that ballot had been axiomatic, the most basic of civic duties. Now, if otherwise good citizens—upstanding, civic-minded, white middle-class and elite clubwomen and businessmen—did not, as one newspaper editor put it, "bestir themselves" to vote, then what exactly did it mean to be a good citizen? How were citizens and governance connected? And how could good citizens be distinguished from bad? By 1924, the failure of Americans to go to the polls had become a pressing public problem, one that threatened the practice of democracy as it had been known for nearly a hundred years and one that raised disturbing questions about the definition of citizenship itself. As civic activists worked to improve turnout in the 1920s, they would help to remake civic relationships between whites and blacks, men and women, natives and newcomers, workers and the middle and upper classes. They would also help to remake the very meanings of citizenship itself.[1]

"Rough Water and Half the Crew Not Working": Nonvoting Becomes a Public Problem

"It is a national disgrace," the *Philadelphia Inquirer* railed in 1924, "that less than 50 per cent of those who were qualified should have voted at the last Presidential election." In the 1920s the failure of Americans to turn out at the polls emerged as an issue of intense public concern. Alarmed at new numbers showing that less than half the eligible electorate cast ballots in the last presidential election, vast numbers of civic leaders—including government officials, clubwomen, veterans, ministers, business elites, newspaper editors, radio commentators, and intellectuals, most of them elite or broadly middle-class and white—deemed the problem of nonvoting an embarrassment to democracy and a threat to good government. This was no time for complacency. With war, recession, radicalism, and race wars a recent memory, amidst ardent campaigns to curb immigration and ensure "100 per cent Americanism" among both immigrants and natives, an apathetic citizenry posed an urgent problem indeed. As Pulitzer Prize–winning cartoonist J. N. "Ding" Darling put it in 1924, it was like being in "rough water and half the crew not working" (see fig. 4).[2]

Criticism of nonvoters in newspaper editorials, magazine articles, political cartoons, and civic group roundtables was profuse; the patriotism, even the Americanness of nonvoters was called into doubt. No one could fail to cast a ballot, Republican party chair Will H. Hays charged, and "at the same time be a 100 per cent American." Critics of nonvoting spared no invective. "Idiots, paupers, vagrants, and the insane" were barred by law from the polls, the editors of a popular middle-class magazine argued, "yet every election . . . witnesses the spectacle of Americans voluntarily and deliberately putting themselves in the same class with criminals, imbeciles, and tramps." Reformers deplored nonvoting, among them woman suffragist Carrie Chapman Catt, who worried that new female voters might forget "the millions of women who lived, labored and died that [women] might have the vote." Scholars weighed in, too. Professor Charles Merriam of the University of Chicago's political science department indicted the nonvoter as "the greatest grafter in America." Arthur Schlesinger and Erik Eriksson likened the trend toward nonparticipation to a devastating "creeping paralysis." Even Robert and Helen Lynd remarked upon it in *Middletown,* their pathbreaking study of Muncie, Indiana, a study which won a popular as well as an academic readership. In the downward trend of voter turnout, they argued, "Middletown's experience parallels that of the country at large."[3]

Americans read about nonvoting, studied it, even tuned their radios to speeches about it. In newspapers, magazines, and pamphlets, Washington lawyer Simon Michelet publicized his finding that almost half of eligible Americans failed to "perform their civic duty as electors." In Wisconsin, Maryland, Georgia, Montana, and California, concerned clubwomen and businessmen investigated the turnout situation in their states. From the studios of WRNY in New York, Eleanor Roosevelt reminded listeners that "patriotism is a question of peace time as well as war time" and that "voting and taking an interest in government is patriotism." Local organizations sponsored radio talks in Dallas, Chicago, Atlanta, and elsewhere on the topic of nonvoting. Nonvoting was the frequent topic of political cartoons as well, sometimes published locally, often distributed broadly through syndication. In one cartoon that received wide play, the wildly popular wartime figure of Uncle Sam interrogated the reader. With his trademark stern look and accusing finger, he asked, "Are You a Vote Slacker?"[4]

In the aftermath of World War I, these "civic slackers" and "poll dodgers" were blamed for a long list of civic ills. The war raised suspicions about the enemy within that continued in the 1920s. The wartime Espionage Act, Sedition Act, immigration restrictions, and "100 percent Americanism" campaigns were transformed, in the postwar period, into the Red Scare, new immigration quotas, and naturalization campaigns. In a climate in which outsiders were seen as dangerous and radicalism still seemed a threat, conservatives believed that apathy at the polls was downright dangerous. "If the non-voting citizen . . . does not re-assert his rights, he is going to find his Government some day nothing more than a soviet of organized selfishness," railed the American Legion. Asked to comment on the problem of nonvoting, NAM member and corporate president Frank Disston conveyed the opinion of many: "Enemies of American institutions and American prosperity are at work. Friends of American institutions and American prosperity cannot afford to sleep."[5]

Nonvoting also seemed to threaten the booming prosperity of the twenties. After the postwar recession, the country enjoyed unprecedented economic expansion. The gross national product swelled from $38 billion before the war to $85 billion by mid-decade. As the consumer culture that had been emerging unevenly since the 1880s matured, consumers of every class enjoyed a more abundant and inexpensive range of consumer innovations—automobiles, installment purchases, home appliances, radios, and "talkies"—despite the uncertainties of employment that plagued workers. Businessmen argued that prosperity would continue only if taxes remained low and regulation remained lax, policies that businessmen's votes were needed to ensure. As Coleman du Pont, soon to be a senator from Delaware, put it, "the man who thinks so little of his country . . . [and] its continued prosperity . . . that he forsakes his civic duties by failing to vote . . . is as big a slacker as the boy who refused to shoulder a musket during the war."[6]

Progressives joined conservatives in worrying about the ills posed by civic apathy. The war shattered the shifting coalition of progressive reformers that had busted trusts, curbed political corruption, Taylorized production processes, and built bureaucracies. Some elements of the coalition, however, regrouped after the war to fight again. Newly enfranchised women worked to ban child labor, preserve international peace, and care for mothers and infants. Senator George Norris pushed for public control of electric power at Muscle Shoals, Alabama. Political corruption inspired fresh outrage when Teapot Dome and the rest of the Harding-era scandals came to light. Reformers knew that past gains could be preserved and good government assured only by voters' continued vigilance. One political cartoonist framed the issue in the terms of Jonathan Swift's *Gulliver's Travels*. "If Only Gulliver Would Wake Up!" the artist lamented, as Gulliver ("The Citizen Who Don't Vote") slept while Lilliputians "Graft" and "Boss" picked his pockets.[7]

If progressives were troubled by nonvoting, progressive women had special reason for concern. Seventy years of agitation had finally won in

1920 the ratification of a constitutional amendment to enfranchise women. Reformers had promised big improvements should women receive the vote—a thorough "housecleaning" to sweep away political corruption and a new and bigger wave of reform. With the Nineteenth Amendment in place, suffragists were acutely aware that they were being tested. The early returns were an enormous disappointment and the criticism came swiftly. "Whether [women] like it or not, the suffrage is theirs, and they cannot refuse to vote without shirking the obligation of an enfranchised citizen," accused a New York paper. The American Legion posed the troubling question, "Are Our Women Slacking?" The reformers worried desperately that woman suffrage would be labeled a failure. As one supporter in Minneapolis pleaded, "What, oh what, is Suffrage if you women will not vote?"[8]

Whatever their politics, concerned citizens agreed that nonvoting was dangerous for democracy. In a political cartoon in a Seattle paper, the ever-vigilant figure of Columbia warned that "the Nation is in Peril! Not from a Foreign foe, in arms, but from Neglect of Duty by American Citizens." The *Wilmington News* argued that low turnout showed "a lack of concern in [sic] civic duties and neglect of them" and could shake "the very foundation of a republic." League leader Maud Wood Park captured this urgency: "Our country is seriously imperilled [sic] by . . . the apathy of enfranchised men and women, and the danger that threatens is greater than the menace of any armed enemy. . . . Our country is too large, too varied, too rich, ever to be conquered, but it can be wrecked from within. It can cease to possess a democratic government . . . and become an autocracy ruled by the vicious or stupid few, and every man or woman who fails to vote this year contributes all that is in his power to such an overthrow of the institutions our forefathers left to us."[9]

By 1924, the failure of Americans to go to the polls had emerged as a pressing public problem indeed.

"The Descending Curve of American Democracy": The Historic Decline in Voter Turnout

It had not always been this way. Even in the relatively recent past, voters had turned out at the polls at much higher rates. Much of the credit for higher participation through the late nineteenth century belonged to political parties, organizations that connected ordinary people to governance and helped to make politics meaningful to them. When in the late 1890s parties began to decay under the stresses and strains of realignment and

reform, voter participation also began to decline, a trend that one popular magazine labeled "the descending curve of American democracy."
By the 1920s, turnout had reached its lowest level in almost a hundred
years.[10]

Through most of the nineteenth century, a broad franchise underpinned high turnouts. By the late 1820s, most states had repealed property requirements; many also loosened residency requirements, and then
found even these relaxed requirements difficult to enforce. At midcentury, in the thirty-one states with alien suffrage, even noncitizen aliens,
such as "declarants," men who had taken out first papers and announced
their intent to naturalize, cast ballots alongside native-born white men.
The result was that for most of the nineteenth century, white men of
every class and ethnic background, including many noncitizens, were
eligible to cast votes. Highly inclusive by class and ethnicity, this regime
was sharply bounded by sex and race, excluding for most of the nineteenth century women and people of color. Enfranchisement for most of
the nineteenth century coincided neatly with whiteness and maleness.[11]

Political parties mobilized this broad pool of eligibles to produce extraordinary turnouts. For the better part of the nineteenth century, in the
"party period" from the 1830s through the 1890s, political parties provided both a structure and a culture that promoted broad voter participation. Parties supplied the nuts-and-bolts organization to mobilize voters and imbued voting with importance.[12]

Party structures supported participation in a variety of ways. By the
late 1830s, political parties had knit together a comprehensive network
of national, state, county, and local organizations that penetrated even
the smallest communities. In this way parties reached people where they
lived. Party officials provided a personal touch. Every community had
its precinct captains who solicited the votes of supporters, checked to
see that they went to the polls, and rewarded loyal voting. The regular
rhythms of the election cycle kept these organizations well-oiled; since
elections in the nineteenth century took place much more frequently
than today, the next campaign was always just around the corner. Intense competition enhanced turnout further still. Before and after the
Civil War, the strength of the parties nationally was closely matched,
and tight races both stimulated interest by voters and pushed party
chieftains to achieve the fullest possible vote. Thus Whigs and Democrats before the Civil War and Republicans and Democrats after it
brought politics home to the people they served. They counted on nuts-
and-bolts organization, not mere exhortation, to get people to the polls.[13]

Parties were also at the center of a partisan political culture that made voting meaningful to ordinary people. In the party period, partisan identity was important. Party loyalties were strong, treasured in families and passed on to future generations. From Irish Catholic Democrats to rockribbed Republicans descended from the Puritans, partisan identities were intertwined with ethnic and religious identities. The institutions that supported ethnic and religious identities—churches, lodges, schools, even marriages—did double duty and reinforced party loyalties as well.[14]

The public location of party festivities enhanced participation further still. In the party period, campaigns were public affairs. On city streets, at courthouse squares, in open fields outside town, party supporters gathered to celebrate and cheer. Ever since the vigorous "Log Cabin" campaign of William Henry Harrison in 1840, political campaigns had bustled with pageantry, drama, and spectacle. Political clubs entertained onlookers with minstrel shows, brass bands, oratory, and oddities such as the "Whig Ball," a sphere thirteen feet in diameter made of poplar boards and muslin that drew enormous crowds in Ohio, Massachusetts, South Carolina, and Georgia as it was rolled from rally to rally. After the Civil War, uniformed companies of partisans marched through the streets in a military fashion, lighting the way with torches and raising banners to the sky. Sometimes rallies and processions were so large that attendance was measured in acres rather than by a head count. Surely the line between voters and nonvoters was sharp, and yet even some who were excluded from the suffrage had a role to play. Women attended rallies and were courted for the "moral standing" they could confer on a particular party. Young men joined marching companies long before they were old enough to vote.[15]

Party leaders and candidates could be counted on to attend these events. No party could claim to be "the People's choice" without "going down to the People" in ceremonies that ratified the party's platform and candidates. Their presence was crucial, for it made the connection between voting and governance visible and immediate. At party rallies, with their speeches, heckling, and debates, the reciprocal power of voters and leaders to influence each other was plain for all to see.[16]

All these public festivities culminated on election day. Election days were festival days; workplaces closed and families gathered in town for outdoor barbecues with singing, speechifying, and, of course, voting. Candidates paraded through the streets while sideshow acts featuring fortune tellers and stilt-walkers entertained the crowds. In the days before secret ballots the act of voting was itself a public affair as men stood before their families, neighbors, and coworkers and placed their ballots in one of the boxes, each plainly marked for a particular party. Enthusiastic partisanship was something to be proud of; loyal partisans, men who had firm convictions rather than mere opinions, were the "salt of the nation." Parades and barbecues, festivals and balloting were gatherings of the community at large—a cross-class, multiethnic sign of a public, participatory political culture.[17]

In this context, the act of voting was meaningful, important, and useful. At a time when partisan identity was bound up with ethnic and religious identity, and when campaigning and balloting took place in a social, public way, voting was not merely an expression of political choice but an assertion of membership in the community. As Michael McGerr put it, ballots cast in this context helped each voter feel like "a member of a well-defined community rather than . . . an unimportant figure lost on a sea of electors." Voting was not only about candidates, policies, and electoral outcomes; it also was a ritual full of personal and communal meaning, a testament to the voter's ethnic roots, his manliness, his religious beliefs, his legitimacy as a citizen.[18]

Together, party organization and partisan political culture produced remarkable turnouts. From the 1840s to the 1890s, national voter turnout in presidential elections consistently exceeded seventy percent. In the last quarter of the nineteenth century, turnout crested at an average that exceeded seventy-five percent. Indiana, New Jersey, Ohio, and Iowa led the nation in those years in participation at the polls, averaging a whopping ninety-two percent between 1874 and the depression of the 1890s. Certainly there were regional differences, with participation in the South lagging behind the rest of the nation. Even in the South, however, turnout in the fifteen years after the Civil War averaged nearly seventy percent. In the party period, the situation was clear: almost everyone who could vote, did (see fig. 5).[19]

At the turn of the century, much of this ceased to be true. Profound changes in the structure and culture of electoral politics produced devastating consequences for voter turnout. The rules of enfranchisement were revised, party organizations deteriorated, rallies became smaller and speeches fewer, and ardent partisanship, for many, fell into disrepute. Three factors account for most of the drop in turnout rates: the imposition of legal hurdles to voting, the enfranchisement of women, and above all, the transformation of political parties.

Beginning in the late nineteenth century and continuing even into the 1920s, states enacted sharp new restrictions on suffrage. After the collapse of Reconstruction in 1877, white southerners worked to build a hegemonic Democratic regime to end black suffrage and secure white supremacy. When in the 1890s the Force Bill and the populist insurgency threatened these goals, the push to disenfranchise both African Americans and Republican-leaning whites accelerated. Determined white elites turned to a dizzying array of devices to curb voting—poll taxes, literacy tests, "eight-box" balloting procedures, white primaries, amendments to state constitutions, and, when legal means failed, old-fashioned fraud, harassment, and outright violence. They succeeded spectacularly in rolling back—in many places virtually eliminating—not only voting by African Americans but also competition to the Democratic party regime.[20]

Disenfranchisement took other forms in other parts of the country, where progressives hoped to eliminate corruption and insure the fitness of the urban electorate. Immigrants, ethnics, and workers were the most frequent targets of these efforts. Michigan and Wyoming were the first to repeal alien suffrage, and the twenty-nine other states with similar statutes all repealed them by the early 1920s. Residency requirements were extended and more strictly enforced both inside and outside the South; states now often required a year's residency in order for a citizen to vote, but in the South and in Rhode Island new residents were required to live in the locality for as long as two years. Literacy and other educational tests became standard in the South—and in California, Connecticut, Arizona, Oklahoma, Oregon, Delaware, Massachusetts, Maine, New Hampshire, New York, Washington, and Wyoming. By the end of the 1920s, forty-six states required some sort of registration for at least some of their voters, usually city-dwellers. Personal registration, in which prospective voters were obliged to present themselves to clerks, usually had to be renewed, even as often as every year. A third of the states restricted the registration period to seven days or less. These changes disproportionately disenfranchised people who lacked the papers or the reading and English-language skills to keep track of complicated registration procedures, in particular immigrants, ethnics, and workers.[21]

If restrictions on voting depressed turnout, expansion of the suffrage had the same effect. Although some states had granted women partial or even presidential suffrage prior to 1920, in a single stroke the Nineteenth Amendment achieved the full enfranchisement of women nationwide. The pool of potential voters thus practically doubled overnight, and most women were eligible to cast their first ballots for president in 1920.

Newly enfranchised women—many of them unfamiliar with the process and still uncertain whether political participation was proper for respectable ladies—did not match men in attendance at the polls. In 1920 in Illinois, the only state that tabulated voting returns by sex, forty-seven percent of eligible women turned out compared to seventy-four percent of eligible men. Scholars estimate that women's turnout in the 1920s lagged twenty to thirty percentage points behind men's. Though precise figures are unavailable due to a dearth of vote tabulations by sex, it is clear that woman suffrage contributed to the overall turnout decline.[22]

New registration requirements and woman suffrage surely contributed to the decline in voter turnout, but these two factors do not account for the whole decrease, or even most of it. In some places turnout declined *before* the new legal constraints were imposed; elsewhere, turnout declined where legal constraints were never imposed at all. Turnout everywhere had already started to sag before the Nineteenth Amendment became law, making a broader, more systemic explanation necessary. The answer lies in the transformation of the institutions that had supported high turnout in the first place—the turn-of-the-century transformation of political parties.[23]

Changes in the alignment of the two-party system, antiparty progressive reforms, and the deterioration of partisan political culture all worked to depress turnout. In the north and west, incumbent Democrats were blamed for the economic devastation of the depression of 1893–1896 and Republicans scored lopsided victories. With their newfound strength, Republicans abandoned a biracial "black and tan" strategy in the South and withdrew from the political scene there, leaving the field to Democrats. As a consequence of this realignment, a competitive, national political system became uncompetitive and sectionalized, each party dominating a different region of the country. This realignment retained its shape for thirty years and its characteristic uncompetitiveness dramatically depressed turnout in both North and South. As a businessman who studied nonvoting in 1924 in his own town of Washington, Pennsylvania, put it, "the average voter was not interested in whether Coolidge [won] . . . by five hundred thousand [votes] or five hundred thousand and one."[24]

The progressive movement of the turn of the century, too, weakened parties and depressed turnout. Business elites, reforming women, and others who found the political parties unreceptive to their concerns echoed the arguments of the nineteenth-century Mugwumps and advanced a searing critique of party politics. Party corruption was a staple of muckraking exposés, and a broad set of reforms cut away the bases of party power. Patronage jobs were reclassified as civil service; primary elections gave voters rather than party leaders the power to nominate party representatives; secret ballots replaced what was left of public voting; and government-printed ballots replaced the party-printed forms that had made split-ticket voting cumbersome. By eliminating the incentives that parties had used to lure voters to the polls and impairing their ability to insure loyalty, these reforms undermined the parties' power to mobilize voters.

Partisan political culture was another casualty of weakened party organizations. The progressives' critique of parties was accompanied by a critique of partisanship as independent, "thinking" voting replaced party-based voting as the civic ideal. After the depression-induced realignment of the 1890s, many more voters than ever before began to vote their pocketbook rather than their heritage, and ethnic and religious identities increasingly cut across rather than reinforced partisan identities. Ticket-splitting and independent voting became commonplace. But along with less party voting went less voting altogether. When the attachments to parties became weaker, voting became less important and turnout sagged.

By the 1920s, much of the exuberance of campaigns and elections had also disappeared as the trappings of campaigning and voting became more sedate and serious. A more sober "educational style" of campaigning had largely replaced boisterous partisan theater; public gatherings around candidates became less frequent, and speeches became shorter and drew smaller crowds. In the place of public gatherings, the national parties mailed campaign literature to voters at home. The campaign literature generated by huge party "literary bureaus" made elaborate arguments about the issues and appealed to voters' "reason" rather than their ethnic or religious identity. Campaigning took on an intellectual tenor; the proper disposition for voting became serious and studious, the cool, reasoned analysis of candidates and issues.[25]

With the advent of the "educational style" came a much more private approach to campaigning and voting. When parties mailed literature to homes, the venue for campaigning moved from public spaces to private ones. Pamphlets displaced speeches as a campaign medium; readers encountered campaign appeals as individuals rather than in assembly. As public meetings between candidates and voters became less frequent, the connection between voting and governance became less obvious. Literature did not allow the interaction that public forums once had: now candidates directed information *toward* voters—always trying to gauge their demands, to be sure, but without the same opportunities for voters to influence their leaders visibly and directly. Even the mechanics of voting had become more private and individualized: secret ballots, cast by a person alone behind a curtain, had replaced the public and communal ceremony of voting.

In this context, the meaning of voting was no longer so clear. Voting was as useful as it had ever been; casting a ballot accomplished exactly as much in the 1920s as it had in the 1880s, because rarely, in either time period, did a single vote change an election's outcome. But if voting was as useful as ever, it was not perceived to be nearly as important. As the connections between partisanship and religious and ethnic background weakened, as campaigns constructed citizens as individuals instead of as groups, as public voting in front of neighbors was replaced by secret ballots, the act of voting was separated from the context of community and lost its meaning as an expression of personal, social, and civic identity. The educational style of campaigning was less boisterous, less colorful, less engaging, and less accessible, too. The cross-class, multiethnic gatherings disappeared as the process moved indoors to private spaces, transforming what had been a shared, public process to one that was increasingly atomized and privatized. Stripped of the social context that had once given it meaning, the significance of voting for individuals, for communities, for governance itself, was no longer clear.

The cumulative result of these changes, from disenfranchisement to woman suffrage to the deterioration of party structures and partisan political culture, was the beginning of a long-term slide in voter participation. Nationally, turnout dipped to an average of sixty-five percent between 1900 and the Great War. In the South, the drop in participation was drastic and steep, as barely a third of the electorate continued to go to the polls. Even outside the South, however, turnout slipped from historic highs to an average of seventy-four percent (see fig. 5).

After the war the turnout picture grew worse. In 1920, turnout slumped to forty-nine percent—the first presidential election in eighty years in which a majority of the electorate failed to vote. In 1924 turnout bottomed out as slightly fewer than forty-nine percent of eligible voters cast ballots. Again, the South lagged far behind the rest of the nation. In the eight states of the deep South, a mere sixteen percent of eligible voters turned out at the polls.

This slide was interrupted in midcentury by the New Deal realignment. In 1928 the excitement Alfred E. Smith generated among immigrants, "drys," and southerners stimulated a higher turnout of fifty-seven percent nationwide. Although participation still lagged at twenty-three percent in the deep South, even that constituted a considerable improvement. Interest in voting accelerated with the Great Depression of the 1930s, and Franklin Roosevelt built a strong Democratic coalition that mobilized voters for a generation, producing turnouts that in most years hovered around sixty percent. The effect of the New Deal realignment on turnout, however, was only temporary. In the 1960s turnout resumed its slow downward slide, fluctuating around fifty-five percent for much of the 1970s and 1980s. In 1996, for the first time since the 1920s, turnout slipped once again below the fifty-percent mark, rebounding only slightly in 2000.[26]

The early 1920s thus stands out as an unusual historical moment with respect to voter turnout. Voter turnout in the 1920s was the lowest of any decade over a span of 160 years; such levels had not been seen since the 1830s and were not duplicated for another seventy years. But such levels were clearly part of a broader trend of long-term decline, a trend that the New Deal realignment arrested for a time but did not reverse. In short, the basic pattern of nonparticipation was set in the 1890s; the effect on voter turnout of the deterioration of parties and partisanship was realized most fully in the 1920s. These changes produced a vexing situation: ironically, as the suffrage *expanded* in the late nineteenth and early twentieth centuries, in percentage terms the active electorate actually *shrank*.

In the 1920s, the trouble was clear: half the electorate was staying home on election day. The implications were serious: mass nonvoting endangered prosperity, reform, and perhaps even democracy itself. But who was to blame? Newspapers lambasted nonvoters, business conservatives berated them, woman suffragists decried them. But who, exactly, was the problem? Who were these "civic slackers" and "poll dodgers"?

The Misrepresentation of the Problem of Nonvoting and the Discursive Construction of Civic Dominance

When clubwomen, business leaders, and newspaper editors criticized nonvoters in articles, disparaged them in cartoons, and reproached them in editorials, who did they identify as the culprits? They could have characterized nonvoters in any number of ways, as highly educated or poorly educated, for example, or Democrats or Republicans, or "us" or "them"; there is no reason why a hundred different commentators should not have come up with a hundred different descriptions, based, perhaps, on what each had observed close to home. Nonvoters need not have been described in any patterned way at all.

But, in fact, they were. Although it is true that in the vast commentary on nonvoting many different descriptions of nonvoters were offered, these were merely "background noise" to a set of remarkably clear and consistent characterizations built upon specific attributes of class, gender, race, and ethnicity. Reforming women, organized businessmen, radio commentators, and editors felt sure they knew who nonvoters were, and in newspapers large and small, in popular magazines, and in the records of civic clubs, they persistently described nonvoters as—and surely believed them to be, like "the most dangerous man in America"— middle class or elite in status, gendered male and female in distinct ways, usually native born, and unfailingly white.

There was only one problem: this characterization of nonvoters was wrong. In the demobilization of the electorate that was a defining feature of the early "third political era," the period that followed the realignment of the 1890s and preceded the New Deal realignment of the 1930s, the empirical data showed clearly that middle-class and elite white men were *least* likely to fail to vote.[27] In broad terms, voters were disproportionately middle and upper class; nonvoters were disproportionately working class. Voters were most often native born and white; nonvoters were most likely to be African American, foreign born, or distinctively ethnic. Voters were more likely to be male; nonvoters were more likely to be female. Nonetheless, activists in the GOTV campaigns, and thousands of editors, publishers, and commentators in newspapers, magazines, and radio, consistently produced and reproduced representations of nonvoters in which the falsehood of nonvoting by middle-class and elite whites, especially men, was constructed as a serious public problem while the real problem of nonvoting by racial minorities, workers, and some women was not.

Certainly the politics of race, class, and gender were at play here, but in the broadest possible terms, why did these people—well-informed and well-meaning activists—get it so wrong, and what does that show? In the misrepresentation of problem nonvoters in GOTV campaigns, in the "play" between representation and fact, lies a map of power relations that reveals who had the power to define the issue of nonvoting as a public problem and how that power was propagated and institutionalized. Why was the problem of nonvoting framed in the particular way that it was? Why did that particular version of the problem prevail in "the public sphere" of discussion and debate?

Surely the problem of nonvoting might have been framed in other ways and, indeed, in some quarters it was: organized groups of women, workers, racial minorities, and ethnic Americans articulated alternative interpretations of the problem of nonvoting, interpretations that in fact much more closely resembled the truth. The availability of more truthful versions of the problem of nonvoting makes the discursive dominance of the false version all the more interesting: it dramatically demonstrates the power of middle-class and elite whites in and around the GOTV campaigns to make their definition of the problem "the" definition, a definition they disseminated so widely and so consistently that it became dominant, naturalized as a seeming consensus, a consensus that then served as the basis for a massive effort to eradicate the problem. Untangling this process sheds light on the agency and process behind the creation of a "public meaning," in this case some of the meanings of citizenship in the early twentieth-century United States. It offers a way to analyze a crucial dynamic through which discursive dominance was built, civic hierarchies were shaped, and a political culture was "made."

The demobilization of the electorate was no generalized, across-the-board phenomenon; voters did not drop out of the electorate in a random or evenly distributed way. Rather, as scholarship at the time suggested and more recent research has confirmed, by the 1920s the pool of nonvoters was sharply skewed by class, race, ethnicity, gender, age, and region.

Low-income voters were much less likely than high-income voters to turn out at the polls. A 1925 study of one Ohio town found that people who lived in neighborhoods that survey-takers categorized as "poor" voted at only two-thirds the rate of residents of what they deemed "fair," "good," or "very good" areas. Relative newcomers—immigrants and their native-born children—voted at a lower rate than native-born citizens; in urban Philadelphia, for example, a city in which a majority of potential voters in 1920 were born abroad, turnout dropped by nearly half in the first two decades of the twentieth century. Newly enfranchised women were far more likely than men to stay away on election day and turned out at perhaps two-thirds the rate of men. Youthful voters were more likely to refrain from participating than older voters. Voters who attained their majority after 1900 were about half as likely to vote as their elders. The figures for voters attaining their majority after 1920 were even lower. Region, too, made a great deal of difference. Demobilization was most severe in the deep South; by 1920, less than a third of the eligible electorate there was still voting. Among blacks, turnout across the region was virtually zero. Thus the identity of nonvoters in the 1920s was sharply skewed: nonvoters were disproportionately poor and working class, ethnic, African American, female, young, and southern.[28]

These skewed patterns of nonparticipation have been identified more recently by researchers using sophisticated regression techniques and extensive databases. But their findings confirmed and refined the picture of nonvoting as it was understood in the 1920s, much of which was generated and publicized by researchers and activists connected to the GOTV campaigns. Charles Merriam and Harold F. Gosnell, in what one historian called "the public debut" of the "Chicago School" of political science, brought innovative research methods to bear on the problem of low turnout. *Non-Voting: Causes and Methods of Control* (1924) used random sampling techniques and categorical variables to survey six thousand eligible voters from diverse precincts who failed to cast ballots in the 1923 Chicago election for mayor, and supplemented that data set with interviews of several hundred local party leaders and elected officials. They found that women, immigrants, African Americans, and youthful citizens were the most likely to be "habitual non-voters," wealthier citizens and native-born whites the least likely. Their work received wide scholarly recognition and was also a topic of interest in publications such as *The New Republic* that reached a broader, educated audience.[29]

Studies of nonvoting by Simon Michelet received even wider public play. An attorney, Republican activist, former secretary to Senator Knute Nelson of Minnesota, and founder of the Washington, D.C.–based "National Get-Out-the-Vote Club," Michelet calculated turnout rates for every state and identified African Americans in the South and women as the largest groups of nonvoters. Between 1920 and 1932 Michelet published in pamphlet form more than twenty studies on turnout and distributed them widely to public officials, party leaders, civic leaders, and newspaper editors. GOTV activists in particular were well aware of Michelet's work; copies of his pamphlets turn up frequently in their archives. More importantly, his work was the subject of articles in a wide range of newspapers and magazines, including the *New York Times,* the *Grand Rapids (Mich.) Chronicle,* the *Minneapolis Sunday Tribune,* the *Birmingham (Ala.) Herald,* and *Nation's Business.* The researchers of the day lacked the databases and regression techniques that future researchers would use to identify turnout patterns with more precision, but clearly they succeeded in identifying in broad outline an accurate demographic profile of nonvoters in the 1920s, and clearly their ideas were an important part of the public discussion of nonvoting.[30]

In the representation of the problem nonvoter that dominated mainstream newspapers, middlebrow leisure magazines, GOTV radio talks, and the records of middle-class civic clubs, one set of characterizations prevailed: using occupation, dress, deportment, speech, leisure pursuits, skin color, and gender to define difference, the problem nonvoter was consistently described and depicted as middle or upper class, native-born, white, and gendered male or female in particular ways.

In the representations of the problem nonvoter, class, gender, ethnicity, and race coincided, constituted, and reinforced each other in complicated ways. Above all, the problem nonvoter was described as a businessman. There were innumerable ways for men to earn a living in the 1920s, but when commentators described the occupation of the typical nonvoting man, they almost invariably described him as a businessman. "The business men of this country," wrote the president of a major insurance company to former Democratic presidential candidate and NCF leader Alton B. Parker, "have a vital interest in the affairs of government, . . . and I am afraid it is the business men who have been neglecting their duties" to vote. Intelligence and seriousness served as class markers and were seen as vital to both good business and good citizenship; it was a shame, then, complained NCF leader John Hays Hammond to a group of fellow businessmen, that "a great body" of the nation's "most serviceable men" made themselves into "absentee citizens." "It is safe to presume," agreed an NAM member, "that the quiet but indifferent people who stay at home on election days comprise a large majority of the class of sensible thinkers." The class skew to the misrepresentation of the problem of nonvoting men was just as evident in some of the proposed solutions: at a time when some businesses still shut their doors on election day and when many people associated the game of golf with the country club set, activists in New York, Rhode Island, Pennsylvania, Ohio, and Alabama all proposed trying to boost turnout by forcing golf courses to close on election day.[31]

Nonvoting women were likewise consistently described not as workers but as middle- or upper-class women or housewives. Thus a writer in the *Ladies' Home Journal* worried specifically that it was women who traveled in the "very best circles" who were failing to vote. Editors of an Alabama newspaper called upon the clubwoman to "lay aside her golf stick" to "go and express herself as a real citizen of the great American Commonwealth." Adele Clark, a national officer of the League from Virginia, acknowledged that poll taxes might impair some women's access to the ballot but believed that "the bother of remembering" to pay them was "the most serious" barrier to access. "Many women of the south," she argued, "are accustomed to having all their taxes paid by trust companies or other legal agents, and these gentlemen, unaccustomed to the detail of a poll tax for women, forget it." Of course, this was not the problem for most women, but only for those with trust funds or "legal agents"; her description of the problem did not acknowledge the far greater number of nonvoters among middle- and working-class women at all.[32]

If commentators on nonvoting had much to say about class, they made few direct comments about ethnicity or race: whiteness and unhyphenated "100 per cent American"-ness seem to have been so safely assumed to be attributes of the problem nonvoter that no explicit comment to that effect was necessary. Rather, when these civic leaders invoked ethnicity or race, they usually did so in ways that constituted the problem nonvoter as native-born and white. As one contributor to *Collier's Weekly* provoked, "Are You an Election Day Alien?" Simon Michelet disparaged the groups ineligible for the suffrage as not only "convicts" and the "insane" but also "aliens, colored illiterates, Indians [and] Orientals," suggesting, it seems, that respectable native-born white citizens would not want to find themselves likened to these groups.[33]

Throughout the representations of problem nonvoters, the class, racial, and ethnic hierarchies were reasonably straightforward: middle- and upper-class qualities were portrayed as "good," working-class qualities as "bad"; whiteness and native-born status were "good," ethnicity and immigrant status were "bad." The hierarchies with respect to gender, however, were conveyed in more complicated ways, reflecting women's ambiguous civic status as a group that was sometimes privileged, sometimes subordinated. Gender classifications did not automatically mark a citizen as either good or bad: neither men nor women were singled out and blamed for low turnout. Rather, male and female nonvoters were characterized and criticized in gendered ways: gender difference functioned as a code that distinguished good citizenship from bad.

Gendered hierarchies were clear in the reasons given for the failure of each sex to vote. Men who failed to vote were routinely described as men who neglected their civic duties to tend to the demands of business. John Edgerton chastised NAM members, decrying their tendency to "make excuses as to how busy [they] are and shirk these transcendent responsibilities." *Collier's* expressed the same concern: "If John Jones has

a share in a humble concern dedicated to the production of dog bis-
cuit[s] . . . , he follows its affairs with feverish intensity. . . . Yet John
Jones pays no attention whatsoever to his rights and interests as a share-
holder in the greatest business the world has ever known—the Government of the United States." Negligence underpinned each of these
charges; when men failed to vote because they were busy with business,
they failed to vote out of neglect.[34]

While men's absence from the polls was chalked up to neglect, nonvoting by women was blamed on pettiness and incompetence. Women
were portrayed as being too pure to participate in politics or too absorbed with trivial matters such as fashion to take the time to vote. In
an address to the Daughters of the American Revolution, President
Coolidge criticized women who failed to vote "because of a curious assumption of superiority to this elementary duty of the citizen. They presume to be rather too good, too exclusive, to soil their hands with the
work of politics. Such an attitude," he continued, "cannot too vigorously
be condemned." Simon Michelet counted among the reasons for female
nonvoting the misplaced priorities of young women for whom "parties
and the varied amusements of youth doubtless made a more powerful
appeal than the prosaic business of registering and voting." *Collier's* argued that women did not vote because they "sh[ied] at revealing their
ages" to registrars while men, by contrast, could not "spare the time." In
the representation of the female nonvoter, vanity and self-absorption got
in the way of civic duty.[35]

Nonvoting women were also characterized as incompetent and irra-
tional in political matters—ill-informed about the candidates, ignorant
about the issues, even incapable of mastering the mechanics of casting a
ballot. A Utica, New York, businessman concluded that women there
who did not vote "do not understand the issues of the campaign, and
become either confused or out of patience with the amount of words
that are printed and spoken and are unable to decide for whom they
wish to vote." A Racine, Wisconsin, businessmen's group informally surveyed nonvoters there and believed that women did not want to vote
"without being told how to do it." Summing up the criticisms of many,
New York reformer Mary Garrett Hay remarked that "women who are
too good, too lazy, too silly, too indifferent to vote are shirking a sacred
duty."[36]

Gender was thus a crucial component of the description of nonvoters.
Both men and women were harshly criticized for failing to vote, but they
were criticized on vastly different grounds. Men were busy; women were

vain. Men were neglectful; women were incompetent. Nonvoting men were harshly criticized, to be sure, but they were criticized for their neglect, not for their pettiness or unfitness. These differences were not mere discrepancies; rather, they expressed and imposed a sharp civic hierarchy between the sexes. They suggested that men were perfectly suited to vote, that they were perfectly legitimate members of a self-governing polity. The problem was not that men could not be good voters, but rather that they fell short on execution. Female nonvoters, on the other hand, were described as incompetent or ill-informed; they were not, or not yet, perfectly suited to vote. In this representation, women would need some work before they could become fully legitimate members of the political order.

When male and female nonvoters were placed side by side in the commentary on nonvoting, the hierarchy between them became obvious, and women almost always suffered in the comparison. This gendered hierarchy was especially apparent in some of the language used to describe nonvoters. Throughout the commentaries on nonvoting, one gendered epithet, the "stay-at-home vote," appeared again and again. The pejorative was applied not only to nonvoting women, who might be expected to be found at home, but also to nonvoting men. The Michigan Women's Christian Temperance Union, for example, was "appall[ed]" at "the number of stay-at-home voters. . . . How can a man or woman be a 100 per cent American and neglect this great duty and privilege?" The ultraconservative business publication *Open Shop Review* lambasted "men at home, who never vote, and to that extent are not citizens." A political cartoon published in a Birmingham, Alabama, newspaper depicted an adolescent boy who was apparently being left at home while three women of the house went out to vote. "You might make yourself useful while we're away and remove the breakfast dishes. I wish you'd make the beds too" (see fig. 6).[37]

The "stay-at-home" epithet linked domesticity and voting, and used gender to represent the difference between good citizenship and bad. When it was applied to nonvoting women, it associated them with the negative attributes of poor housekeepers—apathy, laziness, slovenliness—and implied that they were poor "civic housekeepers" as well. But when the label was applied to nonvoting men, it feminized them, challenged their masculinity, and stripped them of the privilege usually associated with their gender. After all, for a teenage boy, a boy who was practically a man, to be asked to tidy up the house while the women-folk went out to vote—well, that was "Life's Darkest Moment." Gender, in short, supplied a subtle code by which civic hierarchy was expressed and imposed.

At the same time that newspapers, magazines, elected officials, and others criticized women for failing to vote, at the same time they used femininity and domesticity to describe the attributes of poor citizens, they also charged women with voting poorly. Some of this was rooted in familiar criticisms that women voters were petty or incompetent. Part of it grew out of anxiety by some over how this huge, inexperienced, newly empowered pool of voters would perform. The *Richmond (Va.) Times-Dispatch* frankly admitted to "misgivings in many quarters as to the manner" in which newly enfranchised women would "exercise their power." As late as 1928 a political cartoon in the *Chicago Tribune* rued women's participation because it made election time "an Uncomfortable Season of the Year for the Men Folks." If nonvoting by women was a problem, sometimes voting was, too.[38]

In some respects, the situation of women differed from that of other groups with low turnout rates at the polls. If the problem of women's nonvoting was visible in the public sphere of discussion and debate, the problem of nonvoting by minorities, workers, immigrants, and ethnic Americans was not. Throughout these representations of the problem nonvoter, the real problems of nonvoting—disenfranchisement for African Americans, ineligibility for Asian immigrants, low rates of participation for workers and ethnics—rarely entered into the discussion at all. Ironically, it was *voting* by these groups, rather than nonvoting, that was cast as a public problem. If nonparticipation by middle-class or elite, white, native-born men and sometimes women was treated as a problem, so too was *participation* by workers, ethnics, minorities, and sometimes women as well. Supplementing the commentary on the problem of nonvoting was an extensive commentary on the poor quality of current voters, voters who were not the right sort of people or who did not approach voting in the proper way. These people were not problem nonvoters, but problem voters instead.

Intellectual elites offered a chorus of complaint about the quality of the current electorate, complaints in which they criticized the civic qualities of class and racial and ethnic "others." Declaring "a crisis in democracy," William McDougall, William Allen White, Walter Lippmann, H. L. Mencken, and others worried not simply that Americans were failing to vote, but that America might not be "safe for democracy" at all. Ethnic and racial minorities bore much of the blame for this, as William Allen White blasted the "lower racial plasms" that made up the "moron majority." But few ordinary folk met their standard of civic competence; how could any average citizen, in Walter Lippmann's phrase, be "omni-competent" to vote wisely on the vast range of important public issues?[39]

Other business and political leaders shared these concerns and lodged their complaints about the class, race, and ethnicity of problem voters in language that was sometimes subtly coded but unmistakable in its intent. "Here we are with universal suffrage," complained E. E. Loomis, president of the Lehigh Valley Railroad Company, and the people with "education," "initiative, energy and enterprise" are "sitting back and letting many of those without any of their attainments make laws which all must obey." President Coolidge issued an election day warning that only a full turnout by "the people who have something at stake" could protect against the illicit power of "organized minorities." NAM member C. W. Asbury strongly agreed. High turnout by "radicals" would only emphasize "the neglect and carelessness among the sober, serious and clear-thinking men and women in all walks of life." The *Atlanta Constitution* reported with concern a decision by a federal judge in Tulsa, Oklahoma, to permit "unregistered Negroes" to vote. These commentators drew sharp distinctions between problem nonvoters and problem voters, between the business classes and the working classes, between true Americans and radical immigrants, between whites and blacks.[40]

Here, too, class was entangled with ethnicity and race and marked by deportment and demeanor. In a period in which political machines were identified with urban ethnics, workers, and immigrants, a political cartoon published in a Syracuse, New York, newspaper contrasted figures labelled "Machine Politics," "Corruption," and "Vice"—swarthy, almost simian-looking men—with the stylish, respectably married, unmistakably white "Mr. and Mrs. Good Citizen." The former would be sure to "register and vote early." As for "Mr. and Mrs. Good Citizen," would they? (See fig. 7.) Part of the problem was not simply that they voted, but that they voted in a partisan way. Urban ethnics and workers were routinely criticized as party hacks who lacked the ability or will to make political decisions with cool, independent reason. Among those who voted in 1920, *Collier's* ventured, "it is safe to say that the larger percentage were herded by party workers rather than moved by civic consciousness." Loyal partisans, a business journal argued, were "control[led]" by party bosses, to the detriment of the public good. From the point of view of middle-class and elite whites, ethnics and workers were the wrong sort of people and they made political decisions in the wrong way. If nonvoting by middle-class and elite, white, native-born men and women was constructed as an important public problem in the 1920s, voting by workers, minorities, ethnics, and sometimes women was a critical corollary.[41]

In the characterizations of problem voters and problem nonvoters, a reasonably accurate picture of the identity of voters and nonvoters was strikingly absent. Problem voters and problem nonvoters shared one key characteristic: *both were identified more by their personal attributes*—class, gender, race, ethnicity, and their approach to voting—*than by whether or not they actually voted*. Problem nonvoters were middle or upper class; problem voters were working class. Problem nonvoters were petty women and politically independent but neglectful men; problem voters were unthinking partisans who were sure to show up at the polls. Problem nonvoters were white and "100 per cent American"; problem voters were racial minorities or hyphenate Americans. These characterizations of problem nonvoters and problem voters were not random or arbitrary; rather, they were distinctly and consistently patterned along lines of class, gender, ethnicity, and race and signalled not merely difference but hierarchy. Thus middle-class and elite white civic leaders sorted citizens into two groups, problem nonvoters and problem voters—"thinking" people and "unthinking" people, the fit and the unfit, the worthy and the unworthy.

Such was the interpretation of the problem of nonvoting that dominated the public sphere of discourse and debate. These characterizations of problem nonvoters and problem voters reflected the opinions of the people who made them; unsurprisingly, these editors, clubwomen, and businessmen, who were for the most part middle or upper class and white, defined as worthy citizens people who looked much like themselves. Not everyone, however, saw the issue the same way. Some of the people whose participation was labelled a problem—organized groups of workers, African Americans, immigrant and ethnic Americans, and women—contested this interpretation and constructed alternatives to it, alternatives that not only asserted their civic worthiness but also more accurately reflected the real problem of nonvoting.

These groups embraced a range of oppositional strategies, arguing that they too met the standards of good citizenship, or that different standards should apply, or asserting outright the legitimacy of voting to protect their interests. Some among them embraced the civic vision propagated by middle-class and elite white civic leaders but argued that they too met the standards. Thus a group of Italian American leaders in

New York agreed with the National Civic Federation that the trend toward nonvoting was "most disturbing" and pledged their "sincere loyalty as citizens of this great country" to stop it. Clubwomen frequently made this argument as well, pointing out, as League leader Belle Sherwin did, that women who had taken civics classes were "just as interested in their political duty as men, and vote just about as generally," and that, as civic "angels" with a reputation for selflessness and virtue, women were in some ways superior to men as citizens. Samuel Gompers, the elder statesman of the American Federation of Labor, likewise argued that workers ought to be included in the category of civic worthies when he asserted that workers were true Americans and that any real democracy needed their votes. While it was undoubtedly true that "trade union members are as faithful to the duties of citizenship as those in any other sphere of American life, . . . " he argued, "the fact must be that many thousands of trade unionists have failed to vote." "The success of democracy," Gompers continued, "can be assured only by intelligent participation in the selection of officials and the making of national decisions by an overwhelming majority of the people"—trade unionists included.[42]

Some African American leaders embraced the same strategy, adopting the dominant characterization of the problem of nonvoting and applying it to their own communities. "Don't be a slacker . . . in this duty of citizenship," urged an Alabama newspaper published by and for the black citizens of Birmingham. These leaders also criticized men in the community who were "busily engaged in making money" and did not have "ten minutes to spare for registration in order to become voting citizens." Though the words may have sounded the same, the context made the meanings very different, for in a time and place in which racial hierarchies were sharply drawn and often violently enforced, to assert that one shared the dominant group's problem was to assert a certain equality, to level the distance and hierarchy that separated the groups.[43]

Others took a different tack and explicitly framed the problem of nonvoting in other ways, urging GOTV activists to address what they saw as the real problems. Some African American activists, for example, took the opportunity presented by the GOTV campaigns to reiterate their argument that the real problem of nonvoting was their own exclusion from the ballot box. John Hope, president of Morehouse College in Atlanta, condemned the "sad abridgement of political rights" experienced by African Americans and warned that the country would "not have full safety until all of its citizens . . . may enjoy all the political privileges that the country affords to any one" of them. Mary McLeod Bethune, then president of the National Association of Colored Women, encouraged African Americans to make "intelligent use of the ballot" and praised the efforts of member organizations to fix "state difficulties" and "to defend the rights and privileges of Negroes everywhere." By framing the problem in different terms, African American leaders challenged the legitimacy of the dominant hierarchy that cast them as unworthy citizens.[44]

Some groups went further, putting forward an entirely different set of civic values by boldly arguing that their group needed to use the ballot to advance its own interests. Thus the labor paper in Birmingham bitterly pointed out that the struggle of "working men" to "keep a little meat and bread at home" and fight "the land lord and other creditors" was "the direct result of inattention and carelessness on the part of the worker in neglecting to qualify himself to cast his ballot." Some foreign-born and ethnic voters rejected the independent style pushed by the GOTV campaigns, instead asserting that loyal partisanship was a perfectly legitimate approach to voting. Merriam and Gosnell encountered this attitude often in the ethnic neighborhoods of Chicago. They found immigrants who "freely admitted" that they relied on parties to tell them which candidates deserved their votes. Such was the case of a "Russian pocket-book maker" who had taken "an active part in politics as soon as he was naturalized because of the insistence of the Democratic precinct captain." This man "believed one should repay a politician for favors by voting for his man." By asserting their Americanness and the validity of their partisan worldview, ethnics challenged the terms by which they were excluded from the ranks of worthy citizens.[45]

In each of these ways, politically marginalized communities articulated alternative versions of the problem of nonvoting and challenged the discursive dominance of the prevailing interpretation. The institutional location of these critiques is significant, for they were most often generated in organizations that these groups controlled—ethnic associations, black colleges, labor unions, women's clubs—and aired in "counterpublics"—ethnic newspapers, African American newspapers, labor newspapers, club meetings—that belonged to and served their communities. In this case, as in so many others, separate institutions served as incubators for resistance, functioning as sites from which to challenge the power relations embedded in the prevailing discourse.[46]

Important as these alternative understandings of the problem of nonvoting were, they never dominated the "public" sphere of discussion and debate. Clubwomen's arguments were part of the public discussion of nonvoting, but other versions of the problem were practically absent from the pages of daily newspapers, popular magazines, or civic club minutes. Middle-class and elite whites, who for the most part did not belong to Italian American societies, who generally did not follow the goings-on at historically black colleges or read labor papers, were to that extent insulated from these alternative views. Alternative understandings of the problem of nonvoting were largely confined to the communities that generated them. On this issue, at this time, the "public" sphere of discussion and debate was not very public—that is, accessible, inclusive— at all. Here, "public" really meant "dominant" instead.

In this process of meaning-making, women worked from a precarious position of privilege. Middle-class and elite white clubwomen enjoyed a visibility in the public sphere on this issue and a voice in public discussions of nonvoting that African Americans, workers, and immigrant and ethnic Americans did not. Their visibility, however, did not always translate into privilege. Women citizens were often the target of criticism, as femininity and domesticity were often linked, in words and pictures, with negative civic traits.

But whether or not middle-class and elite whites were exposed to alternative views, few outside the communities of workers, ethnics, and minorities lamented the absence of these groups from the polls. Women's absence from the polls received plenty of ink, but the absence of less powerful groups did not. The disappearance of African Americans in the South from the electorate, the withdrawal of workers from the polls, the delegitimization of ethnic political participation simply were not constructed as public problems by the more powerful white, middle- and upper-class editors, clubwomen, and businessmen whose discussion defined the issue in "public" debate. Sometimes relatively disempowered communities successfully influence, challenge, or even define public discourse on issues of importance, but in this case that did not happen. On this issue, at this time, these groups did not succeed in framing the larger "public" debate; they did not possess the discursive or institutional power to make their interpretations prevail.[47]

This dynamic also explains why GOTV activists firmly embraced what looks like such a mistaken understanding of the problem of nonvoting. The GOTV activists did not misrepresent the actual identity of voters and nonvoters because they were confused about the facts or because they did not know, for example, that African Americans had been virtually eliminated from the southern electorate. Indeed, in their view, they did not misrepresent the problem at all. For most of the people behind the GOTV campaigns, the problem really was that too many middle-class and elite whites did not vote and that too many potentially radical—and certainly unworthy—workers, African Americans, immigrants, ethnics, or women did vote. For them, the disappearance from the electorate of people whom they believed to be unqualified or unworthy was no cause for lament. Even the best scholarly evidence did not persuade these educated activists to abandon their view. The *New York Times* reported that when Professor William B. Munro, Harvard professor of government and then president of the American Political Science Association, spoke to a meeting of the National Municipal League in 1927 and pointed out that "the common impression is erroneous" and that "every study that has been made indicates that the best showing at the polls is regularly made by the best neighborhoods," he was "sharply challenged" by Adele Clark, a GOTV activist and League vice president who in previous correspondence had actually referred to Michelet's voting data by name. The lack of participation by African Americans, workers, immigrants, and ethnic Americans was not a problem for GOTV leaders; nor, for some, was the low rate of participation by women. Rather, the problem was the slip in participation by middle-class and elite white men, and, for some, the low rate of participation by middle-class and elite white women. That is why GOTV campaigners worked to close golf courses rather than boxing clubs on election day, and why they put up posters in tennis clubs rather than settlement houses.[48]

Thus, the representation of the problem of nonvoting that prevailed in public discourse actually *inverted* the empirical facts of nonvoting in the 1920s. Nonvoters were characterized as middle and upper class, but in fact they were more likely to be working class. They were portrayed as white, but they were more likely to be black. They were described as native-born, but they were more likely to be foreign-born. They were most often depicted as male, but they were more likely to be female. Their classification as either a problem nonvoter or problem voter depended much more upon their personal attributes—class, gender, ethnicity, and race— than upon whether or not they actually voted.

The misrepresentation of nonvoters as middle-class and elite whites prevailed in countless publications and in every region of the country. It prevailed despite widely publicized evidence to the contrary. It prevailed despite the presence of more truthful alternatives put forward by less powerful groups. The disparity between the actual identity of nonvoters and their representation in the public sphere, between the nonvoter in fact and "The Most Dangerous Man in America," could hardly have been greater. What did it mean, and what does it show?

Broadly, the misrepresentation of the problem of nonvoting helps to explain how an inclusive system of universal suffrage generated an exclusive political culture. Responding to the expansion of the electorate as a crisis, the white businessmen and clubwomen of the GOTV campaigns constructed themselves as model citizens, using newspapers, magazines, cartoons, and club discussions to articulate a set of new civic hierarchies that privileged their political participation and delegitimized the participation of others. They displaced the civic hierarchies of the party period of the nineteenth century, a regime in which white men of any class status or ethnic background, including aliens, and, briefly, African American men, acted as fully legitimate citizens, and replaced it with a regime in which the highest levels of civic privilege were reserved for people who were white, ethnically unmarked, and middle or upper class. They defined good citizens as people who were middle or upper class and white, and some created room amongst the worthies for newly enfranchised women who shared those qualities. This does not mean that white middle-class and elite women had achieved full civic parity with their male counterparts; rather, gender continued to function as a code to subtly sort and grade the ranks of worthy citizenship further still—elevating, for example, female voters who demonstrated "masculine" rationality at the polls and disparaging male nonvoters as effeminate "stay-at-homes." The GOTV activists worked, in short, to fortify the civic distinctions between middle-class and elite whites and others; they based the campaigns not upon a factual description of who nonvoters really were, but upon a value judgment of who they thought voters ought to be.

This cultural coding of citizenship hierarchies was vitally important because it furnished civic distinctions which the Constitution no longer supplied. In a nineteenth-century world of white male suffrage, the suffrage itself had served to distinguish fully legitimate citizens from others; in the party period, the law was enough. The Fifteenth and Nineteenth Amendments, however, collapsed these distinctions between citizens. In a world of nearly universal suffrage, when the Constitution no longer distinguished at the polls between men and women or between whites and blacks, middle-class and elite whites worked to restore through culture some of the civic hierarchies that had been disestablished in law.

They did so in part by dominating the issue of nonvoting in the 1920s. Middle-class and elite whites had the power to define the issue in a way that privileged them, and they had sufficient power to do so in the face of evidence to the contrary and challenges from other groups. They succeeded in constructing themselves as the civic center and relegating others to the civic margins. They made their interpretation of the problem of nonvoting visible and other interpretations invisible, producing what appeared to be a consensus on the issue. By dominating the institutions that comprised the arena for "public" debate—the mainstream newspapers, middlebrow magazines, and civic groups that served in this period as platforms for the definition and discussion of public problems—middle-class and elite white men and sometimes women succeeded in reshaping some of the "public meanings" of citizenship in the United States of the early twentieth-century. They made their definition of the problem of nonvoting "the" definition—the definition that prevailed in "public" discourse, and the definition upon which a massive national effort to remedy the problem was based.

"A WHOLE FLEET OF CAMPAIGNS"

The Get-Out-the-Vote Campaigns in Overview

2

"Register So You Can Vote November 8th." In 1927, on Fountain Square in downtown Cincinnati, the local League of Women Voters erected an immense billboard to summon citizens to civic duty. "Civic thermometers" put the tally of registered voters in public view; each city ward's "thermometer" would rise as the registration numbers climbed. Properly hatted, standing tall, these women hoped their work would propel registration "Over The Top" (see fig. 8).

In the mid-1920s, concerned citizens such as these squarely confronted the problem of civic apathy. In 1923 and 1924, clubwomen and businessmen in every part of the country launched a series of nonpartisan drives to boost voter turnout. In the "Get-Out-the-Vote" or GOTV campaigns, these civic activists enlisted, as one participant put it, "every conceivable agency" to improve attendance at the polls: they advertised in magazines and newspapers and cultivated the support of publishers and editors; they sponsored civics classes and taught citizens how to mark ballots; they helped rewrite laws governing registration and voting; they recruited allies from veterans groups, schools, churches, and synagogues. The GOTV campaigns, in Michael McGerr's phrase, "caught on quickly." By the summer of 1924, they had multiplied into "a whole fleet of campaigns," a full-scale "patriotic crusade."[1]

This crusade took place on a truly stunning scale. The total number of national organizations, state and local organizations, state and local chapters of

national organizations, and individuals involved is uncounted, and perhaps uncountable. A leading GOTV group put the number of participating organizations at more than three thousand. I have counted nearly
a thousand, and certainly I have not found them all. The fullest list of
participants in a single city is for St. Louis, where one organizer named
eighty-nine participating groups while acknowledging the incomplete-
ness of the list. What is certain is that in forty-seven of the forty-eight
states, in the countryside and in urban centers and in towns of every
size, the GOTV campaigns were vigorous, active, and visible.[2]

The large number of participants, however, does not mean that everyone participated. Patterns in the identity of the activists and in the tim-
ing and organization of the campaigns stand out clearly. Most GOTV activists were broadly middle class—the businessmen's wives who met for
club lunches, the shopkeepers who posted placards in store windows,
the insurance salesmen who dropped off literature while collecting premiums. With a few notable exceptions, most vote activists were also
white. Most groups put forward their biggest efforts in the presidential
election of 1924, though many worked intensively in off-year congressional, state, or municipal elections in the mid-1920s and in the presidential election of 1928. At the national level, for the most part, GOTV
groups cooperated in only the most limited ways, sending a representative to attend another group's meeting, for example, or passing resolutions of support. At the local level, by contrast, organizations often cooperated closely, working together to plan and carry out the campaigns.

Participating groups, too, spanned the ideological spectrum from the
far right to the not-so-far left, from ultraconservatives in the National Security League to reforming women who also worked for issues such as
disarmament and an end to child labor. Some GOTV activists were political independents; some, such as Alton B. Parker and Sarah Schuyler
Butler, held positions of leadership in the Democratic and Republican
organizations. Even deeply committed partisans, however, put party
loyalties aside to express support for GOTV. As President Coolidge put
it in a 1924 speech, "I am much less concerned for what party, what
policies and what candidates you vote, than that you shall vote." GOTV
was a nonpartisan affair, and political parties played virtually no role in
the campaigns.[3]

Participants varied, too, in their level of involvement in the campaigns
and in the way in which they got involved in the first place. While local
chapters often followed the lead of their national organizations, a few
took up the GOTV mission quite on their own, winning the attention of

those at the central offices and shaping the program of the national organizations from the bottom up. Some groups did no more than pass a resolution of support and then promptly file the resolution away. Some, however, devoted enormous resources to the campaigns—by conducting thousands of citizenship training classes; by printing and mailing posters and stickers in quantities of millions; by advertising in publications with mass readerships; and by dedicating a full-time professional staff to the project. Among the many committed organizations, five stood out. No group dedicated greater resources to the GOTV campaigns than the League of Women Voters, the National Association of Manufacturers, the National Civic Federation, the American Legion, and *Collier's* magazine.

Most campaigns trumpeted two goals: to "bring out one hundred per cent of the vote" and to "make that vote an intelligent one." They did not actually expect perfect turnout, of course. Rather, most groups set a more attainable goal of seventy-five percent turnout in the presidential election, half again as high as the 1920 turnout figure. As the League put it, that seemed to be "a reasonable increase." GOTV activists also hoped to improve the caliber of the electorate by encouraging, in the words of Maud Wood Park, the "conscientious, discriminating, intelligent use of the ballot."[4]

These two goals complemented one another and indeed were often conflated in the statements of the activists, and yet they depended upon very different assumptions, which, in turn, produced different types of campaigns. The quantitative goal addressed the problem of the problem nonvoter; people who were simply failing to vote needed to be reminded, prodded, or inspired. For this problem, the answer was publicity: the campaigns needed to draw attention to the importance of voting and build enthusiasm for it. By contrast, the qualitative goal focused on the problem of the problem voter. Here the "quality" of the voter, his or her fitness to cast a ballot, was the issue. On balance, problem voters received less attention from GOTV groups, and were usually the targets of campaigns to edify and "improve" them. Here, citizenship education was the key—classes on civics, history, and the "Essentials of Good Government."[5]

These two goals, quantitative and qualitative, coexisted in many efforts to get out the vote for the duration of the campaigns. Over time, however, their relative importance shifted. For most groups, simply increasing turnout was the top priority in 1924, and as a result the early campaigns emphasized publicity and sloganeering. In 1928, by contrast, campaigns worked harder to educate citizens while also increasing turnout. Toward the end of the decade, therefore, the GOTV campaigns took on a more sober, instructional tone.

The GOTV activists also shared a set of themes and a common civic vocabulary. Whatever their differences, the campaigners embraced a common commitment to what they saw as patriotism and nonpartisanship. Ultraconservative businessmen and reforming women alike recalled the sacrifices of the recent world war and called on citizens now to take up a ballot rather than a gun. Election day, as a cartoon in a Providence, Rhode Island, paper put it, was "The Next Defence Day." The campaigners shared, too, a certain civic rhetoric, a recourse to the flexible language of progressivism. GOTV activists of every political stripe invoked democracy, civic duty, and even efficiency in urging voters to the polls. That many groups used the same words does not, of course, imply that they fully agreed on every nuance of their meanings. But whatever the differences among the groups, a progressive vocabulary proved capacious and accommodating and lent the vote campaigns a measure of unity and coherence.[6]

Taken together, these differences and similarities make clear that the GOTV campaigns operated not as a centralized and unified movement, but rather as a series of independently organized and fluid campaigns that cohered around certain civic themes. The task of this chapter, then, is to paint the big picture—to identify who participated in the GOTV campaigns and who did not; to describe the methods they used; to explore the difference that gender and region made in the content and tenor of the campaigns; to articulate the themes and language they employed; and, finally, to assess the extent to which the campaigns met their goals.

A Roster of Middle-Class Respectability: A Profile of the GOTV Activists

Women's organizations, together with men's business groups, formed the backbone of the GOTV effort. Clubwomen were the first to take up the cause, and their work through national organizations and local affiliates as well as other local groups brought GOTV to communities in every region of the country. The League of Women Voters was the most active of these; at the local level, the League often formed the nucleus of a local campaign.

Beyond the League, however, a wide array of women's organizations—service clubs, mothers' groups, religious organizations, reform groups, and social clubs—also took active roles in the GOTV campaigns.

The General Federation of Women's Clubs (GFWC), with some three thousand affiliates, conducted a national survey of GOTV efforts and urged member organizations to get involved. Hundreds of GFWC affiliates answered the call, among them the New York Federation of Women's Clubs, which in 1924 petitioned four hundred other clubs averaging more than one thousand members apiece to register and vote. The General Federation of Business and Professional Women's Clubs also supported the campaigns, and groups representing professional women, such as the Women Lawyers' Association of New York and the Advertising Women of New York, spoke at GOTV meetings and donated money to the cause. Women's City Clubs, such as those in Chicago and Detroit, aired radio programs on the importance of voting and gathered supporters at GOTV dinners. Local units of the Young Women's Christian Association (YWCA) often supplied space for citizenship classes, while mothers' groups, such as the Montgomery, Alabama, Mothers' Club, and parent-teacher organizations, such as the Minnesota Council of Parents and Teachers Associations and the four hundred local chapters of the Pennsylvania Congress of Parent-Teachers, pledged one hundred percent turnout by their members. The Daughters of the American Revolution (DAR) endorsed the campaigns in 1924 and 1926; President-General Minnie Latham "harped on" GOTV in her speeches and reports, and the DAR magazine published articles on the importance of voting. The Women's Christian Temperance Union (WCTU) cooperated with the campaigns as well, and state and local chapters such as those in Michigan, St. Louis, and Birmingham and Gadsden, Alabama, sponsored telephone canvasses and tag days. The Ladies of the Maccabees, a women's benefit association, endorsed the GOTV cause, as did the national councils of the American Association of University Women, the American Home Economics Association, and the Girls' Friendly Society.[7]

Businessmen also embraced the vote campaigns with enthusiasm and worked to improve turnout amongst colleagues, employees, and the community at large. The NAM was the most active of these, but other businessmen's groups at the local and national levels took on important roles as well. The U.S. Chamber of Commerce, for example, publicized GOTV conferences and pledged to sponsor one of its own. The roster of local chambers of commerce that worked to get out the vote is impressive: Philadelphia and Chicago; Baltimore and Buffalo; Denver and Tampa; Richmond and Spokane; Asheville, North Carolina; Amsterdam, New York; Burlington, Vermont; Billings, Montana; San Diego; Jersey City; Salt Lake City—and dozens more.[8]

Other business organizations also joined in. The International Kiwanis club distributed GOTV material to local chapters and asked them to join efforts in their local communities. The San Francisco chapter of Kiwanis responded by tagging voters on election day, the Aurora, Illinois, chapter by announcing plans to publish the names of ballot slackers. The Retail Dry Goods Association and the Building Trades Employers' Association wrote checks, while the president of the Northern States Life Insurance Company wrote the president of "every life insurance company in America" and asked him to "Do [His] Part" by reminding policyholders to "exercise their right of suffrage." The Junior Chamber of Commerce, the group today called the "Jaycees," reported that one hundred local chapters did GOTV work between 1924 and 1926, while the California Development Association said that it had enlisted the support of "practically all commercial organizations in California" and planned to award a "Better Citizenship Cup" to the community "securing the highest voting percentage in California." The American Bankers Association, the Motion Picture Producers and Distributors Association, Rotary International, the National Council of Traveling Salesmen's Associations, the United Engineering Society, and the International Association of Casualty and Surety Underwriters also endorsed the cause.[9]

Though women's groups and business organizations took the lead in the GOTV campaigns, many sorts of civic groups also played an important part. The Boy Scouts of America joined the campaigns to demonstrate their "love for . . . country." Chief Scout Executive James B. West enlisted the help of 685,500 "boys in khaki" as well as two million former members to get out the vote by conducting tag days, distributing literature and canvassing door to door, often in cooperation with other community organizations. The National Security League, the organization of superpatriots headed by S. Stanwood Menken, produced and distributed GOTV buttons, often with custom imprints. J. C. Snyder, president of the National Fraternal Congress of America, asked fraternal societies everywhere to embrace the voting cause. International Civitan, the Elks, the Lions, the Masons, and the National Order of DeMolay (the Masons' group for young men, with chapters in fifteen hundred cities), also endorsed GOTV.[10]

Likewise, religious groups also worked to convert civic slackers into active citizens. The United Society of Christian Endeavor, a Christian ministry group that claimed five hundred thousand members, promised an "organized canvass of every church in the United States." When the National Council of Jewish Women asked its fifty thousand members to add GOTV to their regular program of religious education and social welfare work, local "sections" responded enthusiastically. The Birmingham, Alabama, section joined forces with the local Young Men's Hebrew Association for a telephone canvass while the Altoona, Pennsylvania, section invited a GOTV speaker to a monthly meeting. The Savannah, Georgia, section assisted the local League of Women Voters with a registration drive, while a section from Connecticut organized a "motor corps" to transport voters to the polls. The Knights of Columbus, the American Board of Applied Christianity, and the Federal Council of Churches of Christ also endorsed GOTV.[11]

Similarly, religious publications worked to inspire citizens to go to the polls. The *Homiletic Review,* a monthly "repository of sermons" published by Funk and Wagnalls, launched a crusade to "Get-Out-the-Christian-Vote." Pastors representing two hundred thousand worshippers signed pledge cards and promised to work for one hundred percent turnout in their congregations. President Calvin Coolidge specifically endorsed the *Homiletic Review* campaign and praised the effort to get "all of the church-going community to go to the polls." The *Christian Herald,* an interdenominational weekly newspaper with a circulation of nearly two hundred and twenty thousand, contacted "virtually every Protestant clergyman in the country" and asked him to devote a section of the October 26, 1924, sermon to a "discussion of the obligations of citizenship strictly along nonpartisan lines." The paper also sponsored a voter turnout contest and awarded the winning church a trip for one person to attend the presidential inaugural celebration in Washington. Of the 1,175 churches that entered the contest, the First Methodist Episcopal Church of Colfax, Iowa, won by getting every one of its 277 adult members to the polls. Several other contestants—the First Baptist Church of Huntington, Indiana; the First Congregational Church of Long Pine, Nebraska; the Fruitdale Baptist Church of Fruitdale, South Dakota; and the First Congregational Church of Sylvan, Washington—also reported perfect attendance at the polls.[12]

Military organizations also joined the battle against civic apathy. The American Legion was the driving force behind the 1926 vote campaigns. In conjunction with the NCF, the Legion sponsored GOTV organizing conferences in hundreds of cities on or around September 21, 1926. The range of cities that held conferences was impressive: San Francisco; Chicago; Philadelphia; New York; New Orleans; Oklahoma City; Peoria; Louisville; Boise; Daytona Beach; Santa Barbara; Youngstown, Ohio; Portland, Maine; Casper, Wyoming; and many others.[13]

In addition to the Legion, several other military associations also supported the cause. The Military Order of the World War, an officers' organization, wrote checks, sent representatives to meetings, and asked local chapters to "exercise their good efforts" to urge citizens "to use their voting privilege." The women of the Service Star Legion resolved at their convention in Pittsburgh in October 1923 to "make use of the ballot" and to "exert our influence to have other women do likewise, that we may strengthen our power for good." The Military Order of the Loyal Legion, the Navy League, and the Reserve Officers' Association likewise endorsed the cause.[14]

Occasionally GOTV groups, rather than work through existing organizations, formed new organizations dedicated specifically to higher turnout. Most often, as in the case of the Non-Partisan Co-ordinating Council of New York in 1924, these groups were umbrella organizations that coordinated the GOTV efforts of their constituent groups. On other occasions they formed freestanding organizations, as in New York's Committee on Increase of Registration to Vote in 1926.[15]

One such independent group aspired to national prominence. In July 1924, Simon Michelet, the Republican lawyer and activist, launched the "National Get-Out-the-Vote Club." Michelet envisioned a national network of clubs with branches in every state and congressional district composed of citizen-volunteers who pledged their "active service to the cause of securing a full registration and ballot." Michelet assembled a prestigious advisory board that included Colonel Theodore Roosevelt Jr., Assistant Secretary of the Navy and son of the former president; Democratic National Committee member and party socialite Florence Harriman; Republican National Committee member and anti-Prohibitionist Pauline Sabin; and a half dozen senators. Michelet hoped the clubs would educate citizens about the importance of voting, supply speakers for public events, and distribute data and GOTV literature. In this last task Michelet's efforts were most successful: his pamphlets on "Absentee Voting in the 48 States," "Voting a Civic Duty," and other topics were widely distributed and publicized. In forming local clubs Michelet succeeded least: the count seems to have stopped at one, possibly two.[16]

Publicity was a crucial part of the GOTV campaigns, and the GOTV groups worked hard to cultivate the support of editors and publishers. Their efforts were wildly successful, and many daily newspapers, trade journals, literary reviews, and middlebrow magazines gave the campaigns frequent and favorable coverage. Some even adopted the cause of the campaigns themselves. In this *Collier's* led the way, promoting the cause in 1924 with articles, advertising space, editorials, and a national Get-Out-the-Vote contest.

Many other publications, however, gathered support for the campaigns through the pages of their newspapers and magazines. The Scripps newspaper chain, with twenty million readers, promised a "publicity campaign" of grand proportions, including a "great series of editorials" urging the importance of voting. One ad sponsored by Scripps appeared in *Collier's* with the blazing headline that "PANIC [HAS] HIT THE FLOP HOUSE VOTE" in cities in which Scripps-Howard papers had been campaigning against political corruption. The League of Women Voters and the NAM in particular used sophisticated press operations to win wide editorial support for the campaigns. In 1924, the NAM sent press kits to "every single daily newspaper in the country" and urged each to "publish editorials emphasizing the need for all eligible voters [to go] to the polls." The response was overwhelming: NAM reported that "hundreds" publicized the campaigns with news stories, "hundreds" more with favorable editorials that often praised the NAM by name. Papers large and small endorsed the GOTV campaigns, among them the *New York Times,* the *St. Louis Post,* the *Philadelphia North American,* the *Des Moines Register,* the *Indianapolis Star,* the *Bangor (Maine) Commercial,* the *Anaconda (Mont.) Standard,* and many others.[17]

The "Other" GOTV Campaigns: The Limited Involvement of Workers and Racial and Ethnic Minorities

Though most GOTV activists were middle class and white, there were some important exceptions. A small number of workers, ethnic Americans, and African Americans, organized through labor unions, fraternal societies, church groups and the like, also joined in the work of the GOTV campaigns. Most of them saw themselves as solidly middle class; most worked in the campaigns to turn out people like themselves. Their GOTV participation, however, was usually quite limited in scope, involving, for example, passing a resolution but little in the way of publicity or education efforts. Their efforts constituted only a small part of the overall effort, and they did not assume leading roles in the national campaigns. Nonetheless, their work is important because it shows some of the ways in which they negotiated the civic hierarchies between themselves and more powerful middle-class and elite whites. Sometimes these "other" groups used GOTV to contest the notion that they were lesser citizens or "problem voters"; sometimes they used it to try to secure for themselves some of the middle-class and elite privilege that the campaigns helped to communicate and confer.

Most of organized labor's participation in the vote campaigns took the form of endorsements. The American Federation of Labor (A. F. of L.), the Women's Trade Union League, the National Education Association, the International Molder's Union, and the International Union of Elevator Constructors were among the labor groups that expressed support for the campaigns.[18]

Samuel Gompers, a founding member of the National Civic Federation as well as president of the A. F. of L., spoke out loudly on the importance of voting. Not long before his death he called on "the whole trade union movement" to "begin now and keep constantly at the job of educating trade unionists and non-trade unionists alike to what is a paramount duty in every election—the casting of a vote by every person eligible to vote." Other labor leaders echoed Gompers's sentiment and pledged the support of their organizations. Thomas McMahon, international president of the United Textile Workers of America, reported to the NCF that his group was "in hearty accord" with the vote cause. The Operative Plasterers' and Cement Finishers' International Association endorsed the campaigns, and its president, Edward McGivern, promised to notify locals through the organization's monthly circular. The Glass Bottle Blowers Association, another A. F. of L. affiliate, expressed support for the joint NCF/American Legion campaigns in 1926 and offered to encourage locals to participate. The South Carolina League supplied a speaker to at least one union meeting.[19]

These instances stand out because they were unusual. The occasions on which GOTV supporters reached out to unorganized or so-called "unskilled" workers, however, were downright rare. The A. F. of L. in particular, and much of organized labor in the 1920s, was the province of highly skilled high-status tradesmen, "better-paid artisans" whom some scholars have described as more middle class than working class. In any case, efforts by GOTV activists inside and outside the labor movement rarely extended to the unorganized, "unskilled," often relatively recent arrivals who filled the factories of mass production. The extensive documentation of the GOTV campaigns offers up only a few instances: the work of the Boston League of Women Voters to post GOTV notices in factory restrooms, for example, or the project of the Boy Scouts in Wichita, Kansas, to carry GOTV fliers "to the mills and packing houses" because the workers there "may not have phones." Organized labor's involvement in GOTV at the community level was notably absent, as was any significant participation by or for unorganized workers.[20]

Almost as striking were the limits that labor put on its participation in the vote campaigns and the extent to which union participation was less than what it seemed. William Green, who succeeded Gompers in 1925 as the A. F. of L.'s president, did not share Gompers's enthusiasm for the cause. While Green endorsed the NCF's 1926 GOTV effort, he balked at its rather modest request that he let locals know about the endorsement and urge them to participate. And while many labor publications published articles on GOTV—the *Machinists Monthly Journal,* the *Journal of Electrical Workers and Operators,* the *Boilermakers' Journal,* and the *Brotherhood of Locomotive Firemen and Enginemen's Magazine,* for example—these articles were written neither by union members nor by the staffs of these magazines but rather by the LWV's Publicity Department. In some cases the articles were published under the byline of League president Maud Wood Park, in other cases without attribution at all. And in no case did these articles suggest a working-class perspective on the GOTV campaigns, for example, urging workers to vote to advance their class interests. In every case they urged voting on the generic grounds of civic duty.[21]

What stands out is the limit—often the absence—of labor involvement in the GOTV campaigns, in contrast to the deep involvement of civic organizations of almost every other kind. Despite the number of labor groups that endorsed the campaigns, few aided in the actual work of reaching out to citizens with advertisements or civic education. The attempts to reach unorganized workers and unskilled workers, by unions or anyone else, were even more limited; indeed, they were practically nonexistent. And there is no evidence of any GOTV campaign initiated by unorganized or unskilled workers themselves.

Why these sharp limits? Labor records do not explicitly say why these groups did not get involved, even when they were invited to do so. Plausible explanations, however, are not hard to find. Business groups were convinced that "radicals and other highly organized bodies," as one NAM member put it, already turned out "a high percentage of the total eligibles among their numbers"; they certainly were not interested in turning out more workers. For its part, in 1924 the A. F. of L leadership was deeply committed to electing Robert La Follette to the presidency; a campaign simply to turn out more voters was not what they had in mind.[22]

But beyond these reasons, organized labor in the 1920s would hardly have found many of the GOTV groups to be congenial partners. While the NAM was busy mobilizing businessmen for the vote campaigns, it was also busting unions in "American Plan" campaigns to promote open shops and company unions. Crowell-Collier Publishers also had a terrible track record with labor, evident in the lockout of the International Typographical Union in 1923 at the magazine's main printing plant in Springfield, Ohio. In the context of such bitter relations between labor and management in the 1920s, there was little prospect that the two would join forces, even on a campaign that was supposed to promote the public good.

Campaigns to turn out immigrant and ethnic voters were unusual, if only because GOTV leaders saw no need to turn out more "problem voters." On the occasions when GOTV groups did work in immigrant and ethnic communities, they usually worked to inform and "improve" these voters rather than simply get them to vote. The Boston League, for example, posted information in fifty settlement houses on how to vote, while local chapters of the National Council of Jewish Women chose to stress "the importance of the ballot" in "Immigrant Education" classes. On rare occasions, GOTV groups reached out to immigrant voters in their native languages; the Milwaukee County League, for one, succeeded in securing the cooperation of "all the newspapers"—the "foreign papers as well as the American"—while the St. Louis League noted that foreign-language newspapers there had been "particularly helpful in calling the attention of new citizens" to the registration campaign.[23]

If GOTV campaigns *for* ethnic Americans were infrequent, GOTV campaigns *by* ethnic Americans were downright rare. From time to time ethnic community leaders took the GOTV message into their communities themselves. The Polish League of Irvington, New Jersey, for example, distributed three thousand copies of a Polish-language GOTV flier. Thirty-seven leaders of the Italian American community in New York, including a state legislator, a state Supreme Court judge, and several bankers and Catholic priests, wrote the NCF with an offer to "co-operate with your patriotic endeavor to re-awaken the political consciousness of the American people." These GOTV activists were not struggling immigrants; their membership in the League of Women Voters and their professions marked them as solidly middle class. Their efforts made the point that they considered themselves good citizens and not "problem voters." They turned the GOTV campaigns into one more opportunity to prove that they were real Americans, even if they had been born abroad.[24]

GOTV posed a distinctive set of possibilities and problems for African Americans. In the North, GOTV might have helped recent arrivals from the rural South to learn more about their new opportunities for political participation and to navigate the complexities of registration and ballot-marking. In the South, where the majority of African Americans still lived, the GOTV campaigns took place in the context of disenfranchisement. Literacy tests, poll taxes, and a climate of violence surely shaped the way African Americans participated in and experienced the campaigns. Perhaps GOTV could have offered southern African Americans another vehicle through which to contest disenfranchisement. Perhaps some interpreted the campaigns as a promise that white GOTV groups would join them in that effort. Surely many derided the calls to "vote as you please, but vote"—could there be a crueler joke? Perhaps some hoped to use the civic education programs to "certify" members of the community as the good citizens they already knew themselves to be, and from there pass the literacy tests in a way that that no registrar could deny and which some whites might even respect. Some must have feared the attention that visible aspirations to vote might bring. Some may have simply figured that the campaigns must not apply to them.

The Nineteenth Amendment complicated the situation further still. African American women worked hard for woman suffrage through the National Association of Colored Women and its "Suffrage Department," the Woman's Convention of the National Baptist Convention, the African American sororities Alpha Kappa Alpha and Delta Sigma Theta, women's Republican clubs, and other organizations, often doing so over the protest of white suffragists who considered their support a political liability or who believed they were unfit for suffrage at all. When African American women were enfranchised by the Nineteenth Amendment— and they believed it *did* enfranchise them—they hoped to use the ballot not only to promote policies of "social motherhood" and to give politics a good "housecleaning" but to act publicly and visibly in defense of their communities and even to win back the political rights of which African American men had been stripped. As Charlotte Hawkins Brown, president of the North Carolina Association of Colored Women's Clubs, argued, for "the emancipation of the race from this political thralldom, woman suffrage [is] our only hope."[25]

The early 1920s thus stand out as a crucial political moment for African American women in the South. At a time of great persecution, the Nineteenth Amendment opened up new possibilities. The scholarship, still preliminary as to how the Nineteenth Amendment was actually implemented and experienced, suggests that African Americans, women and men, attempted in 1920 to register "en masse," mobilizing

in church and club meetings in the days before poll books opened, training for tests to interpret the Constitution, and approaching registrars as
a group. While most, apparently, were turned away—unable to pass literacy tests to suit the registrar, or made to stand in line until closing
time, or bluntly told that election officials simply "were not going to register any colored men or women"—many in fact succeeded in registering and/or voting—perhaps a thousand in North Carolina in 1920, for
example, and twenty-five hundred in Nashville the same year. What
happened to this tenuous exercise of political rights later in the decade
is unclear; one account argues that in North Carolina, "black women and
men registered in ever-increasing numbers throughout the 1920s," while
another claims that "throughout the South" African American women
quickly became the targets of disenfranchisement and "lost the vote
within less than a decade." This much is clear: the 1920s were a crucial
political moment for African Americans in the South, for the bounds of
black disenfranchisement were then being tested in a way that had not
been true for a generation.[26]

This was the context, North and South, in which GOTV transpired.
The GOTV campaigns took place at a time when northern blacks sought
a place in the political system and when African American women and
men in the South, taking advantage of the cracks in the edifice of white
supremacy created by the Nineteenth Amendment, were staking out and
trying to defend their new sliver of access to the ballot, and perhaps, despite their best efforts, watching it slip away.

Clearly this was a time of urgency, but the GOTV campaigns did very
little to benefit the black community. GOTV campaigns by or for African
Americans were unusual, in part because the leading GOTV groups barely
acknowledged the existence of disenfranchisement and hardly saw greater
participation by "problem voters" as something to be encouraged. These
groups were also uninterested in dealing with the delicate issue of disenfranchisement: to organizations looking for broad support, a debate on
the merits of black political participation was entirely unwelcome. The
National Civic Federation was very explicit on this matter; fearing that it
might "raise the color-line question," the NCF planned in 1926 to omit
from a series of national GOTV coordinating meetings any organizations
in "the nine so-called 'slave states.'" When, through a clerical error, invitations went out to southern groups anyway, NCF leaders breathed a sigh
of relief when the invitations elicited "no bad results."[27]

Despite reticence on the part of national GOTV leaders, some African
Americans did take up GOTV, usually clubwomen working through

service groups or churches. The National Association of Colored Women (NACW), for example, with its elite and middle-class membership, promoted the vote cause. In her biennial account of NACW activities, Association president Mary McLeod Bethune reported that "while we are nonpartisan, we have sought to encourage the intelligent use of the ballot" in order to "bravely shar[e] our great responsibility in protecting the life of our commonwealth." The Alabama Federation of Colored Women echoed the sentiment in 1929 when it resolved to "recommend a broad citizenship program and urge our women to take part in all civic and community activities."[28]

Beyond this, in the north, some local leaders did pursue efforts at GOTV by and in African American communities despite the lack of enthusiasm in the national organizations. Irene Goins, president of the Chicago chapter of the Douglass League, an African American League chapter named after Frederick Douglass, reported that her members had been "sincere in [their] efforts" and had "confined" their work "to educating the women of this district to the great need of registering and voting." The Douglass League's GOTV work included a door-to-door canvass, talks at churches and clubs, and, Goins reported proudly, "citizenship schools, which we feel were second to none." The Chicago Federation of Colored Women likewise offered a citizenship education program.[29]

In a few cases, white groups also conducted GOTV work in African American communities. The New York League of Women Voters regularly supplied GOTV speakers to outside organizations; occasionally, they supplied them to African American groups, as when Dr. Katherine Bement Davis addressed the "Colored Branch of the YWCA" in 1924. Similarly, the president of the League of Women Voters of the Oranges in northern New Jersey conducted at the Oakwood Avenue "colored branch" of the YWCA a "rather unusual" series of lectures and workshops, one of which was a "get-out-the-vote meeting" at which "civic responsibility" was to be discussed.[30]

In the South, some African American leaders cautiously took up GOTV in their communities. In Birmingham, for example, several African American women's clubs—the Cosmos Club, Inter Se, the Joy Crafters and the Pierian Club—all took part in a GOTV meeting sponsored by the county League of Women Voters. Businessmen and publishers took up GOTV as well. Birmingham's African American newspaper urged members of the community to register to vote, arguing on the editorial page that "thousands of Negro men and women of this district are prepared to register. The opportunity is here," it continued. "We should seize it as the great hope for our protection and the security of our commonwealth."[31]

To some, the tenor and character of GOTV work by African Americans in the South may seem disappointing, even deficient. They barely mentioned the racialized and brutal policies of disenfranchisement—the unfair laws and the violence—that blocked them from the polls. Color-blind calls exhorting African Americans simply to get out and vote ("The opportunity is here") seem wildly out of touch. Nor did they use the campaigns to challenge the class hierarchies that excluded so many more from the polls, failing, for example, to protest the poll taxes that made voting by poorer African Americans all but impossible. This is not to say that African American organizations failed to protest disenfranchisement or work to restore their rights. Outside the GOTV campaigns, many community leaders worked vigorously to restore equity at the ballot box. Many took bold positions, squarely asserting, as did W. E. B. Du Bois in the pages of *The Crisis,* that African Americans were "not free to vote." Within the GOTV campaigns, however, African American civic leaders did not explicitly work to end the poll taxes and literacy tests that barred their community from the polls; indeed, often they called for energetic compliance with them, calling in a 1924 newspaper opinion piece, for example, for a "poll tax and registration crusade throughout the length and breadth of the state." They did not use the campaigns to push for an end to the barriers to black voting; they called on members of the community, rather, to overcome barriers and go to the polls and vote.[32]

This approach may also be read as a calculated and cautious choice. Surely it demonstrates one way that this group used the "weapons of the weak"; to call on community members to accept the system and succeed within it rather than change it helped them to avoid reprisals. But this approach also accomplished something more. These community leaders pursued, it seems, not a distinctively race-conscious politics but rather a "politics of respectability." By adopting a strategy of "we, too"—"we, too" can meet the standards for civic worthiness that whites claim only they can meet—they were asserting that they were the civic equals of whites, that they were fully fit to exercise the responsibilities and privileges of citizenship on the same terms as anyone else. Such an approach by the community's "best women and men" might not only earn them a place in the civic order, but perhaps also open the way for the African American community at large. After all, if the "ideal 'Race Man' . . ." could "serve as an example to whites of the true nature of African Americans," they might "in turn make it easier for others of [the] race to succeed."[33]

On balance, it is hard to fault southern middle-class and elite African Americans for not doing more. At a time in which violence was always near, many chose to tread carefully; even vague statements and benign-looking meetings surely put them at risk. And in a time of such sharp racial hierarchies, African Americans who asserted that they were intelligent voters and respectable citizens were essentially asserting that they were the civic equals of whites. In the 1920s South, that was no small thing.

Thus the involvement of "other" groups in GOTV was plainly limited. GOTV leaders rarely worked to turn out workers, ethnics, or African Americans because these were precisely the people whose status as good citizens was seen as suspect. No leader from these "other" groups assumed a leadership post in the national campaigns. At the local level, however, in scattered and important examples, middle-class and elite community leaders did from time to time take on GOTV work at home. In it they saw a chance to show themselves to be respectable citizens; with it they hoped to earn a measure of civic equality.

There is one group that might have been expected to join the GOTV campaigns with great enthusiasm. Political parties had long borne the responsibility for getting voters to the polls and, for most of the nineteenth century, had compiled a stunning record of success. GOTV groups, committed as they were to nonpartisanship, might have learned much from parties about the nuts and bolts of boosting turnout; the parties, in turn, might have profited from the influx of new voters that the vote groups promised to produce. There is ample reason to expect political parties to have been intensely involved in the vote campaigns.

But, in fact, they were not. The relationship between the GOTV groups and the parties was surprisingly and strictly limited. Prominent partisans loudly endorsed the vote campaigns, but the official party organizations remained strangely silent. Rarely did GOTV groups and the parties cooperate in any concrete way. Just as striking was the reluctance of vote groups to use the methods, such as precinct canvasses, that parties had used to turn out voters so effectively for so long. Despite their shared interests, the GOTV groups did little to cooperate with the Democratic and Republican Parties, and the parties did little to cooperate with them.

This is all the more remarkable given the substantial overlap between the ranks of party activists and GOTV supporters. Many prominent partisans actively promoted GOTV. Alton B. Parker, head of the National Civic Federation during the GOTV campaigns, had been the Democratic nominee for president in 1904. Elihu Root, Republican and former secretary of state and senator, also took the podium on behalf of the NCF vote campaigns. Eleanor Roosevelt, deeply involved at that time in the New York State Democratic Party, and Sarah Schuyler Butler, Vice Chair of the New York State Republican Committee, were paired as speakers at NCF functions, while Emily Newell Blair, vice chair of the Democratic National Committee, and Harriet Taylor Upton, vice chair of the Executive Committee of the Republican National Committee, issued a joint statement in 1924 in support of GOTV. Key figures in the League's GOTV movement campaigned vigorously in the 1928 presidential race. Maud Wood Park and Caroline Slade took leaves of absence from the League to campaign for Herbert Hoover, while Florence Whitney chaired the Women's Independent Committee for Alfred E. Smith.[34]

These examples should not mislead. Substantial as the overlap between prominent partisans and GOTV leaders might have been, on no occasion did any party leader, in his or her capacity as a party leader, endorse GOTV or work on behalf of the campaigns. When party leaders spoke out in praise of the vote campaigns, they did so as individual activists and not on behalf of their parties.

At the national level, the parties did not cooperate with GOTV in any capacity. Neither the Democratic nor the Republican National Committees (DNC and RNC, for short) joined in the vote campaigns. Indeed, even at the local level, cooperation between parties and GOTV was unusual. Examples of such collaboration are scattered and include small donations to the local GOTV coordinating committee in New York City by representatives of both Tammany Hall and the Republican County Committee, for example, and the simple listing of the "West End Woman's Republican Club" in the "Honor Roll of [GOTV] Co-Operating Organizations" in St. Louis.[35]

Even without an explicit tie to the parties, it would have been possible for GOTV groups to use party methods. From time to time GOTV groups in fact spoke about the importance of the party-style canvass— compiling lists of potential voters, precinct by precinct; checking those lists against the rolls of registered voters; buttonholing unregistered citizens to get them to enroll; following up on election day to see that they had in fact voted; even physically transporting them to the polls. In truth, however, very few GOTV groups actually did this kind of work. A few local Leagues organized systematic, thorough canvasses— Saginaw, Michigan, for example, was praised for perfecting a system of "block organization." Many vote groups skipped the canvass but offered transportation to citizens who requested it, Legion posts in Huntington Beach and Santa Ana, California and League chapters in Virginia, St. Louis, and New London, Connecticut, among them. The best the other groups could do was occasionally speak an approving word on behalf of party-style canvassing, but some GOTV groups—*Collier's* and the NAM, for example—did not do even that.[36]

What stands out here is not the strength of the connection between political parties and GOTV, but its weakness. GOTV groups put minuscule effort into party methods compared to advertising or education. Some party leaders said they supported GOTV, but not in their capacity as party leaders. Indeed, the relationship between GOTV groups and political parties was fraught with tension, not cooperation, and for very good reasons. GOTV groups abhorred partisanship, even though at times they appreciated the functions that parties performed. And parties saw GOTV as emanating from unfriendly quarters and possibly introducing an uncomfortable uncertainty into the electoral process.

Some GOTV groups conceded that political parties were an essential fixture of a democratic system. The League of Women Voters made the study of parties a basic part of its citizenship education curriculum, encouraging local Leagues everywhere to "Know Your Parties." The NAM and *Collier's* even mimicked parties when they put out "platforms" of recommendations on policy issues such as government efficiency and the postwar economy.[37]

GOTV activists concluded that parties could be positive, but partisanship was not. Vote groups were unsparing in their condemnation of "unthinking" party-line voting. Partisanship, *Collier's* editors argued, "drag[ged] good judgment in the dust." Good people who stayed away from the polls unwittingly empowered party machines, added a Legion editorial, because their absence permitted "professional panderers of the ballot box" to control a small number of unthinking voters and thus to "brazenly" manipulate the public's business in unscrupulous ways. To many of the middle- and upper-class reformers of the vote campaigns, partisanship was not a time-honored commitment to a political philosophy. To them it was illegitimate, a profound corruption of civic virtue. Good citizens, they felt sure, were above such blind loyalties. "Country, not Party," the Legion professed as its motto. "Policies, not Politics."[38]

Political parties distrusted nonpartisanship as much as GOTV groups distrusted partisanship. Publicly, the Democratic and Republican parties maintained a studied silence on the topic of GOTV despite the fact that vote activists kept them well apprised of their work. DNC and RNC files are full of GOTV reports and recommendations that were acknowledged merely with polite notes of thanks. When GOTV touched on the issue of parties, political leaders tactfully refused requests for help, as when President Coolidge's secretary declined Ralph Easley's request that the president issue a statement urging every citizen to join a party; that, Bascom Slemp said, was a "controversial question." The parties knew about the vote campaigns and elected to keep them at a cool distance.[39]

There were plenty of reasons for the parties' guarded response. Many of the people who ran the GOTV campaigns were people with whom the parties had fought long-running battles. Progressive reformers, plentiful in the GOTV ranks, had after all made a career out of bashing parties. *Collier's* attacks on partisanship—condemning it, for example, as a frame of mind befitting "inferior" and "unscrupulous men"—did not win them any friends amongst party leaders. The LWV aroused suspicion of a different sort: in the uncertain days after woman suffrage, some party leaders worried that the League aspired to be a third party, a woman's party. Furthermore, simply increasing the number of voters held little appeal. The parties' interest lay in increasing the number of their own supporters, not increasing the number of voters in general without knowing which party these new voters would support. In other words, GOTV did them no particular good—and potentially a great deal of harm.[40]

Mutual distrust, therefore, accounts for the carefully circumscribed relationship between the vote reformers and the parties. Even as they courted the support of parties, GOTV groups professed their disdain for partisanship; the parties, understandably, were not interested in participating in such a project and, indeed, remained suspicious of their motives. As a consequence, throughout the 1920s, the political parties and the vote campaigns cooperated almost not at all.

In sum, then, the list of participants in the GOTV campaigns reads like a roster of middle-class respectability. White clubwomen and businessmen took charge, organizing and executing the campaigns on the national level and in a stunning range of cities and towns. Other organizations—religious groups, veterans' groups, and boys' and girls' clubs among them—also played substantial roles.

But in the ranks of the GOTV organizers there were also a few surprises. Some whose participation might have been expected, like political parties, were largely absent. And some whose participation might have been surprising, such as southerners and African Americans, were in fact present. Immigrants and ethnic Americans, workers, and minorities, however, participated only at the margins: their efforts were unusual and small in scale in comparison to the efforts of others. Most of the GOTV activists were middle class and white; for the most part, the campaigns belonged to them.

"Hurrah Campaigns" and Citizenship Schools: The Methods of the GOTV Campaigns

When the vote activists made use of "every conceivable agency," they embraced tactics from the sober to the spectacular, from the everyday to the extraordinary. They posted notices in newspapers; they dropped leaflets from airplanes; they lectured on literacy tests; they practiced punching ballots. Their methods varied widely, to be sure, but most of their work can be classified into one of two broad categories: either they *advertised* to make citizens more conscious of the need to vote, or they *educated* to make citizens more conscientious in the exercise of their duties.

Advertising or publicity campaigns were predicated upon the premise that the problem of low turnout was a problem of awareness. Dubbed by one leader a "hurrah scheme of campaigning," advertising-style campaigns worked to increase the number of voters by announcing that registration or election days were at hand and calling upon citizens to get themselves to the polls. Publicity campaigns were primarily campaigns of exhortation: they neither transformed nor reformed the voter, but rather simply asked him or her to go to the polls.[41]

Advertising-style campaigns included, to be sure, advertising. Businesses took out GOTV ads in newspapers or incorporated reminders to vote into their regular advertising. Gilchrist's department store in Boston, for example, amidst copy touting sale prices on "Black Beauty Comfort Shoes" and "Larger Women's Dresses," urged readers to "BE SURE TO VOTE." The R. A. Tiernan Typewriter Company in southern California reminded readers that the "WELFARE of our NATION Depends Upon You! So Do Your DUTY Tuesday and VOTE!"[42]

GOTV advertising also took other forms. The Junior Chamber of Commerce imprinted special bottle caps and paper collars with GOTV slogans and had them placed on home-delivered milk bottles in ninety-two cities. Billboards and bank and store window displays in New York, St. Louis, Grand Rapids, Cincinnati, and elsewhere reminded citizens of the upcoming election. Publicity stunts, such as the airdrop of leaflets in 1926 from an airplane high above downtown Atlanta, stirred excitement for the cause.[43]

Publicity campaigns extended beyond commercial advertising and included a wide range of ways to inform and remind. Telephone operators in New Jersey, for example, asked election day callers whether they had voted or not. "Telephone trees" accomplished a similar purpose, including one in St. Louis in which a thousand volunteers offered to place GOTV calls to one hundred persons apiece. Automobile caravans, such as those in Pennsylvania and Minnesota in which GOTV campaigners traveled and staged rallies in town after town, worked in the same way. The point of each of these tactics was the same: to remind citizens that the election was near and to build enthusiasm for civic duty.[44]

GOTV publicity campaigns consciously drew their inspiration from the work of the Creel Committee. Shortly after the United States entered World War I, President Woodrow Wilson charged George Creel and the Committee on Public Information (CPI) with mobilizing public support for the war. The CPI created and conducted publicity campaigns to sell war bonds, recruit volunteers for military service, conserve supplies, and shape public opinion. Half a decade later, the GOTV campaigns used many of the same techniques to promote voting: advertising in newspapers and magazines and on billboards; posters and cards for display in store and car windows; speakers for club gatherings and movie audiences in the style of "Four Minute Men"; exhibits at state fairs; and movies and slides. Indeed, some of the groups that had worked with Creel later served in the vote campaigns, too, among them the Chamber of Commerce, the Boy Scouts, and the YMCA. The GOTV groups' reliance upon advertising and publicity techniques meant that their work resembled less the turnout efforts of the political parties than the Creel Committee's publicity campaigns.[45]

The educational campaigns of the GOTV activists operated on a different premise than the advertising campaigns. Rooted in a progressive faith in civic improvement and expertise, the GOTV education campaigns presupposed that nonvoters needed to be transformed or reformed before they cast their ballots. Educated, expert citizens would not only go to the polls; they would go to the polls and vote "intelligently." Vote activists hoped that education would increase not just the quantity of voters, but their "quality" as well.

To meet this goal, GOTV activists enlisted the support of professional educators. The League asked the National Education Association (NEA) to join, pleading that "we shall need every blackboard in the country and every teacher to help get out the vote." GOTV citizenship training efforts were often conducted as formal educational programs. The League of

Women Voters, the American Legion, and others developed specialized curricula and teaching materials for use in voter education programs. GOTV activists reinforced their commitment to education by situating citizenship classes in educational settings such as grade school and college classrooms.[46]

Together, these two tactics, publicity and education, accounted for most of the work of the GOTV campaigns. Some activities, of course, were both at once. Worried that formal education might be a tough sell, GOTV activists often blended educational programs with entertainment. GOTV plays were a popular part of League functions, plays in the spirit of the New Jersey League's *A Day at the Polls,* a "delightful comedy" that illustrated "the careless errors made by voters and election officials." The Milwaukee County League took a similar tack when it entered a float in the city's "Court of Neptune Pageant" in 1926. The event, which "attracted thousands to Milwaukee," gave the League "another opportunity . . . to make its plea for greater responsibility in citizenship." The float, which featured League members posed in a civic tableau around a GOTV poster, even won third place, and continued to draw audiences when it was displayed at the festival's "water carnival."[47]

Frequently GOTV organizers used the two tactics, advertising and education, in tandem. Thus activists in St. Louis in 1924 publicized the need to register and vote with car posters (50,000 of them), window posters (50,000), GOTV letter stickers (150,000), and reminder slips in pay envelopes (300,000), while also educating city residents by providing speakers at some two hundred meetings of community groups.[48]

Both approaches were part of the vote campaigns throughout the 1920s. They were not, however, found in every election cycle in the same proportion. Both publicity and education were crucial in both the 1924 and 1928 campaigns, but the balance between them shifted over time. Many groups emphasized publicity in 1924. When these efforts produced dismal results, many activists came to the conclusion that "hurrah campaigns" were insufficient to motivate citizens to vote. After 1924, GOTV leaders recognized that low voter turnout was a protracted problem and began to put more weight on citizenship education. That, they hoped, might offer an enduring solution.

Rubber Stamps and Radio Teas: The Power of Gender in the GOTV Campaigns

Gender might have counted for little in the vote campaigns. Even GOTV groups with mostly single-sex memberships—the American Legion, the

National Association of Manufacturers, the League of Women Voters, among others—carried GOTV work far beyond their own ranks, and none restricted their efforts to turning out only one sex.

Nonetheless, gender cut a powerful figure in nearly every aspect of the campaigns. Not only did the vote activists offer gendered explanations for nonvoting by women and men; in a very basic way, gender served as an organizing principle of the campaigns. For the most part, women worked with women and men with men. And when each group took up the work of publicity and education, each did so using methods that made sense to them given their gendered experiences as women and men.

The campaigns in fact were largely organized along gender lines. Most women worked to get out the vote through women's groups, usually service or religious groups such as the YWCA, the National Council of Jewish Women, Girls' Friendly Societies, the National Congress of Mothers, women's city clubs, and WCTU chapters. Men's efforts, by contrast, were concentrated in men's groups, primarily business, trade, and service organizations such as the Chamber of Commerce, the Motion Picture Producers and Distributors of America, the Navy League, the American Bankers Association, Lions clubs, and employers' associations.

Just as the structure of the GOTV campaigns was gendered, so too were the methods they used. Women's efforts, for example, often entwined GOTV events with women's ways of socializing. One League member recommended "tea-parties, luncheons, dinners, fashion shows, baby-shows, pageants, parades, dramatics, performances of school-children, bakery sales, [and] fairs" as ways to attract women to programs on voting and good citizenship. These events integrated civic activism into the social worlds of middle-class clubwomen. Get-Out-the-Vote luncheons and teas were common and took place in Pittsburgh; Milwaukee; Omaha; Charles City, Iowa; Westchester County, New York; and elsewhere. "Radio Teas," gatherings of League members and their friends "around the receiving sets" during broadcasts of programs on citizenship and voting, were a favorite in New York City.[49]

Other GOTV efforts linked the turnout campaigns to women's household roles as mothers and hostesses. The Brooklyn League sponsored a baby derby and adorned toddlers with sashes emblazoned with voting slogans. The Federated Clubwomen of San Francisco registered young mothers at a baby clinic. The League's "First Voter" parties were a popular way to mark women's civic coming of age. The "birthday party" thrown for first-time voters by the League in Norwich, New York, in 1928 showed some of the possibilities. Guests were seated at "twelve tables trimmed to represent the twelve months of the year," each decorated with "a tiny birthday cake surmounted by one candle." Each table was the charge of a young host or hostess who had been "instructed" in the "art of presiding at a banquet." Guests were treated to a dinner followed by music and messages of congratulations from local officials. At evening's end, they were sent home with "favors"—"indexed copies of the United States Constitution tied with red, white and blue ribbon." By drawing on their roles as hostesses and mothers, the Get-Out-the-Vote activists worked to infuse civic duty with domesticity.[50]

Men's work in the vote campaigns drew upon their own gendered experiences, in particular their experiences in business. Most men's groups favored reaching nonvoters by what might be called "business methods." Businessmen urged employees to vote in company newsletters, turned club luncheons into Get-Out-the-Vote meetings, and posted voting reminders at country clubs where they gathered to play tennis and golf. Kiwanis headquarters sent GOTV literature to its twelve hundred clubs across the nation, while the NAM printed thousands of red, white, and blue stickers urging "Vote as You Please, But—Vote!" and asked members to paste them onto business correspondence, packages, and pay envelopes. The Junior Chamber of Commerce supplied members with rubber stamps bearing voting slogans and asked them to stamp outgoing mail so as to reach "12,000,000 in this way" alone. These methods not only drew upon men's experience as businessmen; they actually incorporated the Get-Out-the-Vote message into the nation's business routine.[51]

Gender thus shaped not only the organization of the GOTV campaigns but their methods as well. The women and men of the GOTV campaigns usually worked in same-sex groups to spread the message of more active citizenship. By linking the campaigns to family roles on the one hand and to business methods on the other, GOTV reformers infused the campaigns with some of the meanings of gender.

"Will You Vote, Dixie Land?" Regional Variations in the Vote Campaigns

GOTV supporters campaigned actively in every region of the country—in the East, Midwest, and West, as well as in the border states and even the deep South. There were, however, significant regional differences in the quantity of the campaigns, and sometimes in their character as well.

The campaigns were most common in the East and Midwest, least common in the mountain West and South. GOTV activity on some scale took place in Billings, Butte, and Great Falls, Montana; Ogden and Salt Lake City, Utah; Denver and Colorado Springs, Colorado; Boise, Idaho; Carson City, Nevada; Casper, Wyoming; Phoenix, Arizona; and Roswell, New Mexico. None of these campaigns, however, appears to have amounted to much. In the mountain West, the early enfranchisement of women may have undercut the infrastructure upon which the vote campaigns were built: most communities with big campaigns were home to active chapters of the League of Women Voters, and since women as a rule had won suffrage early in the mountain West, the League, which was the successor to the National American Woman Suffrage Association (NAWSA), was relatively weak there.[52]

The South presented an entirely different situation. The South had far lower turnout, and far greater obstacles to changing that, than any other region. The unique complex of circumstances there—a hegemonic Democratic party, an especially restrictive system of poll taxes and literacy tests, and a history of extreme and sustained political violence and intimidation—held turnout in the South far below that of the rest of the nation, and made improvement there vastly more difficult.

The southern campaigns to boost turnout also touched most directly upon sensitive questions of political power. Southern whites could have had much to fear from the vote campaigns. Who in fact did vote reformers there hope to turn out? Did they hope to buttress white rule by turning out more of the white Democrats that the system privileged? Or did they intend to challenge that system by turning out more African Americans and upland whites, people who might well contest hierarchies of race and class by voting Republican? Campaigns to raise voter turnout in the South had the potential to question the power arrangements of the races and classes over which the Democratic party stood guard.

Despite these complexities, a significant number of GOTV campaigns took place in the South. Large and vibrant campaigns took place in Birmingham, Richmond, and Atlanta, and GOTV work on a smaller scale also took place in Dallas, Fort Worth, Shreveport, Montgomery, Norfolk, Lynchburg, Roanoke, and Savannah, as well as in the towns of Concord, Franklin, and Highlands, North Carolina; and Cherrydale and Petersburg, Virginia.[53]

GOTV campaigns in the South, however, were mostly white affairs. Notwithstanding occasional GOTV efforts by southern African Americans, the much more numerous campaigns by southern white clubwomen and businessmen worked to reinforce the region's system of race and class oppression. Campaigns to get out the vote in the South often included, as they did in Dallas and Birmingham, campaigns to encourage the payment of poll taxes, provoking no comment at all upon the legitimacy of a system that disenfranchised the poor. While GOTV campaigns in Michigan and New York worked to simplify the registration process, southern campaigns urged registration without uttering a word about the especially convoluted and even arbitrary registration practices in the region. GOTV everywhere enforced and institutionalized civic hierarchies of race and class; in the South, GOTV worked to fortify a regime in which those hierarchies took a regionally distinctive form.[54]

From time to time, southern GOTV campaigns took on a distinctive regional stamp as southern GOTV activists created slogans or songs with a particular regional resonance. Southern activists employed a variety of linguistic devices to issue their calls for higher turnout without explicitly invoking race. Calls for higher turnout by "qualified voters" were common, but the GOTV groups used other terminology as well. For example, the Mecklenburg County, North Carolina, League devised a slogan, "Loyalty in voting," that cleverly invoked both loyalty to the all-white Democratic party as well as a more generic sense of patriotism and civic duty. Southern GOTV groups also sang a song to the melody of "Dixie":

> 'Way down south in the land of cotton,
> Love of country's not forgotten,
> Will you vote? Will you vote?
> Will you vote, Dixie Land?
> . . .
> Get out the vote in Dixie.
> Hurray! Hurray!
> The South will proudly take her stand
> There'll be no slackers in her land,
> We'll vote. We'll vote,
> We all will vote in Dixie.[55]

"We all will vote in Dixie" did not, of course, mean that they really hoped that "all" would vote. That was true in GOTV campaigns across the country, and it was true in the South. Everywhere the GOTV campaigns worked to reinforce the civic privilege of whites over blacks, the middle classes over the working classes. In the South, the GOTV campaigns worked to reinforce their own particular power regime.

Keeping the Faith: Patriotism and Nonpartisanship
as GOTV Themes

Certainly there were many differences amongst those who worked to get out the vote, including differences of ideology, gender, and region. Indeed, some of the major participants were so far apart ideologically that on issues other than voter turnout—the peace movement, for example, and the proposed constitutional amendment to ban child labor—they fought fiercely. The differences between groups were significant enough that, at the national level at least, the major GOTV organizations for the most part declined to cooperate in any substantial way.[56]

Nonetheless, the work of the GOTV activists employed a shared set of themes and a common civic vocabulary. Whatever their differences, the vote activists promoted the campaigns as an enterprise in patriotism and nonpartisanship, and did so in the terms of a progressive-sounding language of democracy, civic duty, and efficiency. That they embraced the same themes and used the same sorts of words does not necessarily mean that they fully agreed on what these things meant: the Red-bashing that the National Civic Federation regarded as a patriotic duty seemed not at all patriotic to the members of the League, the WCTU, and others whom they smeared as "bolshevists." Rather, these themes and phrases were capacious enough that they accommodated differences in meaning and helped give the campaigns a sense of unity and coherence.

Almost every participating group described voting as the preeminent duty of the patriotic citizen. Rituals and heroes of the recent war were pressed into service in a new campaign against "civic slackers." The Fife and Drum Corps of Boise, Idaho, for instance, led a parade of citizens to City Hall on registration day. Elsewhere, radio stations sounded "To the Colors" to encourage citizens to report for duty at the polls. General John J. Pershing himself "enthusiastically approve[d]" of the GOTV cause. Even the most emotional patriotic symbols of the war found new service in the GOTV campaigns. The umbrella coordinating committee in New York, for example, conducted GOTV business on letterhead that reprinted a moving stanza from "In Flanders Fields" and asked readers to "Vote Election-day" to "Keep the Faith" with those who had made the supreme sacrifice. This sober exercise of patriotic duty called for a serious, nonpartisan tone. As a magazine's editors put it, *"Collier's* does not presume to instruct how votes should be cast. *It does urge that votes shall be cast."*[57]

Nonpartisanship and patriotism were themes upon which GOTV groups could agree. Their common reliance upon a progressive-sounding language of democracy, civic duty, and efficiency harmonized the campaigns further still. Calls to civic duty permeated the literature of the GOTV campaigns; as President Coolidge put it in his endorsement of the National Civic Federation's efforts, "Every American citizen ought to be properly impressed with the duty of casting his ballot." Simon Michelet even designated turnout an index of "voter efficiency." Some participants invoked democracy and civic duty with such utter earnestness that their efforts sound almost naïve today. Consider the lyrics of a song composed for the League of Women Voters campaign, which they sang to the tune of "O Tannenbaum":

> Awake, and hear your country's call,
> Come out and vote, come out and vote.
> Corruption thrives when polls are small,
> Come out and vote, come out and vote.
> Corruption's plans come and forestall,
> End rule by half, have rule by all.
> Democracy, you shall not fall!
> We'll come and vote, we'll come and vote.[58]

Certainly differences between GOTV groups remained. This shared progressive vocabulary, however, gave a highly decentralized set of civic campaigns a measure of coherence and unity. It papered over differences that divided the major GOTV groups at the national level, and it promoted real cooperation between GOTV groups at the local level. After the war as before, the progressive elements of the civic culture proved accommodating and flexible.

The Painful Surprise: The Failure of the GOTV Campaigns

With a commitment to patriotism and nonpartisanship and a progressive inflection, the GOTV campaigners pitched their cause to millions in every region of the country. Publicity materials—twenty-five million NAM stickers and pamphlets, for example, and a half-million display posters put out by *Collier's* ("Register! Vote! Don't Be A Parlor Patriot. Don't Be A Rocking-Chair Paul Revere.") flooded mailboxes and filled shop windows. Press releases were mailed to "every single daily in the country," and advertisements and articles were carried in magazines—the *Saturday Evening Post,* the *Ladies' Home Journal, Literary Digest*—that together boasted many millions of readers. No wonder GOTV leaders believed the campaigns had a vast reach. As *Collier's* put it, "To-day there is not a literate man or woman entitled to plead ignorance" of the importance of voting.[59]

Nevertheless, when the votes were counted, the numbers showed that in their stated goal of boosting turnout the GOTV campaigns had failed miserably. In 1924, forty-nine percent of eligibles went to the polls, far short of the seventy-five percent goal, and, by some calculations—what an embarrassment—a few tenths of a percentage point lower than in 1920. Some states, it was true, posted increases over the previous presidential election, but the states that showed the greatest gains, Wyoming and Mississippi, had negligible GOTV campaigns, really almost none at all. Confronted with these results, the best response that organizers could muster was that without their efforts, things surely would have been worse. Ralph Easley tried to put the best face on it in a letter to eight Sunday newspapers in New York. "All the unselfish and sacrificing work . . . must have added hundreds of thousands, if not millions, of voters to the list." "Had they not voted," he continued, "there would have been a bigger slump in the vote." The frustration continued in 1928 when, in a year of fewer and smaller GOTV campaigns, voter turnout increased to 61 percent—a substantial boost, to be sure, though still far short of what the GOTV activists had in mind, and not something for which they dared take credit.[60]

Privately, the GOTV groups expressed deep disappointment that so much hard work had accomplished so little. The NCF dubbed the campaigns the "Get-Out-the-Vote fiasco," while an officer of the Boston Chamber of Commerce rued the "painfully surprising" results. After the failure of 1924, GOTV leaders reevaluated and retooled for future campaigns. An NCF officer urged a writer for the Associated Press to look ahead. "It will be a surprise to the country," he told him, "to learn how ineffectual the 'Hurrah' scheme of campaign to improve turnout really is; but . . . the earlier we learn that, the sooner we shall 'get down to brass tacks'" and find a more effective way to boost participation at the polls. In fact, the NCF and other groups placed greater emphasis on voter education and less on straight publicity in the 1926 and 1928 campaigns, though without ever achieving the sorts of results for which they had hoped.[61]

Why did the campaigns meet with such failure? Part of the answer lies in the irony that the GOTV groups invested very little effort in actually getting out the vote. They advertised and educated on a massive scale to persuade people of the importance of voting, but did little to actually follow through. They rarely checked registration lists, or canvassed, or transported voters to the polls. Rather than simply bring voters to the polls, GOTV activists wanted to inspire and transform them into people who would want to bring themselves. For all the extraordinary efforts the vote groups made to boost turnout, very little energy in the Get-Out-the-Vote campaigns was spent on the nuts and bolts of actually getting voters out.

This does not mean that the middle-class and elite whites of the GOTV campaigns were disingenuous or unthinking. Rather, it speaks volumes about the civic values they embraced. They believed that good citizenship consisted in behaving in certain ways, ways that they believed they demonstrated and lived, ways that they expected advertising and education to promote in others. In 1923 and 1924, however, the League of Women Voters, the National Association of Manufacturers, the National Civic Federation, the American Legion and *Collier's* magazine geared up with confidence that they could change the nation's track record of turnout. Because these groups did the most to push the problem of nonvoting onto the public agenda and shape the efforts to combat it, the specifics of their campaigns warrant a closer look.

"VOTE AS YOU PLEASE—BUT VOTE!"

The Leadership of the Get-Out-the-Vote Campaigns

"VOTE AS YOU PLEASE—BUT VOTE," the stickers urged, patriotically presented in red, white, and blue (see fig. 9). Businessmen, factory owners, and merchants from coast to coast brought the GOTV message to colleagues, customers, and employees by pasting these stickers on business correspondence, newsletters, employee pay envelopes, and customers' parcels. Once the GOTV emblem of a single business group, the "Vote as you please" slogan and the tricolor graphic were soon employed by a broad range of GOTV groups and even by advertisers selling products that had nothing to do with the campaigns. "Vote as you please," in short, became a testament to the reach and penetration of the GOTV campaigns.

The "Vote As You Please" slogan was coined by the National Association of Manufacturers, one of the leading Get-Out-the-Vote groups. In the profusion of the GOTV campaigns, five organizations stood out for the extraordinary scope and scale of their work. The League of Women Voters, the National Association of Manufacturers, *Collier's* magazine, the National Civic Federation, and the American Legion spearheaded the biggest and most important GOTV campaigns. Each made GOTV a top priority within the organization, devoting substantial resources to the cause and organizing campaigns on a national scale. These groups comprised the campaigns' activist core.

Three of these groups—the League, the NAM, and *Collier's*—claimed to have inaugurated the GOTV movement; the League, however, was the only group with a legitimate claim to that distinction. Rather, each of these three groups took up GOTV independently, and each devised a plan of action and executed it autonomously. Collaboration amongst the national GOTV leaders was unusual: at the national level, only the National Civic Federation and the American Legion cooperated closely.

Though the campaigns were independently conceived and run, they were synchronized by the rhythm of the election cycle. The biggest campaigns took place in presidential election years, in particular in 1924. In off years, many GOTV groups ran smaller campaigns to turn out voters for congressional or city elections or stepped back to assess their past work and plan for future elections. Over the years leadership roles shifted from group to group. The League, the NAM, and *Collier's* all did their most intensive GOTV work in 1924. After 1924 the NAM and *Collier's* largely abandoned the project, but the National Civic Federation and the American Legion stepped in and in 1926 put on their largest campaigns. Only the League of Women Voters sustained a serious commitment to GOTV throughout the period, conducting substantial and intensive campaigns in 1924, 1926, and 1928.

These, then, were the campaigns of the groups that did the most to lead GOTV. Why did each take up the cause? What precisely did each do to turn out more voters? How did each shape the overall campaigns, and how, in turn, was each shaped by them? Finally, in the aggregate, what did their efforts add up to?

"Let Us Come to Our Citizens' Duty 100% Strong": The Vote Campaigns of the League of Women Voters

In April 1923, the League of Women Voters, assembled in convention in Des Moines, Iowa, set new goals for the organization by passing two resolutions. The women agreed first that

> *Whereas,* in the last Presidential election less than fifty per cent of the men and women eligible to vote actually voted, *therefore be it resolved,* that the National League of Women Voters call upon the public-spirited men and women of all political parties and in every section of the United States to take part in a campaign for efficient citizenship to the end that at the next Presidential election at least seventy-five per cent of the voters accept the responsibility and the privilege of self government and cast their ballots according to the best information they can obtain.[1]

They then agreed that "*Whereas*, the realization of that purpose rests upon clear ideas of Government and Politics in the minds of energetic men and women," they were further "*resolved*" that "each state League undertake a plan of study" of election laws, legislatures, and the "machinery" of government "with a view to full participation by the electorate."[2]

With these two resolutions the League of Women Voters inaugurated the GOTV campaigns and assumed a preeminent role in them. The League was fully engaged in GOTV in April 1923, more than a year before any of the other major groups adopted the cause. It boasted a skilled national leadership comprised of women with long histories of political involvement. It staffed the national headquarters with professional administrators, researchers, and publicists. By 1928 it had established a solid organizational base comprised of Leagues in forty-five states and Hawaii and the District of Columbia plus hundreds of city and county Leagues, all knit together in a federal style. Conventions and frequent publications helped stitch together a coherent organization and encouraged consistency in purpose and practice. Alone among the major groups the League sustained its commitment to GOTV, kicking off the campaigns in 1923 and persisting with them through 1928. No group did more to shape the campaigns' tenor and form.[3]

If no group did more to mold the vote campaigns, no group was more thoroughly molded by them. The GOTV campaigns left a lasting mark on the League's public identity and mission. At a time when the organization was new, the vote campaigns gave it high visibility and a sterling reputation. "No one activity of the League," a League committee recalled later, brought it "anything like the publicity which attended the Get-Out-the-Vote campaign of 1924. From coast to Coast [*sic*]," newspaper clippings about their work "poured back" along with "abundant editorial comment almost wholly favorable."[4]

The vote campaigns also did much to help the League to refine its public purpose. At its conception after World War I, the League embraced two goals, to "foster education in citizenship" and to "support improved legislation." The vote campaigns helped the League satisfy the first goal; lobbying for progressive causes such as maternal and child health legislation and a constitutional amendment to ban child labor helped it meet the second. But consensus on legislative goals proved difficult to sustain and by the early 1920s the League had shifted much of the work of lobbying to other organizations, such as the Women's Joint Congressional Committee. However, the problem of an uninformed, apathetic citizenry remained, and the League addressed it with vigor in the vote campaigns, first as a special, election-year project and then increasingly as the heart of the League's day-to-day work. The vote campaigns were a formative experience for the League, an early step in its evolution into an organization dedicated to "informing and galvanizing the electorate . . . on a nonpartisan basis."[5]

The League's approach to the vote campaigns was rooted in its origins, structure, and membership. Formed in 1919 as an auxiliary of the National American Woman Suffrage Association as the Nineteenth Amendment neared final ratification, the League was launched as an independent organization at NAWSA's Victory Convention in 1920. Maud Wood Park, a summa cum laude graduate of Radcliffe and president of the Massachusetts Woman Suffrage Association, was the organization's first president and served until 1924. Park was succeeded by Belle Sherwin, who served as president until 1934. Sherwin, the daughter of the founder of the Sherwin-Williams paint company, was likewise cut from a progressive tradition. Educated at Wellesley, she taught English in settlement houses in her native Cleveland, organized the Consumers' League and Women's City Clubs there, and chaired the Ohio Women's Committee of the wartime Council on National Defense during World War I. Sherwin's selection as president shows the importance the League placed on the vote campaigns; after all, Sherwin had chaired the Committee on Efficiency in Government, the committee which had orchestrated the first vote campaigns. Both Sherwin and Park were close associates of Carrie Chapman Catt.[6]

The League's interest in the vote campaigns thus lay in its origins: the women who had worked so hard to win woman suffrage were determined to see it used. The poor turnout of women voters in 1920 sent "shock waves of disappointment" through the suffragist community. If women did not turn out to vote, if they did not even show up, what hope was there that they could "clean up" politics or launch a fresh wave of progressive reform? Indeed, what hope was there that women would be taken seriously in politics at all? The opportunity was historic—and it was also very much in danger of being lost. The promise of a large pool of new voters, Maud Wood Park argued, voters who were "untrammeled by carelessly made political affiliations" and without "bad political tendencies to undo," would last "only a few years" and would "never come again." The former suffragists knew that the stakes were high: the success of woman suffrage—indeed, the very legitimacy of women as full voting citizens—was on the line. "I implore you to register," Catt pleaded in 1928 to her female radio listeners. "Let us come to our citizens' duty 100% strong."[7]

The former suffragists' concerns, however, were not limited to women. The numbers showed that low turnout could not be blamed on them alone, and many were less than impressed by the "low standards of citizenship found among men." Clearly, League women argued, it was "just as important to get out the men-vote as the women-vote." In the GOTV campaigns, that was what they set out to do.[8]

The GOTV campaigns became the League's "chief activity" in 1924, improved participation at the polls its "foremost goal." With the presidential election fast approaching, the League put its full weight into educational and publicity work. It sponsored civics classes to teach the mechanics of governance. It publicized the elections and stressed the importance of voting in leaflets, cartoons, poetry, and songs, all deliberately "popular in form." It dispatched campaign secretary Minnie Fisher Cunningham on a national speaking tour. It asked local Leagues to compile lists of registered voters and to canvass precincts. It asked other organizations, such as the YWCA, the Federated Council of Churches of Christ in America, and the National Education Association, to help.[9]

The League had sponsored civics classes and workshops from its very first days, but in the months before the 1924 election it greatly intensified its efforts. It developed civics quizzes ("Know Your Town," "Know Your State," and "Know Your Nation") and encouraged local Leagues to make a project of finding out the answers. These quizzes in effect served as a standardized curriculum for civics education among League members. The League sponsored workshops for the voting public on registration procedures, ballot-marking, and the use of voting machines. A whole range of institutes, seminars, and demonstrations rounded out the League's program of civic education. Between 1923 and 1925 the League sponsored some four hundred formal citizenship schools, some with as many as a thousand participants, and many more workshops and demonstrations. All were designed to improve the information levels of voters and increase their attendance at the polls.[10]

To complement its educational efforts, the League publicized the election and the importance of voting with press releases, posters, pamphlets, and contests. Elizabeth Hauser headed the League's Publicity Department for most of this period, and largely through her efforts the League issued regular press releases, articles, and photographs about GOTV. Much of this material was supplied to news outlets in camera-ready form, a practice that made it easy for newspapers to publish their material. Newswires regularly carried the League's GOTV news. The League also purchased a few pages in each issue of *The Woman Citizen* and in election years filled them with reports of GOTV.[11]

The national office also promoted the GOTV message with two graphics: a simple nine-by-twelve-inch poster of the word "*Vote*" superimposed upon a ballot box, and a more elaborate illustration of the "Seven Steep Steps" to "Efficient Citizenship." In 1924 and after, the League distributed the "Vote" poster widely, selling it at a small profit to state Leagues and other GOTV groups. This poster surfaced in shop windows, bank lobbies, business offices, and fair booths. The "Seven Steep Steps" graphic was usually reserved for newspapers and League publications. It outlined the League's GOTV program succinctly, urging readers to support candidate forums and precinct campaigns.[12]

In the summer of 1924 the League was also approached with "a remarkable advertising proposition" by the Frederic J. Haskin Company, an information bureau maintained in Washington by the newspaper industry. Haskin offered to print a GOTV booklet, publicize it in the nation's newspapers, and fill mail-in requests for it. The League jumped at the chance and composed "The ABC of Voting," twenty pages of state-by-state registration requirements, nonvoting numbers, suggestions for further reading (including League literature), and pithy reminders ("541,778 Voters Failed to Vote in 1920 in Louisiana. Are You Satisfied With These Figures?"). Haskin produced fifty thousand copies of the booklet and announced its availability "on front pages across the country."[13]

The League further publicized the vote campaigns by pushing its way onto the nation's editorial pages. In 1924 it announced a Get-Out-the-Vote cartoon contest with a prize of $250 to be paid to the artist who drew the published cartoon "best calculated to arouse general interest and increase attendance at the polls." The League appointed a distinguished panel of judges to assess the entries, among them William Allen White, Katharine Ludington, Bruce Bliven of *The New Republic,* and Anna Steese Richardson of *The Woman's Home Companion.*[14]

Artists and newspapers responded enthusiastically. A long list of papers published contest entries—the *Chicago Tribune,* the *Los Angeles Times,* the *Pittsburgh Press,* the *Des Moines Register,* and the *Atlanta Constitution;* smaller papers like the *Seattle Times,* the *Oklahoma City Times,* the *Niagara Falls Gazette,* and the *Wichita Eagle;* even the *Lima (Ohio) News* and the *Bluefield (W.Va.) Daily Telegraph;* and many more. Oz Black of the *Lincoln (Nebr.) Star* won the prize with a cartoon that depicted a horse, "The Half of Us Which Votes," pulling a heavy cart up a hill while a second horse, "The Half Which Does Not Vote," held the cart back.[15]

The League's GOTV efforts culminated in a contest to award a silver loving cup—"one of the handsomest among American trophies"—to the state League that produced the greatest percentage increase in turnout. The national League passed out to the press and to every state League a photo of Belle Sherwin posing proudly with the trophy; state Leagues sent out their own press releases announcing their plans to capture the prize. In the end thirty-five state Leagues competed for the cup, which was awarded in 1925 to the California League in a lavish ceremony at the national convention in Richmond.[16]

League efforts did not stop at the top; indeed, the headquarters worked hard to enlist the help of local chapters and outside organizations. To accomplish this, the national headquarters issued a forty-page handbook, "Get Out the Vote—Why, When, How." The handbook explained the League's mission in the campaigns ("to restore majority rule in this country"), enumerated turnout goals for every state, and supplied samples of GOTV fliers and posters. It provided talking points for speakers ("The country will be in a bad way if the national backbone cannot have a little starch put into it, if the voters cannot be made to see that it is the part of good citizenship . . . to vote"); it detailed procedures for conducting a party-style precinct canvass; it furnished examples of GOTV work already in progress ("In Minneapolis a registration booth was mounted on a truck and taken through the residential district"); and it suggested slogans for fliers ("*Stop* and ask yourself whether you will *look* like a good citizen if you do not *listen* to your country's call for voters and vote"). Between 1924 and 1926 the League distributed seventy-five hundred copies of the handbook to state and local Leagues and other organizations, including the American Federation of Labor, the Women's Christian Temperance Union, the Women's Trade Union League, the American Association of University Women, the National Municipal League, the National Council of Jewish Women, the Pan-Hellenic Conference, the National Farmers' Union, and the National Grange.[17]

Using both the suggestions of the League handbook and their own homegrown ideas, women in state and local Leagues eagerly embraced GOTV work. League ladies in Grand Rapids, Michigan, decorated cars and passed out "dodgers" or leaflets. The Delaware League recruited the governor to speak at an "outdoor mass meeting" while the Oregon League contacted voters by telephone. The Geneva, New York, League applauded Eleanor Roosevelt's speech there on the importance of "getting women, especially, out to vote." The Toledo League found no project "more interesting or more worth while" than the ballot-marking classes it conducted "in the homes of Polish, Syrian and Bulgarian women." The El Paso, Texas, League sent out five thousand fliers, affixed stickers to milk bottles, and conducted a candidates' forum complete with Spanish-language translation. State Leagues in Michigan, Wisconsin, and Alabama offered their own trophies for the best GOTV work by a county or local League; in a state like Alabama that had not "the faintest hope" of winning the national cup, a state-level contest provided incentive and opportunities for recognition.[18]

Leagues in a few communities—Minneapolis; Saginaw, Michigan; Webster Groves, Missouri; parts of New York—put on the party-style precinct organization campaigns that the national headquarters had recommended. Most locals, however, stuck to advertising or education. Some LWV efforts, admittedly, were rather meager: the Leagues in Bismarck, North Dakota, and Great Falls, Montana, for example, did little more than get up a meeting or two. But some Leagues orchestrated campaigns that were utterly grand in scale: the Illinois organization distributed one hundred thousand pieces of GOTV literature, blitzed 118 daily newspapers across the state with a series of ten press releases, and broadcast fourteen radio talks on the importance of voting. Whatever the scale of their efforts, the League's presence in so many communities made GOTV a local fact. League chapters helped translate the grand designs of the national leaders into campaigns with roots in the community.[19]

The League, in short, did much to make the vote campaigns visible. When turnout did not increase in 1924, the campaigns' failure was just as visible. Women in particular were excoriated for their low turnout, the value of woman suffrage pointedly questioned. The League rushed to defend the enfranchisement of women, arguing repeatedly that "woman suffrage has been anything but a failure." It was hardly reasonable, Maud Wood Park argued, to expect women voters "over-night to straighten out tangles over which generations of men had worked in vain." Despite the disappointing numbers, a League committee argued that surely "the final intensive campaign of getting out the voters was unimportant in comparison to the value of the educational work which preceded." League women had done little to improve the quantity of voting citizens, it was true, but they felt sure they had done much to improve their quality.[20]

Despite these disappointments, the project was too important to abandon. In 1925, the League worked to rethink the GOTV effort. It col-

lected official return figures from secretaries of state to pinpoint the results of the last election. It polled state Leagues to inquire about their
own GOTV efforts and why they thought they had succeeded or failed.
It also asked a "Committee of Nine," chaired by Florence Whitney of
New York and established at the 1926 convention in Richmond, Virginia, to review the evidence and recommend a course of action. Whitney's committee recommended that the League return to the organization's original mission of civic education and link the campaigns to the
League's permanent program. The permanent institutionalization of the
GOTV program became the new goal: GOTV work should not be allowed to "interfere with regular League work," but rather should be
"built" into "the program of the organization." From this point forward,
GOTV would be no ancillary project, but rather an ongoing demonstration of the organization's basic mission.[21]

In 1926 the League made changes and moved squarely in this direction. Rather than continue to orchestrate a GOTV campaign out of central headquarters, the national office refashioned itself into a resource for
affiliates. It designed and distributed ten thousand copies of a GOTV
poster; set up a prize-winning exhibit at the U.S. Sesquicentennial Exposition in Philadelphia; publicized state and local campaigns in the pages
of the *Woman Citizen;* and served as a clearinghouse for information.[22]

Though the National confined its GOTV work to these tasks in the off
year, some state and local Leagues in 1926 "carried on very vigorously."
The California League, for example, printed up red, white, and blue
posters reminding citizens that "November Second is the day you attend
to State Business — *Vote Early.*" The New London, Connecticut, League
conducted a house-to-house canvass and held a "school for voters" in an
empty storefront, while the Wayne County, Michigan, League brought
in Eleanor Roosevelt to speak at a dinner for first-time voters. The Ramsey County, Minnesota, League presented a play by one of its members;
in *The Voter's Dream,* a woman "in the home, occupied with philan-
thropic interests and indifferent to her responsibilities as a voter," learned
"the error of her ways." The Atlanta League distributed a total of thirty-
five thousand fliers, fifteen thousand tags, and one thousand posters,
and prepared to award a silver trophy to the Georgia chapter that turned
out the most voters.[23]

The results of their efforts in 1926 were even less impressive than before. Forty-five states reported a drop in turnout from 1924, most of
them on the order of twenty-five or thirty percentage points, a pattern
typical of off-year elections but not well understood at the time. The

persistent low turnout made the League's ongoing study of nonvoting more urgent than ever; it simply had to get a handle on the problem before taking up GOTV work again. The League decided to conduct its own community studies of nonvoting, patterned explicitly on the work of Professor Ben A. Arneson. League women spent the winter of 1926–1927 surveying households and scanning voting records in communities in five states.[24]

In the meantime, local and state Leagues on their own initiative again took up GOTV in the off-year elections of 1927, among them Leagues in Toledo, St. Louis, Kentucky, and South Dakota. The national office continued to conduct citizenship schools, holding them in Arizona, California, Kansas, New Hampshire, New York, North Dakota, and Washington state. Most of the League's efforts in 1927, however, were geared toward preparing for the presidential election of 1928. To that end, while the community studies were in progress, the League undertook its most comprehensive review of the problem of nonvoting yet.[25]

In April 1927, the League presented its findings on the causes and character of nonvoting. Their own studies confirmed the scholarship of the day: fewer women voted than men, and higher education seemed to be linked to higher turnout. They also concluded that publicity-style campaigns were ill-suited to fix the problem of nonvoting because "indifference may be the largest single factor in the 'Stay-At-Home-Vote,' but back of 'indifference' lies . . . a failure of education." While the vote campaigns might still include an "appeal to those individuals who need only to be reminded that the vote is theirs and the time has come to use it," the effectiveness of the campaigns was likely to depend far more upon an effective program of "political education." Citizenship education, the League concluded, must be made the clear priority. The League released these results to the press but also took their data straight to the top: on April 30, 1927, a League delegation presented the findings in a meeting at the White House to President Calvin Coolidge.[26]

With these preparations and their "considered experience," the League approached GOTV in 1928 with much more modest expectations. It announced from the outset that "it is not to be expected that the size of the total vote on election day, small or large, will in any sense be a measure of the success of the League's contribution"; educational goals resisted such easy measurement. But while quantitative measures—the amount of literature distributed, for example—clearly indicate that the League's vote campaigns were smaller in 1928 than in 1924, the 1928 vote campaigns were also much more fully integrated into the League's overall agenda: this time the League appointed no special staff to the project and made little effort to enlist the aid of other groups. The emphasis in 1928 was placed squarely on education, and the result was a GOTV campaign that was at once "less spectacular" and "more realistic."[27]

To this end, the headquarters issued a new 1928 GOTV handbook, a manual focused squarely on the ins and outs of civic education. This time the handbook contained not clever stories of the promotional work done by various locals, but detailed instructions on how to conduct one-day "Voters' Schools" and the proper way to compose, tabulate, and publicize candidate questionnaires.[28]

The League also continued its program of citizenship schools and continued to regard "no part" of its work "with more satisfaction." Around 1928 the League switched from a retail to a wholesale strategy, easing out of the business of training citizens directly and easing into a system of "model" or "demonstration" schools at which League leaders would be taught how to set up schools themselves. Mrs. W. W. Ramsey, a League vice president, traveled widely and conducted model schools in St. Louis, Kansas City, and Joplin, Missouri; Grand Island and Lincoln, Nebraska; Topeka and Wichita, Kansas; Tulsa, Oklahoma; Fairmont, Wheeling, and Morgantown, West Virginia; Davenport, Iowa; and Madison, South Dakota. The wholesale approach helped the League boost its capacity to educate citizens: League women estimated that the "pupils" of the Kansas City model school alone taught six thousand citizens before election day.[29]

The League also prepared new materials to reflect its greater emphasis on education, sometimes borrowing the work of local chapters. To improve turnout in city elections, for example, the Toledo League in 1927 designed and professionally produced a GOTV filmstrip, a "Minute Movie." The League headquarters applauded the filmstrip as "a most promising medium for much of the education work which we shall have to do in the coming year to get out the vote," and encouraged League women everywhere to obtain copies for the 1928 campaign.[30]

The League's major innovation in the 1928 campaigns, however, was its use of radio as an educational medium. Local Leagues, in particular the New York and Chicago chapters, had been experimenting with radio for civic education since 1924. At the invitation of National Broadcasting Company president Merlin H. Aylesworth, the League developed plans to broadcast a far-reaching and regularly scheduled program.[31]

On January 3, 1928, the "Voter's Campaign Information Service" made its debut. In the broadcast premiere, League President Belle Sherwin explained the purpose and format of the program. Strictly "unpartisan" in orientation, the League hoped the program would lead "the voting public . . . to think responsibly about the merits of campaign issues and finally to more general and responsible voting." Each program would feature guest speakers who staked out opposing sides of a current issue. The League was also prepared to mix civic education with entertainment: the inaugural program included a few Christmas numbers and ended with a rousing rendition of the "Star Spangled Banner."[32]

The half-hour "Voters' Service" aired weekly on Tuesday nights. It was broadcast alternately from the studios of WEAF in New York and WRC in the District of Columbia. Some twenty-one radio stations, from Maine to Texas to Nebraska, carried the first program. Other stations later picked up the show, among them WGN in Chicago. The programs presented some of the leading public figures of the day, including Franklin Roosevelt, Walter Lippmann, and Henry Wallace.[33]

The League expected radio to help them reach League women; it certainly urged members to convene or to gather at tea and listen to the broadcasts. But it also hoped to communicate to a much broader audience, and in this it seems to have succeeded. NBC estimated the program's audience at fifteen million listeners, and League women were elated at fan mail from "teachers, farmers, business men, laborers, housewives and students," a "cross-section of the country." The American Library Association gladly filled requests for a reading list that it had prepared to accompany the broadcast. Members of Congress and newspaper editors applauded the program in speeches and editorials, the *New York Herald*, for example, commending the League for providing a "valuable" tool for civic education. The widely praised Voters' Service remained on the air for another five years.[34]

In the vote campaigns of 1928, as in 1924, local Leagues took up GOTV work with enthusiasm. The St. Louis League aired talks over radio station KWK in order to "get out an informed vote" and posted "civic thermometers" in public places to display increases in registration. Leagues in Connecticut arranged candidates' meetings, "political spelldowns," new voters' parties, and information booths. The New Jersey League sponsored a talk by party representatives that "colored women voters" were "especially urged to attend," and also filled eleven thousand requests for pamphlets on changes in state voting laws. The Dallas, Texas, League urged citizens to pay their poll taxes in a campaign that included radio spots, a film shown at local movie theaters, and booths staffed by tax collectors and League women at the "four largest department stores." The Michigan League distributed forty thousand copies of a pamphlet that tapped into the car craze with an extended motoring metaphor. Readers were reminded that the destination of "Political Highways" was the election of public officials; they were urged to mind registration regulations, the "Traffic Laws" of good citizenship, and to beware of "Detours That Lead Astray," such as golf and the movies.[35]

If local Leagues did not deemphasize publicity methods as thoroughly as their national leaders might have liked, still they poured great energy into GOTV. Their efforts, it seemed, were better rewarded in 1928 when voter turnout climbed, according to League calculations, to sixty-one percent. Still, humbled by poor results in past years, the League was reluctant to declare victory and claim credit. Rather, it took the improvement as a sign that its strategy of educating the public was working. When League leaders assessed the campaigns of 1928, they renewed the group's commitment to civic education and affirmed every recommendation of the Committee of Nine, adding only the suggestion that the League make fuller use of radio "to bring to the voter information on issues, candidates and election procedure." As Vice President Ramsey put it, "What has been begun is to be continued." In short, the League decided to stay the new course.[36]

The League did much for GOTV, to be sure, but GOTV also did much for the League. For most of the 1920s the GOTV campaigns constituted the most important work of the League of Women Voters. What began as its biggest project, its "chief activity," became the organization's basic charge, so much so that by 1927 League leaders could declare that its "continuous day by day work" to increase "intelligent participation in government" was its "real Get-Out-the-Vote campaign."[37]

"A Stockholder's Meeting of the U.S.A.": The Vote Campaigns of the National Association of Manufacturers

"We . . . urge all eligible voters, irrespective of political leanings, to go out and vote—vote as they please—but vote!" With this announcement on July 6, 1924, National Association of Manufacturers president John E. Edgerton inaugurated the group's GOTV effort. The NAM conducted one of the premier vote campaigns of 1924, and it did much to shape the campaigns' public identity. It supplied GOTV groups with mass quantities of literature, some twenty-five million pieces, and it created and popularized the campaigns' signature slogan, "Vote As You Please—But Vote!"[38]

From its genesis the NAM was a business lobby. Founded in 1895, the Association emerged in the 1900s and 1910s as a leading opponent of progressive labor reforms. A hundred thousand members strong by 1924, most of whom were small and mid-size manufacturers of auto parts, textiles and the like, the NAM lobbied tirelessly to block wage and hour reforms, reduce regulation and taxes, and promote the open shop. The NAM also worked to polish the business community's public image. A professional public relations staff put out press releases with regularity, taking credit for some ten thousand newspaper stories a year.[39]

The NAM, however, was much more than a lobby, for a lobby would have had no compelling reason to invest in a civic issue so far removed from the bottom line. The men of the NAM saw themselves as the natural leadership class, as people uniquely suited to leading roles in civic life. Edgerton laid this out plainly in a 1920 convention speech to members. "Manufacturers as a class are better equipped by experience for effective service as citizens than any other class." They are "broad in their sympathies and tolerant in their attitude toward the weaknesses of their fellow men," he explained. "It is within our power to contribute most materially to the leading of this country." NAM member and corporate officer Harrie C. White concurred that "leadership carries with it responsibilities," one of which was to awaken a sense of duty to vote "among those best fitted to exercise it." This leadership capacity made it only fitting that the NAM should spearhead a project such as GOTV. Businessmen saw themselves as model citizens, as just the right people to shape the civic behavior of others. As NAM members put it proudly in a convention statement, "We mould men while we make commodities."[40]

If the vote campaigns seemed an ideal outlet for the business community's civic leadership, the political circumstances of the summer of 1924 made its involvement positively urgent. A Red specter lingered in some conservative corners, and when Progressive Senator Robert "Fighting Bob" La Follette emerged as a serious presidential candidate, NAM members were spurred to action. La Follette, they believed, represented radicalism, class division, and a serious threat to their prerogatives as businessmen. His "so-called Progressives," they argued, were really "Anarchists, Socialists, Communists, and Bolshevists." Sympathizers spoke of "Fighting Bob" in the same breath as "Lenine [sic] and Trotsky." It was bad enough that La Follette was pulling labor to the polls; far more threatening was what they saw as his frontal assault upon the prerogatives of capital, especially his support of the public ownership of railroads and water power and his proposal to empower Congress to override the decisions of a Supreme Court that in the 1920s had been a bulwark against against wage and hour reforms.[41]

The businessmen did not believe that La Follette would outright win. Rather, they worried that he might attract enough support to force the election into the House of Representatives, where anything could happen. Wild scenarios were bandied about in the press: La Follette had "united the Socialist vote, the I.W.W. vote and the Farmer-Labor vote of the west." Combined with the vote "of the unthinking people"—voters who might be seduced by his blatant appeals to class—La Follette might be able to block a majority in the electoral college, throw the election to the House, prevail there by some sinister machinations, or perhaps permit the election of someone even worse, such as Charles Bryan, the governor of Nebraska, Democratic vice-presidential nominee, and brother of the hated William Jennings Bryan.[42]

The problem, then, was that while "the great majority of the people are conservative, . . . a very large percentage of that group take [sic] no interest in political affairs." These were precisely the people whose votes were needed to save the nation from "La Folletism," and the people the NAM set out to rouse in the GOTV campaigns. As strongly opposed to La Follette as the NAM was, it nonetheless refrained in the campaigns from direct partisan advocacy. It believed that it could afford to. Confident that the ranks of nonvoters were filled with "sensible thinkers," the NAM could ask them to "vote as they pleased" and expect that to translate into support for the Republican Calvin Coolidge, or at least the Wall Street lawyer John W. Davis. The businessmen fully expected that "this great offensive . . . against the ballot-slackers" would "result in a national administration, safe and sane."[43]

Thus, two days after Senator La Follette accepted the nomination of Progressives assembled in convention at Cleveland, the NAM jumped into the GOTV campaigns. It urged members to talk to colleagues at "luncheon clubs" such as Kiwanis and Rotary and at golf and tennis country clubs. It asked them to deliver "five-minute talks" at movie theaters or over the radio. It suggested they "appeal to employees in group meetings" and transport workers to the polls. It also lined up the support of other organizations, and claimed to have brought some three thousand groups into "the manufacturers' national [GOTV] effort." Finally, it publicized the campaigns with great effectiveness: the press packets it sent to "every single daily newspaper in the country" generated "hundreds" of news stories and "hundreds" more editorials in a wide range of papers including the *New York Sun,* the *Des Moines Register,* the *Philadelphia North American,* the *Indianapolis Star,* the *Gadsden (Ala.) Journal,* the *Biddeford (Maine) Journal,* and the *Hoquiam Washingtonian.*[44]

The NAM's greatest contribution to the vote campaigns, however, was to produce and distribute GOTV literature in mass quantities. The Association put out nearly twenty-five million posters, fliers, leaflets, and stickers, making it the largest single supplier of GOTV literature. It sent a supply to every member, and also to other GOTV groups in quantity, including "several hundred thousand" pieces to the American Legion and "great quantities" to the Boy Scouts for a house-to-house canvass in "all parts of the country." Two pieces accounted for most of the literature put out by the NAM: the sticker urging citizens to "Vote As You Please," and a leaflet calling them to a "Stockholder's Meeting of the U.S.A."[45]

The stickers commanded attention on business correspondence, newsletters, employee pay envelopes, and customer's parcels. But more than just the sticker, the slogan stuck too. "Vote As You Please, but *Vote!*" or close variants showed up in political cartoons in newspapers in Syracuse, Oklahoma City, and Los Angeles. Other GOTV groups also adopted it, perhaps without knowing its provenance. The League of Women Voters used it in a poster, the Brooklyn-Manhattan Transit Corporation on the front page of an employee newsletter. The Lansing, Michigan, Chamber of Commerce produced its own version of the sticker, adding its name to the bottom. Decentralized as they were, the GOTV campaigns shared a slogan, and that slogan was "Vote As You Please, but *Vote!*"[46]

Indeed, "Vote As You Please" took on a life outside the GOTV campaigns altogether. At times it was appropriated for newspaper advertisements for consumer goods and commercial entertainment. A furniture store in Santa Ana, California, headlined a newspaper ad with a summons to "Vote As You Please Tomorrow—But Vote!" Readers of the *Denver Post* and the *St. Louis Post-Dispatch* were asked to "Vote as You Please, But be Sure to Buy American Beauty Macaroni Products." An ad for the National Theater in Richmond, Virginia, reproduced the format and typeface of the NAM sticker and asked readers to "Vote As You Please" but also to "Be American To The Core" by coming to see *Janice Meredith,* a movie starring Marion Davies and Tyrone Power. These usages are remarkable, for they powerfully show that the GOTV campaigns had penetrated the public discourse of the time. Advertisers used the slogan because they believed that customers would be familiar with it, and they believed that customers would be familiar with it because GOTV groups had publicized it far and wide.[47]

The leaflet argued the NAM's case more fully. On the cover it announced a *"Stockholders Meeting Of The U.S.A."* on *"November 4"* and asked the reader to "Attend and Vote!" Inside, it enumerated the number of "Ballot Slackers" in every state and bluntly asked readers if they might be among those who had "failed to perform their full duty as citizens." The vast numbers of nonvoters posed "a menace to our institutions and our government" that "every thinking person" would want to fix. "Go to the polls yourself, talk to your friends, associates and neighbors and line up a great army of voters on November 4."[48]

Perhaps the most revealing part of the leaflet is the extended metaphor it used to describe the relationship between business and government. "The Fathers of our Constitution," it claimed, ". . . made you a participating stockholder in the greatest corporation in the world—the United States of America—and gave you the privilege of personal representation in the conduct of its affairs." The election was a "stockholders meeting" at which the nation's business would be decided. The stockholders metaphor was a commonplace in the GOTV campaigns and in the public discourse of the period. It equated decision makers in the private sector with decision makers in the public sphere. It conveyed the conviction of businessmen that their status as owners in the private sector gave them legitimacy in the public sector, that business ownership entitled them to a sort of proprietorship in the civic sphere. It expressed the belief, hammered home in many articles and editorials of the period, that government ought to be run like a business. If their model held, civic life would be transformed into an imitation of business life.[49]

The NAM stockholders folder surfaced in other GOTV campaigns, especially those of the League of Women Voters. The Pennsylvania League dropped "thousands" of copies of the leaflet from an airplane, while the Indiana and Saginaw County, Michigan, Leagues reproduced it in their bulletins. A political cartoon in a farmers' newspaper from Kansas with a circulation of 500,000 showed a "stockholders meeting" notice being delivered in a house-to-house canvass by Uncle Sam.[50]

The metaphor also surfaced in GOTV editorials in *Collier's* in 1924, and in *Nation's Business* and the publication of the Georgia League of Women Voters in 1928. The "100% Register and Vote League" of Los Angeles warned that "no proxies" would "be recognized at the big stockholders meetings of the Citizens of the United States." Vote activists in

Chicago characterized city elections there as a "Stockholders' Meeting for Citizens of Chicago."[51]

The "stockholders" metaphor and "Vote As You Please" slogan persisted beyond 1924, but for the most part the NAM's commitment to GOTV did not. The Association conducted only an in-house campaign in 1926, sending "Vote As You Please" posters to members for display in their factories but declining offers to cooperate with other groups in a broader campaign. And, despite promises of a "revival" of the 1924 effort for the next presidential election, the records for 1928 show no evidence of any GOTV work at all.[52]

After 1924 the NAM largely terminated its involvement in the vote campaigns—and for good reason. Given its goals in 1924, no further work was needed. The Coolidge landslide had frustrated La Follette's antibusiness schemes; indeed, the senator died in 1925 and no "radical" threat on the scale of his presidential bid materialized for the rest of the decade. The NAM announced with relief that the "sensible thinkers" did not disappoint. The election results showed clearly that "the citizens remain[ed] the upholders of recognized American principles" and that "radicalism" had been "repulsed." Association leaders also noted, evidently pleased, that the vote campaigns had been a public relations boon, bringing an "unusual amount of praise and genuine interest in the Association." Every major GOTV group tried to put the best face on the election results of 1924; alone among them, the NAM could count the vote campaigns a genuine success.[53]

Collier's *Magazine: "The Year of the Big Vote"*

"The election figures of 1920 stirred us like a fire bell in the night," wrote the editors of *Collier's Weekly* in the last issue before the 1924 election. Alarmed by the nation's terrible "habit of civic indifference," the editorial board embarked on a publicity campaign of sloganeering and salesmanship to generate excitement for the election and boost turnout at the polls. A big-name leisure magazine with more than a million readers a week, *Collier's* brought to GOTV both state-of-the-art publicity techniques and a reputation for progressive reform. Working under the leadership of John B. Kennedy, the associate editor who handled much of the magazine's GOTV work, *Collier's* gave much ink to the vote campaigns in 1924 in articles, editorials, and advertisements.[54]

Collier's was a weekly magazine of current events and fiction. In a period when magazine readership was highly stratified by class, *Collier's* was one of the most popular middle-class publications. Its circulation of just over a million copies a week exceeded that of *Good Housekeeping* or *National Geographic;* indeed, only a handful of publications, such as the *Saturday Evening Post,* could boast a larger readership. A "new magazine" in the phrase of Christopher Wilson, *Collier's* was thoroughly modern in format and style: its articles were short and punchy, and it sported a color cover, lots of pictures, and abundant advertising. William Allen White, Ida Tarbell, and George Creel contributed to its pages, and some of its staff members, among them Bruce Barton, Edward Anthony, and Robert Goldsmith, went on to positions of importance in politics.[55]

Though the magazine's mainstay was light leisure reading, civic issues cropped up often in its pages. In the 1920s the magazine addressed public issues such as immigration, party corruption, and prohibition. In election years it filled pages with prognostications and profiles of public figures in an "up close and personal" style: articles on "My Neighbor Woodrow Wilson" or "That Charm of Mrs. Coolidge" promoted the politics of personality. Like many publications of its kind, the magazine felt keenly that it had a duty to inform. *Collier's* believed it could best "fulfill its obligation" to "citizen-readers" by "sincerely studying and impartially presenting the facts about the great national issues of government—and about our men in public life." Readers would then be ready to "use the ballot faithfully and intelligently" to uphold "American ideals, aims, and principles."[56]

In the early 1920s, however, *Collier's* did not merely inform: it intervened directly in civic affairs. Between 1920 and 1923 the magazine repeatedly took on substantial civic projects with a reformer's zeal, conducting a door-to-door straw poll of a quarter million subscribers to produce "a correct picture" of public opinion "not adulterated by political propaganda," and, in a remarkable one-page proposal, devising a new system of municipal government and offering staff support to any city willing to try it. The magazine's self-appointed role as a civic authority stemmed from its political independence. Without ties to any party or candidate, *Collier's* believed it could break the stranglehold of political corruption and restore government in the public interest. During the GOTV campaign in 1924 *Collier's* even appended the phrase "In the interests of better citizenship" to its title graphic on GOTV ads: *Collier's* good government credentials were part of its very identity. In the early 1920s, *Collier's* saw itself as not merely a messenger, but as an agent in the civic sphere.[57]

The GOTV campaigns perfectly illustrated the magazine's extraordinary sense of civic agency. In the early 1920s *Collier's* had warned often of the evils of "civic indifference" and called attention to the twin dangers of the problem nonvoter ("the right class of people do not vote") and problem voter (the "moron majority"). In 1924, believing themselves the first to undertake such work, the editorial board elected to "make Get-Out-The-Vote the major piece of work" for the magazine for the year. This degree of support for the campaigns distinguished *Collier's* from other publications; while many magazines commended the vote campaigns in editorials or articles, *Collier's* alone made GOTV its mission.[58]

The *Collier's* 1924 vote campaign was conducted largely in the pages of the magazine. It published a half-dozen feature articles in the summer and fall, frequent editorials between May and November, and a series of three full-page advertisements in the final weeks before the election. Letters to the editor and brief boxed reminders likewise kept the issue before readers. *Collier's* supplemented the print campaign by supplying literature to other vote groups (three million citizen pledge cards, and a half million posters for chain stores and banks) and by securing pledges from fifty radio stations to broadcast GOTV announcements. Despite the fact that in 1923 *Collier's* organized a door-to-door canvass of hundreds of thousands of subscribers to conduct a presidential poll, at no time did the magazine try to canvass precincts for GOTV. This shows how firmly the magazine's editors believed that low turnout was a problem of "civic indifference," a problem that a promotional campaign of slogans ("Make 1924 the Year of the Big Vote"), salesmanship, and contests could dispel.[59]

Collier's used full-page GOTV advertisements to urge citizens to "step forward to stem the tide of retrogression in civic duty." Articles and editorials likened the election to a sales campaign, the voter to a smart shopper. "[T]he majority of our people have good sense." "[T]o sell the voter something, you must have the goods."[60]

Collier's also hoped a nationwide citizenship contest would generate enthusiasm for voting. In September of 1924 the magazine announced that it would present a trophy to the state that produced the largest proportional increase in turnout. A prestige piece custom-made by Tiffany's, the trophy was intended to "awaken the public conscience and stir every voter to action." "Which state will win?" one of its GOTV ads asked breathlessly. "Your vote will count!"[61]

By election day, *Collier's* had thoroughly promoted, packaged, and sold its message of active citizenship, a message that other publications and GOTV supporters picked up and amplified. The *New York Times* published several stories on the *Collier's* campaign and GOTV groups reprinted the *Collier's* pledge card. Ads announced that all three presidential candidates and at least eight state governors endorsed the *Collier's* campaign; some, including Walter Pierce of Oregon, Albert Ritchie of Maryland, and Alfred E. Smith of New York, issued their own GOTV proclamations or statements of support, adding to the ripple effect.[62]

With articles and editorials in its own pages, millions of pledge cards and half a million posters, and a contest endorsed by prominent political figures, *Collier's* insisted that it had done the "utmost" to encourage voters to turn out. Election day would show "whether the delinquent half of the voters of our country *can* be aroused to active citizenship." If turnout failed to rebound, editors warned in a final pre-election editorial, the future of participatory democracy looked bleak. "If the dreary, depressing figures of 1920 are to be written again, it means that the habit of civic indifference has become fixed, and that Bunker Hill and Valley Forge have lost all significance." To *Collier's,* there was a great deal on the line on November 4.[63]

When turnout was tallied, *Collier's* estimated that turnout had increased by 4.2 percent—a modest result, given that they had put forth their "utmost" effort, and a claim that was not even accurate. Disappointed and embarrassed, the magazine asserted a feeble claim of success—the results did show a "general proportional increase" in turnout, despite the fact that twenty of the forty-eight states "actually show[ed] a decline"—and hurried back to the fiction and lighter fare that had been its mainstay. After promoting the citizenship contest in prime advertising space, *Collier's* buried the story announcing Wyoming as the trophy winner on page 30 of a later issue. After that, it never mentioned the vote campaigns again.[64]

In 1924 *Collier's* had responded to the problem of nonvoting as to a "fire bell in the night." After the disappointment of the GOTV campaign, nonvoting apparently ceased to be so alarming. For the rest of the decade the magazine dutifully reminded readers to "go to the voting places resolved to do your duty with all intelligence and all loyalty," but it never again attempted another vote campaign. Indeed, it never attempted another civic experiment of such size. It was as if, utterly embarrassed and chastened by defeat, the magazine retired its vision of itself as a powerful agent in the civic sphere. *Collier's* continued to meet its responsibility to inform, addressing public issues, especially the prohibition question, and extensively covering the 1928 presidential race. But its days as a civic leader were over. It was enough, the magazine's editors decided, to present "the facts and the opinions" on the issues of the day.[65]

"The Only Way of Carrying on Democracy": The Party-Centered Vote Campaigns of the National Civic Federation

In the off-year elections of 1926, the leadership of the GOTV campaigns shifted to the National Civic Federation. Founded at the turn of the century to mediate labor disputes, by the 1920s the NCF had become a bastion of antiradical activism. Federation leaders hoped higher turnout could turn back the Red Menace, and in that spirit educated, advertised, and formed alliances. Unique among the major GOTV groups, the NCF hoped to boost turnout by revitalizing political parties.

At the turn of the century, amidst vast industrial expansion, large-scale business consolidation, and bloody repression of worker protest, the NCF was formed to "raise the level" of labor relations. A tripartite organization comprised of leaders of business, labor, and government, the NCF was founded in 1900 as a forum in which moderates from all sides could meet to resolve differences. For twenty years the hallmark of the Federation was moderation, and the organization counted amongst its successes its help in settling strikes (among them the 1902 coal strike) and in winning passage of workers' compensation laws. After World War I the NCF abandoned its temperate tone and passionately pursued an antiradical agenda, working in the 1920s to strengthen immigration restrictions and opposing the World Court. The Federation's interest in citizenship projects, including GOTV, stemmed in part from its commitment to antiradicalism.[66]

In all its work, the NCF capitalized on the civic stature of the organization's leaders. These were men who were deeply engaged in civic affairs; more precisely, they were men who had spent a lifetime working in and through political parties. Republican Elihu Root, now the honorary chair of the Federation's GOTV work, was the philosophical godfather of the NCF vote campaigns; his speeches as far back as 1907 on the problem of political participation in an industrial society "constitute[d] practically the foundation" of the Federation's GOTV work. Alton B. Parker, former chief justice of the New York Supreme Court, Democratic party presidential nominee in 1904, and legal counsel to the American Federation of Labor in the *Danbury Hatters* and *Buck Stove and Range* cases, served as president of the NCF in the 1920s and presided over the vote campaign project in 1924. John Hays Hammond, the Yale-educated "World Famous Mining Engineer," lifelong Republican, and "intimate" friend of Presidents Harding and Coolidge, chaired the Federation's Departments on Political Education and Active Citizenship and headed up the 1926 vote campaigns. The NCF also assembled a GOTV advisory committee, the roster of which reads like a "Who's Who" of civic and party leadership of the period, including Charles Evans Hughes, former Illinois governor Frank O. Lowden, and Columbia University President Nicholas Murray Butler.[67]

The heartbeat of the Federation's GOTV and citizenship projects, however, was the man who was "always the Federation's central figure," Ralph M. Easley. A newspaperman by background, Easley founded the Chicago Civic Federation in 1894 and then the National Civic Federation, serving as its executive secretary until his death in 1939. Energetic and skilled as an agenda-setter and administrator, Easley was also a dedicated and well-connected Republican. The NCF's shift to the right was in some measure the product of his own convictions: from the end of World War I until his death in 1939, Easley remained "obsessed" with the threat of radicalism and pledged all his energies to stop it.[68]

If leadership was the NCF's strength, organization was its weakness. The Federation was no grass-roots group; its only office was in New York. There the NCF conducted a local GOTV campaign with the active support of many local leaders. Given its lack of "real machinery," however, the NCF had to rely upon allies for GOTV work elsewhere.[69]

Before the NCF moved to the fore of the GOTV campaigns in 1926, it gained some experience in the campaigns of 1924. Acting on a resolution passed during the previous year, the NCF warned that voting was a civic necessity—all the more so in a time marked by "fear of Reds." At the NCF's annual meeting in April 1924, members adopted a two-part agenda. In the short term, the Federation would join the League of Women Voters, the National Association of Manufacturers, and others in a campaign to register and turn out voters for the fall elections. Over the long term, however, it resolved to attack the problem of nonparticipation at its roots. Members were convinced that the reluctance of good citizens to work actively in party organizations permitted corruption and enabled parties to march poor citizens, rather than good ones, to the polls. Improving turnout, therefore, meant revitalizing the party system by bringing good citizens to bear at each stage of the electoral process, from primaries to platform-writing to the general election. The press of time made a push to renew the party system impossible before November; for 1924, the NCF conceded, "it was not going to be practicable to push a drive for participation in party politics." Over the long term, however, the Federation planned to put parties at the center of the GOTV agenda. It hoped that "a widespread understanding of the principles and methods of party government" would induce voters "to become active in their respective party organizations."[70]

Though it limited its commitment to GOTV in 1924, the NCF counted the vote campaigns among the year's "outstanding activities." It created a committee to take charge of the campaigns and then issued pamphlets, put out publicity, studied registration laws, lined up allies and endorsements, and helped run a grass-roots campaign in the city of New York.[71]

To "launch the [GOTV] drive on a national scale," the NCF turned to organized business. Lacking a decentralized structure of its own, the Federation asked chambers of commerce in six hundred cities to lead GOTV work in their communities. President Parker's request, issued by mail in August of 1924, received "a most enthusiastic response": Chambers in "several hundred cities" reported that they would get to work right away.[72]

The Manchester, New Hampshire, Chamber, for example, distributed GOTV stickers and posters, while the West View Borough Chamber near Pittsburgh put up a hundred posters and delivered a circular to every home. The Lincoln, Nebraska, Chamber coordinated its GOTV work with other local groups, including the League of Women Voters, Rotary, Kiwanis, Lions, Pathfinders, "Knife and Fork," Cosmopolitan Business and Professional Women's League, Altrusa Club, American Legion, and Sons of Veterans clubs. To Federation members, the Chamber was a perfect partner: after all, businessmen were precisely the sort of people they believed were failing to vote and precisely the kind of people whose votes were most needed. As Haley Fiske put it in correspondence with the Federation, "it is the business men who have been neglecting their duties. Any movement which will stir them up . . . ought to be in every way encouraged."[73]

Other enthusiastic allies, Easley reported, were "springing up overnight." A range of national organizations endorsed the Federation campaigns, including the DAR, Rotary International, Civitan clubs ("Builders of Good Citizenship"), and the American Board of Applied Christianity. At Parker's request, the Military Order of the World War appointed a national GOTV committee and asked local chapters to "exercise their good efforts" to support the cause, and the International Association of Casualty and Surety Underwriters set up a committee to oversee GOTV efforts.[74]

The NCF also succeeded in generating other GOTV activity at the local level. The administrative chairman of the Federation campaigns, J. A. Hall, reported with pleasure that the people of Sayre, Pennsylvania, had "followed our entire program." Factories throughout the Lehigh Valley blew their whistles on election day, fire trucks paraded through town, and "men with megaphones rode through the streets urging people to vote." In Burlington, Vermont, chimes rang out "The Star-Spangled Banner" to remind citizens to go to the polls. Voters in Milford, Delaware, attended "special patriotic [church] services," while "as far north as North Dakota" GOTV supporters advertised in newspapers, blasted factory whistles, and sounded sirens "every hour."[75]

Finally, in 1924 the NCF laid the groundwork for a future effort to invigorate parties. It contacted local and national party leaders and urged Chamber men to approach local party officials, "first thing." More importantly, Federation leaders began to make a concerted case for the importance of parties in American political life. It was imperative, they insisted, that good people join parties to clean them up and "purify the American party system." An infusion of new members, especially white and middle-class businessmen, would make parties "really representative of the best elements of our citizenry."[76]

When the votes were in, the NCF fared no better in the election of 1924 than any other GOTV group. Easley tallied up the membership of participating organizations with disbelief—the Federal Council of Churches of Christ, with one hundred and fifty thousand preachers and presumably millions of faithful, the DAR with two thousand chapters, the American Legion with eleven thousand posts—these groups had worked intensively on GOTV for months. "And then," fretted Easley, "what happened? Apparently, nothing!" In public, of course, the NCF put a positive spin on its efforts. The vote campaigns, it claimed in a press release, had "partially checked" the downward trend in voter turnout. It was a comfort that the 1924 campaigns were not the sort of campaigns the NCF really had wanted to run; with more time, a more comprehensive, party-centered program would be possible. The Federation's best attempt, its members believed, lay ahead.[77]

To affirm its continuing commitment to GOTV, in early 1925 the NCF elevated the temporary committee that had run the 1924 campaign to a full-fledged, permanent "Department on Political Education." The department's principal task was to focus squarely on political parties. Again the NCF contacted state party officials, this time to inquire about the particulars of party membership in their states and to ask for their input on the problem of nonvoting. By then, the Federation's commitment to political parties had earned it the "whole-hearted approval" of party leaders: both Republican National Committee chair William Butler and his Democratic counterpart, Clement Shaver, conveyed their enthusiastic support.[78]

When the full Department on Political Education convened in January of 1926, Federation members met to develop a strategy for the fall elections that could lay the groundwork for an even bigger effort in the presidential year of 1928. For two days a range of speakers—Governor Alfred E. Smith of New York, American Federation of Labor officer Matthew Woll, a high school civics teacher from Pittsburgh—presented their suggestions. Some thirty organizations sent delegates to the meeting, among them the NAM, the American Political Science Association, the Order of DeMolay, and the American Legion. In March, the American Legion, with posts in "every community," was selected as the Federation's GOTV partner. As an assembly of patriots rather than of partisans, the Legion could "command the greatest support and the least opposition from all groups." The Legion, they agreed, would "act for" the NCF and bring the vote campaigns to the grass roots, uniting communities behind the banner of civic duty.[79]

In the 1926 campaigns the Legion handled the day-to-day mechanics of GOTV conferences and local campaigns; from its headquarters, the Federation publicized the effort and collected endorsements. The NCF mailed press kits to thirty newspapers in the East and Midwest and asked each to "advise us editorially" on the campaign's prospects and progress. It supplied GOTV literature to cooperating organizations and landed the endorsement of trade groups, service organizations, labor unions, and public officials. The National Education Association, for example, "extend[ed] its good-will and support" to the undertaking, while the Navy League praised the NCF's "highly important work." The United Textile Workers expressed its "hearty accord" with the project, as did the International Molders' Union. The League for American Citizenship, an immigrant organization, pledged "every ounce of cooperation." The National Grange and the National Council of Traveling Salesmen's Associations also supported the effort. Congressmen Theodore Burton (Republican, Ohio), Emanuel Celler (Democrat, New York), and Albert R. Hall (Republican, Indiana), Senator Edward I. Edwards (Democrat, New Jersey), and Governor Franklin S. Billings (Republican, Vermont) all sent letters of support.[80]

From its headquarters, the Federation also made the case for the importance of political parties. In April 1926, the NCF issued a "declaration" linking the problem of nonvoting to the problem of nonparticipation in parties. "It is a disquieting fact that scarcely one-half of the citizens privileged to become voters exercise the elective franchise. Fewer participate in the primaries at which party candidates are chosen, while fewer still are active members of their own party organization through which party policies and programs are determined." This was no way to run a democracy. "Such lethargy . . . makes minority rule inescapable." The Federation issued a call to action: "Since our government rests primarily upon the foundation of political parties, it is clearly the duty of every citizen to aid in the maintenance of that Government through enrollment in a political party, active participation in the framing of its policies, and in the nomination and election of its candidates." "This," and nothing less, was "the true goal of political education."[81]

The campaign of 1926 was the campaign the NCF had dreamt of. It was well planned, thoroughly decentralized, and squarely focused on parties. When election day came and turnout still failed to improve, Federation leaders were disappointed indeed. They analyzed the outcome with brutal honesty. "Face the facts," Hammond said in a public statement. The numbers "fail[ed] to reveal any cause for [con]gratulation," except perhaps the small consolation that "without such an effort, the results would have been much more disheartening. It was now clear"—abundantly so—"that holding meetings, voting resolutions, [and] securing newspaper, radio and pulpit publicity" would "not accomplish the end sought."[82]

The off-year elections of 1926 were supposed to have charted a course for even larger campaigns in 1928; instead, they turned out to be the NCF's last large-scale GOTV effort. In 1927 the Federation revisited without enthusiasm the problems of nonvoting and parties and issued a few more reports, weakly promising yet "more intensive" and "more practical" GOTV programs. It dabbled in civic education and suggested that cities form "local joint committees on active citizenship" to educate citizens and convince them of the importance of parties and voting.[83]

The NCF's GOTV efforts in 1928, however, were half-hearted and uneven. This time the Federation enlisted the help not of the Legion but of local real estate boards and the General Federation of Women's Clubs, and did little work with them beyond cosponsoring a high school essay contest on GOTV themes. In a few locations the NCF supported significant campaigns, in particular in New York City, its own backyard. The campaigns, however, paled in comparison to their efforts in 1926 or even 1924. With a few exceptions, after 1926 the NCF largely withdrew from the national GOTV scene.[84]

The 1920s were the Federation's waning years, and in some respects the vote campaign of 1926 was the organization's last hurrah. In the 1930s the NCF drifted into obscurity, resurfacing briefly in the 1940s only in the wake of war. Once at the forefront of progressive labor-industry policymaking, by the 1930s much of the organization's influence had dissipated. In its twilight years the Federation did little more than issue pamphlets on the dangers of radicalism. With the conclusion of the GOTV campaigns, its days as a force for civic renewal were over.

"Ballots and Not Bullets": The Vote Campaigns of the American Legion

The American Legion's GOTV campaign was born of a unique partnership. In 1926, it stepped forward to provide the National Civic Federation with an ally that could deliver the GOTV message to the grass roots. Though the Legion did GOTV work through much of the decade, it put forward its biggest effort for the off-year elections of 1926. For the Legion, GOTV was an easy extension of its work "for God and Country."

As the nation's leading lobbying and service organization for veterans of World War I, the Legion was supremely positioned to lead the advance against "civic slackers." With nearly seven hundred thousand members organized into a network of eleven thousand local "posts," state-level "Departments," and a National Headquarters, the Legion enjoyed a broad presence in the field, a centralized national command, and enormous credibility in the public eye. Legion men were genuine patriots, men who had proven themselves to be the best of citizens with sacrifice and blood. Back on American soil, the veterans were determined to use their wartime service to propel themselves to their proper place at the forefront of civic and community leadership. They did so with a conservative bent and sturdy credentials as "truly and thoroughly American" "ideal leader type[s]," the type that, as the membership of the organization generally demonstrated, was broadly middle class, male, and white.[85]

The Legion pursued a broad agenda in the 1920s, including employment and government benefits for returning servicemen, naturalization for immigrants, civics education for children, and antiradicalism for all. Permeating every project, however, was the Legion's commitment to "one hundred per cent Americanism," a concept that was apparently so self-evident to Legion men that it never warranted explicit definition. The Legion put its ideals into practice through the work of its Americanism Commission, which in the 1920s provided state and local Legions with materials for teaching citizenship skills, sponsored a thousand Boy Scout troops, and organized one hundred thousand boys into baseball teams.[86]

"Americanism" was likewise the driving force behind the Legion's commitment to GOTV. Defending the democratic process resonated keenly with men who had sacrificed in the war, and they felt obliged to instill the same sense of duty in others. "Every man or woman in America who takes his or her place in active politics is a peacetime soldier in a great world-wide battle for free self-government," they proclaimed. Americans could best preserve hard-won freedoms "by voting—and voting with intelligence."[87]

Legion men first took up GOTV work in 1923 when, after a rousing convention address by General John J. Pershing, they determined to urge every member to "cast his vote at all elections" and to "impress upon citizens generally the necessity and duty of voting." The national convention the next year in St. Paul directed the Americanism Commission to undertake a GOTV campaign. That year Legion leaders lent their support to other GOTV groups: former National Commander Hanford MacNider, for example, served on the Advisory Committee of Simon Michelet's National Get-Out-the-Vote Club. Local posts also publicized the campaigns and set up car pools to transport voters to the polls. In New York, Legionnaires handed out car cards urging citizens to "KEEP THE FAITH" and "VOTE ELECTION DAY." The California Department expected two thousand members to enlist in its GOTV efforts, which included a speakers' bureau. Indeed, California was home to a substantial Legion GOTV campaign. A GOTV contest in Orange County, for example, spurred participation by local posts. The Huntington Beach post lined up fifteen cars to carry voters to the polls, while the Santa Ana Auxiliary tagged citizens who promised to vote.[88]

The Legion reserved its greatest offensive against the ballot slackers for 1926. In May it accepted the NCF's invitation to become a full partner in the GOTV effort. The Federation supplied the Legion with GOTV literature and several thousand dollars to defray expenses. The Legion in turn supplied manpower and a grass-roots organization.[89]

The heart of the 1926 Legion campaign was its effort to orchestrate a mighty wave of GOTV planning meetings at the local level. On September 21, "hundreds of Legion posts" gathered local business, labor, civic, and women's groups at "community conferences." These conferences were charged with working out "ways and means" of running publicity and citizenship education campaigns and appointing a local "Permanent Joint Committee on Political Education" in each community to study "the machinery and work of political parties" and "the duties of citizens in relation thereto." The Legion supported the party agenda of the NCF and hoped to persuade citizens not only to vote, but also to sign up "with some party" and do "their share of the party work." The goal was to get out the vote, to be sure, but Legionnaires hoped to "go much further than that" and "get at the roots of the non-voting evil" by educating citizens and building a permanent infrastructure of purified parties.[90]

The conference campaign drew the support of national organizations and leading public figures alike. The U.S. Chamber of Commerce, the American Federation of Labor, the General Federation of Women's Clubs, Rotary, Kiwanis, Knights of Columbus, and Elks all endorsed the conference approach. Many other groups cooperated in concrete and explicit ways. Frank Land, Grand Scribe of the Order of DeMolay, pledged his group's cooperation "to the fullest extent" and requested a supply of literature he could send to DeMolay chapters in nearly fifteen hundred cities. Grace Brosseau, president-general of the DAR, called the conference scheme "highly patriotic" and asked DAR chapters to participate fully. The Legion campaigns won kudos at the highest levels. President Coolidge congratulated Legionnaires on their work. He was "gratified," he approvingly wrote, "to know that, in co-operating with The National Civic Federation, you are throwing the splendid resources of your organization into the important work of arousing our citizens to take part in elections." "Too much stress," he added, "cannot be laid on the necessity of 'getting out the vote.' "[91]

The Legion later reported that conferences took place in hundreds, perhaps thousands of cities. Meetings were held in every part of the country, including Philadelphia, Cleveland, New Orleans, Nashville, Omaha, Peoria, San Bernardino, Phoenix, Daytona Beach, and Marietta, Ohio. Mayor William E. Dever kicked off the meeting at City Hall in Chicago. The NCF reported that the meetings in San Francisco, Seattle, Kansas City, and St. Louis were positively "corking."[92]

The Legion-sponsored conferences spawned grass-roots GOTV campaigns on an impressive scale. The David Wisted post of Duluth, Minnesota, for example, distributed forty thousand tags to voters, and then sponsored a contest in which thirty thousand school children collected the tags from parents and neighbors. The class that collected the most tags was rewarded with a silver trophy and a "theater party." An Ohio post persuaded a local drugstore to slip into customers' parcels GOTV reminder cards imprinted with the Legion name; some fifty thousand cards were distributed in this way. The Floyd L. Perry Post of Miami, Oklahoma, "summon[ed] all slackers to the polls" with a full-page newspaper ad. The conferences drew together community groups and helped them share strategies, literature, and enthusiasm. More than any other means, Legion-sponsored conferences provided the framework for local GOTV work in 1926.[93]

Given the intensity of their efforts, the Americanism Commission found the results of the 1926 elections "disheartening." Like others, however, the Legion found consolation in the thought that civic education took time. It was "only through such educational efforts," the Americanism Commission reported in 1927, that "our citizenship will be permanently awakened to the dangers of citizen inertia and indifference." That, they were sure, made the project worthwhile.[94]

The Legionnaires resumed GOTV in later years on a smaller scale, reminding a failing public that, even in 1928, "making the world—and our own [be]loved country—'safe for democracy' is as big an issue" as it had been during the war. "The fight is just as real, . . . though it is waged with ballots and not bullets." In the presidential election that year, the Legion again drew attention to the duty to vote with articles, editorials, and cartoons and resolved to pursue GOTV within an agenda of "political education." Scattered Legion groups worked to get out the vote in their own communities, among them the Park Slope, Brooklyn post, which made use of speakers and signs (see fig. 10), and the Ladies' Auxiliary of Greenville, Pennsylvania, which won a $100 prize from the local paper for a campaign that paired a precinct canvass with a babysitting service.[95]

On a smaller scale, in fact, the Legion maintained its interest in voter turnout well beyond the 1920s, issuing reminders to vote at least through the mid-1950s. Intensive, organization-wide efforts to boost turnout, however, ended with the 1926 campaign, and GOTV and political education dropped out of the Americanism Commission agenda as early as 1929. The Americanism Commission pursued other projects—more Boy Scout troops and baseball teams, plus a new focus on local emergency relief services and "local councils of defense." In these ways, the Legion continued, in the years after GOTV, to affirm its commitment to "Americanism."[96]

Collectively, the five major GOTV campaigns brought the GOTV message to every region of the country. Between them they passed out millions of posters and pamphlets, broadcast voting reminders in communities from coast to coast, and taught the basics of civics to many thousands of potential voters. Though for the most part they worked independently, reflecting their different motives and organizational capacities, they shared both a common goal—to increase the quantity and quality of voter turnout—and a common set of civic values that privileged whiteness and middle-class and elite status.

The major vote groups varied in their motives and methods. They were spurred to act by concerns ranging from the League's anguish over the unrealized potential of woman suffrage to the NAM's dread of resurgent radicalism. While each group made use of publicity and education, each also struck a different balance between the two—League women, for example, relying heavily on civic instruction while the modern publicists of *Collier's*, for the most part, opted instead for advertising methods. The balance between advertising and education across the campaigns also shifted over time, as most groups favored publicity methods at first but eventually placed more faith in the power of education. The internal organization of the participants likewise predisposed them to certain types of campaigns: the Legion, with its extensive network of local posts, could deliver the GOTV message directly to communities, while the Civic Federation, ensconced in its headquarters in New York, had no choice but to work from the top down.

Clearly, most of the major GOTV groups came to their activism independently. They cooperated little, and coordinated their efforts even less. With the major exception of the joint NCF/American Legion effort in 1926, at the national level the leading GOTV groups did little more than supply literature to one another and occasionally correspond or confer. Indeed, even these contacts resulted in angry charges of stolen ideas, insufficient acknowledgements, and assorted misrepresentation. For groups that were often fiercely at odds on other issues, little more could have been expected. The military patriots of the Legion could not abide the peace activists of the League; the League and the NAM were at loggerheads over the issue of child labor.[97]

For all their independence from one another—indeed, despite their many differences—the major GOTV groups had a great deal in common. Most of the major campaigns found themselves urging citizens to "Vote As You Please—But *Vote!*" The diffusion of the NAM slogan amongst vote groups with different agendas and little relationship to one another shows how widely the GOTV message circulated in the media of the day. It also shows what a powerful force for cohesion the progressive language of duty and nonpartisanship could be, unifying behind a single phrase even groups with opposing agendas.

The use of the NAM slogan outside the vote campaigns is even more revealing. The repeated invocation to "Vote As You Please" for macaroni and movies is powerful evidence that the vote campaigns had attained a high level of visibility in the public sphere. Clearly their calls for better citizenship had become part of the public discourse of the day; clearly GOTV groups had attained a significant public presence.

More important than their shared slogan, however, was the common conviction of campaign leaders that they were the sort of people who should lead. When middle-class and elite whites prefaced their GOTV work by describing themselves as women untainted "by carelessly made political affiliations," as businessmen "better equipped" to be good citizens "than any other class," as the Legion's "ideal leader type[s]," they were clearly stating that they saw themselves as the people fit to lead, and saw "others" as people who needed to be led. Whatever their differences, the major GOTV groups shared the bonds of color and class, and worked from the assumption that these characteristics legitimized their leadership in the civic sphere. They used the GOTV campaigns to articulate and propagate a set of civic values they held in common, values that put them at the top of the civic hierarchy.

"GOOD FOR AT LEAST 100 VOTES"

The Get-Out-the-Vote Campaigns at the Local Level

On the day before the September primary, the Grand Rapids, Michigan, League of Women Voters sponsored a parade to drum up enthusiasm at the polls. "With the Firemen's band at its head," a procession of twenty-five cars "decorated in patriotic colors and bearing pennants with slogans admonishing all voters to use their voting privilege" made its way through the city's business districts (see fig. 11). Despite the pouring rain, "factories and shops" and schools "furnished spectators and applause" along the length of the two-hour route.[1]

The GOTV campaigns were not just a top-down affair. Local campaigns such as the one in Grand Rapids were numerous, vigorous, and often departed from the dictates of national organizations. Local GOTV leaders always had considerable autonomy to conduct the campaigns as they saw fit, and local efforts varied widely in their methods, participation, and reach. Some towns put up only small efforts, while others mobilized massive resources. In many areas clubwomen were the driving force behind efforts to organize, while in others businessmen assumed the leadership roles. Some campaigns took place in relatively homogenous communities; others were organized in cities with great ethnic, class, and racial diversity. Some campaigns took place in towns where political parties were relatively weak, while others were situated in cities with powerful party machines.

The three case studies that follow investigate how the GOTV campaigns played out in the context of local political institutions, cultures, and practices. New York City, Birmingham, Alabama, and Grand Rapids, Michigan, were all home to large and well-developed GOTV campaigns, and together the three illustrate an assortment of organizational and cultural settings in which the campaigns took place. In New York, GOTV activists faced an enormous and diverse population including many thousands of immigrants and a powerful Democratic political machine. In Birmingham, where political participation was the almost exclusive preserve of whites, the campaigns raised tantalizing questions about exactly whose votes organizers hoped to "get out." In Grand Rapids, a manufacturing center and Michigan's second largest city, GOTV groups operated within the context of ethnic, racial, and economic diversity and of a Republican-dominated two-party system.

In each case study, a variety of sources held the key to understanding the local campaigns: organization records and publications, political party records and publications, large-circulation daily newspapers, and newspapers that served distinct communities in the city. Who did the work of GOTV in each locale, and what form did it take? To what extent did the national campaigns penetrate each city and the diverse communities there? What sort of reception did local GOTV activists receive? Though the national campaigns failed to boost turnout, did intense, local campaigns work? These case studies offer the opportunity to examine the reach and the limits of the GOTV campaigns, and to see how they were shaped by local political leaders, institutions, and practices.

"Improve the Electorate by Education": The GOTV Campaigns in New York City

The Get-Out-the-Vote campaigns in New York City were born out of frustration with machine politics. In the 1920s Tammany Hall reigned supreme. Democratic voters outnumbered Republicans by two to one, and the machine succeeded in electing every mayor between 1917, when Tammany reclaimed victory over the Fusion movement backed by John Purroy Mitchell, and 1933, when Republican and City Fusion candidate Fiorello LaGuardia won by running on a platform of reform. Especially after the death in 1924 of boss Charles Francis Murphy, extortion, contract-rigging, protection rackets, and office-selling reached heights that were indecent even by Tammany's relaxed standards, so much so that scandal would eventually drive Mayor Jimmy Walker, first elected in 1925, from office. Tired of being outvoted by the coalitions of

Irish, Italians, Jews, and workers whose party loyalties kept Tammany in power, the native-born elite whites who dominated the city's civic and business communities saw GOTV as a way to challenge the machine. Recalling one of the city's many graft cases, John Hays Hammond of the National Civic Federation in 1926 blamed the sorry state of city politics on the indifference of New York's "decent" citizens. The frequent scandals, the *New York Times* reported, "represent the apathy toward law and decency of the majority of American citizens and emphasize the necessity for the 'get-out-the-vote campaign.' " The GOTV campaigns, in short, were a vehicle through which the city's clubwomen and economic elites, "status-centered" elites in Theodore Lowi's phrase, could challenge the power of the city's "party-centered" elites.[2]

Certainly GOTV activists in New York wanted to improve turnout by "decent" citizens, and to that end they embarked upon vigorous and widespread advertising campaigns. Hopelessly outnumbered by loyally Democratic ethnic and working-class voters, however, anti-machine elites could never hope to prevail solely by boosting participation amongst their own. GOTV organizers in New York believed that "problem voters" posed a serious problem and undertook to transform working-class, minority, and ethnic voters from loyal partisans into people who behaved like independent and "intelligent" citizens. "You don't want merely numbers on election day," Representative Ogden Mills, Republican candidate for governor, declared at the city's "community conference" sponsored by the NCF and the American Legion at City Hall in September 1926. "You want an intelligent vote. You don't want the voters to vote as a leader tells them to do," he explained. "You want them to be so well informed that they will tell the leader what to do."[3]

For that reason, GOTV activists in New York put a great deal of energy into civic education. They hoped that familiarizing voters with how the system worked and teaching them to emphasize issues would break down Democratic loyalties and detach civic participation from neighborhood, ethnic, and class identities. Their best hope, in the words of the New York League of Women Voters, was to try to "improve the electorate by education." While GOTV activists in New York employed both advertising and education in abundance, civic education was of special importance in the campaigns there.[4]

The sheer number and range of groups that participated in GOTV citizenship education programs in New York City was probably the greatest anywhere. The list included the New York League of Women Voters, the American Legion and its many neighborhood posts, the New York

City Council of Jewish Women, the New York Teachers' Council, YWCAs, the Metropolitan Life Insurance Company, the Council on Adult Education for the Foreign Born, the public schools, colleges and universities, journalists, assorted elected officials, mothers' clubs, department stores, and even some party officials. Their educational efforts took a variety of forms: they sponsored talks on "The Duties and Privileges of Voters" at colleges, YWCAs, club meetings, and churches; they passed out handbills detailing the candidates' positions on issues; they set up information booths furnished with party platforms, "Digest[s] of New York Election Laws," and maps of election districts; they developed "Education by Radio" and broadcast talks on "Registration and Enrollment"; they offered a summer school on government and politics for women at Columbia University; they even created a "Correspondence Course on Citizenship" to educate new women voters by mail. These efforts to educate voters worked to replace local party leaders with elite "experts" as sources of civic authority. They also worked to replace a politics organized around neighborhoods with politics organized around institutions, such as downtown department stores, and the dominant daily newspapers, where elites had more influence.[5]

The extent of their efforts at civic education in many respects put New Yorkers at the head of the class. Not only was the city home to immense and repeated GOTV campaigns—in every year between 1924 and 1929, in municipal and state as well as federal elections, and in every borough, above all in Manhattan—but many national GOTV leaders lived in the city and helped to run the local as well as the national campaigns. Florence Whitney, James West, Alton B. Parker, Ralph Easley, and others used the city as a kind of laboratory to test and model the strategies they hoped groups across the country would adopt. National organizations with offices or headquarters in New York, such as the National Security League and the Traveling Salesman's Association, did GOTV work in the city and also took it on the road. The NCF was particularly important in this respect, for it was both at the center of local organizing in New York and a major sponsor of the national campaigns. When GOTV groups held their national conventions in the city, as when the NAM met at the Waldorf-Astoria in October 1926, it may have sharpened the local focus on nonvoting and efforts to remedy it. For these reasons, the GOTV campaigns in New York were exceptionally energetic and exceptionally powerful in influencing the shape of GOTV beyond the Hudson.[6]

When GOTV leaders in New York looked around, they saw problem voters in abundance. The biggest city in America in the 1920s with more than five and a half million residents, New York was home to both extra-ordinary ethnic and racial diversity and the nation's oldest political machine. More than a third of the city's residents in 1920 had been born outside the country, and of these fewer than forty percent had been naturalized. Immigrants to the city hailed from all over the world, with the largest percentages of foreign-born whites coming from Russia (24 percent), Italy (20 percent), and Ireland (10 percent). Rooted in the city's Irish American community, New York was home to one of the strongest party machines in Tammany Hall. If partisan organization and ritual had faded in many parts of the nation, in New York party politics was still robust. Precinct captains and assembly district leaders still organized voters person by person, and vibrant neighborhood-based political clubs still anchored machine loyalties. Even torchlight parades, long disappeared in other areas, from time to time still filled city streets. Ethnic and working-class voters and strong party ties were central facts of political life in New York, and the GOTV campaigns there were dedicated to reforming both.[7]

Party affiliation per se did not trouble GOTV activists, for many of them were affiliated themselves. It was the ties to Tammany and the power of workers and ethnics who banded together under its auspices that they saw as cause for concern. Certainly there were prominent partisans amongst the GOTV leadership in New York; they included Ida Slack of the General Federation of Women's Clubs, herself a Republican candidate for office in 1925; Pauline Sabin, president of the Women's National Republican Club, a founding member of the governing board of the NCF's new Department of Political Education, the NCF body charged with running the national GOTV campaigns after 1925; and Elihu Root, former secretary of state and Republican senator from New York. Hoover's New York supporters in 1928 included League Vice President Caroline Slade, Carrie Chapman Catt, the NCF's John Hays Hammond and Ralph Easley, Anna Steese Richardson of the Good Citizenship Bureau of the *Woman's Home Companion,* the League's Katherine B. Davis, and Sarah Schuyler Butler, all of whom were active in GOTV. La Follette supporters in 1924 included Catt and Harriot Stanton Blatch, both of whom represented New York at the Conference for Progressive Political Action that nominated La Follette for the presidency. Democrats too were counted amongst New York's GOTV leadership, among them Alton B. Parker of the NCF, League member Mrs. J. Ramsey Reese, and Governor Smith himself. Eleanor Roosevelt, then vice-chair of the Women's Division of the New York State Democratic Committee,

Figure 1. A nineteenth-century middlebrow leisure magazine celebrated voting by white working men. Paul Frenzeny, "The October Elections—Pennsylvania Miners at the Polls," *Harper's Weekly*, 26 October 1872, 836.

Figure 2. By the 1920s, representations of good citizens had changed. Here, another middlebrow weekly depicted voters, including a woman, as stylishly upper middle class. George Bream, *Collier's Weekly*, 4 November 1922, front cover.

Figure 3. Commentators found the failure of elite white men to vote alarming. Gale, "The Most Dangerous Man in America," published in the *Los Angeles Times*, 21 October 1924, and found in series II of the Papers of the League of Women Voters, Manuscript Division, Library of Congress, Washington, D.C. Copyright, *Los Angeles Times*. Reprinted with permission.

Figure 4. With the Red Scare a recent memory, Get-Out-the-Vote commentators worried that the absence of businessmen from the polls gave radicals undue influence. J. N. "Ding" Darling, "Rough Water and Half the Crew Not Working," *Collier's Weekly*, 2 August 1924, 19. The cartoon also appeared in *Current Opinion*, September 1924, 249.

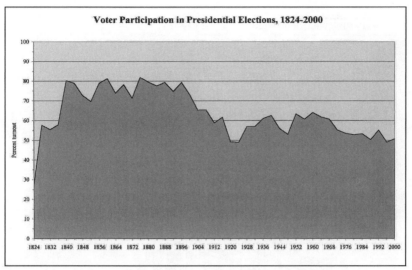

Figure 5. Voter Participation in Presidential Elections, 1824–2000. U.S. Bureau of the Census, *Historical Statistics of the United States*, Part II (Washington, D.C.: U.S. Government Printing Office, 1975), 1067–68, 1071–72; U.S. Bureau of the Census, *Statistical Abstract Online*, table 458, http://www.census.gov/prod/www/statistical-abstract-us.html; *Washington Post,* 9 November 2000, A35.

Figure 6. Get-Out-the-Vote commentators often labeled nonvoters "stay-at-homes," an epithet that challenged women's claim that their domestic responsibilities equipped them for civic duties while also criticizing men by feminizing them. Webster, "Life's Darkest Moment," *Birmingham Age-Herald*, 4 November 1926, 16. Copyright, *The Birmingham News*, 2003. All rights reserved. Printed with permission.

Figure 7. Workers and ethnic Americans were often depicted not as upright citizens but as corrupt "problem voters." Vic Lambdin, "These Men Will Register and Vote Early," 1924, published in the *Syracuse Herald*, series II, LWV Papers.

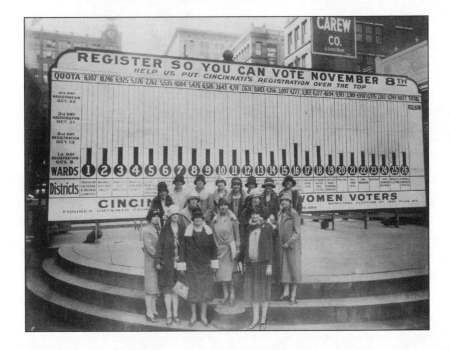

Figure 9. "VOTE As You Please, But VOTE" became the slogan of the Get-Out-the-Vote campaigns. Cover, *American Industries*, October 1924, available at the Hagley Museum and Library. Courtesy National Association of Manufacturers.

Figure 10. A Brooklyn post of the American Legion used speakers and signs to boost turnout for the November 1928 election. *American Legion Monthly*, January 1929, 37. Photo reprinted with permission, *The American Legion Magazine*, copyright January 1929.

Figure 8. (*facing page*) On Fountain Square in downtown Cincinnati, League women displayed a challenge to citizens in each city ward to get out and vote. "Register So You Can Vote November 8th," 1927, from the Prints and Photographs Division, Library of Congress, Washington, D.C. Courtesy League of Women Voters of the United States.

Figure 11. Members of the Grand Rapids League of Women Voters proudly displayed an entry in the city's Get-Out-the-Vote parade. Pictured are Florence Shelley, Grace Van Hoesen, Callie Amberg, and Mrs. Amberg's children, David and Mary. "Good Citizens Vote!" *Grand Rapids Herald*, 9 September 1924. Courtesy Grand Rapids History and Special Collections Center, Archives, Grand Rapids Public Library, Grand Rapids, Michigan.

Figure 12. Department stores integrated GOTV messages into their advertisements, such as this one for Paul Steketee and Sons Department Store in Grand Rapids, Michigan. *Grand Rapids Herald*, 4 November 1924, 6.

Figure 13. *The San Francisco Chronicle* appealed for advertising by highlighting the good citizenship of its businessmen readers. *Nation's Business*, May 1927, 143. *Nation's Business* was the publication of the Chamber of Commerce of the United States.

Mr. Solid Citizen

Mr. Solid Citizen . . . married . . . Dad to a bright youngster or two . . . fond of golf, motoring, baseball and radio. In business for himself or holding a position of responsibility. Buyer of everything from structural steel to kiddie cars. This is Mr. Solid Citizen: address, any city in the United States.

Mr. Solid Citizen votes regularly. He knows there are a few things about his government that could stand improvement but he doesn't believe the remedy rests with wild-eyed theorists or that waving a red flag will help. In New York he reads the *Times*—and in San Francisco he reads *The Chronicle*. His family read it too—and his family are accomplished spenders!

Mr. Solid Citizen is a busy man and it's easier to talk to his clerks than to himself—but not so profitable. A direct route to his attention is *The San Francisco Chronicle*. For 62 years *The Chronicle* has been the business man's conception of an interesting and informative newspaper. San Franciscans and residents of Northern California read it regularly—with due profit to advertisers.

You talk to buying power when you advertise in the

San Francisco Chronicle

Representatives:
Williams, Lawrence & Cresmer, 285 Madison Ave., New York City; 360 No. Michigan Ave., Chicago; R. J. Bidwell Co., Times Bldg., Los Angeles; Henry White, Stuart Bldg., Seattle.

Figure 14. Herbert Hoover solicited votes in his 1928 presidential bid by screening campaign movies on transportable trucks. Transport Publicity Company, 1928, Herbert Hoover Presidential Library, West Branch, Iowa.

Figure 15. Advertisers such as the Ziegfeld Theater constructed buying as a metaphor for voting. *New York Herald-Tribune*, 5 November 1928, 12.

Figure 16. Women's roles as consumers sometimes undermined, rather than reinforced, their claims to good consumer citizenship. Here, artist Dorman H. Smith depicted a woman as a petulant and immature citizen who treated the right to vote no more seriously than she would a fashion accessory. "A Thing of Beauty Should Be a Joy Forever," reprinted from the *Muncie Evening Press*, 29 September 1924, 4. The cartoon also appeared in the *Gary Post Tribune*, the *Akron Press*, and four other newspapers.

explained their task. "In some localities where groups of voters are 'got out' by this or that organization or faction the less desirable element in a community may be the deciding factor in an election." She added, "If the noncontrolled majority stays at home[,] victory for the others is made easy." The remedy? "A full vote in every community is the most direct way of combating undesirable political forces."[8]

Indeed, GOTV leaders recognized early that participation in parties was unavoidable if they were to succeed. Independents could not vote in primaries; only voters registered in a party could. By flooding the parties with new and "more intelligent" members, GOTV groups hoped to press the parties to put up better candidates at the primaries so that there would be someone worth voting for in the general election. Thus the New York League urged every voter to abide by the following vow: to "connect myself with the political party which most nearly represents my views on public questions, and to exert my influence within the party to bring about the nomination of good men for office and the endorsement of measures for the public weal."[9]

To address the issue of problem voters, at the invitation of Alton B. Parker and the National Civic Federation, representatives of forty-two organizations convened at the Hotel Astor in September of 1924 to form a "clearing house to coordinate the activities of all the organizations working to get out a big vote." The "Non-Partisan Coordinating Council" (NPCC) became the umbrella organization for the GOTV work of dozens of groups, including the Merchant's Association of New York, the American Federation of Labor, the Knights of Columbus, the New York City Federation of Women's Clubs, the Retail Dry Goods Association, the Boy Scouts and Girl Scouts, the New York Federation of Churches, the Fifth Avenue Association, the Women Lawyers' Association, the American Board of Applied Christianity, the Sons of the American Revolution, the League of Advertising Women, the Washington Heights WCTU, Rotary clubs in the Bronx and Staten Island, and the Brooklyn Civitas Club. Party representatives from a smattering of local Republican and Democratic clubs, the Republican Committee of New York County, and even Tammany Hall from time to time dropped in on these meetings, though none held leadership posts and none attended meetings regularly.[10]

These groups put forth extraordinary efforts. The New York Federation of Women's Clubs sent out GOTV mailings to its four hundred member clubs, each of which boasted between one and two thousand members. The Brooklyn Chamber alone distributed twenty-five thousand

GOTV posters. The New York League urged members to "Vote as You please, but Vote!" while also passing out literature produced by *Collier's* and the NAM. The Bronx Women's Club held a GOTV luncheon, while the Mother's Club of Queens held a GOTV talk at Public School 36. Indeed, the NPCC claimed that its member organizations represented nearly a million voters. Newspapers reinforced their message and reminded readers that "Today's The Day! Do Your Duty And Visit The Polls—Early." The NPCC even issued a "call for buglers everywhere in the city" to "join in calling the assembly" when registration sites opened. Their work earned widespread praise. Democratic nominee John Davis commended it as being of "the highest merit," while Speaker of the New York State Assembly H. Edmund Machold remarked that the campaigns "cannot help but tend for better government in the interest of all the people."[11]

Much of the GOTV work in New York in 1924 focused on what one organizer termed "intelligent educational work." The New York League of Women Voters urged all local Leagues in the state to launch a program of citizenship education and supplied them with a "Working Kit for Vote-Getters" that spelled out the civic values they hoped to persuade people to embrace. "When few vote, elections may easily be swung for personal gain" by bosses who lined their pockets or workers who traded loyalty for a job. The "minority vote is a controlled vote" and "puts the power in the hands of the machine rather than of the people." "The people," as the League saw it, ought to be basing political judgments on "unbiased" information learned in classes, lectures, and workshops rather than on loyalties to family, faith, neighborhood, or party. They ought to reason through issues and give priority to abstractions like the intricate workings of the three branches of government, rather than uphold neighborhood ties or focus on narrow personal concerns. Elsewhere the League recommended enlisting university professors, "local men and women who are responsible and non-partisan students of public affairs," and League officers and other "experts secured by them" as teachers for these classes, thus substituting "experts" for bosses as political authorities. These programs offered an alternative to machine models of good civic behavior and hoped to transform "problem voters" into "intelligent" citizens.[12]

Educational efforts spread far and wide. The New York Council of Jewish Women invited Caroline Slade to address a meeting of their club, an organization that boasted 5,500 members and "always" turned out two or three thousand members at meetings. The New York Teachers' Council pronounced themselves "in thorough sympathy with every effort" to "bring out one hundred per cent. of the vote," advising further that "every effort should be made to make that vote an intelligent one." The League sponsored a citizenship school at Columbia University and another "Institute of Politics" at Erasmus Hall High School in Brooklyn. At the Brooklyn event, attendees could learn about "Our Democracy—That 38% Vote in Kings County" from Professor Raymond Moley of Columbia and "Party Responsibility in Getting Out the Vote" from Sarah Schuyler Butler. Radio addresses reached countless more with the information they needed to cast "informed" votes, from Senator Nathan Straus Jr.'s October address on WEAF on "Citizens and Slackers," to the New York public school school system's Director of Civics Frank Rexford's talk on WNYC on the duty to vote, to Mrs. Walter Timme's speech on WGBF on "Why I am Going to Vote." Each of these efforts would produce, they hoped, a fuller and more intelligent vote. "The people of New York have never failed to answer when they have been called upon to serve the country," the NPCC wrote in a letter to the editor of the *New York Times* near the close of the registration period. "They must not fail now."[13]

Lively GOTV work continued in New York in the municipal, county, state, and congressional elections of 1925, 1926, and 1927. In 1925 criticism of civic slackers continued at a shrill pitch. Businessmen were once again targets, as when Republican candidate for Mayor Frank D. Waterman expressed his frustration with fellow businessmen who "complain of the manner in which the city affairs are conducted" but "fall down when they are called upon to assist in remedying the situations they deplore." Religious leaders took a critical tone, too. At a meeting of the New York Baptist Ministers Conference, the Reverend Dr. Charles Sears, superintendent of the New York Baptist City Mission Society, chided "church members [who] are tremendously neglectful of the ballot and by their neglect have contributed to the mismanagement of our cities. . . . It is not sufficient for Christians to say, 'Not a thing to do with it.' " "Not the red-hot, misguided Socialist, but the cold-blooded, hard-shelled indifferentist who neither registers nor votes is the greatest obstacle to securing good government," argued Alfred W. Martin in an October address to the Society for Ethical Culture. Simon Michelet continued the censure of the "stay-at-home vote" and pointed out that the United States ranked "far below the leading European nations" in voter turnout. Newspapers continued to call for citizens to register and vote, the *New York Times* insisting that "it is for every man and woman entitled to register to choose between being a good citizen and being a slacker and a shirker." In the efforts to educate voters, the League persisted most faithfully of all.

In 1925 it continued to pass out handbills to inform voters of the positions of candidates on the issues and the particulars of when and how to register and vote, and continued to broadcast radio talks with titles such as "Registration and Enrolment" and "Why Vote."[14]

In 1926, as reform-minded papers warned that Georgy Olvany, Tammany's leader, would "spare no efforts to get every Democratic voter registered," GOTVers in New York brought a renewed focus on the need to reform parties. "Instead of a 'Get Out the Vote' slogan," Ralph Easley said, "we ought to have a 'Get Into the Party' slogan." In this spirit, a wide array of groups took up GOTV again in 1926. The NCF and American Legion demonstrated their strategy of cooperation by cosponsoring the city's "community conference." In proceedings that were broadcast live on WNYC, representatives from more than one hundred local organizations formed themselves into the New York City Committee on Active Citizenship (NYCAC). Heavyweights in the city's women's club and business communities were elected to head the organization, including Robert Adamson, a banker and leader of the Merchants Association of New York; Henry H. Curran, U.S. commissioner of immigration at Ellis Island and a member of the City Club; and Mrs. William Dick Sporborg of the New York City Federation of Women's Clubs. Representatives from the American Federation of Labor, the New York Teachers' Council, the Greater New York Federation of Churches, the Catholic Women's League, the League for American Citizenship, area Chambers of Commerce, the Lions Club, and the NCF and American Legion all served on the executive committee. Mayor Jimmy Walker opened the proceedings by wishing the organizers well and declaring his "firm conviction that every eligible voter should belong to a political party." At the same conference John Hays Hammond of the NCF stressed that remaking the parties from the inside and turning out a better class of voters was the solution to poor municipal governance. "One hears a great deal about party corruption, of ruthless machines and insidious bosses, who lurk in each party to defraud the public. . . . I do not deny that there has been much of that in the past, . . . but, if so, there never was an instance where the remedy was not plain."[15]

The Committee on Active Citizenship oversaw the GOTV efforts in the city in 1926 and placed the emphasis squarely on civic education. They won a pledge of "whole-hearted co-operation" from the New York City Superintendent of Schools to prepare students for their future roles as voters and to urge their parents to "register, enroll and vote" too. Member groups printed party platforms, passed out voting information to shoppers, and lobbied for changes to New York election law to make it easier for potential voters to register. Republican assemblyman Phelps Phelps (that in fact was his name) introduced a bill to fine citizens who did not register, noting that "we are continually hearing complaints that the right class of men are not elected to govern our cities and States. . . . In many cases the people who take this attitude are usually found wanting when the registration books are open." GOTV groups again took to the airwaves to present addresses called "Registration" and "Why Vote?"[16]

The Committee on Active Citizenship continued its campaigns dedicated to "wiping out this deplorable record" in the municipal and state elections of 1927. Now with seventy-five member organizations, they hoped to breathe "new life" into GOTV efforts. They added Haley Fiske of the Metropolitan Life Insurance Company and Laura Cauble of the Woman's Democratic Club to their list of officers. The NCF surveyed NYCAC member groups to find out why some people still failed to vote, only to find that these groups had not yet succeeded in getting one hundred percent of their own members to turn out. This time, GOTV leaders decided to work on getting "members of [their] own organization[s] [to] meet their civic obligations by registering, enrolling, attending primaries, [and] voting at elections," a move that highlighted their intent to stimulate turnout by the "right sorts." Member groups continued to sponsor radio talks and distribute literature with registration and election information. Organizations such as the New York Kiwanis Club and the Greater New York Federation of Churches held informational meetings to press the message, as United States Attorney Charles H. Tuttle put it at a dinner given in his honor, that "every election is a summons to the colors." GOTV groups continued to sponsor educational meetings such as the one on "The Duties and Privileges of Voters" organized by the Manhattan 13th Assembly District chapter of the League of Women Voters, in which Sarah Schuyler Butler, Belle Moskowitz, and Mrs. Charles Tiffany spoke to members at the Barnard College Gymnasium. The city also featured "New Voters" at the Fourth of July celebration on City Hall Plaza. Mayor Jimmy Walker handed out certificates to "native and foreign born first voters," and the program was broadcast live over WNYC. Some twenty thousand New Yorkers attended the reception that followed as guests of the "Mayor's Committee on Independence Day Reception [for] First Voters."[17]

The GOTV campaigns continued in 1928, but on a substantially smaller scale. Here and there some of the keenest participants continued to sponsor public events and educational programs. This time Governor

Al Smith addressed the crowds at the city's Fourth of July celebration, singling out five thousand new voters in the crowd and urging them to "vote and to give study to the platforms of the major political parties." The NCF put out press releases with lengthy statements on why "A Better and Bigger Vote [Is] Needed to Preserve our Democracy." The Park Slope post of the American Legion in Brooklyn organized a car campaign, while Legion posts in the city used a short film to remind citizens to "Do what you please on election day—but cast your ballot first." The Republican Business Men, Inc. issued from their headquarters on West 40th Street a statement urging golf courses around the country to close on election day. The League of Women Voters persisted, too, the state League issuing in pamphlet form a "Correspondence Course on Citizenship for Women" that focused mostly on "The Use and Abuse of Party." The League continued its GOTV efforts in radio, and from New York on the final broadcast before election day gave John Hays Hammond the last word. "We cannot take lightly the responsibility of citizenship. . . . Eternal vigilance in political affairs is the price we must pay for good government."[18]

To New Yorkers involved in GOTV throughout the 1920s, the issue of "problem voters" loomed large. They had already worked to reduce their numbers. Both the New York League of Women Voters and the state American Legion had enthusiastically backed Albany's successful push to require proof of literacy for all who became eligible to vote in or after 1922. But clearly more needed to be done to weaken the partisanship and reform the "blind voting" that GOTV activists charged was characteristic of ethnics, immigrants, workers, and racial minorities. "The job of supervising"—supervising—"the millions of voters represented in the racial groups of the country," one observer wrote in a letter to the editor of the Times, required much more.[19]

Thus GOTV groups in New York worked to reform, reconstruct, and remake the civic identities and behaviors of the ethnics, workers, immigrants, and racial minorities whose political participation they regarded as a problem. In 1924 the League of Women Voters lined up Henry Curran for one of its radio broadcasts on WEAF. On at least three occasions it sent speakers to the "Colored Branch" of the YWCA in Harlem to discuss how and why to vote. The Non-Partisan Coordinating Council also "most earnestly urged" every city employer to "bring this important obligation to the attention of his employes . . . in the most forceful manner possible." In 1926 the Brooklyn LWV announced that it would schedule a speech by Mary Paddon on "The Immigrant Woman as Voter" at its annual convention at the Hotel St. George. In 1927 the New York LWV reported that it was "taking a deeper interest" in the citizenship of naturalized and immigrant women and setting up new lines of cooperation with the Council on Adult Education for the Foreign Born. It followed up by passing out guides to naturalization at information booths around the city.[20]

In a few cases, newspapers and organizations serving ethnic communities took up GOTV themselves. The *Jewish Daily News* articulated the familiar critique that the right sort of people were not voting and that their lack of interest encouraged governmental corruption. In 1924 the editors decried the failure of "the so-called best people in each community" to turn out at the polls. They "claim that it is useless to cast a ballot since the professional politicians run the country." Such an attitude would not do. Noting that "the shout has now gone forth to get the vote out and non-partisan organizations have been formed to stimulate civic pride," the paper urged citizens to join in and "go to the polls and vote." An election-eve editorial reinforced the message. "Don't be a slacker. Don't stay at home tomorrow and then call yourself a good citizen. Vote intelligently." The paper repeated the message in the campaigns of 1926. "So long as citizens are not interested the cheap politicians and the grafters will continue to rule to the detriment of the country at large. . . . There must be an intelligent study of public affairs. That is essential. And then there must be voting. So tomorrow do not neglect to cast your vote." To a similar end, in 1927 the East Side Post of the American Legion, with members born in Russia, Poland, Italy, Austria, Germany, and twenty-seven other countries, reported with pride that it had sponsored classes on "Americanism" for newly naturalized immigrants and also backed half a dozen Boy Scout troops. The Hebrew Educational Society in Brooklyn likewise offered "classes in citizenship and civics" along with courses in Jewish history, psychology, and dressmaking. Prominent Italian Americans in the city agreed with an NCF report on nonvoting that the problem had to be "dealt with vigorously if our democratic institutions are to endure."[21]

These, however, were exceptions rather than the rule. Representatives of the city's minority or ethnic and working-class communities held no leadership positions in the GOTV campaigns, and organizations and institutions with roots in these communities were rarely involved in GOTV at all. From time to time they welcomed the city's GOTV leaders to their meetings, but calls of their own for "intelligent" and nonpartisan voting were few and far between. The GOTV graphics that were so plentiful in the major dailies were not to be found at all in the newspapers that specifically served the city's ethnic and minority communities, and when calls to "vote as you please, but vote" appeared at all in African American, Jewish, and Irish American newspapers, they appeared alongside, and were often outnumbered by, calls to vote for a particular party or to advance the group. Often, leaders in minority communities flatly rejected charges that their communities voted in unthinking and blindly partisan ways. They maintained, rather, that they voted in accordance with their interests, as every good voter should. In no sense was GOTV a project of New York's ethnic, minority, or working-class communities. To the extent that GOTV was present in these communities at all, it came from the outside.

This pattern was clear in the city's Irish American community. Irish American voters denied that they voted as thoughtless partisans and ardently defended the legitimacy of voting in their class and ethnic interests. A Catholic priest and professor asserted in a New York paper that Irish American voters "care no longer for labels but for the principles, facts and records of the candidates for office." The editors of the *Irish World and American Industrial Liberator,* a long-running New York paper with a national and international orientation, argued that "there was a time when the so-called 'Irish vote'" was ignored in American politics because one political party "was sure of it" and "the other had no hopes of winning it." That, the editors claimed, was no longer true; blind partisanship was waning. Irish "Democrats or Republicans or Progressives" are "examining for themselves the merits or demerits of the political issues" they faced at the polls. "They are voters and not mere ballot casters." The paper supported La Follette for president and Smith for governor in the same year, praising them for their support for the working man and their opposition to the Ku Klux Klan. The editors opposed the 1924 Demo-cratic presidential nominee, John W. Davis, on complementary grounds; as a former U.S. ambassador to Great Britain and lawyer who worked on behalf of coal companies to jail strikers in the 1902 strike in West Virginia, Davis was no friend of the Irish worker. These were proper grounds upon which citizens ought to choose a candidate. "Universal suffrage," the editors asserted, gives voters the power "to protect themselves against any injustice done them through the government becoming the agent of unscrupulous and greedy profiteers. All they have to do is to use their ballots to strip of power any administration which . . . favors specitl [sic] interests at the expense of Abraham Lincoln's 'plain people.' "[22]

The city's African American leaders took the same position. The *New York Amsterdam News,* for example, regularly listed the places and times at which citizens could register and vote, occasionally adding that readers were "at liberty to belong to any party and vote for the men you consider the right ones." More often, however, the paper's editors urged readers to vote not to promote abstract nonpartisan ideals but to protest Tammany's corruption, to elect Republicans, and to advance the race. "Every citizen of the United States, white or black, owes it to himself to register and vote," the editors argued, but "the Negro, American born and West Indian[,] has other reasons for a strict exercise of the right of suffrage." Local Republicans had nominated African American candidates for alderman and assemblyman, candidates who would likely "be elected to office if every redblooded Negro in the district will register and vote for them." "Keep elective representation for the Negro, by the Negro"—that was what voting could accomplish for them. In 1923, while urging the reader to "go to the polls and discharge his duty as a citizen of the State and Nation," the paper also implored voters to rebuff Tammany's attempts to divide the black vote by giving African American Democrats a handful of patronage jobs. "Don't be fooled. Everywhere there are evidences of the price the community is paying for these jobs. Bootleggers, robbers, murderers, petty thieves and houses of ill fame are doing a thriving business . . . and in too many instances receiving protection at the hands of corrupt politicians." Mindful of Marcus Garvey's efforts to meld immigrant and native-born blacks into one potent political force, the editors called for unity within the community and urged southern-born blacks to register and vote and West Indian immigrants to naturalize and do the same. With their combined efforts, "a colored man could be sent to Congress with ease," something that would not be achieved until Adam Clayton Powell Jr. was elected in 1944. When the *Amsterdam News* asked readers to "BECOME NATURALIZED, REGISTER And VOTE!," it made the case for race-conscious political action, not for nonpartisan GOTV.[23]

Across these communities, the limits of GOTV are clear. Sometimes newspapers editorialized on GOTV in the abstract; rarely, however, did they report on GOTV work taking place in their communities, suggesting either that such work was receiving little public notice or that it simply was not being done. Rarely did members of these communities serve as leaders in citywide efforts; ethnic associations are notably absent from the membership of the NPCC or the NYCAC. Clearly their efforts at GOTV were small and, where they existed, they were separate from the biggest organized efforts in the city. Occasionally the slogans and arguments popularized by the main GOTV groups showed up in the public statements of these groups, statements that it was the "better classes" who were failing to vote, or that citizens who failed to vote were "stay-at-homes," but the literature of the major groups—the NAM pamphlets, the red-white-and-blue stickers, the LWV graphics—did not. Sometimes the ideal of the "intelligent," or nonpartisan, voter was praised on the editorial pages of papers that catered to these communities. More often, however, these communities saw the ballot as a tool to be used to advance their class, ethnic, and racial interests. While the dominant dailies promoted practically nothing other than the civic ideal of independence and intelligence, that approach to voting was only one of many, and hardly the most common, promoted in the ethnic, racial, and working-class press.

For all their efforts to educate voters, the GOTV campaigns in New York gave supporters little to cheer about. Their attempts to replace party bosses with "neutral experts" as sources of information and authority, their campaigns to reform parties from the inside out, even their bid to boost turnout amongst their own club memberships scarcely made the turnout numbers budge. Campaign leaders bemoaned the lack of dramatic results. Turnout in the five boroughs rose from about fifty-three percent in 1920 to fifty-eight percent in 1924; using different numbers, the NCF estimated the increase in turnout at about three percent. After all their hard work, the GOTV campaigns in the city had wrought very little. The *New York Times* reported the results a bit more generously, but could only conclude that the GOTV campaigns had caused "voting indifference" to decrease "slightly."[24]

In this machine city, the numbers showed clearly that Tammany had won and GOTVers had lost. Massive campaigns of civic education, campaigns intended to undermine the neighborhood basis of politics and to detach voters' political loyalties from their ethnic, religious, and class identities, did not make a dent in the power of the Democratic machine. Neighborhoods were crucial to the practice of "politics as usual" in New York, but not to GOTV. Vote activists tried to organize politics on a different basis, substituting editorials in the *New York Times* for conversations in political clubs, exchanging signs at Saks for personal relationships. GOTV messages penetrated ethnic, minority, and working-class communities in only the most limited ways, and there they met not warm welcomes but confident claims to the contrary, that partisan or class- or race-based voting was good. Ethnic Americans and workers continued to comprise the majority, and they remained loyal to the institutions that they saw as sources of identity, pride, and power.

"Good for at Least 100 Votes": The GOTV Campaigns in Birmingham

In January 1924, Birmingham, Alabama's leading African American newspaper carried an advertisement for "Madam C. J. Walker's Toilet Preparations," the hair straighteners and beauty products that made the entrepreneur a millionaire. The advertisement featured, however, not her products but rather a contest to choose a church pastor to "make a trip to the Holy Land at our expense." The ad listed ministers by name and invited readers to "find your favorite candidate." And how were readers to register their choice? "Vote for him," the ad explained, by mailing in "the coupons found in each package" of Madam C. J. Walker products. Every purchase was "good for at least 100 votes," the more expensive products worth even more. With the purchase of these "high class toilettes," the balloting would begin.[25]

For a group of citizens largely excluded from the franchise, the irony was palpable. African Americans here could vote for a prize for a pastor at a time when few could overcome the barriers to cast ballots for a president. But access to even this ballot was mediated by the culture of consumption: here coupons constituted ballots, and one literally had to make a purchase to cast a vote. In the context of a political system in which class status was a powerful predictor of political participation, and in which ballot box–stuffing was practically standard procedure if a race threatened to be close, the extent of one's participation in the contest was directly linked to the extent of one's consumption: the more a customer spent on Madam C. J. Walker's products, the more votes he or she was entitled to cast.

In the Birmingham of the 1920s, voting and buying were linked in complicated ways in product advertisements, newspaper editorials, and in the Get-Out-the-Vote campaigns. Birmingham was home to the largest GOTV campaigns in the South, campaigns comprised of "tag days," citizenship schools, radio spots, and political cartoons. These campaigns were the work of dozens of community groups, both black and white, and, to a lesser extent, of organized labor as well. In big ways in the fall of 1924, and in smaller but significant ways in 1926 and 1928, the citizens of Birmingham took up with great seriousness "the burning question of Get-Out-the-Vote."[26]

The existence of a large GOTV campaign in the South itself raises "burning question[s]." Indeed, the early twentieth-century South presented a peculiar setting for campaigns to boost turnout. In a period and place in which mass disenfranchisement of blacks and poor people was enshrined in state constitutions, in which the dominance of the Democratic party usually made the outcome of elections a foregone conclusion, and in which racial hierarchies in particular, in the civic sphere and elsewhere, were sharply drawn, frequently challenged, and often violently enforced, what did it mean to "get out the vote"? How did the GOTV campaigns, with their broad call to "vote as you please, but vote," bend and warp under the pressures of race and class politics in the South? In short, what did it mean to get out the vote in a place in which many locals clearly did not want to get *everyone* out to vote?[27]

If the South seemed an unlikely setting for GOTV work, Birmingham was the most likely among southern locales. Founded after the close of the Civil War near natural deposits of iron ore, limestone, and coal, Birmingham was born for business. As the nation's demand for steel grew, so too did Birmingham, the city's population around the turn of the century quadrupling in twenty years. Of the city's approximately 179,000 residents in 1920, nearly forty percent were African American, and perhaps twenty thousand worked in the mines and mills. Heavy industry also attracted foreign-born laborers, including substantial numbers of Italians and Russians. Though immigrants comprised only four percent of the city's population, their presence triggered "intense programs of 'Americanization.' " Birmingham's workers, foreign-born and otherwise, were not without a measure of political power; in Congressman George Huddleston and City Commissioner William Harrison they found energetic advocates. Organized labor in Birmingham, however, never recovered from failed miners' strikes in 1908, 1919, and again in 1920, strikes that the National Guard was called out to crush. Not until the 1930s did Birmingham see a sharp upswing in organizing activity.[28]

The city's largest employers, the men who ran Tennessee Coal and Iron (TCI), Republic Steel, Sloss-Sheffield Steel and Iron, and the Ingalls Iron Works, made up the city's leadership class. Exceptionally well organized in clubs and trade associations in a city that, as historian Blaine Brownell put it, "had no prewar aristocracy in the first place," Birmingham's business leaders directed the economic and civic affairs of the city with exceptional freedom. The city's business leadership and phenomenal growth were important parts of its public image—in the 1920s, Birmingham was home to the tallest skyscraper in the South—and the subject of endless boosterism. At the great civic pageant in 1921 celebrating the fiftieth anniversary of the city's founding, the character of Birmingham's founding father, "Colonel" James R. Powell, surveyed the city and pronounced it good. Birmingham, he proclaimed, was the

"Magic City of the World, the marvel of the South"—no, "the dream of the Hemisphere, the vision of all Mankind." Puffery, the businessman's rhetoric of advertising and promotion, was a well-established part of Birmingham's civic language.[29]

It was Birmingham's businessmen, together with their clubwomen wives, who directed the city's GOTV campaigns. O. L. Bunn, secretary and manager of the Birmingham Chamber of Commerce, proudly responded to an early appeal by the NCF that he was already "circularizing the membership" to boost voter turnout. The Birmingham-based Alabama Textile Company displayed the NAM's "Vote As You Please" posters, while a local paper reported on Met Life's national campaign. The International Association of Civitan Clubs, founded and headquartered in Birmingham, urged members to register and vote. After experimenting with GOTV work in 1924, the Junior Chamber made GOTV the club's "major activity" two years later. It sent "Four minute speakers" to business groups and fraternal organizations, furnished local movie theaters with GOTV slides, and solicited the cooperation of area employers, many of whom responded with letters "pledging their support to the movement." In 1924 and again in 1927 and 1928, the Junior Chamber also broadcast on local station WBRC "to remind the qualified voter of his duty to go to the polls." The Get-Out-the-Vote activists also counted the Exchange Club, the Farm Bureau, the American Legion, and the Alabama Mining Institute among their business supporters.[30]

Clubwomen embraced GOTV with even greater enthusiasm through campaigns organized by Pattie Ruffner Jacobs, Jeannette Adams, and Mollie Dowd. Jacobs, a Democratic party activist and one of the leading suffragists in the South, served as the first president of the Alabama Equal Suffrage Association before becoming a vice president of the national League of Women Voters. Jacobs chaired the Efficiency in Government committee of the Jefferson County LWV and used her position to help organize GOTV campaigns across the state. Adams, a vice president of the Jefferson County League and president of the Alabama League in 1926, was the wife of the vice president of the Birmingham Chamber of Commerce and served as a link between the two groups. Dowd served as secretary of the Alabama League while remaining active in the Jefferson County organization, helping to tie together local and state efforts. In the 1930s, Dowd would go on to serve as a labor conciliator for the state of Alabama.[31]

A thousand members strong, the "lively and active" Jefferson County League passed out GOTV fliers spelling out eligibility requirements and collected poll taxes at area department and drugstores. They distributed twenty-five thousand tags bearing the "Vote as you please" slogan to passersby in downtown Birmingham and in twenty-two counties across the state. In 1924, Alabama League ladies even entered the national League's silver cup contest, not because they had the "faintest hope of getting the cup" but because they wanted to be "good sports." In 1928, the Jefferson County League ordered both the national League's GOTV doll exhibit and GOTV "slide film," displaying the first in the windows of the First National Bank building downtown and screening the second at a League booth at the annual "Birmingham-Made" Exposition. Two things were missing from the League's local campaign: radio (the National League's weekly program on the NBC radio network was "almost impossible to get," Mollie Dowd reported); and a grass-roots precinct campaign.[32]

The Jefferson County League cooperated closely with other groups, supplying them with literature and office space and helping to coordinate their efforts. The statewide Non-Partisan Committee to Get Out the Vote operated out of League headquarters at Birmingham's Hillman Hotel. The League also gathered some two hundred and fifty representatives of cooperating groups for joint planning meetings in September and October of 1924. The Jefferson County League supplied other groups with copies of "Seven Steep Steps" and won the cooperation of both the state librarians' organization (which slipped fifty thousand leaflets urging readers to "Vote Nov. 4th" into correspondence and the books that patrons borrowed) and the Alabama Child Welfare Department (which distributed a thousand leaflets as enclosures in correspondence). The Birmingham Business and Professional Women's Club, the Eastern Star, the Council of Jewish Women, and the Women's Christian Temperance Union likewise joined in the local campaigns.[33]

Clubwomen and businessmen in Birmingham recruited other organizations to the cause—the Birmingham newspapers, which railed regularly against the "stay-at-home vote"; the DAR; fraternal organizations; and the American Legion and the American Legion Auxiliary, the latter of which argued that even women who were "not yet in sympathy with woman suffrage" had a "moral obligation as citizens of this Republic to vote." Religious communities joined in, too. Dr. James E. Dillard, pastor of the Southside Baptist Church, served on a statewide GOTV committee, as did Rabbi Morris Newfield, the Hungarian-born leader of Birmingham's Temple Emanu-El and one of the city's most prominent racial progressives. The Birmingham section of the National Council of Jewish

Women staffed a poll-tax collection booth and canvassed voters by telephone with the aid of the Young Men's Hebrew Association. The Alabama League declared November 2, 1924, "get-out-the-vote Sunday" and asked religious leaders to offer "special prayers, sermons and announcements."[34]

Even politically marginalized groups in Birmingham participated in GOTV. In the African American community as elsewhere, middle-class and elite businessmen and clubwomen took the lead. Under the direction of editor and manager Oscar W. Adams, the *Birmingham Reporter,* the largest African American newspaper in Birmingham as well as the "Official Organ of the Masons, Eastern Stars and Knights of Pythias," published occasional reminders to vote, including a boxed reminder before the 1924 general election, in the NAM's phrase, to "Vote as you please— but vote!" The paper likewise published detailed instructions on the procedures for paying poll taxes.[35]

Above all, the *Reporter* editorialized often on the importance of black voting. An op-ed piece by Mary E. Clarke urged a "poll tax and registration crusade throughout the length and breadth of the state"; voting, after all, was the most "sublime duty" of citizenship. Other editorials echoed her call. "Birmingham needs more voting citizens," declared the February 1926 edition. "Our problems are too grave and the possibilities too great to refrain from exercising all the rights and privileges known to good citizenship." The use of the word "refrain" is jarring; certainly these writers were aware of the barriers to black voting. "The Negro, truly, has great oppositions to overcome," a *Reporter* editorial wrote plainly on another occasion. But they placed much of the responsibility for black participation on the black community itself. "There are numbers of Negroes in Birmingham who can qualify for registration, who will be registered if they qualify and who could both qualify and register if they would try." These editorials did not openly criticize the poll tax system, the intimidation, or the violence that kept African Americans from the polls. Rather, they couched their complaints in coded language that criticized the "gravest injustice" done to African Americans. Frequently these community leaders argued, in terms that echo Booker T. Washington, that full citizenship could be earned and that it was in fact near at hand. As Birmingham's William H. Clarke put it in a 1924 editorial:

> Let us start anew a general citizenship drive in every city, section, county and state. Let us employ with increased vigor and force . . . the teaching profession to furnish intelligence and guidance in our

efforts . . . [and] the church with its splendid union and formidable strength. Let these foster, encourage and push forward the present necessary movement among us; and before the present generation passes from the busy scenes of active life, you will see the race begin to reach forth and regain in all its fullness . . . the coveted prize of full American citizenship which it won and lost in the latter half of the 19th century.[36]

African American clubwomen in Birmingham explicitly embraced the GOTV campaigns. Clubs such as the Joy Crafters, Inter Se, the Cosmos Circle, and the Sinovadad club served as important social outlets for middle-class and elite African American women. Rooted in church and religiously inspired, the clubs often met in church buildings and their minutes frequently recorded prayers and hymns as part of club proceedings. The Sinovadad club in particular drew from the highest echelons of African American society in Birmingham. Founded in 1925, it was comprised of but twenty-four members "prominent in the social and club life of the community" but it contributed to the state Federation of Colored Women three state officers and more financial support than any other Birmingham club. The Sinovadad club easily turned out three hundred guests at social functions and served as a patron of the Birmingham YWCA, the Community Chest, and the Old Folks Home.[37]

In the fall of 1924, a small number of African American women's clubs, including the Joy Crafters, Inter Se, and Cosmos Circle clubs, accepted the invitation of the Jefferson County League of Women Voters to take part in a GOTV meeting. All of these clubs were members of the Alabama Federation of Colored Women, the state affiliate of the National Association of Colored Women. In 1925, Nellie (Mrs. A. M.) Brown of Birmingham succeeded Margaret Murray (Mrs. Booker T.) Washington as president of the Alabama Federation of Colored Women. Under Brown's leadership, the Alabama Federation resolved three times before 1929 to improve the citizenship of its members, recommending one year that members adopt "a broad citizenship program" and, in another, that they take up "a serious study of citizenship under a competent leader." Like so many others, leaders in this African American community also called for "intelligent" political participation and the expert exercise of civic duties. By attending joint planning meetings and passing resolutions, African American clubwomen clearly participated in the Birmingham campaigns.[38]

Organized workers also played a role in Birmingham's GOTV campaigns. In the 1920s South, Birmingham was something of a labor town.

The local *Labor Advocate* was the official organ of both the Birmingham Trades Council and the Alabama State Federation of Labor. Birmingham was also where labor's candidate in 1924, Senator La Follette, chose to set up the southern regional headquarters for his presidential campaign.

Organized labor in Birmingham, as elsewhere, had often urged workers to register and vote with, for example, banner headlines urging readers to "Pay Your Poll Tax on or Before Next Wednesday if You Wish to Vote This Year." But unlike other GOTV groups in Birmingham, the Trades Council addressed explicitly and forcefully the radical potential of full voter turnout. For years the *Labor Advocate* had urged workers to "*Qualify Yourselves To Vote, And Then Go Out And Vote For Your Kind Of People, And Then Evil Legislation Against You Will Cease. Wake Up, You Sluggards, Wake Up!*" The paper took the GOTV campaigns very seriously. In 1924, the editors noted that "*Lots Of Folks Are Urging 'Get Out The Vote.'* " They continued, bellowing that "*We Don't Hear Very Much Of It From Certain Elements* to whom it would mean defeat to really get out the vote." Labor promoted GOTV in Birmingham in class-conscious terms rarely heard in the campaigns. Confronted with evidence that the wealthy clearly pursued their own interests, "any laboring man . . . can see why he and every member of his family who is eligible should pay their poll tax and be real American citizens." "Why Not 'Our' Government," the paper queried, instead of, apparently, "theirs"?[39]

That organized labor in Birmingham gave strong editorial support to the GOTV campaigns is clear; repeatedly it pressed readers to "*Pay That Poll Tax Now* and be *A Real American.*" What rank-and-file workers may have done to get out the vote is less clear. Minutes and newspaper reports of meetings of various locals show a few instances in which the GOTV message was directly raised with workers. At a January 1924 meeting of Painters No. 57, for example, guest speaker Jefferson county registrar L. K. Bowen argued that "it was just as essential for a union man to have his paid up tax receipts and register ticket as for him to carry his union card." And appended to the minutes of a January 1924 meeting of the Birmingham Trades Council was a pointed reminder to "pay your Poll Tax *Today.*" Whatever the level of rank-and-file GOTV activity, it is clear that local labor leaders brought news of national GOTV campaigns to the attention of their members. In 1926, the *Labor Advocate* praised the National Civic Federation's GOTV campaign for "Tackling a Tough Job." In 1928, it reprinted the NCF's GOTV piece, "A Call to Civic Duty," in full.[40]

The emphasis on "intelligent voting," evident everywhere in the GOTV campaigns, took on special meaning in the southern context of the Birmingham campaigns. In Birmingham as elsewhere, civic education was an important part of the GOTV effort. League ladies, for example, sponsored citizenship schools at Gadsden, Guntersville, and at Auburn University, sharing with women "Five Easy Lessons In Citizenship," including "What Every Woman Should Know About Making a President."[41]

But unlike GOTV campaigns in other regions of the country, the Birmingham campaigns placed an explicit emphasis on getting out a certain segment of the potential electorate, a group they termed "qualified voters." This resort to "qualified voters"—meaning, presumably, people who had passed literacy tests, registered, and paid poll taxes—was a way of speaking about the electorate while excluding "problem voters"— African Americans in particular, and poor people in general. In this thinly veiled way, the GOTV campaigns in Birmingham addressed themselves to people who were middle class and white. With this discursive manipulation, middle-class and elite southern whites embedded "intelligent citizenship" in a hierarchy of race and class.[42]

At the same time as businessmen and clubwomen urged Birminghamians to go to the polls, as African American clubwomen resolved to undertake a "serious study of citizenship," as labor leaders asked workers to *Go Out And Vote For Your Kind Of People,* the vote campaigns and newspapers also were filled with language that linked citizenship to consumption. Advertisements that described voting in terms of buying, such as the Madam C. J. Walker ad, appeared regularly in the Birmingham press. The Guarantee Shoe Company, for example, described its "Super-Value Men's Shoes" as " 'Strong Campaigners.' " With their long-lasting quality, it was "no wonder so many men [were] 'electing' them to fill their shoe needs, term after term!" Sokol Brothers furniture store featured its liberal credit policy and announced that thousands of customers had already "elected" to do business there. "Why not you, too?" The program for a 1924 Alabama League citizenship school boasted advertisements from local merchants declaring that "Good Citizenship and Good Merchandise Go Hand in Hand." Each of these advertisements paired buying and voting and discursively linked consumption to citizenship.[43]

This linkage notwithstanding, voter turnout in Jefferson County in the 1920s remained extremely low. Solid turnout figures for Birmingham are hard to come by, but by any measure, they clearly remained very low. After a significant improvement in turnout in 1920—an increase to 19 percent in 1920 over 7 percent in 1916—turnout in Jefferson County dipped in 1924 to just under 14 percent and stayed there in 1928. Of course, different methods of calculating the figures indicate very different results. By narrowing the base of possible voters to "qualified" voters—again, most likely white adults who had registered and paid poll taxes—the Alabama League claimed in 1924 to have achieved a turnout rate of fifty-five percent.[44]

With inflated claims such as these, the GOTV leaders of Birmingham congratulated themselves on a job well done. "All the work in this campaign," Amelia Fisk wrote her GOTV coworkers, had been "thoroughly worth while," not only because it seemed to increase turnout, but because it "focused public attention on the great need for arousing the interest of the voters in their franchise as the safeguard [of] our government." If these campaigns failed to boost turnout in a meaningful way, different communities within the city used them to reinforce or contest civic hierarchies of race and class. By directing their efforts toward "qualified" voters, middle-class and elite white civic leaders in Birmingham used the GOTV campaigns to reinforce the class and racial hierarchies of the 1920s South. For middle-class African Americans in the city, GOTV probably took on different meanings. Unfree to speak plainly or convinced that the path to progress lay in showing they could be good citizens on the terms established by whites, African Americans likely viewed their very presence in the GOTV campaigns as undermining the assumptions of white supremacy upon which white participation in the campaigns was premised. In other words, the campaigns gave them a relatively safe way to communicate their conviction that they were entitled to vote. By contrast, labor's work in GOTV expressed a militancy that African Americans may have felt they could not afford. In all these ways, the Birmingham campaigns show how local actors transformed the GOTV campaigns initiated by national organizations into campaigns that served their own purposes.[45]

Selling the City on Citizenship: GOTV in Grand Rapids, Michigan

In the city's third year of working to get out the vote, the Citizens' League of Grand Rapids, Michigan, a coalition of groups working for municipal reform, recalled the words of advertising expert Edward Bernays: "Good government can be sold to a community just as any other commodity can be sold. . . . It is an intangible product . . . but no more intangible than the creation of a desire for breakfast foods, or a new style in hats. . . . It . . . represents the acceptance of a new idea, . . . and . . . is comparable in every respect to the sale of any other commodity to the public."[46]

The Citizens' League joined more than thirty local organizations in an effort to "sell" the city on the importance of high turnout. Conducted every year from 1924 to 1928, the GOTV campaigns in Grand Rapids were among the most extensive local vote campaigns anywhere. Organizers in the Grand Rapids League of Women Voters and the Association (Chamber) of Commerce joined forces with the city's leading newspapers (future senator Arthur Vandenberg's *Herald* and its competitor, the *Press*) to boost participation at the polls. They advertised and publicized the importance of voting; they posted GOTV placards in shop windows and passed out a hundred thousand GOTV fliers; they attracted attention with a rousing pre-primary parade. In Grand Rapids, advertising methods constituted the core of the local campaigns to get out the vote.

The leaders of the Grand Rapids vote campaigns had extensive experience in local organizing; many were soon tapped for positions of importance in state and national organizations. The Grand Rapids LWV was a leader among Michigan Leagues; its founders, including Mrs. Clay Hollister, a vice president of the Michigan League from 1924 to 1926 and the wife of the president of the Old National Bank of Grand Rapids, and Helen Russell, who served as president of the Michigan General Federation of Women's Clubs from 1922 to 1924, had been major organizers in the Michigan women's suffrage movement, which succeeded in passing a referendum in 1918. Teacher Dorothy Judd became president of the Michigan League in 1928; thanks in considerable measure to her efforts, Michigan in 1929 enacted a permanent voter registration law. Judd went on to chair the National League's Department of Efficiency in Government from 1930 to 1932. The work of these and other GOTV leaders and their organizations won the notice of national vote campaign leaders: Belle Sherwin applauded the "intention, performance and careful execution" of the Grand Rapids GOTV campaigns and called them "a model" for campaigns everywhere.[47]

Grand Rapids was a model city in more ways than one. The second largest city in the state with one hundred and forty thousand residents, Grand Rapids was home to a bustling business community noted for its boosterism and "pep." The city was "the recognized center of the furniture industry in the United States" and, later, the birthplace of Amway as well. In the "city built on wood," some seventy factories in the 1920s turned out high-quality furnishings for businesses and homes, while auto parts manufacture constituted an increasingly important segment of the local economy. Some fifteen thousand city residents—many of them of Dutch ancestry, but many Poles, Germans, Swedes, and Canadians as well—found employment in these two industries. Fragmented by ethnic and religious diversity, workers in Grand Rapids had a long history of failed collective action but succeeded spectacularly in acquiring homes of their own: the people of Grand Rapids liked to publicize the fact that their city had the second highest rate of home ownership in the nation. A city of joiners as well as of homeowners, the citizens of Grand Rapids also prided themselves on their civic involvement. The Association of Commerce boasted nineteen hundred members, the Woman's Club twelve hundred. As the city's Advertising Club phrased it in promotional pamphlets, Grand Rapids was "A Good Place to Live."[48]

The GOTV campaign of 1924 was not the first attempt to boost turnout in Grand Rapids. In 1918 and again in 1919, the Grand Rapids Americanization Society (a wartime umbrella organization of reform groups), the local War Board, the local Woman's Committee on National Defense, and the area Trades and Labor Council worked to naturalize aliens and increase turnout amongst safely "Americanized" new citizens, newly enfranchised women, and the city's Dutch establishment. Between 1924 and 1928, many of the same groups revisited the problem of nonvoting, in much the same spirit as before. "The light vote, the alien, and the radical problems," local GOTV activist Frank Dykema argued, made it imperative that the city's middle-class and elite leaders turn out at full strength. The Association of Commerce echoed the sentiment: "Business men especially should appreciate the franchise privilege" and turn out "so that the majority may rule."[49]

The clubwomen of Grand Rapids joined businessmen in the 1924 campaigns. Grace Van Hoesen, Dorothy Judd, and Callie Amberg of the Grand Rapids LWV were the mobilizing forces behind the local campaigns. Van Hoesen was a businesswoman and a losing candidate in the 1923 race for city commissioner; before the end of the decade, she would win election as a Kent county supervisor. Judd taught civics at Grand Rapids Central High School after graduating from Vassar and became a leader of the local League in 1926. Amberg was the wife of Julius Amberg, a highly regarded young attorney in town.

Under the leadership of these women, the League planned and executed much of the 1924 campaigns. It printed and helped pass out one hundred and thirty thousand "dodgers" in stores, factories, hotels, and banks. It organized a "mass meeting" at the downtown Pantlind Hotel for citizens to meet and question candidates for office. It sponsored a parade of fire trucks and decorated cars to raise interest in the September primary. The League also enlisted the help of dozens of other local groups, among them the DAR, the Women's University Club, and the YWCA. A telephone campaign and postcard reminders rounded out the League's campaign. Between leaflets, store-window displays, and the parade, publicity methods dominated the League's GOTV work.[50]

If the League did the legwork of the publicity campaigns, the department stores advertised the cause with great enthusiasm. Herpolsheimer Company, "Western Michigan's Greatest Store," and Paul Steketee and Sons, in its sixty-second year, vied with each other not only in the variety and quality of their merchandise but in the ardor with which they called citizens to the polls. In full-page ads featuring mah-jongg sets and election day specials on men's union suits ("Note When You Vote—The necessity for choosing your clothing with as much care as your candidate"), the city's leading merchants also reminded citizens of their civic duties. Herpolsheimer's pressed citizens to pledge to "register and to make that registration good with [the] vote" and announced in a banner headline that "Voters Will Round Out Polling Day With a Round of Shopping!" Steketee's reminded readers that "Today is the Most Important Day for Every United States Citizen" and challenged them to "plan to cast an intelligent ballot." The ad urged readers—and potential customers—to "do your part to insure the selection of the proper leaders" to "guarantee . . . peace and prosperity to the country" (see fig. 12). For these merchants, good shopping and good citizenship went together. The department stores of Grand Rapids made good citizenship their business.[51]

Other groups eagerly joined in the League's campaign. The Federation of Women's Clubs, with its twenty-two member clubs, distributed a thousand "show-window placards" to city merchants. The Association of Commerce turned to snappy slogans—the NAM's slogan, in fact—and urged citizens to "Vote November 4th[,] Vote As You Please But Vote." Teachers in the Grand Rapids public school system urged the young students to "ask dad and mother if they've voted yet." The *Grand Rapids Chronicle* noted the nonvoting studies of Simon Michelet and roundly condemned the "stay-at-homes." The Grand Rapids Woman's Club and Knights of Columbus hosted GOTV speakers, while an industry publication, the *Furniture Manufacturer and Artisan,* applauded the civic activism of Charles Sligh, president of Sligh Furniture Company and Republican candidate for governor. The *Grand Rapids Herald* urged voting with a banner headline above the masthead: "Vote Today—Do Your Duty As a Citizen—Vote Today."[52]

If these business groups and women's clubs joined in the GOTV activities with great enthusiasm, groups of other kinds did not. Participation in the Grand Rapids vote campaign by organized labor seems to have been limited to a single editorial in the local labor newspaper in each presidential election year. Indeed, the local labor press did not even report on GOTV activities in the community. The minutes of the Trades and Labor Council, the American Federation of Labor group in Grand Rapids, show no evidence of GOTV work. The local Polish weekly, *Echo Tygodnioew,* used no GOTV graphics or slogans. Local and state political parties likewise played only marginal roles in the campaigns; though the names of the local women's political clubs (the Women's Woodrow Wilson Club, the Grand Rapids Women's Lincoln Club, the Grand Rapids Women's Republican Club) appear amongst the list of sponsoring organizations on GOTV leaflets, no further evidence of their involvement surfaces anywhere else. The records of the state Republican and Democratic parties make no mention of GOTV.[53]

The apparent nonparticipation of working-class, ethnic, and party organizations notwithstanding, if in 1924 the GOTV campaigns in Grand Rapids were big, in 1928 they were even bigger. Again the League of Women Voters took the lead, working with the Association of Commerce and others to publicize the cause "through the newspapers, [and] through the schools, department stores, signs at time clocks in factories, [and] enclosures in laundry packages." Again the women lined up the support of other groups, and again they blanketed the city with fliers reminding citizens to "register now and be sure that you can cast your vote in the fall." The League also sponsored a "school for voters" at the Woman's City Club in October and helped to run a three-day statewide citizenship school at Michigan State College (now University) in East Lansing. The Grand Rapids League hosted a "New Voter's Birthday Party" that drew two hundred young women, "bobby soxers" in the sponsor's phrase, and welcomed them to the responsibilities of citizenship with an evening of skits and talks by party representatives. The Civic Round Table, a new umbrella group of the presidents of local organizations, also took up the cause, organizing a "citizenship rally" to get "out a larger and more representative vote on election day." And local clubs once again sponsored talks on the importance of voting, the Woman's Club, for example, urging members to vote and "vote intelligently." Together these efforts, "almost heroic" in scale, left the Association to hazard that "no one" could remain "uninformed." The Michigan League was certainly impressed: in 1928 it awarded the Grand Rapids League a silver loving cup for conducting the best vote campaign of any League in the state.[54]

Enthusiastic as the campaigns were, the election results in Grand Rapids showed that the campaigns there were no more successful than the campaigns nationwide. Despite congratulatory reports in the newspapers and accounts of great achievements—the secretary of the Association of Commerce told the NCF that the 1924 campaigns produced "by far the greatest [turnout] in the history of Grand Rapids"—the numbers showed nothing to cheer about. Turnout in Kent County in 1924 rose less than a percentage point over the 1920 figure, to fifty-nine percent. In 1928, turnout even dipped slightly to fifty-five percent.[55]

The Grand Rapids campaigns were distinguished not by their results but by their methods. Certainly GOTV leaders there tipped their hats to civic education, increasingly so in 1928 when the League established citizenship schools. For most of the period, however, most of their efforts focused squarely on publicity. They paraded cars plastered with GOTV posters; they handed out leaflets in banks and hotels; they posted "show-window placards" in stores; they incorporated GOTV reminders into department-store advertising. Advertising and publicity methods constituted the core of the Grand Rapids vote campaigns, linking political culture to consumer culture in a variety of ways.

As these case studies show, the GOTV campaigns were much more than a set of well-meaning memos filed away at the headquarters of the leading national organizations. Local communities took up GOTV with gusto, mobilizing sometimes thousands of volunteers and gaining visibility with front-page newspaper coverage and downtown parades. In each of these cases, groups other than the NAM adopted the "Vote as you please" slogan as their own, showing without a doubt that the national message had penetrated deeply into local communities. In every case local GOTV organizers used the campaigns to address local issues and concerns. In New York, business and social elites used GOTV to fight the Tammany machine; in Birmingham, middle-class and elite whites used GOTV to reinforce the racial and class hierarchies of "qualified" citizenship while workers and elite African Americans used the same campaigns to undermine them; and in Grand Rapids, businessmen and clubwomen used GOTV to continue the work of "Americanization" begun during the war.

Certainly these case studies show significant similarities. In every community white businessmen and clubwomen were at the center of the GOTV effort. They were the ones who sponsored community meetings and passed out tags reminding citizens to vote. In no city did minorities, workers, or ethnic Americans take up GOTV on the scale of white businessmen and clubwomen. In every city, these groups stood at the margins of the campaigns, sometimes involved in comparatively limited ways—hosting a speaker or publishing an editorial—but they played no part in making overall campaign strategy and often were not involved at all. And in every case, no matter how intense the local effort, the campaigns failed to boost turnout in a significant way.

But these case studies show substantial differences between local campaigns as well. Workers, ethnic Americans, and African Americans responded to the GOTV campaigns in a wide range of ways. Sometimes they seem to have had almost no contact with the campaigns, as the paucity of evidence of GOTV among union members in Grand Rapids suggests. Sometimes they were relatively welcoming of the message, as when the Jewish press in New York issued its own calls to "vote intelligently." Sometimes they twisted the campaigns to their own ends, as when African American clubwomen in Birmingham subtly sent the message that they believed themselves to be civic equals by holding themselves to the same standards of citizenship that their white neighbors claimed to espouse. And sometimes they rejected the campaigns' claims altogether, as when Irish American voters in New York insisted that to vote for the Democratic machine *was* to vote intelligently. GOTV leaders at the national level knew what they intended the campaigns to look like; they could not, however, control how local communities would conduct them or how local citizens would respond.

In local communities and on a national scale, then, the campaigns to get out the vote were an important feature of the political landscape of the 1920s. What, broadly, can they teach us about politics, culture, and power in this period? How did the vote campaigns use civic education programs to operationalize and institutionalize their civic values? How did the campaigns connect the culture of consumption to the practice of good citizenship? And what did the campaigns reveal about how the fading world of parties would be replaced?

THE EXPERT CITIZEN

Civic Education and the Remaking of Civic Hierarchies

5

In the 1920s, the Metropolitan Life Insurance Company took an intense interest in improving the civic qualities of immigrants. Met Life agents personally met newly landed immigrants at the boat, put them in touch with relatives, boarded them on trains bound for their final destinations, and hired a Washington lobbyist to help with difficult legal cases. To ensure that their guidance continued after the immigrants reached their new homes, agents sent lists of the names of new arrivals to colleagues in branch offices who followed up and encouraged the newcomers to become citizens. Met Life agents then organized classes in "American language" and "Civics," sometimes teaching them in their own offices, and celebrated when they eventually accompanied their charges to naturalization ceremonies. These businessmen of Met Life, who claimed to have helped at least eighteen thousand immigrants in these ways, believed they had a civic duty to educate newcomers and show them how to become "true Americans."[1]

Citizenship training programs such as those organized by Met Life were a commonplace in the 1920s, a feature of campaigns to "Americanize" immigrants and improve the civic qualities of native-born citizens alike and an extension of wartime efforts to promote "100% Americanism." Rooted in nativism, a progressive affinity for expertise and education, and earlier ideas of an "informed citizenry," civic education programs took square aim at reforming problem voters and often focused on partisan voters in particular. Organizations such as the

Jewish Welfare Board, the Daughters of the American Revolution, and the U.S. Chamber of Commerce prepared manuals, sponsored night schools, or dispatched "home-teachers." As Robert Wiebe put it, in the early twentieth century, middle-class Americans became convinced that "citizenship did not simply happen; it had to be made to happen."[2]

GOTV organizers believed that civic education was a critical tool in treating problems of voter turnout. "As regards the abstention from voting," John Hays Hammond and a partner wrote in 1923, "the remedy may in part be found by devoting more attention in our schools and colleges"—and, Hammond would later conclude, other forums—"to the subject of civic duty." Education, they argued, "is the key to the situation." In the course of the campaigns, GOTV groups designed and directed some of the most extensive citizenship training programs in the country. Together, the business community, especially NAM members and the Metropolitan Life Insurance Company; the American Legion; and the League of Women Voters conducted literally thousands of classes, seminars, institutes, and workshops. Some collected and publicized candidate surveys and party platforms, laying out the choices side by side to encourage comparison; some created, evaluated, and disseminated curricula; some paid for employees to attend citizenship "boot camps" to train them for good citizenship as well as national preparedness. Unlike many groups, GOTV groups used civic education to work both with aliens, whom they hoped to help negotiate the process of naturalization, and with current citizens, whose civic virtue they hoped to improve. These initiatives, they reasoned, would not simply boost turnout, but transform citizens into informed and rational voters. They hoped that this work, as Hammond put it, would produce "an increase in the number of intelligent voters."[3]

"Intelligent voting" was an important goal of citizenship education programs, not only in the GOTV campaigns but beyond them as well. The call for a more intelligent voting citizenry in the 1920s was broad and wide. League ladies in Cleveland prepared an education campaign that would give members "an opportunity to have normal or elementary courses in citizenship" so that they might gain "a knowledge of the facts which underlie the questions put to every voter today." The National Council of Jewish Women declared its intention in 1927 to foster "the development of an intelligent citizenry among Council members themselves, teaching and preaching." The editors of *Collier's* believed that the magazine, by meeting its obligation to present "the facts about the great national issues of government," could help Americans "use the ballot faithfully and intelligently." The Merchant's Association of New York agreed that the "continued existence and successful operation of our representative form of government" depended upon "the active and intelligent participation by all citizens" in "exercising regularly the right of ballot." Merchants also got into the game, as when the Toof Laundry Company in Concord, New Hampshire, claimed in its advertisements that sending out the wash gave "the women of America the opportunity to attain the leisure necessary to vote intelligently." Civic educators agreed with Maud Wood Park that "the conscientious, discriminating, intelligent use of the ballot should be part of the very fabric of life itself."[4]

While advocates of civic education rarely defined "intelligent voting" explicitly, the content of their programs indicates that they hoped to produce citizens who were knowledgeable about civics, who rejected blind partisanship and voted independently on the issues, and who could competently perform the mechanics of casting a ballot. The American Legion, for example, in 1921 endorsed a joint effort with the National Education Association to encourage more emphasis on the Constitution in school curricula. The New York League of Women Voters' "Correspondence Course on Citizenship for Women" included sections on "The Structure of Government" and "Your Vote and How to Use It." The National Council of Jewish Women counted among its goals the task of educating Jewish women about the importance of issues concerning "the health of their families, the cost of living, [and] pure air" and that "only through the ballot can they register their opinions and thereby secure results." The national League of Women Voters provided state and local Leagues with curriculum materials to help members to "Know Your Party." The set of twenty questions prompted the reader to ponder "who prepares the platform and determines the policies of your party" and asked if he or she had "carefully considered which political party to join" and "found satisfactory ground for your choice?" The NAM counted among their achievements in the 1924 GOTV campaigns the fact that they had "started regular campaigns of education in national administration" promoting "the non-partisan urge to 'Vote as you please, but Vote.' " The national League further recommended that state and local chapters continue to hold "Voters Schools" that offered "demonstrations of the machinery of voting."[5]

Much more was at stake in citizenship education programs, however, than making sure people understood how a bill becomes a law or how to pull a lever in a voting booth. The civic education programs of the GOTV campaigns and others conveyed important ideas about civic authority and legitimacy—who had it, what issues were important, and how those issues ought to be understood. By organizing hierarchical relationships between the people who did the teaching and the people who were taught, by prescribing only a narrow range of issues and actions as legitimate, and by identifying legitimacy with whiteness and middle-class and elite status, civic education programs worked to propagate middle-class and elite white ways of being citizens and to assert their civic privilege over workers, African Americans, ethnic Americans, and sometimes women. The concept they used to justify this, and which they used citizenship education programs to promote, was the idea of "expert citizenship."

To help reform problem voters, GOTV groups turned to the field of education to endorse, design, and implement their programs. Early on, GOTV groups enlisted professional educators in their cause. NEA president F. G. Blair pledged the union's "good-will and support in making [the] program a success." College presidents also spoke out in favor of GOTV. R. L. Wilbur, president of Stanford University, joined the Advisory Council of the National Civic Federation and promised to work for GOTV through a local American Legion post. The president of Bennington College in Vermont addressed the national League at a conference on nonvoting in 1929. Charles A. Lory, president of Colorado State Agricultural College in Fort Collins, Colorado, similarly endorsed the cause.[6]

GOTV citizenship training efforts often took shape as formal educational programs. The League of Women Voters, the American Legion, and others developed specialized curricula and teaching materials for use in voter education programs. The chair of the American Citizenship committee of the Iowa League, for example, prescribed in a pamphlet the courses that a citizenship school should contain, among them classes on the "Machinery of Government," which included instruction on the units of government from the local township to the federal level, and "The Next Election," which covered the caucus system, primaries, party conventions, registration, and balloting procedures. The League also trained citizenship teachers with a national program of "Seven Steep Steps" to "Efficient Citizenship," a packet of materials that instructed GOTV educators to "hold pre-election meetings and invite all candidates to speak" and to "collect and give out unpartisan information on candidates and issues." Some League-sponsored citizenship training schools even issued certificates to honor and credential those who completed courses.[7]

Locating their education efforts in classroom settings reinforced the educational message. GOTV classes for adults were routinely held at grade schools, high schools, colleges, and universities. Vote activists also used school children to try to reach parents. Teachers in New York, for example, sent GOTV literature home with children, while the superintendent of schools in Grand Rapids, Michigan, asked classroom teachers to conduct a contest to see which homeroom could get the most parents to vote. In Ohio and Virginia, cooperative extension services, state and county programs to teach modern agricultural and homemaking practices to farmers and rural women, set up study groups at which rural women could learn about township and county government. The use of familiar educational settings and formal curricula, with the seal of approval of trained educators, gave GOTV civic education efforts an aura of credibility and professionalism.[8]

GOTV civic education programs by businessmen, the American Legion, and the League of Women Voters stood out for the wide scope of their efforts. The business community, so active in the campaigns to get out the vote, articulated a clear and consistent definition of good citizenship in the 1920s. In publications, speeches, and community work and in the GOTV campaigns themselves, business leaders argued that businessmen were model citizens and that they made up the natural leadership class. Corporate presidents agreed that "unless a man is successful in business or professional life, he is certainly not capable of running the Government." The Birmingham Chamber of Commerce declared itself a "virile, informed[,] strongly managed guardian and promoter of public welfare." Indeed, businessmen argued that businessmen ought to, and in some measure had, supplanted politicians as civic leaders. As an officer in the U.S. Chamber put it, "the American business man is today the most influential person in the nation. . . . His precedessors in leadership, the soldier and the politician, created the problems and then proved unable to solve them. Their failure opened the way to him."[9]

Given their natural leadership capacity, business leaders embraced the project of citizenship education with enthusiasm. Their efforts in the field were extensive but sharply bounded. In the many publications and record collections I have examined that document their far-reaching efforts to educate citizens, there appears not a single example of businessmen working to educate other businessmen. They exhorted their fellow businessmen to be good citizens or criticized them for their civic shortcomings, but on no occasion did they try to educate them to be good citizens. They always educated others, often their own employees. The NAM, for example, asked large employers to insert voting reminder slips in pay envelopes and bills. O. L. Stone, the general manager of Associated Industries of Massachusetts, maintained that manufacturers had a duty to "see that their employees [were] naturalized and registered and that they vote[d]" at elections. The McKeesport, Pennsylvania, Chamber sent every member a GOTV placard and urged him to "place before [his] employes" information on the specifics of registration and polling "to equip them to vote." Jesse Isidor Straus, president of Macy's department store, appealed to his seventy-five hundred employees to "make their voices articulate at the ballot box," slipped GOTV material into pay envelopes, and opened the Manhattan store late to enable employees to vote before coming to work. In Chicago, a department store in the downtown Loop dispatched female employees in half-hour shifts to the Woman's City Club to receive "instruction" on voting. At a time when "welfare capitalists" were assuming a degree of responsibility for the health care, education, and even recreation of their employees, some employers also assumed responsibility for educating employees so that they might be "fairly informed as to the issues to be voted upon."[10]

Businessmen sometimes worked to educate not only their workers but their customers as well. One of the most extensive campaigns to educate customers was that conducted by the Metropolitan Life Insurance Company. With thirty million policyholders, Met Life was one of the largest corporate providers of life insurance to working-class families. Not only did the company sponsor an award-winning advertising campaign in major magazines to promote voting; it also used its salesmen to deliver civic information and advice with a personal touch.

Twenty thousand Met Life agents visited policyholders at their homes every week to collect premiums and to check on living conditions, and, while they were there, they handed out pamphlets, booklets, and copies of the company magazine for policyholders, *The Metropolitan.* The magazine instructed customers on topics such as cleanliness and proper nutrition, and, in a piece on GOTV in 1924, informed readers that "the vote is a duty of citizenship." One of the booklets, "How to Take Out Your First Papers," an "Easy Book in Plain English for the Coming Citizen," featured sections called "Why Become a Citizen" and "Learn English" and suggested that readers ask their agent if they needed more information. The booklet also defined the characteristics of "The True American" as someone who, for example, "believes that 'All men are created free and equal,' " and that "there are no classes in America," and who also "obeys the rule of the majority." Company representatives literally handed out instructional pamphlets at the pier, pamphlets that were intended to "promote a knowledge of the lives of great Americans whose example may lead the future citizen to a respect for and love of the flag and the tradition it symbolizes." In 1923 in the company's "Home Sweet Home" campaign, Met Life urged local officials and businessmen to set up a program to naturalize every foreign-born resident in their town, much as the company's Norristown, Pennsylvania, branch had done. Through hand-delivered information and a personal touch, the company worked to position itself as a major source of civic information for immigrant and working-class customers.[11]

Met Life and the broader business community promoted a vision of good citizenship built on hierarchies of class and gender. They used their position as businessmen to assert their competence to educate not each other—their class peers—but their customers and the employees who worked under them. Class and gender intersected in their construction of citizenship: the people who did the teaching—employers and salespeople—were overwhelmingly if not exclusively male, while the people who were taught—employees or working-class customers— might be male or female, but were always of a lower-class status. The act of instructing was bounded by gender, the act of receiving instruction by class. Men taught; customers and workers were taught.

Citizenship training programs by the American Legion promoted a similar set of civic hierarchies. The Legion's efforts upheld the soldier as the civic ideal—white male soldiers in general, and soldiers-turned-businessmen in particular. The Legion's Americanism Commission worked to propagate "the ideals of true Americanism" with public celebrations of patriotic holidays, essay and oratory contests, memorials, and lessons in the proper treatment of the flag. It sponsored Boy Scout troops and established an extensive baseball program for high school boys. Finally, the Americanism Commission ran citizenship training schools for new citizens as well as the Legion's Get-Out-the-Vote campaigns.[12]

Most of the Legion's efforts at civic education reinforced a distinctly masculine vision of good citizenship. For these veterans, the good soldier was the good citizen. The Legion encouraged members to get involved in politics to "show the world what a good citizen the soldier makes." For soldier-citizens, even voting was characterized as a masculine act; veterans were urged to take a "virile, he-man part in every election." Like the business community, the Legion recognized the good businessman as a model type: indeed, in the Legionnaire the identities of the good soldier and the good businessman often merged. The Legion magazine described the upstanding citizenship of its members with pride: "Today, the young service men of six years ago are advancing all along the line. Go into almost any bank in almost any town and note the men who are assuming the key positions in the financial affairs of their community. Go into almost any store in almost any town. If the owner is a young man, he's almost sure to be a Legionnaire. Check over a list of the lawyers and physicians and dentists of any community and note particularly the fact that the Legion button and outstanding reputation among the younger leaders go together."[13]

The Legion did not deny that women and minorities had a claim to citizenship. They did, however, define citizenship for these groups in restrictive and contradictory ways. Women who had served in World War I were formally invited to join the Legion, but most women active in the Legion had not served in the Armed Forces themselves but had husbands, fathers, or brothers who had. American Legion Auxiliaries, often paired with "bachelor" Legion posts, served the veterans and the community by "safeguard[ing] the girls of the community," commemorating holidays, visiting disabled veterans, and working with other women's groups for community "uplift." In short, women's membership in the organization and their call to community service was relational and cast in domestic, family-oriented terms.[14]

African American servicemen were also invited to join the Legion, and most of those who joined formed separate posts. Occasionally the Legion spoke reverently of the service rendered by black soldiers, but more often the Legion magazine described them in derogatory terms, much as the minstrel shows of the day did. Even an article praising black soldiers and reminding readers that "they also served" described them also as shiftless, stupid, and endlessly amusing. Military service had forged white men into good citizens, but it apparently did not impart those qualities to everyone who served.[15]

Within a year of its founding, the Legion began an all-out campaign to convert aliens into citizens. Starting in 1920, the national headquarters urged all local posts to conduct Americanization activities. The headquarters secured the names and destinations of immigrants entering through Ellis Island and forwarded them to local posts so that members might call on them and encourage them to become citizens. In ten thousand pamphlets the headquarters also urged posts to offer English and civics classes, conduct naturalization ceremonies, and advocate the exclusive use of

English in public schools. Hundreds of posts, like those in Guilford, Connecticut, Moxee City, Washington, and Logansport, Indiana, took up these suggestions and taught immigrants in formal education programs and night schools. As early as 1921 the Legion claimed credit for the passage of English-only education laws in twenty-five states.[16]

Native-born citizens, too, were targets of the Legion citizenship campaign. Americanism projects worked to give Americans a more thorough knowledge of history, good citizenship, and the law. The Legion asked Congress to urge the states to make the study of history, civics, and the Constitution mandatory in schools, and succeeded in getting such laws passed in at least five states.[17]

Americanism programs for youth also worked to cultivate civic manhood. The Legion headquarters praised the Pennsylvania Department, or state chapter, for its effort to recognize the "best all-around boy" among high school seniors. The winner—the boy who exhibited scholastic achievement and athletic prowess as well as "qualities of manhood, truth, courage, devotion to duty, sympathy for . . . the weak, . . . and fellowship"—would surely have the "makings of a solid American in him." Baseball was another way to develop the qualities of good citizenship in boys. By 1928, one hundred thousand boys, including the children of immigrants, were playing Legion baseball each summer, while their sponsors hoped that the boys would "acquire from the lessons of leadership, loyalty and team work learned on the baseball diamond the qualities which will make them better citizens of tomorrow."[18]

The ideal of the citizen-soldier was embraced far beyond the Legion's own membership. Other citizenship education programs, in particular the Civilian Military Training Corps (CMTC), promoted the same view. The CMTC was created by the National Defense Act of 1920 to train young civilian men in the basics of military service. Both native- and foreign-born men attended these "boot camps" at Camp Devens, Massachusetts; Camp Custer, Michigan; and twenty-eight other sites. The program was intended not only to train a reserve of men who might serve in a military emergency, but also to educate them in "the privileges, duties, and responsibilities of American citizenship." As one lieutenant colonel put it, the trainees were "instructed as to the institutions of our government" to help "make them intelligent citizens and voters. It is our hope that some day all of the men of the country will have had this training, at which time we will not only have voters, but intelligent voters." By the mid-1920s nearly forty thousand men attended these summer camps each year, among them President Coolidge's two sons. Met Life sent some of its employees and the American Legion supported the program enthusiastically. The masculine, soldierly model of ideal citizenship was thus reaffirmed and propagated.[19]

The Legion's citizenship education efforts, then, constructed a hierarchy of citizenships out of differences in gender, race, and class. Masculine citizenship—as soldier, businessman, or young athlete—was privileged in the attention it received and the status it held. Soldiers, drawn from diverse class backgrounds, could all stake a claim to privileged citizenship, yet even among them the businessmen enjoyed elevated status. African Americans and women could be citizens, it was true, but they lacked the prized qualities and status of civic manhood. Immigrants were people to be taught and converted, and American veterans were the people qualified to teach them. Baseball provided a route to good citizenship for native-born and immigrant boys. Both natives and immigrants needed civic education to be good citizens, making clear the value the Legion placed on "information" and "expertise."

To promote "the political education of the new women voters (but not excluding men)," the League of Women Voters launched the most sophisticated program of citizenship education among GOTV groups. At the Victory Convention celebrating the ratification of the Nineteenth Amendment, Carrie Chapman Catt herself initiated the League's first program of civic education in time for the 1920 election. The League soon institutionalized its commitment to citizenship education in its Department on Efficiency in Government. By 1929, the League had conducted 1,165 citizenship training schools, reaching, League leaders believed, hundreds of thousands of citizens. These programs articulated an ideal of woman citizenship that stressed political independence and an informed approach to public issues. The ideal woman citizen might be married with children or single, and perhaps a clubwoman, but she was always independent and well informed.[20]

The League's citizenship training efforts were comprised of several programs. They organized women into small "Study Groups," taught them the mechanics of casting ballots in "Ballot Marking Classes," surveyed the techniques of poll-watching in day-long "Voters' Schools," lectured on public issues and the institutions of government in "Citizenship Schools," and offered advanced, "post-graduate" training in three-day "Institutes." In 1928, League women expanded their classroom to reach a still larger audience with their "Voters' Radio Service" over the NBC radio network. By the late 1920s, civic education had become such an important part of the League's mission that when League officers contracted with a Washington publicity agency to produce a filmstrip to tell the story of "*The National League Of Women Voters*—What It Is and How It Came to Be," its civic education programs, rooted in the Get-Out-the-Vote campaigns, were proudly featured in the organization's history. The "day-by-day, all-the-year-round educational work of the League [proceeds] in its local branches throughout the land." In San Francisco; Chicago; Providence, Rhode Island; Asheville, North Carolina; Laconia, New Hampshire; Canandaigua, New York; and elsewhere, Leagues sponsored "School[s] of Politics" on "The Federal Constitution" and "All-Day Conference[s]" on "The Direct Primary." Indeed, by 1930, the League described citizenship education as its main mission, an emphasis the organization retains to this day.[21]

Two sorts of people most often taught the League's citizenship classes: clubwomen and academics. The national headquarters maintained a full staff of professionals under the supervision of Minnie Fisher Cunningham. Their job was to plan citizenship schools and help state and local leagues to plan their own. Eventually the League sponsored seven to ten regional institutes per year for the teachers of citizenship schools, so that the League might reach a wider audience through a multiplier effect. At the state and local level League leaders themselves taught the sessions. League leaders also brought in professors of political science and history, usually men, to lecture at their citizenship schools. At the first school organized by Carrie Chapman Catt, prominent scholars such as Charles Merriam and Ernst Freund took the lecture stand. Both kinds of teachers, clubwomen and academics, were experts in matters of civics and government; their specialized training or academic degrees, in addition to their class status and race, qualified them to teach. Both kinds of teachers were models of the League's ideal of the informed citizen.[22]

The League reached out to diverse groups of women with their citizenship education efforts. Although women needed instruction in order to exercise their new franchise intelligently, the League continued the suffragists' critique of "the low standards of citizenship found among men" and encouraged them to participate as well. Nonetheless, women accounted for the vast majority of students at League citizenship schools. The locations of these classes suggest the range of women who took part. School auditoriums, church basements, the "ladies' rooms" (lounges) of banks, settlement houses, "libraries of millionaires," "kitchenette apartments," YWCA halls, women's downtown clubhouses, and "the fearsome halls of great universities" all served as meeting places for citizenship schools, a variety that invited participation by women of different class and ethnic groups. Scattered evidence points specifically to the occasional inclusion of African American and ethnic women. The Federation of Colored Women's Clubs cosponsored classes with the Woman's City Club of Chicago, and the [Frederick] Douglass League chapter in Chicago ran citizenship schools for women of the African American community. Classes were conducted at settlement houses in Illinois and Boston, and League women in Toledo, Ohio, sponsored "ballot-marking classes in the homes" of Eastern European and Middle Eastern women. In Virginia and Ohio, the League reached beyond the city to rural women by sponsoring schools through cooperative extension services. Given the time and expense required to attend classes and the informational channels through which they were promoted, it seems likely that most students of these sessions were white and middle class, like the clubwomen who sponsored them. Nonetheless, the League clearly made an effort to reach beyond these racial and class boundaries. The message was that all women could become good citizens if they acquired the education that good citizenship required.[23]

The League of Women Voters also used radio to reach a wide audience. Their civic education programs on radio were the most extensive and sophisticated radio programs in the GOTV campaigns. Local Leagues experimented with civic education in the new medium and laid the groundwork for what in 1928 would become the National League's radio "Voter's Service," the "citizenship school of the air." In 1924 the California League, for example, broadcast from a San Francisco station three-minute GOTV speeches "by well known persons." In the same year, the Illinois League broadcast fourteen radio talks on GOTV of five to fifteen minutes in length. In 1926, the Atlanta League also broadcast a radio talk on the importance of voting.[24]

The New York League, however, surpassed all others in its use of radio to get out the vote. At least three stations, WEAF, WGBF, and the Gimbel's department store station WGBS, broadcast League talks on GOTV and civic education. Speakers, "expert citizens" all, included public officials, business leaders, and League women. In the fall of 1924, for example, Mrs. Raymond Brown, managing editor of the *Woman Citizen*, spoke on the topic of "When Every Woman Votes," and philanthropist and Macy's co-owner Nathan Straus spoke about "Citizens and Slackers." In the off-year election seasons of 1925 and 1926, WGBS broadcast talks by Nettie Schuler ("Registration and Enrolment"), Caroline Slade ("Why Vote"), Mrs. J. Ramsay Reese ("Registration"), and Dorothy Straus ("Why Vote?").[25]

The 1928 debut of the League's "citizenship school of the air" reflected the culmination of their radio efforts. Fifteen million listeners tuned in to talks on current issues and campaigns by people such as former vice-presidential candidate Franklin D. Roosevelt and Republican National Committeeman Charles Hilles. Listeners were invited to read the list of books supplied by public libraries that accompanied the course.[26]

The programmatic content of the League's citizenship schools, on radio and elsewhere, specified the details of their vision of the model woman citizen. The curriculum outlines of the classes showed what the LWV thought women citizens needed to know, how women should conceive of their citizenship, and why they should vote. Local Leagues asked the national office for curriculum suggestions or devised programs to suit local interests. Even programs developed at the local level, however, usually covered the same topics: the institutions of American politics at the national, state, and local levels; procedures for evaluating candidates and marking ballots; the role of political parties; and issues of current concern.

The Illinois League developed what was widely recognized as one of the best citizenship training programs in the country. It recommended that every citizenship school include the following subjects:

"Essentials of Good Government"
"The City: 'Madam, Who Keeps Your House?' "
"The Public Pocketbook"
"Political Parties and Their Place in Government"
"Marking the Ballot"[27]

Leagues elsewhere taught similar courses. The Iowa State League used the national League's curriculum to teach women to "Know Your Town," "Know Your County," "Know Your State," and "Know Your Nation." The Connecticut League urged women to participate in "Party Government" in order to "Make a Single Vote Count" and introduced attendees to elected officials. A professor from the California Institute of Technology taught a session on "Education for Political Participation" at a League school in Los Angeles while two local women there led a discussion on "Methods of International Co-operation to Prevent War." The Georgia League titled an entire day's session "Woman's Place is in the Home—But, Madam, Who Keeps Your Home?" and offered panels on food and milk inspection, public utilities, and parks and playgrounds.[28]

These courses constructed women as citizens in two different ways. Some courses idealized a feminist woman citizen by asserting that women could understand complicated matters like the structure and function of governments and political parties. Others folded good citizenship into the more traditional conceptions of the roles of wives and mothers by tying issues of governance to things familiar and feminine— social "housekeeping," public "pocketbooks," and the like. In both cases, the League constructed a path to good citizenship for women through education and the acquisition of expertise.[29]

Taken together, the three citizenship education programs—by businessmen, the American Legion, and the League of Women Voters—offered prescriptions for good citizenship that coalesced and fragmented along gender, race, and class lines. The business community and the Legion privileged men as the teachers. For the Legion, which worked hard to nurture civic boyhood into civic manhood, gender was the most crucial of the three components. For the League, education transcended gender: well-qualified men and women were equally regarded as expert. All three groups privileged whiteness among the teachers. All three also privileged whiteness among the taught, suggesting that whites were the most important group to teach, that they were the most teachable, or, perhaps, that other groups were simply unredeemable, even by education. On the issue of race, only the League held out education as a sure means of uplift; African Americans, for example, could aspire to good citizenship if they were sufficiently educated. All three groups incorporated class into their civic ideals. For the business community, which never taught peers, it was the most important of the three components. For the Legion and the League, the privileged status attached to class could be transcended by military service or education.

Despite the variations, embedded in the programs of all three groups was one crucial assumption: citizenship education produced educated citizens, and educated citizens were the best kind. The paths to education and expertise might be different—businessmen secured it through business experience, Legionnaires through soldiering, League women through education—but it was expertise just the same.

Even GOTV groups that lacked the infrastructure to conduct civic education programs at the local level affirmed this ideal of expert citizenship. Before it ever ventured into the GOTV campaigns, *Collier's* had been troubled by the civic behavior of, in William Allen White's phrase, the "moron majority" and urged "intelligent voting" instead. Ruth Farnum, speaking in 1926 on behalf of the New York State Federation of

Women's Clubs at a 1926 NCF planning meeting, appealed to women to undertake personally the task of helping foreign-born citizens to vote and to vote "for the things that our country was created for."

> Ladies, if every one of us would say to ourselves, it is not only my duty to vote but I know two or three people who have not my chances and advantages, don't know what the vote is and perhaps neglect it on that account, and I am going to enlighten them. . . . There are so many people who have the vote who were not born in America, who do not understand what America is and stands for, who will not vote for the things . . . which we hope to uphold; if we will take each one of us two or three or four of those people, we are going to make our land great, noble, invincible.[30]

In a similar embrace of expertise, in the late 1920s the NCF shifted strategies to try to get out a better, rather than a bigger, vote. "Doubling an uninformed vote," it decided, would be "a liability instead of an asset." GOTV groups saw their role as one of imparting "expertise" to people who needed it, for their own good and for the good of the nation.[31]

Political parties posed an awful dilemma for the GOTV activists. They had no problem with political parties as institutions, as the civic infrastructure around which political participation was organized. What they objected to was partisanship, the reflexive loyalty of a voter to a party label, the power of party bosses to manipulate masses of "unthinking voters," the tolerance of corruption and bribery that they were convinced characterized party voting. The vote campaigners hoped to substantially reform the party system, preserving the structure of party organization while stripping citizens of unthinking partisan attachments. When the vote groups saw a place for parties in the GOTV campaigns, they envisioned a system of parties without partisanship, something possible only with civic education.[32]

Most GOTV groups regarded political parties as an essential fixture of a democratic system. The League of Women Voters made the study of parties a basic part of its citizenship education curriculum. The League, the NAM, and the American Legion all lobbied the Democratic and Republican parties regularly to advance their legislative agendas. The NAM and *Collier's* even imitated parties by putting out "platforms" of their own recommendations on policy issues such as government efficiency and the postwar economy. Elihu Root best articulated the reason why parties were crucial in a participatory system of government. In a speech before the Civic Federation's Department of Political Education in 1926, Root argued forcefully that "there has been only one way ever discovered under popular government of securing successful administration and that has been by the voluntary association of people who agree upon . . . major policies for the purpose of enforcing those policies and selecting officers of government who represent those policies." He reiterated: "There has never been any other way found."[33]

Recognizing the importance of political parties, many GOTV groups called on citizens not only to vote, but to join a party and work actively within it. From the beginning the League "urge[d] its members to enroll in the political party of their choice." "The only way to get things done in this country," Carrie Chapman Catt advised successful suffragists gathered in convention in 1920, was "to get [women] on the inside of the political party." Indeed, participation in parties was the only way to make voting worthwhile, for without the input of good citizens at party primaries and conventions, there was no way to ensure that good candidates would survive until the general election. "How futile are these drives to 'get the vote out,'" Ralph Easley wrote, "when, on reaching the polls, the voters find that they have only the choice of two tickets, both of which may be equally bad." GOTV groups in search of more voters and better voting could not avoid confronting the issue of political parties.[34]

Important as the vote groups believed parties to be, they were unsparing in their condemnation of "unthinking" party-line voting. Partisan voters were problem voters, because partisanship was everything that good citizenship was not—unprincipled, undiscriminating, even downright un-American. Collier's lashed out at party voting repeatedly. Voters who were delivered by party bosses were hardly "moved by civic consciousness." "The apathy of good citizens," added a Legion editorial, empowered party hacks to manipulate public affairs "brazenly and contemptuously" by controlling a small number of voters. To the GOTV activists, partisanship was not a loyalty linked to family, ethnic, or religious identity. To them it was a precious privilege sold cheaply for a petty favor, a base loyalty to shady characters. To the middle-class clubwomen and businessmen who made up the vote groups, partisanship was illegitimate, a civic evil of the highest order.[35]

The challenge, then, was to preserve parties as an institution while purging them of the taint of partisanship. The vote groups hoped to transform the parties and reform them, first by populating them with "respectable" people. A basic purpose of the vote campaigns, the National Civic Federation declared, was "to induce men and women voters of the country to join their respective ward clubs and participate in the running of their party machinery." An infusion of "honest blood" could "clean up the local political clubs" and "get the decent citizenry into the parties."[36]

Indeed, loyal party voters seemed beyond the bounds of "decent citizenry." A *Collier's* author defended his decision to join Tammany Hall by explaining that citizens needed to reclaim the parties from professional politicians—in the process implying that politicians, and perhaps even party members, were not citizens at all. "If a million American citizens were to join the political organizations" and, "within these organizations, declare their wishes," he explained, the next presidential election would be "a citizens' election, not a politicians.' " An influx of good citizens into the parties could "purify the American party system." Indeed, it could positively redeem it. John Edgerton of the NAM called on his fellow businessmen to "not only study platforms and records," but to do their "full part toward making both." "There are enough good men in America," he continued, "to save it."[37]

The vote campaigners hoped to reform the parties by infusing them with "honest blood," but also by remaking the bond between citizen and party. In the place of unthinking commitments or a base exchange of loyalty for favors the vote campaigners hoped to elevate citizens to participate out of a more detached sense of civic duty. The Legion, for example, challenged its members to "take a hand in the political affairs of your community" and hold party leaders to the same high "standard exacted of [soldiers] while they were serving their country during the war." At the same time that Legion vote conferences were urging citizens to join a party and participate "in the framing of its policies, and in the nomination and election of its candidates," the Legion was also urging them to assume "the higher duties of citizenship which transcend the fealties and implied obligations of partisanship." Carrie Chapman Catt was sure that women, too, could join the parties without succumbing to "party sophistries." Political parties and good citizenship were not inherently incompatible; for the vote campaigners, however, the relationship between citizens and parties needed to be reconsidered.[38]

Under attack, the parties made at least a token effort to improve their image. Some party women who were veterans of progressive politics but new to the franchise and to party membership worked to make affiliation with a party respectable, an intellectual commitment that honorable citizens could make. They argued that party commitments could be based on reason and introduced to the parties some of the civic education that was taking place in the GOTV campaigns and beyond.

The DNC distributed a four-page discussion of Democratic principles and issue positions "for the benefit of those women who want to base their party affiliation on something more substantial than heredity or environment." Some women's political clubs assumed the style of civic clubs, gathering not in unthinking support of a party label but to study governance and party principles and platforms. The women of the New York State Democratic Committee encouraged women to engage in such "club work" and prepared for them a curriculum covering "Government by Party," current legislation, party organization, and pressing issues such as conservation and foreign policy. They hoped to "not only mobilize Democratic women for service, but attract all liberal minded intelligent women to study and to work for better conditions in local, state and national government."[39]

In the spring of 1924 an officer of the DNC went further, establishing—with her own funds, and without the financial backing of the national party—the "National School of Democracy," a series of workshops and civics lessons for women. "Women are literally *eating the lessons up,*" Justina Wilson, Director of Education for the DNC, reported, adding that she hoped to enroll ten thousand women in the school before the November election. The Republican party likewise offered a curriculum in "Practical Politics" for women, a set of lessons in which they could learn not only about the party, but about "Americanism," current issues, and the structure of municipal government. Party-based civics classes were hardly the heart of party work in the 1920s; the fact that they were run by women, for women, and without substantial support from the party, attests to that. But they were important because they offered a way to reconcile the conflict between party loyalty and intelligent citizenship. They were an answer to the criticism, leveled by GOTV campaigners and others, that partisanship was by definition ill-informed, unthinking, and illegitimate.[40]

Rather than simply bring voters to the polls, the GOTV activists wanted voters to want to bring themselves, and to do so under the "inspiration of a high purpose to serve the nation." They hoped to replace what remained of the partisan attachments of old with a nonpartisan, and, they thought, more noble sense of civic duty. They hoped to substitute the nonpartisan or detached partisan civic style valued by white, middle-class, and elite clubwomen and businessmen for other, more partisan, ways of being a citizen. To this end, they defined nonpartisanship or thinking partisanship as proper behavior for a good citizen and a reflexive attachment to party as improper. Simply put, to the vote campaigners, intelligent partisanship was legitimate, blind party loyalty was not, and civic education was the key to transforming the latter into the former.[41]

The GOTV groups were hardly the first citizens to value education; familiarity with law, languages, and history, for example, was one reason that many in colonial times believed that the gentry were due deference. Nor were the GOTV groups the first to prize "expertise" in citizenship; certainly Mugwumps, woman suffragists, and progressives of every stripe had been promoting it, or something like it, for decades. The world war, however, brought new urgency to the issue, and the GOTV groups made substantial contributions to the broad postwar push to use civic education to promote Americanism and Americanization. The Legion and the League operated on an ongoing basis and on a national scale. They and other GOTV groups organized intensive efforts in local communities; they employed a wide range of methods, from essay contests to filmstrips to boot camps; they wrote curricula and taught teachers; and they worked to improve the citizenship of adults and youth and native-born citizens and immigrants alike. The ideal of expert citizenship was reflected in, promoted by, and in considerable measure institutionalized by the Get-Out-the-Vote campaigns. With the advent of expert citizenship, the progressive cult of expertise—which had already reorganized business, restructured municipal administration, and created the professions—remade the criteria by which good citizenship was marked.

Expertise occupied an awkward position as the gateway to citizenship, poised on the boundary between inclusion and exclusion. On the one hand, for groups like businessmen, expertise was embedded in their privileged identities: they did not need citizenship education to be expert citizens. On the other hand, expertise was something that anyone, in theory, could acquire. Marginalized groups could use citizenship education to assert a claim to civic legitimacy. Mary McLeod Bethune, president of the National Association of Colored Women, praised the group's efforts "to encourage the intelligent use of the ballot" as well as "to defend the rights and privileges of Negroes everywhere"—goals it regarded as complementary, not competing. Samuel Gompers asserted that workers, too, could be expert citizens by arguing that "intelligent participation" by an "overwhelming majority" of Americans was the only way to preserve democracy. By accepting the terms of expert citizenship, marginalized groups could assert equality with the most privileged groups and justify their legitimacy in making public decisions.[42]

In practice, however, expert citizenship functioned more to exclude than to include. Radicalism, class consciousness, race consciousness, and ethnic identity had no place in expert citizenship; citizenship training courses excluded these perspectives and designated them as out of bounds. And whatever the theoretical possibilities, many of the workers, immigrants, minorities, and women whom the experts deemed in need of education could not or did not seek the validation conferred by formal training. Some certainly embraced or even created alternative constructions of citizenship that asserted a claim to civic legitimacy on different grounds—for example, a style of citizenship built upon party loyalty, which still flourished in cities with urban machines. But the fact is that in the 1920s the sheer number of nonvoters in these groups was staggering, and there is direct evidence that the charge of illegitimacy embedded in the values of expert citizenship had reached these groups and was one of the reasons they excluded themselves from the polls.[43]

In their 1924 study of nonvoting, Charles Merriam and Harold Gosnell published summaries of interviews with nonvoters in Chicago. They attributed much of the nonvoting among workers, African Americans, women, and foreign-born citizens who spoke little English to "ignorance" and "timidity." A close reading of the stories of these nonvoters, as Merriam and Gosnell tell them, suggests that "timidity" meant not shyness or reserve but rather a feeling of incompetence and illegitimacy. Among Polish men in the Stockyards district, for example, the researchers remarked that "many of the men worked such long hours that they were too tired to read about politics when they came in and did not wish to vote unintelligently." They cited the case of "Mrs. Turner, a young laundress who had moved from Mobile to Chicago," who "deplored the fact that so many colored people voted without knowing what they were doing." A "Mrs. Q, who was both a business woman and a housewife," said that she "did not vote because she did not have time to go carefully into the history and qualifications of the candidates" and she "did not believe anyone should vote unless they knew . . . what they were doing." Even a woman who read party platforms and newspapers, "a Swedish washerwoman," declined to vote because "unless she was certain of what she was doing, she did not feel that she should vote." In case after case, Merriam and Gosnell found potential voters who understood what middle-class and elite whites such as the GOTV reformers meant by "expert citizenship," and further understood that it did not include them. The ideal of expert citizenship, a basic premise of the GOTV campaigns, helped to delegitimize the participation of non-elite citizens in the electoral process.[44]

With the development and institutionalization of expert citizenship, the gulf between the nineteenth-century good citizen and the twentieth-century good citizen grew vast indeed. In the nineteenth century, any person with the privileged demographic attributes—whiteness, male-ness, and the age of twenty-one—was readily marked as a fully legitimate good citizen. By the 1920s that was no longer true. Not only did different groups qualify for that status—foreign-born whites were no longer readily included in the privileged group, and now women sometimes were—but the civic meanings of racial, ethnic, class, and gender difference had changed as well. Whiteness was expert; racial otherness was not. Maleness was expert; femaleness often was not. Native-born status was expert; foreign-born, hypenated Americanness was not. Expertise was not simply about how much one knew; it was also a way of designating the privilege of powerful people.

By the 1920s, the formal right to vote was broadly, if imperfectly, distributed among sexes, races, and classes. That right, however, was undercut by a persistent identification in the GOTV campaigns and elsewhere of ethnic, gender, class, and racial otherness with illegitimacy in public decision-making and of "nonpartisanship," "independence," and "rationality" with whiteness, native-born status, masculinity, and wealth. The boundaries of "expert citizenship" were defined not by expertise but rather by racial, class, ethnic, and gender difference and functioned as a way to privilege middle-class and elite white ways of being citizens. In the 1920s, nearly all Americans might technically have enjoyed "equal" access to the ballot, but the authority and the legitimacy of citizenship in the public sphere of discussion and debate were largely reserved for privileged groups.

THE METHODS OF WRIGLEY AND BARNUM

The Get-Out-the-Vote Campaigns and the Commodification

of Political Culture

In 1927, in an advertisement in a businessmen's magazine, the *San Francisco Chronicle* pitched its power to reach consumers by touting the *civic* qualities of its readers. The *Chronicle* promised advertisers that its pages were a good way to catch the eye of "Mr. Solid Citizen," the reader who was at once a husband, father, and businessman. "Mr. Solid Citizen," the ad explained, was "fond of golf, motoring, baseball and radio" and a "buyer of everything from structural steel to kiddie cars." His family—a lovely wife, two well-behaved children—were, like him, "accomplished spenders!" And, as the ad noted pointedly, "Mr. Solid Citizen . . . vote[d] regularly" (see fig. 13).

"Mr. Solid Citizen" offers clear evidence, both in what it says and what it does not, that the political culture of the early twentieth century bore little resemblance to that of the late nineteenth. Though civic hierarchies based on gender difference seemed unchanged—here the only "solid citizen" was a "Mr."—in this idealized civic world there was no sign of the popular politics of the nineteenth century, no evidence of the political parties, the intense partisan loyalties, the festivity, or the broad and legitimate participation of immigrants and workers that defined the party period. In the world of "Mr. Solid Citizen," it was even necessary to point out that being a "solid citizen" required "vot[ing] regularly," something that nineteenth-century citizens, with their long record of high turnout, could safely have assumed. In the place of a multiclass, multiethnic popular politics was an unmistakably sober, upper-middle-class milieu in which the breakfast table was set with linen and the window opened out onto a neighborhood of large homes and tree-lined streets. In the world of "Mr. Solid Citizen," even the language of politics had changed. Gone was the partisan speechmaking and the ardent rhetoric of party loyalty. In its place appeared the modern ad, an ad that spoke simultaneously of "accomplished spend[ing]" and "government," as if "solid citizen[ship]" had anything to do with "buy[ing]."

The GOTV campaigns belonged not to the world of party politics but rather to the world of "Mr. Solid Citizen," a world in which consumption did much to define political culture. Everywhere GOTV activists used print advertising and radio shows to disseminate their message on a mass scale. They set up shop at department stores and movie theaters and asked patrons to register and vote. They enlisted professional admen to devise snappy slogans. They plastered cars with GOTV posters and banners, literally turning the automobile into a vehicle for the cause. In place, personnel, technique, language, ritual, and product, the GOTV groups linked the vote message to consumption, political culture to consumer culture.

In this, the GOTV activists were not alone; indeed, they were not even first. As early as the 1896 presidential campaign of William McKinley, political party elites enlisted the help of public relations professionals and invented "advertised politics." In the 1910s, department stores came out in solid support of the campaign for woman suffrage. Later in the decade, George Creel's Committee on Public Information used advertising to define and communicate how good citizens should behave in time of war. By the 1920s, citizens on election nights routinely took in election returns at the movies. In short, in many ways, on many levels, from the turn of the century forward, political practices became embedded in the places of a culture of consumption dominated by middle-class whites, a transformation I call the commodification of political culture. The GOTV campaigns were remarkable not because they alone forged these links, but because they adeptly illustrate these connections, helped to institutionalize them, and propagated them on a wide scale.[1]

The commodification of political culture had enormous implications for democratic practice. Above all, it changed the way different groups of people stood in relationship to the civic world. Not every group participated in those arenas of a consumer culture dominated by unhyphenated, middle-class and elite whites; not everyone cared to, and not everyone could. A political culture built around a particular culture of consumption put the people who dominated it at the center of the civic order; the commodification of political culture placed middle-class and elite whites at the center of civic affairs and placed workers, ethnics, and African Americans at the periphery. Through the commodification of political culture, middle-class and elite whites shifted the terrain upon which participatory politics was practiced. They moved it to ground they dominated, a place where they could be the civic norm.

Consumer Society in the 1920s

Consumer culture was a defining element of public life in the 1920s, and the 1920s were a defining moment in the development of consumer culture. Though consumer goods and advertising, of course, predated the 1920s, a mature consumer society did not. Not until the 1880s did a national network of railroads, an industrialized system of mass production, and the concentration of growing populations in urban centers make possible a national marketplace. Only at the turn of the century did social and cultural changes—the ascendancy of a "therapeutic ethos" that placed value on leisure, pleasure, and "self-realization," and the broader shift from "character" to "personality" that valued acquisitiveness, indulgence, and surface over thrift, self-restraint, and substance—begin to reflect and promote a social order centered around consumption. After World War I, the range of consumer commodities exploded, mass production and distribution techniques and rising wages made them accessible to a broader populace, and advertising "bec[a]me 'modern.'" Certainly the consumer boom that followed World War II distributed the goods and values of consumer culture even more widely. By the 1920s, however, consumer society had reached a new level of maturity.[2]

Automobiles, home appliances, and cosmetics were among the "glamour industries" of the decade. The number of passenger cars in the United States multiplied from 6.8 million in 1919 to 23.1 million in 1929, as more working-class families joined middle-class families in car ownership. Refrigerators, gas and electric stoves, and vacuum cleaners were marketed heavily in this period to ease women's labor at home. Women's use of makeup became a commonplace rather than a scandal, and the beauty culture, with its beauty shops, cosmetics, and even plastic surgery, became a booming business.[3]

Consumer culture also turned leisure into a commodity. Consumers paid money to be entertained by motion pictures, professional sports (especially baseball and boxing), radio, popular magazines, and tabloid newspapers. Motion pictures became much more popular as movie fans, middle-class as well as working-class, flocked to theaters in record numbers. The number of weekly paid admissions to the movies swelled from forty million in 1922 to sixty-five million in 1928. Hollywood stoked fan interest with the colorful personalities of the studio "star system" and technical innovations such as "talkies."[4]

Radio was both a communications medium and a consumer commodity at the same time. Sales of "crystal sets" or receivers, limited to $60 million in 1922, grew to a whopping $843 million in 1929. And although in the early days of broadcasting radio stations were sometimes owned by churches, labor unions, and foreign-language community groups, commercial stations that operated for profit and paid the bills with some type of advertising were always part of the mix. As early as 1926, NBC linked listeners from coast to coast in the first commercial radio network. With the creation of the Federal Communications Commission in 1927, commercial broadcasters soon dominated the airwaves.[5]

By the mid-1920s, leisure magazines had become staple reading fare in middle-class American homes. Among Middletowners, for example, the Lynds found that ninety-seven percent of "business class" homes took at least one magazine. The new "mass market" magazines differed from their predecessors in several respects. Not only did publications like the *Saturday Evening Post, McClure's,* and the *Ladies' Home Journal* contain more advertising than their stodgier predecessors; articles, too, were written in the direct, punchy language of a sales pitch. Reading material often catered to distinct class tastes. Business-class readers favored *The Atlantic* and *World's Work,* while *True Story* found a large readership amongst workers and women. First published in 1919, by 1926 *True Story* could boast a circulation of nearly two million readers. Given the degree of class stratification in the magazine trade, relatively few publications, such as the *Saturday Evening Post,* appealed to a broad cross-class audience.[6]

Tabloid newspapers also skyrocketed in popularity. The *New York Daily News,* first published in 1919, two years later claimed the largest circulation of any daily newspaper in the country. By the middle of the decade, tabloid papers were succeeding in a dozen cities under publishers such as William Randolph Hearst. The growth of newspaper chains—Hearst, Scripps-Howard, and others—increasingly standardized the content of newspapers by distributing widely the same news copy, comics, and advice columns.[7]

Some consumers, especially middle-class whites, found new places to shop in the 1920s. Chain stores such as J. C. Penney, Piggly Wiggly, and the National Tea Company introduced self-service shopping, branded products, and fixed pricing to middle-class neighborhoods. Department stores, palaces of consumption since the 1890s, expanded to offer an even broader array of goods and services. By the 1920s, department stores functioned not only as merchants of clothing and housewares, but as entertainment venues and civic centers too. Between the walls of a department store shoppers could often find a women's lounge (much like a club, with a comfortable parlor stocked with reading material), a post office, a beauty salon, a travel agency, a theater or concert hall, public meeting rooms, and space for art exhibits. Gimbel Brothers in New York boasted its own radio station, WGBS, and in 1920 Bloomingdale's even added a zoo. With trend-setting merchandise, popular attractions, showy windows, and spectacular displays, department stores acted as merchants of consumer culture itself.

Advertisers further articulated a middle-class vision of consumer society. "Madison Avenue," a creation of the 1920s, promoted not only specific products but the values of a consumer society as well. The amount of money spent on advertising to stimulate demand and channel desire more than doubled between 1914 and 1919 and doubled again to a whopping $3 billion by 1929. In the creative hands of Albert D. Lasker, Edward Bernays, Bruce Barton, and other pioneers of promotion, public relations became a distinct profession and advertising acquired a modern flair.[8]

Advertisers and publicity professionals in this period used a range of techniques to promote products and build a sense of personal connection between the seller and the consumer. Endorsements and testimonials, often by actors, cast celebrities as authorities. Print ads that included coupons—not the cents-off coupons of today, but small forms the reader could send in to request information or samples—helped advertisers identify individual consumers with precision. Brightly colored, gummed stickers, like the red ones Western Union pasted to telegrams ("Results count. Western Union Telegrams bring results") changed everyday business correspondence into advertisements, while slogans simplified the seller's message with memorable, punchy prose. Publicity stunts generated attention and excitement on a grand scale. Airplanes emblazoned store or product names in the sky or rained sales fliers on consumers in shopping districts below. A decade that popularized contests in flagpole-sitting and marathon dancing also used contests, such as bake-offs, to promote particular products.[9]

These "modern" ads differed significantly from their nineteenth-century counterparts. Unlike earlier ads, which typically announced a product's availability and described its function and use, modern ads attributed to products the power to impart subjective qualities such as status, happiness, fulfillment, and style. They prescribed for the reader the reaction the seller wanted her to have, rather than simply present information and leave the conclusion up to her. In these ways modern advertising furnished the act of consumption itself with "personality" and aggressively marketed a social vision in which consumption served as a main source of identity and value.

Advertisers likewise encouraged workers to emulate their own middle-class and distinctly managerial values. Advertisements encouraged compliance by emphasizing scrutiny and speaking in an authoritative tone. They pressed the consumer to acknowledge an ever-expanding range of "needs" and defined only certain kinds of behavior as "correct." Advertisements preached to consumers the gospel of "personal efficiency"—fulfillment and redemption through time-saving, pleasure-maximizing, improvement-minded consumption. In this new culture of consumption, promoters used advertisements to craft "narratives of adjustment" and urged consumers to embrace modern, middle-class values for themselves.[10]

That was the advertisers' wish. The extent to which consumers complied is another matter. Place, race, ethnicity, gender, and class mediated the ways and extent to which people embraced, resisted, negotiated, or reshaped the economic and cultural changes in their midst. Farmers, for example, worked "to create their own forms of modernity" by rigging automobiles to power corn shellers; similarly, they transplanted "the venerated custom of rural visiting" onto telephone party lines. Workers bought cars and movie tickets in huge numbers—and resisted chain stores and branded products at the same time. Italian Americans might attend a professional baseball game, the nation's pastime, and then return home and use a phonograph to play music from the old country. The result was hardly the single, homogenous, mass culture of consumption that advertisers depicted and producers desired—more, perhaps, a patchwork of multiple, diverse cultures of consumption.[11]

For all these communities, however, consumer culture in its many forms constituted a crucial part of public life. In the 1920s, more than ever before, consumer culture supplied many of the public spaces, such as shops and movie theaters, in which people encountered one another in their lives away from home and work. It supplied the media, such as radio and tabloid newspapers, through which they learned about public affairs. It helped to redefine public space as department stores came to "anchor" downtowns much as courthouses and city halls had once done. Department stores became symbols of civic identity and attracted tourists much as any monument of civic importance; when a tourist group from South Carolina in this time period made a visit to Boston, they put only two stops on their itinerary: Bunker Hill and Filene's. Consumer culture occupied a prominent place in the public life of the 1920s.[12]

In this new consumer society, middle-class and elite, native-born whites occupied a special place. Certainly they accounted for many of the leisured women and businessmen whose shopping, production, and marketing helped to fuel a consumer economy. But these same people also dominated depictions of America's "typical consumers" and—curiously, at the same time—were upheld as the consuming ideal. At a time when less than two percent of the nation's population played golf, Bruce Barton's advertising firm, Batten, Barton, Durstein and Osborn (BBDO), described the American people as "one hundred and thirty million people, all living about the same kind of lives" who desired simply "comfort, pleasure, . . . and more distance off the tee." While working-class men might appear in ads as delivery men or mechanics who demonstrated a product's use, "an unspoken law," Roland Marchand argued in his extensive analysis of 1920s magazine ads, "decreed that the protagonist (and consumer surrogate) in every ad must be depicted as middle class." Minorities appeared rarely, and then only as servants—African American cooks preparing Cream of Wheat for others to eat—or as negative examples—a " 'Mexican' washerwoman" serving as an "archaic [foil] for modern washing methods" in a series of ads for Proctor and Gamble. Even women, the people who could be counted upon to do most of the household shopping, were portrayed as being at their consuming best when they made purchasing decisions with supposedly masculine and businesslike rationality, as did an ad that likened a wife to a corporate buyer. In the consumer society, middle-class whites were the picture of typical, modern, and idealized consumption, while "others" were invisible or un-modern at best.[13]

The institutions, products, places, and language of the new consumer society, with all their gendered, classed, and raced complexities, served as both medium and message for the publicity portions of the GOTV campaigns. GOTV groups put out print ads that bore all the hallmarks of modern advertising; they turned movie patrons into captive audiences for GOTV talks; they used automobiles to carry their message; they used radio to publicize the cause. In doing so, the GOTV campaigns showed how the commodification of political culture was remaking the civic world.

In "Rainbow Colors": Advertising the GOTV Campaigns

GOTV campaigners turned often to advertising and publicity to market their message of good citizenship. Sometimes they enlisted the help of professional promoters and conducted major campaigns in the national media. More often, at the local level, they handed out fliers, collected coupons, and staged publicity stunts. At both the national and local levels, every time the vote reformers used advertising and publicity they connected politics to one of the major institutions of consumer culture.

Occasionally GOTV organizers directly tapped the expertise of the advertising industry. Public relations pioneer Ivy Lee addressed the Manhattan League in 1925 to share "An Advertiser's Views on Selling Good Government." Clubs of advertising professionals in St. Louis and New York took an active part in local campaigns. In New York, for example, the Direct Advertising Association designed and produced car posters in quantity for the NCF. Car cards urged "Loyal Patriotic, Red-Blooded Americans" to "Answer The Roll Call" on election day and reminded "The Womanhood Of The Nation" that they were "Called To Duty At The Polls."[14]

When the Metropolitan Life Insurance Company embarked on a GOTV publicity campaign, it drew upon considerable experience in civic-minded advertising. In the first decade of the twentieth century, the life insurance industry was rocked by scandal as investigations revealed irresponsible investments, financial coverups, and corrupt dealings with government officials. In part in an effort to salvage their image, in the 1910s Met Life embarked upon great publicity campaigns to demonstrate their corporate good citizenship and educate the public. Met Life dedicated considerable effort to promoting public health with pamphlets on subjects such as safe milk handling and "Teeth, Tonsils and Adenoids." In the early 1920s, it advertised efforts to make "every resident a citizen."[15]

Building upon this background, in 1924 Met Life turned its attention to low voter turnout. In an ad that won top honors from the Associated Advertising Clubs of the World for advertising in the field of insurance, Met Life urged readers to "Vote! . . . You can't avoid it." Either "you will go to the polls and declare your honest opinion on the political issues

involved," or, by your absence, you will "cast a silent vote" against democratic government. The vivid language of advertising turned bland appeals to civic duty into colorful and impassioned pleas. Not forefathers,
but rather "the men whose bleeding feet made red the snows of Valley
Forge" laid upon every American the obligation to vote. The patriots
"gave their lives to win freedom; can you refuse just one day to preserve
it?" If readers marched faithfully to the polls, they could make this "the
year of the biggest vote the United States has ever seen." Company president Haley Fiske concluded the advertisement with an impassioned appeal. "No excuse for failing to vote can pass muster." Whatever election
day brings, "get to the polls and vote!" This ad had an impressive reach,
for it appeared as a full-page spread in the *Saturday Evening Post, Collier's,* and other middlebrow leisure magazines with a combined circulation of more than seventeen million readers.[16]

Met Life used advertising again in 1928 to promote GOTV. With the
war an increasingly distant memory, the company abandoned patriotic
themes and simply urged readers to "Speak Up!" at the polls instead. "No
one else can speak for you on Election Day," the company president
warned. Non-voting left the sober but silent majority, "the real majority," unrepresented. "Only by voting," the ad argued, could such people
"save themselves from the danger of being governed by a minority holding opposite opinions." Unlike the 1924 attempt, this ad promised that
voting produced results; no mere exercise of duty, voting was an effective way to influence public affairs. "Your next President," the ad insisted, was "bound" to use his influence to "bring about the kind of government wanted by those who elected him." Every vote possessed the
power to "help to solve great problems."[17]

Collier's encapsulated its GOTV campaign in a single slogan that appeared repeatedly in its advertising campaign, "Make 1924 the Year of
the Big Vote." Unlike Met Life, *Collier's* made no bow to civic education
but relied solely upon advertising and publicity for GOTV. Not only did
the editors apparently place great faith in the power of publicity; they
also believed that solving public problems was mostly a matter of resolve, making their role one of motivating citizens to get the job done.
Ending the hypocrisy of Prohibition or the stranglehold of the two-party
system just meant "cutting out bluff and bunk and doing the thing
straight for the sake of results." This was, after all, the magazine that had
promised to end municipal inefficiency and corruption with a one-page
reform plan. "You see," wrote a member of the *Collier's* staff, "this business of getting along in politics is simply a matter of common sense."[18]

In the fall of 1924, *Collier's* designed and placed in its own pages—sometimes in prime advertising space such as the inside front cover—elaborate, full-page ads that made the case for the importance of voting. Borrowing from the advertising profession, the *Collier's* ads used standard modern promotional techniques—a slogan, a contest, and endorsements—and, like every good modern ad, laid out the interpretation that editors desired rather than leave it up to the reader.[19]

The *Collier's* ads featured the magazine's national Get-Out-the-Vote contest and promised a handsome reward to the state that produced the greatest proportional increase in turnout. The magazine hoped that the contest would increase voting by offering a strong "stimulus" to "state pride." Sensitive to the criticism that a contest might trivialize what was supposed to be a serious act of citizenship, the magazine worked soberly to "awaken the public conscience and stir every voter to action." Every ad closed with a tag line next to the title graphic that reinforced the magazine's seriousness of purpose: "In the interests of better citizenship—*Collier's.*"[20]

The ads focused intensely on the prize. A drawing of the trophy dominated most of the ads as the headlines—"COLLIER'S VOTING TROPHY," "Your vote will help to win it for your state!"—also stressed the prize. The text described the prize in elaborate, enticing detail. "Surmounted on a walnut base is a globular ballot-box in gold and silver," on which was mounted "a bronze eagle alert," wings outstretched. Made by Tiffany's, the trophy was an "exquisite work," no tacky bauble, but rather "a signal recognition of state pride in good citizenship" that would place the winning state "before the country as an exemplary American commonwealth." Like modern advertisements everywhere, the *Collier's* GOTV ads tried to prescribe the meaning of the trophy rather than let readers decide, and here worked to endow it with prestige to make it an object of desire.[21]

These ads also prescribed the duties of citizenship, sometimes according to the gender of the reader. The ad that featured the voting trophy issued separate appeals to women and men. Women were urged to vote with a lecture: "There is no valid excuse for not exercising your franchise. Convenience, personal antipathy, petty fears—none of these should keep you from the polls." Men, by contrast, were urged to vote with a challenge to their manhood. The nation's security rested upon their shoulders: "How long will you men countenance minority rule, permitting half of the voters to say who shall govern you and who shall spend your money?" Nonvoting women were scolded in a tone generally reserved for children; nonvoting men were challenged to step up and meet their responsibilities as real men. Ads such as these reinforced gender difference and reasserted masculine civic privilege.[22]

Endorsements also added celebrity and credibility to the *Collier's* effort. The voting trophy ad announced proudly that the *Collier's* campaign had secured the support of the three major presidential candidates. President Coolidge wrote that the political system had "no greater need" than higher voter turnout. Democratic nominee John W. Davis praised *Collier's* for "performing a genuine service to the Nation." "Every good citizen," Progressive Robert La Follette added, would "endorse the efforts of *Collier's* to arouse the electorate to the duties and opportunities of citizenship." *Collier's* also secured the endorsements of state governors, including Alfred E. Smith, and printed testimonials from eight of them in a subsequent ad. By displaying the endorsements of prominent elected officials, *Collier's* worked to give its GOTV campaign legitimacy and prestige.[23]

The *Collier's* competition, complete with advertisements, endorsements, a slogan, and a prize, was not the publication's first attempt to promote civic virtue with a contest. The magazine sponsored or supported three other such contests in the years before it took up GOTV. In 1921, magazine editors blamed the postwar recession on the poor attitudes of businessmen and consumers and offered a cash prize for the best stories of good salesmanship. In 1923 it offered to print excerpts from the best entries in the American Peace Award essay contest sponsored by Edward William Bok. In the same year it also entered the debate on prohibition enforcement and offered a cash prize for the best essay on what should be done to fix the widely flouted law.[24]

The GOTV campaign may not have been *Collier's* first civic campaign, but it was its largest effort, and also its last. When the GOTV campaign failed to boost turnout despite the magazine's heavy investment, *Collier's* got out of the business of civic virtue and redefined itself more narrowly as a forum for entertainment. At one time the magazine had defined civic leadership as part of its very identity, even going so far as to append a statement of civic mission to the title graphic. After the failure of the vote campaigns, in 1927 a new phrase appeared where "In the interests of better citizenship" had been before. Now *Collier's* was no civic leader; rather, it was "NEWSY * PICTORIAL * BRIEF." Consumer culture, the magazine found, did not make a very good vehicle for civic virtue. In the late 1920s, the magazine decided that to entertain was virtue enough.[25]

Both *Collier's* and Met Life reached a national audience through the medium of the middle-class leisure magazine. But GOTV advertising and publicity efforts extended well beyond mass marketing by corporate giants to smaller, hometown ad campaigns. The Springfield, Massachusetts, Chamber of Commerce, for example, secured twenty-eight two-column GOTV ads from area businessmen. The Home Makers Club of DeKalb Township, Illinois, reported incorporating advertising into its GOTV strategy, and businessmen in Passaic, New Jersey, similarly indicated that they spent a "considerable" sum of money on vote ads. Chamber members in Canton, Ohio, and Fort Worth, Texas, believed that heavy local newspaper advertising had improved turnout there. Businessman J. C. Richards of Farrell, Pennsylvania, agreed and proudly reported to the National Civic Federation that "your national and our local advertising kept the vote up."[26]

Local GOTV groups used not only print advertising but the full repertoire of marketing techniques, including billboards, fliers, coupons, and stickers. Billboards displayed the GOTV message literally in place of commercial advertising. Organizers in St. Louis posted displays on sixty billboards across the city that "pointed an accusing finger at negligent and indifferent citizens." Handbills and fliers of various sorts had the twin virtues of being cheap to produce and easy to distribute. The St. Louis activists also blanketed the city with two hundred fifty thousand GOTV cards while Atlanta campaigners distributed thirty-five thousand fliers. Vote reformers printed coupons in newspapers for the same reason that commercial advertisers did: to precisely identify members of their target audience. In Wheeling, West Virginia, Toledo, Ohio, and Norwich, New York, organizers asked readers to return GOTV coupons printed in the local papers so that they could extend to them invitations to a "First Voters' Party." Colorful, gummed stickers placed on business letters, packages, and department store parcels made commercial transactions and communications do double duty as GOTV publicity. Vote activists in Winnetka, Illinois, Flint, Michigan, El Paso, Texas, southern California, and elsewhere used stickers, much as the NAM had done, and sometimes on a grand scale. In St. Louis, for example, GOTV reformers affixed one hundred fifty thousand GOTV "letter stickers" on local mail.[27]

Publicity stunts rounded out GOTV groups' promotional strategies. Reformers showered downtown Atlanta with an election day airdrop of GOTV fliers in "rainbow colors." Organizers also used car caravans—parades of automobiles that transported GOTV speakers from town to town—to drive their point home. A Minnesota League convoy travelled from the Canadian border at International Falls to the Iowa state line, then back to the Twin Cities, arriving there on election eve. This cara-van of "League women (and in many cases men voters)" relayed "a real 'torch of democracy' all the way" and invoked the old-fashioned torch-light parade, now turned to a nonpartisan cause. In October 1924, the Pennsylvania League likewise organized a car caravan for a month-long speaking and publicity tour that started in Philadelphia, circled the state, and ended at Bryn Mawr. By grabbing attention and building enthusi-asm, publicity stunts multiplied the impact of GOTV campaign resources and, organizers hoped, made civic duty exciting again.[28]

Automobiles figured into publicity campaigns in other ways. Activists everywhere decorated cars with vote posters and stickers. The League's national headquarters in Washington urged local Leagues to make "car cards" part of their GOTV campaigns. The St. Louis League decked fifty thousand cars with posters reminding citizens to "Register Today." The Winnetka, Illinois, League pasted stickers onto cars, while the Elizabeth, New Jersey, League placed colored handbills on parked cars. The Vir-ginia League distributed fliers through auto clubs. A New Mexico League member raised funds by selling box lunches with GOTV fliers tucked in-side to "motor tourists" who visited area "Indian festivities." In a few places, vote reformers made detailed arrangements for election day trans-portation. Leagues in South Carolina, St. Louis, and Athens, Ohio, for example, organized "motor corps" to ensure that no citizen failed to vote for lack of a ride.[29]

Automobiles served as vehicles for the GOTV campaigns, both liter-ally and metaphorically. In political cartoons of the period, the auto-mobile was a favorite stand-in for sound-running government. In the GOTV campaigns in particular, nonvoters were often depicted as pas-sengers who enjoyed the ride but who could not be counted on to help when the going got tough. In a cartoon that was syndicated to 114 news-papers, "Ding" Darling likened an election to a car trying to negotiate a treacherous road. A tiny man, "the small percent who take their voting duty seriously," tries mightily to control an oversized steering wheel (the "Ballot") while a much larger man, "the big majority who do not vote at all or vote without due consideration," sits in the back, engrossed in the sports page. When the car crashes, it is the nonvoting passenger who grumbles that "the darn thing's no good! It won't stay in the road!" Dar-ling reinforced his point with the title of the cartoon: "It's a wonder there aren't more serious accidents."[30]

With each of these advertising and publicity strategies, at the local as well as the national level, GOTV activists made use of the techniques of modern advertising. Every print ad, contest, coupon, and car caravan strengthened the links between the world of politics and the world of consumption.

Silver Screens and Crystal Sets: Getting Out the Vote with Motion Pictures and Radio

The GOTV campaigns also used commercial entertainment to try to motivate citizens to vote. Far from distracting voters from the duties of citizenship, many GOTV activists believed that motion pictures and radio would prove "most effective aids" in turning out "the Big Vote." These media reached large audiences with ease and could inform and entertain them at the same time. When vote leaders screened GOTV newsreels and broadcast GOTV radio shows, they piggybacked on the popularity of commercial entertainment and put consumer goods and consumer spaces to civic purposes.[31]

Key leaders of the motion picture industry lent their clout to the vote cause. The Motion Picture Producers and Distributors of America, the powerful movie industry trade group led by Will H. Hays, endorsed the GOTV campaigns in 1924. Hays himself made a series of widely reported speeches urging citizens to go to the polls and calling for the disenfranchisement of citizens who repeatedly failed to vote. Sydney Cohen, president of the Motion Picture Theater Owners of America, likewise pledged his support for the GOTV campaigns.[32]

With the backing of key industry leaders, and often at the request of local vote activists, theater owners and managers cooperated broadly with the campaigns. The NAM encouraged local business leaders to speak to movie audiences about the importance of voting. Some vote activists, such as League women in Meriden, Connecticut, set up tables in theater lobbies to register movie patrons. Activists in Atlanta arranged for a GOTV newsreel to be screened at nine theaters, and the League marketed its "slidefilm" nationally for screenings in noncommercial as well as commercial venues. In places such as South Carolina, Morgan County, Illinois, Rockland County, New York, and New York City, theaters showed slides listing local registration and polling information before and between the evening's features. At the request of the Illinois League, the Exhibitors Association of Chicago asked every theater owner in the city to show GOTV slides. Some 220 theaters complied, including at least one theater in every ward of the city. In St. Louis, ninety theaters screened GOTV slides; in Michigan, so did another seventy-five.[33]

Radio, too, comprised a key part of the vote activists' strategy. Radio connected politics to consumer culture from the very beginning: the first broadcast from Pittsburgh's KDKA announced that Warren G. Harding had won the 1920 presidential election. In the GOTV campaigns, local Leagues and other GOTV groups developed the medium's civic uses.

All five of the major GOTV groups used radio. In 1924, the NAM urged businessmen everywhere to air five-minute addresses to stress the importance of voting. The National Civic Federation issued a patriotic call to duty by enlisting New York stations to play "To the Colors" at noon on election day. The National Civic Federation and American Legion arranged for their 1926 joint planning conference in New York to be broadcast live on WNYC. Three years before *Collier's* attempted a magazine format on the air ("*Collier's* Radio Hour"), the magazine secured pledges from fifty radio stations to make announcements urging registration and voting.[34]

The League's GOTV radio programs often interwove educational discussions of civics and current affairs with entertainment. KFRU in Columbia, Missouri, for example, carried the regular Monday night radio citizenship school of the Missouri League. The February 27, 1928, program was typical: sandwiched between a program of "Patriotic Airs" and "Popular Airs" was a discussion by Miss Essie Heyle, Extension Professor of Home Economics at the University of Missouri, on "Why a Homemaker Should be Interested in Voting." In these cases, not only did vote reformers use an important consumer commodity to transmit their message; they spliced their programs with music in an effort to entertain. They combined the GOTV message with leisure and entertainment, a clear sign that political culture and consumer culture were becoming more and more closely linked.[35]

Generally, League ladies aspired to a highbrow tone with broadcasts of "airs" and talks by expert speakers. But on at least one occasion, they worked to reach nonvoters in the vernacular. The Milwaukee County League explicitly dedicated itself to turning out voters among the city's ethnic communities and made foreign-language radio part of its GOTV strategy. The Milwaukee County League broadcast GOTV talks not only in English, but in "German, Italian, Polish, Hungarian and Bohemian" as well. Their efforts were among the few that tried to appeal to ethnic voters on their own terms.[36]

At a time when the radio was a new and popular consumer commodity, and when the definition of the medium was up for grabs, GOTV activists seized the opportunity and used radio to broadcast their civic concerns. For both radio and movies, they used popular commercial entertainments to draw a crowd and then pitched their cause to the audience. They entwined their message with movie features and music to present civic education and entertainment; they also screened "minute movies" to present civic education *as* entertainment. In commercialized leisure, as in advertising, the GOTV campaigns promoted and illustrated the commodification of political culture by linking political practices to consumer culture.

Location, Location, Location: The GOTV Campaigns in Consumer Spaces

GOTV activists repeatedly situated their publicity campaigns in the public spaces of consumer culture, such as department stores, chain stores, beauty parlors, and movie theaters. These strategies linked consumer culture and political culture spatially and created places where people could link their roles as citizens and consumers.

Stores of diverse description—drugstores, bakeries, butcher shops, filling stations—all allowed vote reformers to set up shop on the premises. The Virginia League of Women Voters' state coordinating committee placed fliers in stores and gas stations across the state. Junior Chamber members in Flint, Michigan, persuaded local bakeries to put "Register Now" stickers on bread wrappers. Members of the Elizabeth, New Jersey, League reported that "beauty parlors were . . . our first line of attack" but that they also received "splendid co-operation" from groceries, meat markets, and drugstores—"in fact, nearly every sort of a store approached." Drugstores in the Alabama towns of Fairfield, Ensley, Pratt City, Wauhouma, and Leeds allowed League women to set up tables to collect poll taxes. *Collier's* printed a half million posters specifically for distribution in chain stores ("Register! Vote! Don't Be A Parlor Patriot"), some of which likely showed up in S. S. Kresge stores, the second largest chain of five-and-dime stores in the country.[37]

Department stores exceeded all other shopping venues in their enthusiasm for GOTV. These fashion leaders also styled themselves as civic leaders and, in city after city, incorporated vote messages into their newspaper advertising and supplied GOTV groups with table space, display windows, and even the labor of store employees. Often they allowed League women to set up registration and information booths in prime selling space near entrances, the better to catch customers on their way in or out. Bloomingdale's, Lord and Taylor, Saks Fifth Avenue, and

Abraham and Straus in Manhattan all furnished League women with table space and support, while Gimbel Brothers' WGBS aired, at the League's request, a series of talks on the importance of voting. Department stores across northern New Jersey—Muir's in Orange, Tepper's in Plainfield, and Bamberger's and Hahne's, both in Newark—all accommodated the requests of League women to set up information booths.[38]

The department store campaigns, however, extended far beyond the urban centers of the northeast. The West Virginia League set up booths in "leading department stores" across the state in an effort to "register the shoppers." In 1926, the Atlanta League persuaded nine local department stores to wrap GOTV fliers in customers' parcels. The Ithaca, New York, League planned to distribute literature at a department store, while the Meriden, Connecticut, League expected department store booths to make it "very convenient" for unenrolled citizens to register. The Indianapolis League reported solid results: at local department stores they succeeded in registering more than fifteen hundred new voters.[39]

GOTV activists literally displayed the link between consumer culture and political culture by setting up exhibits in department store windows. Cheap plate glass became available in the 1890s and by the middle of the 1910s "great banks of store windows" were a common feature in cities. Typically, of course, store windows displayed merchandise— interesting and fashionable goods that might entice a passerby to stop and shop. In the vote campaigns, they displayed GOTV posters and paraphernalia instead. The South Carolina League distributed five thousand window cards urging women to "enroll!" The Non-Partisan Coordinating Council in New York asked merchants to display an "honor poster" if they had registered everyone on the premises. In these displays, GOTV materials physically took the place of the usual wares. Store window displays framed civic messages in terms of consumer culture and embedded the GOTV campaigns in it in the most transparent of ways.[40]

In these many ways the GOTV campaigns promoted and illustrated the commodification of political culture. GOTV activities in movie theaters, beauty parlors, chain stores, and department stores—indeed, in the many public spaces dedicated to consumption—turned consumer spaces into civic spaces, too. Print ads and billboards applied the promotional techniques of modern advertising to market the GOTV message. Car caravans and radio teas used the most popular consumer commodities of the day to drum up enthusiasm for the cause. By linking the products, techniques, places, personnel, and language of consumer culture to political practices consistently, systematically, and on a mass scale, the GOTV campaigns helped to define and remake the political culture of the 1920s.

"Aged Man Dies Happy": The Commodification of Political Culture Beyond the Get-Out-the-Vote Campaigns

The commodification of political culture was clearly evident in the Get-Out-the-Vote campaigns. But there is also abundant evidence that the same process was at work outside the vote campaigns and in the decades before and after them. As early as the 1890s, political parties hired public relations professionals to promote candidates. In the Progressive era, department stores actively supported woman suffrage campaigns. During World War I, the government's campaign to shape public opinion and mold civic behavior also used the methods of modern advertising. Around 1920, movie theaters began routinely to incorporate election night announcements of election returns into the evening's entertainment. In the 1920s, newspapers often recounted tales of voting in a tabloid style. In the early decades of the twentieth century, consumer culture left its mark on the institutions and practices of politics far beyond the GOTV campaigns themselves—on political parties and civic spaces, on civic campaigns and political rituals, and on the meanings of citizenship itself.

Political parties showed clearly the influence of consumer culture in the personnel they hired and the campaign methods they used. Since the late 1890s, political parties had been moving in a piecemeal way toward "advertising-" or "merchandising-style" campaigns. Under the leadership of Marc Hanna, George Cortelyou, and others, the parties began systematically to "package" the candidate, stressing his personality over his party identification and managing his image with carefully crafted publicity campaigns. They also began to replace lengthy, textual campaign pamphlets with literature that instead featured pictures and snappy slogans.[41]

Party leaders also explicitly likened campaigning to a sales pitch. Democratic activist Emily Newell Blair argued that an election campaign was "a drive for votes, just as an Ivory Soap advertising campaign" was "a drive for sales." The Women's Division of the Republican party in 1928 told its members that "when you start to win a vote for Mr. Hoover, you become a saleswoman." What were they selling? "An ideal and an opportunity"—the ideal of "citizenship as typified by the ballot," and the "opportunity" to vote for "one of the ablest candidates" ever put before the American electorate. Republican leaders regularly compared campaigning to the advertising and sale of ordinary consumer commodities and defended their use of "the methods of Wrigley" and "Barnum." Glitzy advertising-style campaigns were necessary, they said, if they were to fix one of the "most baffling failures of democracy," the "inertia" that kept half the electorate "away from the polls."[42]

Political parties regularly sought the services of advertising professionals. In the 1910s and 1920s many public relations pioneers went to work for political campaigns. Albert Lasker, the head of the Lord and Thomas agency in Chicago, advised Warren G. Harding on publicity strategy two years before Harding ran for the presidency. Will Hays also brought sophisticated public relations skills to the Harding camp. Born William Harrison Hays (in honor of the father of the president from his home state of Indiana), Hays chaired the Republican National Committee from 1918 to 1921 and managed Harding's presidential campaign before going on to repair the image of the motion picture industry with the Hays Office. Public relations professionals carefully crafted Harding's image by limiting press access to him, supplying the demand for information with newsreels prepared by the campaign, and staging pilgrimages of faithful supporters to visit the candidate at his home in Marion, Ohio. Best of all, they managed to sell this thoroughly modern public relations effort as a folksy, old-fashioned "front porch" campaign.

Eight years later, Belle Moskowitz used her experience as a consultant to Edward Bernays to direct publicity for the presidential campaign of Governor Alfred E. Smith. In the 1928 campaign she bore the primary responsibility for Smith's print and radio advertising and campaign motion pictures. Smith's opponent in 1928, Herbert Hoover, consulted extensively with Bruce Barton and sometimes used speeches written by him. In 1936 Barton would win for himself a seat in Congress as an anti–New Deal Republican. Each of these experts in public relations doubled as an expert in political communications; each built a direct link between the promotion of consumer commodities and the marketing of political candidates.

Presidential campaigns had used slides, newsreels, and movies as early as 1904, and by 1916 movies had become a key part of every major campaign. In the 1920s these films, which were screened in both commercial movie houses and noncommercial venues such as club headquarters and church basements, acquired added sophistication. In the 1928 election, for example, the Hoover campaign released *Master of Emergencies,* a feature-length film that showed Hoover feeding starving Belgians in World War I and comforting flood victims in Mississippi in 1927. To improve distribution, Hoover supporters showed the film not only in the usual places, but also in specially designed movie trucks that brought it straight to the neighborhoods where voters lived or worked (see fig. 14). The Hoover campaign also screened the film at its "Hoover Store" on 45th Street in Manhattan and sent volunteers to stroll the sidewalks in sandwich boards to reel in viewers. Not to be outdone, the Smith campaign screened its own "motion pictures and vitaphone pictures" outdoors on Broadway near Times Square. By using movies to promote candidates, political parties borrowed the commodity form of the motion picture and identified political campaigns with commercial entertainment.[43]

Party-sponsored publicity stunts also borrowed the "methods of Wrigley and Barnum" and put them to political purposes. In 1911, for example, party activists sponsored a race between a donkey and an elephant at that utopia of commercialized working-class leisure, Coney Island. Eleanor Roosevelt was the chief force behind a publicity stunt staged in 1924 by the Women's Division of the New York State Democratic Party. She and her colleagues built "the largest teapot ever," mounted it on a "touring car," and drove it to one hundred Democratic rallies across the state. The teapot, which evoked the Teapot Dome scandals of the Republican administration, "boil[ed] over" with "Republican corruption" on cue and then revealed the Democratic speakers of the day, often Emily Smith (the daughter of Governor Alfred E. Smith), Daisy Harriman, or Eleanor Roosevelt herself. Volunteers passed out campaign literature and miniature pasteboard teapots to the crowds at every stop. In their use of publicity stunts as well as campaign movies and professional advertisers, the political parties thoroughly enmeshed the campaign process in consumer culture.[44]

Long before department stores became involved in GOTV, they served as both civic leaders and civic spaces. Throughout the 1910s, department stores constituted a significant base of support for the woman suffrage campaigns. William Leach has demonstrated that department stores "everywhere" offered their window space to suffragists, who decorated them with displays of literature and banners in the " 'colors of the Suffrage Party.' " Wanamaker's in Philadelphia permitted female employees to march in suffrage parades on company time, while Macy's in 1912 became the designated headquarters for suffragists' supplies such as "marching gowns, bonnets, and hatpins." Carson, Pirie Scott in Chicago, too, welcomed delegates to the 1916 Woman's Party convention with a window display of a wax mannequin suffragist. Ten years before they joined the GOTV campaigns, department stores helped forge the link between consumption and civic participation.[45]

Other campaigns to improve civic virtue also show the connection between consumer culture and political culture. Most notably, the wartime
Committee on Public Information, headed by George Creel, directed a
"vast enterprise in salesmanship" to persuade Americans to back the war
effort in thought and deed. Working in uncharted territory, the Creel
Committee pressed the art of modern advertising into the service of the
war effort by supplying newspapers and magazines with camera-ready
articles and advertisements, producing and distributing posters, window
cards, movies, and slides in huge quantities, and forming public speaking committees. The Creel Committee used modern public relations
techniques to persuade Americans to support the war and urged Americans to consume in a patriotic way—to save their nickels to buy Liberty
Bonds, for example, or to observe "meatless, wheatless" days. By promoting civic behavior with commercial-style advertising, the CPI enmeshed civic virtue in a commercial form.[46]

Like political parties, civic spaces, and civic campaigns, consumer
culture also reshaped key political rituals. In particular in the practices
surrounding "return night," or the announcement of election results, an
important political ritual made use of venues, techniques, and commodities of consumer culture.

In the early nineteenth century, when national election results were
slow to trickle in, many communities scheduled a special "return night" at
the town square or city center, perhaps a week after the election, to announce the results to the community. When the telegraph made election
results available more quickly, newspaper offices became the center of
large election night public gatherings. Results were flashed on a screen or
the side of a building for the crowd to view. Beginning about 1920, return
nights began to incorporate commercial movies into the festivities: newspapers competing for readers worked to entertain the crowds during the
lulls between results. In 1920, for example, the St. Louis *Post-Dispatch*
sponsored an election night movie party that drew thousands of participants. At its downtown offices, election results were projected on a huge
screen stretched over Market Street. Between batches of returns, the screen
showed movies. The paper promised revelers first-rate entertainment: "a
brand new first-run release, Mutt and Jeff in *The Politicians,* a Harold Lloyd
comedy, a review of current events," and "a Charlie Chaplin comedy."[47]

In the 1920s, movie theaters became sites for "return night." Movie
theaters offered special election night shows in which theater personnel
announced election results to audiences before or between screenings.
In Emporia, Kansas, in 1924, for example, the Strand Theater promised

a special "Election Returns Show." The program was to open with a screening of "Single Wives," the "poignant" drama of "gorgeously gowned, . . . well bred, pleasure led darlings" who had been "prizes . . . for the young suitor" but were now "forgotten" wives. The movie would be followed by election returns via the "Strand's Leased Wire," those to be followed by a second film, more election returns, a Stan Laurel comedy, and yet more returns. The splicing of the evening's entertainment with election returns shows very explicitly the weaving of political culture into consumption. Election nights at movie theaters were quite common in this period; the same kind of ads show up in movie listings for theaters in Grand Rapids, Atlanta, Denver, St. Louis, Birmingham, and the hamlet of Bath, New York, as well as New York City, Boston, and San Francisco.[48]

The same weaving of political practices with commercialized entertainment took place in radio and at dance halls. WNYC, WJZ, and WEAF, for example, all "interspersed" election returns "with entertainment of a high caliber," including performances by orchestras, operatic singers, and Broadway stars. The Roseland dance hall, the "Ballroom Of Refinement," promised "Complete Election Returns by direct wire" as well as "Carnival Features" during its "Election Night Frolic." When movie theaters promoted voting, when radio stations combined election returns with performances by Broadway stars, when movie theaters and dance halls delivered election results to paying patrons, consumer culture provided the space, the participants, and the context for one of the basic rituals of the political process.[49]

In the 1920s, as the popularity of tabloid newspapers soared, a tabloid style of storytelling also included accounts of adventures in voting. Typically these stories recounted tales of ballots dramatically cast by the dying as they breathed their last. "Aged Man Dies Happy After Casting His Vote for Coolidge," the *Grand Rapids Herald* reported in 1924. "The hope of casting a ballot for Coolidge and Dawes, candidates on the ticket he had voted for a lifetime," kept James A. Eaton "alive for the last week or more, during which he had been at death's door, with hardly strength enough to whisper that he wanted to see one more Republican victory." The Associated Press newswire publicized the story of Ellis Cutting, a Cedar Rapids, Iowa, man and "the last survivor of the Immortal Light Brigade." Cutting "cast his last vote" for Coolidge and Dawes but, as he was "dying from paralysis, . . . physicians said he probably would not be here to learn whether his vote had helped elect the Republican candidates." Nonetheless, "he was happy in having cast it." These stories cast voters in heroic roles in melodramatic tales; they infused the act of voting with color and drama, and recast it in a tabloid-style trope.[50]

Thus, on many levels, inside the GOTV campaigns and in the political culture at large, the political practices of the 1920s came more and more to resemble key aspects of consumer culture. The evidence—the use of commercial advertising techniques by political parties and the use of advertising personnel in political campaigns; the extensive support by department stores for suffrage and the GOTV campaigns; the advertising campaigns of the Creel Committee to inculcate civic virtue; the incorporation of commercial movies into return night festivities; the construction of tabloid-style voting narratives—is piecemeal, but abundant and consistent. All of it points toward a basic transformation of political culture around the turn of the century in which a broad range of civic practices became embedded in the places and commodities and language of consumer culture.

Certainly political party elites in the late nineteenth century borrowed advertising techniques and fashioned out of them an "advertising style" of political campaigning. The evidence presented here suggests, however, that the borrowings were taking place on a much grander scale. The borrowing of the forms of consumer culture was not limited to political campaigns: it appears quite clearly in other aspects of the political culture of the period—the GOTV campaigns, the rituals of "return night," and tabloid-style voting narratives—as well. The adoption of the techniques of consumer culture was not limited to party elites: other political actors— interest groups and civic groups, partisans and nonpartisans, in urban centers and beyond them—also did the same. Nor was the borrowing limited to advertising: it encompassed movies, department stores, radio, and a wide range of institutions and practices associated with consumer culture. The "advertising style" of political campaigns should be seen as one aspect of a broader process in which the techniques, spaces, and language of political culture came more and more to resemble the techniques, spaces, and language of consumer culture. In short, the transformation of political culture did not occur in a vacuum; like other aspects of American life, political practices reflected the development of a consumer society.

Voting for a Vacuum, Repeating for a Chesterfield: The Voting/Buying Metaphor and the Construction of Consumer Citizenship

The transformation wrought by the commodification of political culture was so far-reaching that in language and sometimes even in practice consumption came to be equated with citizenship itself. When Maud Wood

Park stated that the purpose of the GOTV campaigns was to "'sell' the idea of voting to every possible voter," and when Bruce Barton described advertising as having been "voted for, and elected" to a new position of influence in society, they constructed a metaphor between voting and buying, a metaphor that appeared frequently in the GOTV campaigns and, beyond them, in the advertisements and political cartoons of the day.[51]

This was no small development, for in the process consumer culture also reshaped the way that many citizens constructed their civic identities. The problem of low voter turnout had created a crisis in the meaning of citizenship. If nonvoting was now, apparently, the norm, then just what did it mean to be a good citizen? If citizenship was not necessarily about voting, then what was it about? And how could good citizenship be distinguished from bad? The voting/buying metaphor reveals that, for many, the commodification of political culture replaced a citizenship in which people connected their civic identities to their ethnic, religious, and partisan identities with a citizenship in which people linked their civic identity to their identity as consumers. The commodification of political culture replaced the partisan citizen with the consumer citizen as the new civic ideal.

The concepts of consumption and citizenship had long been intertwined. Boycotts of commodities—or the mass appropriation of them—had historically been used to make a political point. Buying and voting specifically had been paired for some time, as when woman suffragists pointed out that women's experiences as good consumers who made wise choices for their families qualified them to make good political choices, too. By the early twentieth century, parallel images of the consumer and the citizen had constructed a hyphenate, the "consumer-citizen."[52]

The voting/buying metaphor in the GOTV campaigns, product advertisements, and political cartoons of the 1920s pushed the relationship between buying and voting to a different level. Metaphors liken two things by saying that one is the other. The two things are not actually one, or else there would be no need for a metaphor; rather, in language they acquire an identity as very nearly the same thing. The voting/buying metaphor described voting and buying as very nearly the same thing, and melded the two together to create a single identity, a "consumer citizen" without the hyphen. For the consumer citizen, his or her identity as a consumer was tightly bound to his or her identity as a citizen.

The GOTV campaigns, along with other advertisements and political cartoons of the period, created an extended metaphor to identify buying with voting. Shopping was no longer just a rationale or model or analogy for voting; in the 1920s advertisers actually equated buying with voting. This language and the corresponding images appeared regularly in the GOTV campaigns and in publications—general interest, specialized, large and small—at election time in the 1920s.

The voting/buying metaphor appeared often in the publications of GOTV groups. In the midst of the vote campaigns, advertisements in state League of Women Voters' magazines frequently featured the voting/buying metaphor. "A Large Majority of the women have cast their vote for Chicago's favorite FEDERAL ELECTRIC VACUUM CLEANER," announced the Illinois League bulletin. "Cast Your Vote for Merita Bread," urged an ad in a Georgia League publication. A Kansas creamery advised women that "IF YOU WANT TO PICK WINNERS Vote For COPLEY'S ICE CREAM and PEERLESS BUTTER." In a national League convention program, the Halle Brothers department store of Cleveland argued that a store depends upon "voters, who are of course, the customers" just as "truly as does a political party." It advertised with pride that the store had enjoyed "increasingly large 'votes of confidence'" from female shoppers. Each of these ads equated buying with voting.[53]

The voting/buying metaphor also appeared often in the popular press of the day, far beyond the discourse of the GOTV groups. The Haynes Hardware Company of Emporia, Kansas, for example, urged customers to "*Vote*" for the "*One Minute Washer*," the "Women's Choice" in washing machines. Hofheimer's shoe store in Richmond, Virginia, declared that its "'Black Cats' are Elected—the Best $5 Shoe a Man Can Buy!" Phillip Levy and Company, a Richmond furniture store, urged readers that "when casting your ballot for the furnishings of your home, remember the platform of Phillip Levy's. Lowest Prices, Easiest Credit Terms, Best Possible Service." Wallach Brothers of New York urged customers to "Cast [their] ballot[s] for the 'Town weight' overcoat" by Hart, Schaffner, and Marx. The Ziegfield Theater in New York boasted that "*43 Million* registered Americans" had "elected . . . '*Show Boat*' by Kern and Hammerstein America's Outstanding Musical Production of All Time" (see fig. 15). Buying and voting were equated not only to promote good citizenship, but to sell washing machines, clothing, newspapers, and theater tickets.[54]

Some of these ads even looked like ballots. When the Hippodrome Theater in New York announced the vaudeville lineup for a "Special Election Week Pageant Of Wonders," it placed next to the name of each act ("Poodles Hanneford," the "World's Greatest Clown Equestrian," and "Frick and Pope," "Champion Ice Skaters,") an "X," just like the "X" used to mark a ballot. A few ads spun the voting/buying metaphor into a full-fledged narrative. Chesterfield cigarettes recounted a story of a southern voter caught "repeat[ing]" or casting multiple ballots. The ad urged:

> . . . ALL you voters
> WHO WANT to repeat
> DON'T DO it with votes.
> GO TO some smoke shop
> AND CAST a ballot
> FOR CHESTERFIELDS. . . .
> FOUR MILLION smokers
> OF THIS cigarette
> REPEAT REPEATEDLY.
> 'THEY SATISFY.'[55]

This explains why the good consumer and the good citizen during this period looked so much alike. The good consumer was usually portrayed as middle class or elite, white, ethnically unmarked, and a businessman if male and often a wife or mother if female. Similarly, the good citizen was usually portrayed as middle class or elite and white, ethnically unmarked, and a businessman if male and a wife, mother, or clubwoman if female. Both good consumers and good citizens were experts, intelligent people who made rational decisions. The similarity in portrayals of the good consumer and the good citizen was no coincidence: by the 1920s, they had become practically the same person, the consumer citizen.

In a few cases, they in fact *were* the same person. Some activists claimed that buying literally made a person a legitimate participant in public affairs. In a 1923 precursor to its GOTV campaign, *Collier's* recast its magazine subscribers as voting citizens. It polled subscribers in a door-to-door canvass to record their preferences for the next presidential race. A thousand representatives of the magazine visited nearly a quarter of a million subscribing households between May and July. Unlike the popular *Literary Digest* poll, in this canvass only subscribers could vote, a distinction that, *Collier's* argued, eliminated fraud and gave its poll special legitimacy. The decidedly middle-class readers of the magazine constituted, to *Collier's,* "average voters" whose votes would comprise "a correct picture" of public opinion. *Collier's* hoped the poll would circumvent the power of parties to dictate the choice of candidates. In the poll, unlike in actual primary elections, subscriber-voters were free to vote for any candidate: they were "not limited by party restrictions, nor controlled by political machines." In this respect, the *Collier's* poll was presented as being *more* legitimate than a real election, and the participants, true consumer citizens, as more legitimate than real voters. In these cases, consumption helped to make a person a good citizen, a legitimate decision maker in the public sphere.[56]

The metaphorical relationship between buying and voting made the case that the two were very nearly the same thing. So too did the way that the commodification of political culture put people simultaneously in the roles of consumers and citizens. The *Collier's* poll and the Met Life campaign in which agents gave literature to customers did this directly, but it was evident elsewhere as well. Advertisements that employed the voting/buying metaphor or promoted GOTV placed the people who read them in the multiple roles of consumers and citizens as the same time. Moviegoers viewed GOTV slides and listened to "four-minute men" speak from the stage; radio fans listened to talks on the importance of voting; patrons got their election returns at dance halls. Each of these ways of communicating with citizens reached them while they were in the act of consuming. Each constructed the citizen as a consumer at one and the same time.

Not everyone, however, was eligible for consumer citizenship. Access to this privileged status was unevenly distributed along the lines of gender, race, ethnicity, and class. As Marchand put it, on the "'one dollar, one vote' principle[,] . . . some people could cast far more votes than others." Racial minorities and workers, excluded from consuming roles in advertisements, were excluded from consumer citizenship as well. Middle-class white women's position in this civic order was complicated and precarious and their status as consumer citizens reflected this instability. While middle-class white men, especially businessmen, were unfailingly depicted in advertisements and political cartoons as good consumer citizens, middle-class white women were not. Though women did most of the household shopping and were seen by many as the most competent consumers, this did not automatically confer upon them a privileged status in a political culture built around consumption. Occasional depictions of women as silly or confused shoppers undermined the position of political privilege that consuming women might have secured in a consumer society. One entry in the League of Women Voters' GOTV political cartoon contest, for example, portrays the vote as a fashion accessory in the hands of a fickle shopper. She gazes longingly through a store window after "the vote"—a hat—but finds after acquiring it that it is bigger than she had thought and that, indeed, she cannot quite carry it off. The conclusion shows her to be unstable and unreliable, hardly the sort of person suited to the sober responsibilities of good citizenship: "Hats are pretty much of a nuisance after all" (see fig. 16). Businessmen, it seemed, came to good consumer citizenship automatically; women, apparently, did not.[57]

What emerged out of the voting/buying metaphor was a true consumer citizen—not a hyphenate, but a classed, raced, and gendered consumer and citizen melded into a single, exclusive identity. The conflation of buying and voting and the redefinition of citizenship as consumption was sometimes in fact real, as in the *Collier's* straw poll and the Met Life GOTV campaign among its customers. More often, as in advertisements, it was confined to language. This is not to say that in the 1920s buying actually became voting and that people did not know the difference, but the linguistic collapse of the two terms surely signals a real change. It indicates clearly that the status, legitimacy, and authority once conveyed by citizenship and voting and participation in the civic sphere were now conveyed by consumption and buying and participation in consumer culture.

By the 1920s, participation in a white, ethnically unmarked, middle-class and elite culture of consumption was deeply bound up with the problem of political participation. The commodification of political culture redefined civic virtue not as actual participation in politics but as whiteness, middle-class and elite status, and native-born status instead. People who were excluded by class or race or ethnicity from full participation in the portions of a culture of consumption that middle-class and elite whites dominated lacked the same connection to consumption that the dominant groups enjoyed, making it more difficult for them to claim legitimacy as decision makers in the public sphere. Indeed, some may have excluded themselves from participation in the polity; not only did a politics built around other people's consumer identities offer little that was politically relevant to those who crafted their civic identities in other ways, but people who lacked the cultural franchise conferred by middle-class consumption could easily have felt that they lacked the cultural authority to cast ballots in a fully legitimate way. As politics became more deeply connected to middle-class and elite white ways of consuming, the people excluded from full consumer citizenship became the people excluded from fully legitimate political participation.

The GOTV Campaigns and the Politics of Exclusion

Given the large scope and scale of the GOTV publicity efforts, the vote activists made sweeping claims that their advertising campaigns had reached practically everyone. "Everywhere thoughtful people are beginning to get excited over the fact that so many citizens are so little interested in their Government as not to take the trouble even to vote," a *New York Times* reader remarked in a letter to the editor. The editors of the *Anaconda (Montana) Standard* exclaimed that "in no former election year has there been anything like the interest taken in the present campaign." A businessman in Kenosha, Wisconsin, reported that, at least in his community, "never before" had there been "so strenuous a campaign . . . to get out the vote."[58]

Upon closer analysis, however, the situation was much more complicated. While it is certainly true that GOTV publicity must have made its way to millions through magazine ads, "Four Minute Men," and posters plastered on city buses, the publicity campaigns did not distribute the GOTV message evenly to a representative cross-section of Americans. Though there is little direct evidence of the reception of the GOTV campaigns—commentary by observers on what they saw and thought—the way GOTV groups conducted their publicity work makes it clear that they were much more likely to reach and resonate with certain kinds of people than others. In location and style, the GOTV publicity campaigns catered to middle-class, white, native-born citizens with middle-class, white, native-born tastes.

The leisure magazines that supported the GOTV campaigns, for example, were largely white in readership and middle class in style. After all, it was *Collier's*, not *True Story*, that sponsored the GOTV contest and rewarded good citizenship with a prize. When the vote reformers set up registration tables at department store entrances instead of the stores' employee lounges, they made clear that their priority was middle-class consumers rather than working-class clerks. When they chose bank lobbies instead of ethnic lodges to display their posters and pennants, they revealed a preference for a constituency of "Americans" over "hyphenates." The GOTV advertising and publicity campaigns were conspicuously lacking in ethnic or working-class content. The heroes of the 1924 Met Life ad were "the men whose bleeding feet made red the snows of Valley Forge"—literally, red-blooded Americans. This model of the good citizen was the ancient patriot, not the recent arrival. GOTV editorials turned up often in city newspapers popular with the business community, but rarely or not at all in newspapers that catered to ethnic communities and racial minorities. At the same time that the Grand Rapids *Herald* urged readers to "Do Your Duty As a Citizen—Vote Today," the Grand Rapids *Labor News* and the local Polish weekly *Echo Tygodnioew* had little to say about voting at all. And whether in print or on the radio, few GOTV activists tried to reach voters who did not speak English in ways they could understand. Though the vote campaigns could legitimately boast about their presence in many places, the preponderance of GOTV publicity work ended up in places that white, middle-class, native-born citizens would have been the most likely to encounter.[59]

The GOTV campaigns also gave special agency to middle-class consumers. The broad use of automobiles in the vote campaigns conferred a special position of leadership to the people, more middle- than working-class, who owned them. Car ownership expanded dramatically in the 1920s, to be sure, but buying a car, even on Henry Ford's installment plan, remained out of reach for many workers and very difficult for many working-class city dwellers. And while anyone might read a sign pasted on a car window, only car owners could put them on, making middle-class consumers the agents of the GOTV message in a way that less affluent passersby—mere observers—could never be. When consumer commodities became delivery vehicles for civic messages, they carried with them the message that agency in civic life, as in consumption, belonged to the "haves" rather than the "have-nots."

It is true that many of the publicity efforts in the GOTV campaigns were broadly accessible. For example, both middle-class and working-class people and both native-born and foreign-born Americans in this period enjoyed motion pictures and radio in great numbers, if often in different theaters or on different radio stations. Undoubtedly the working-class clerks who slipped GOTV fliers into customers' parcels also read them, and anyone of any background could view a billboard, admire a window display, or see the placard posted on the side of a bus. But when working-class and ethnic Americans encountered League ladies and Chamber men bearing fliers, it must have been clear to them that the GOTV campaigns came largely from people outside their own communities, and were intended largely for people outside their own communities. This middle-class bias was a matter more of omission that commission; there is no evidence that reformers excluded workers, ethnics, or minorities from their publicity campaigns by design. Just the same, there was little about the selection of forums or content that was geared toward or sensitive to working-class, African American, or ethnic audiences. Perhaps few citizens were formally precluded from encountering or responding to a GOTV message, but surely the place and style in which the message was delivered made a great deal of difference in the way it was received or whether it was received at all. Working-class, ethnic, and minority voters may not have been actually excluded from GOTV publicity efforts, but it was abundantly clear that they were not the point.

The Commodification of Political Culture and the Politics of Exclusion

The commodification of political culture, the reproduction of the processes of consumer culture in civic life, rearranged the relationship between politics and consumption in the larger public sphere. For most of the nineteenth century, political practices had been structured by and around political parties; by the 1920s, they were often structured by and around the institutions of consumer culture. For most of the nineteenth century, political activities—meetings, literature displays, election return announcements—took place in distinctly civic spaces such as courthouse squares or town halls; by the 1920s, when these activities took place at all, they took place, or at least also took place, in distinctly consumer spaces such as department stores and movie theaters. For most of the nineteenth century, citizenship was marked by participation in the civic sphere; by the 1920s, increasingly it was marked by participation in a distinctly middle-class culture of consumption.

Certainly the relationship between consumer culture and political practice was complicated. Though politics borrowed much from consumer culture, consumer culture also borrowed from politics. Advertisers who employed the voting/buying metaphor used political practices to legitimize consumer activities. When advertisers asked consumers to "vote" for a vacuum cleaner or to "repeat" for a Chesterfield, they were promoting not only their products but consumption-oriented values as well—the acquisitiveness, other-directedness, and penchant for pleasure that helped to define consumer culture. By the 1920s, the producers' critique of acquisitive, pleasure-seeking values was fading and advertisements such as these reflected and reinforced that. When consumers "voted" for products by buying them, they ratified consumerist values; in consumption as in politics, "votes" conferred legitimacy.

Though the relationship between consumer culture and political culture may have been reciprocal, it was by no means balanced. From the turn of the century forward, to a significant degree, political practice was incorporated into consumer culture. When advertising experts showed party leaders how to communicate with voters in a modern way, when department stores devoted space to the causes of League women, when movie theater owners peppered the evening's entertainment with announcements of election returns, political practices not only became associated with consumer culture; they became embedded in it. Political spaces were not being used for consumption; consumer spaces were being used for politics. Political experts were not hired to market consumer goods; advertising experts were hired to market political candidates. Electoral contests were not used to generate enthusiasm for buying; publicity stunts were used to generate enthusiasm for elections. Politics was not being used to sell movies; movies were being used to sell politics. The political practices of the nineteenth century, the party-centered ways of campaigning and behaving as citizens and delivering election results, were being displaced, replaced, absorbed into the places and language of a culture of consumption. Political culture was increasingly being integrated into a society in which much of public life centered not around civic affairs but around consumption instead.

As political culture became incorporated into selected segments of a culture of consumption, the class, racial, and ethnic biases of that consumer culture became incorporated into the civic order, too. By moving civic activities from town squares and city halls, places at which everyone was entitled to be, to department stores that enshrined middle-class values and catered to elite tastes, middle-class and elite whites traded inclusive civic venues for exclusive ones; every citizen could assert a claim to city hall and think it "theirs," but department stores that sold expensive goods and cultivated a high-class image made it all too easy for have-nots to feel out of place. Consumer products such as radios integrated into the political order only the people who had access to them; consumer commodities used for civic purposes such as cars could give civic agency only to owners. The commodification of political culture literally shifted the ground upon which politics was conducted from inclusive to exclusive spaces, and in the process helped to make politics the province of people who were white and middle class or elite.

To be sure, neither the places nor the language nor the objects of this consumer culture formally excluded anyone from political participation: any person of any class or race or ethnic background was free to register to vote at a table run by League ladies at Bloomingdale's or to respond to a political candidate's advertising-style campaign. But it must have been clear to everyone who was not white, native born, and middle class or elite that these places did not cater to their own communities, that neither the media nor the messages emanated from their own communities, and that none was particularly for their own communities. The commodification of political culture was the product of elite whites and of the white middle classes; it promoted and privileged their ways of being citizens.

Conclusion
THE NEW REGIME

Middle-class and elite whites in the early twentieth century succeeded spectacularly in their efforts to contain the radical potential of universal suffrage. By the 1920s, immigrants, ethnic Americans, and workers had practically disappeared as respectable participants from discussions of civic issues in the large-circulation daily newspapers that comprised in this period a crucial part of "the public sphere" of discourse and debate. A drumbeat of unfavorable depictions of women citizens counterbalanced their familiar portrayal as civic "angels" and undermined their new equality as voting citizens by criticizing their competence to make decisions which men would have to abide. Middlebrow magazines routinely characterized the interests of native-born, middle-class whites as the public good and the interests of immigrants, workers, African Americans, and sometimes women as narrow and particular. Civic education classes described good citizenship in terms that defined "expertise" as whiteness and middle-class or elite status, while advertisements that portrayed businessmen and stylish homemakers as model citizens propagated the idea that people who were elite or middle class ought to be regarded as both the civic ideal and the civic norm.

This was a remarkable achievement, for as recently as a generation earlier the vigorous participation of workers, immigrants, and ethnic Americans in civic life had been a democratic necessity. Workers, ethnic Americans, and noncitizen immigrants *had* participated, fully and fully legitimately, in the electorate of the party period. Their participation was once a defining feature of the political system; by the turn of the century it had become contested ground. The strong system of multiethnic, multiclass political parties that for most of the nineteenth century had welcomed and indeed insisted upon their participation deteriorated rapidly after the realignment of the 1890s, making it possible for the class stratification that in the mid–nineteenth century had come to characterize so many aspects of American life—the workplace, the arts, the layout of urban space— finally to take hold in politics as well.

By the end of the 1920s, a new system of civic hierarchies had displaced much of the old. In the old regime, enfranchisement corresponded neatly to the racial and gender hierarchies that conferred privilege upon white men of every class and ethnic background. African Americans were for the most part excluded from significant roles in civic life, and women occupied subordinate roles as abstractions perched upon parade floats or as critics of, say, temperance policy, but not as people who were empowered to make public decisions for others. In most places, voters needed simply to be male, white, and twenty-one years of age; those qualities alone made them legitimate decision makers for the rest of society.

As more people gained the right to vote, powerful groups worked to change the meaning of enfranchisement. When enfranchisement no longer neatly corresponded to civic privilege, middle-class and elite whites began to mark civic status in new ways. In the new regime, frequently under the banner of "expertise," noncitizen immigrants were banned from the electorate; African Americans in the South remained for the most part disenfranchised; workers and ethnics were pushed to the margins of civic life; and women occupied a range of positions that reflected their unsettled civic status, from working-class and ethnic women who had few resources for exerting civic power in official ways to elite white women who used the power conferred by their class and race to carve out a place for themselves in the most privileged ranks. In the new regime, the pinnacle of civic privilege was reserved for elite and middle-class whites alone.

This political culture of exclusion was achieved in many ways. Courts during the Red Scare, for example, defined the views of left-leaning immigrants as a breach of the boundaries of good citizenship, while "Judge Lynch" continued to enforce segregation, disenfranchisement, and deference. The "American Plan" campaigns by business groups to replace closed shops with open shops curtailed the influence of workers on the job. The continuing use of injunctions to prevent picketing and strikes branded labor activism as a criminal act. The restrictions on immigration passed in 1921 and 1924 dramatically cut the number of new arrivals, while Americanization campaigns by schools, churches, and businesses pressured foreign-born residents to shed ethnic markers and conform to narrow definitions of "Americanness." In the 1920s, these actions and others added up to a multifrontal assault on the ability of workers, immigrants, ethnic Americans, and sometimes women to function as full, and fully legitimate, citizens.

In the making of middle-class and elite white civic dominance the GOTV campaigns played an important part. GOTV reformers did not invent expert citizenship or introduce consumer culture to politics; they did not manufacture, singlehandedly and from scratch, the new system of civic hierarchies that largely displaced the old. They did, however, contribute significantly to these changes and help to promote them further. GOTV groups embraced, for example, the progressive ideal of expert citizenship, articulated it in pamphlets and magazine articles, publicized it with cartoons and contests, and institutionalized it in civic education programs, at every point reinforcing and propagating the idea that workers, immigrants, ethnics, and women needed to be educated before they were fit to exercise their right to make decisions for all.

The GOTV campaigns also helped to promote the commodification of political culture, the paradigm shift from a politics organized around political parties to a politics organized around a dominant culture of consumption. This process likewise helped to shape the new system of civic hierarchies because it placed middle-class and elite whites and the aspects of consumer culture that they dominated at the center of civic life as well. When Met Life placed advertisements in the *Saturday Evening Post* and tried to turn customers into voters, they integrated the techniques, the products, and the language of consumer culture into the practice of politics, much as the Creel Committee had done. Like the commercial advertisers who drew a metaphorical relationship between voting and buying, GOTV groups also helped to transform the basis upon which many people formed their civic identity from a rainbow of ethnic, religious, and partisan affiliations to a single model of the "rational," middle-class or elite, native-born, white consumer citizen. Along with retailers and theater managers, GOTV groups also helped literally to shift the ground upon which politics took place by moving civic activities from inclusive to exclusive spaces—from town squares, for example, where every man could claim he had a right to be, to movie theaters, where a person had to be a customer to be present, or department stores, which catered to people who had money to spend. In short, the GOTV campaigns were thoroughly implicated in the transformations of political culture that took place in the early twentieth century. They were a product of, an example of, and an agent of change.

Middle-class and elite whites did not achieve their place of civic privilege without a fight, and could hardly rest secure that their position would be permanent. Indeed, in the 1920s they faced constant challenges to their place atop the civic hierarchy. African American women in the South who were determined to use the Nineteenth Amendment to better conditions for their communities; immigrant and ethnic Americans who thrilled at the possibility that Al Smith might become president; workers who rallied to Robert La Follette's tireless campaigns to claim a fairer share of the fruits of their labor; feminists who pushed for an equal rights amendment to expand women's newfound equality as voting citizens to all aspects of life—challenges from these groups and others threatened to undermine the special status of privileged groups. This explains why middle-class and elite whites poured so much effort into GOTV, why they felt there was so much at stake. They needed the Get-Out-the-Vote campaigns to reinforce and reaffirm their position of civic privilege. They needed advertising campaigns to get out *their* vote; they needed education campaigns to try to remold problem voters into people who would support the system of civic hierarchies that permitted them to be on top. Under the pressures of the Great Depression, their fears would in fact prove valid, as some of these less-privileged groups would succeed in using the fluidity generated by extraordinary circumstances to make for themselves a New Deal, to rearrange civic hierarchies in more equitable ways, and to reclaim a place in civic life.

The commodification of political culture helped to redefine what constitutes the public sphere. Not only did "the public sphere" of the early twentieth century prove to be not very public; increasingly, it became not very civic either. The public sphere is historical, like everything else, and the GOTV campaigns, low voter turnout, and the commodification of political culture all suggest that during this time the importance of civic life within the public sphere was shrinking. For most of the nineteenth century, the public sphere was built in large measure around politics; politics was the center of public life, and engagement with the political system was one of the key factors that bound together diverse people in society. By the 1920s, none of those things was true; the public sphere was built in large measure around consumption, consumption was the center of public life, and participation in consumer society was one of the factors that bound together diverse people in society. Priorities shifted, and the relative importance of politics and consumption in public life changed. To the extent that politics continued to engage the attention of the public, it often did so in ways—such as adopting the language of advertising for civic causes, or having citizens register to vote in department stores—that integrated it into a consumer society.

There is no straight line between the political culture of the early twentieth century and the political culture of today. Certainly, over the past hundred years much about consumer culture and the practice of politics has changed. Nonetheless, the commodification of political culture is now such an established fact of political life that it hardly attracts notice. In the 1990s, when Ross Perot used infomercials to sell his presidential candidacy, analysts commented often on their cost or on the pie charts, but rarely on their form, a form usually reserved for selling exercise equipment and kitchen gadgets. Likewise, few thought it noteworthy in 2000 when the major presidential candidates offered merchandise for sale on their official website "stores."

The commodification of political culture has left a lasting mark on governance as well. Consumer culture has not supplied a very effective set of institutions for making decisions and implementing policy. Consumer citizenship has proven a poor substitute for the partisan variety it helped to replace: buying does not register people's opinions on the issues of the day, for example, or make politics meaningful to ordinary people. Advertisers do not perform the functions that political parties once fulfilled. They do not offer a process for resolving differences of opinion; they do not cobble together coalitions; they do not forge the majorities that confer legitimacy on electoral outcomes; they do not make policy. None of these developments supplies an infrastructure that mobilizes political participation and makes it meaningful to people; none supplies organizations that connect citizens to the voting booth, or the voting booth to policy outcomes.

The GOTV activists did not address these problems. Above all, they never articulated a vision of a truly participatory democracy. Full turnout would have required much greater participation on the part of the least powerful groups in society—poor people and workers, immigrants and ethnic Americans, African Americans, and women—something that made many uncomfortable then, and that still makes many uncomfortable now. The demands of "expert citizenship," or something like it, still delegitimize political participation on the part of people perfectly qualified to make good judgments. Gender, race, ethnicity, and class continue to demarcate hierarchies in civic legitimacy, so much so that today "civic" is practically synonymous with "middle class" and "white." These issues have certainly evolved, but they are not new. Difference poses a challenge to democracy even yet.

ABBREVIATIONS

ABP	Alton B. Parker
AI	*American Industries,* published by the National Association of Manufacturers
AJHS	American Jewish Historical Society, Waltham, Massachusetts
ALM	*American Legion Monthly*
ALR	American Legion Records, American Legion Library, Indianapolis, Indiana
ALW	*American Legion Weekly*
BAH	*Birmingham Age-Herald,* Birmingham, Alabama
BHL	Bentley Historical Library, Ann Arbor, Michigan
BPL	Birmingham Public Library, Birmingham, Alabama
BS	Belle Sherwin
BSP	Belle Sherwin Papers, Schlesinger Library, Cambridge, Massachusetts
CW	*Collier's Weekly*
DNC	Democratic National Committee
FDRL	Franklin D. Roosevelt Presidential Library, Hyde Park, New York
GR	Grand Rapids, Michigan
GRPL	Grand Rapids Public Library, Grand Rapids, Michigan
HHPL	Herbert Hoover Presidential Library, West Branch, Iowa
JHH	John Hays Hammond
LC	Library of Congress
LWV	League of Women Voters

LWVP	League of Women Voters Papers, Manuscript Division, Library of Congress, Washington, D.C.
Met Life	Metropolitan Life Insurance Company
MLL	Metropolitan Life Insurance Company Library, New York, New York
MWP	Maud Wood Park
MWPP	Maud Wood Park Papers, Schlesinger Library, Cambridge, Massachusetts
NAM	National Association of Manufacturers
NAMR	National Association of Manufacturers Records, Hagley Museum and Library, Wilmington, Delaware
NCFR	National Civic Federation Records, New York Public Library, New York, New York
NYT	*New York Times*
RE	Ralph Easley
RNC	Republican National Committee
ser.	series
WC	*Woman Citizen*
WN	*Weekly News,* published by the New York League of Women Voters

NOTES

Introduction. Making Dominance

1. Harris-Emery Company, "Will You Take This Pledge?" [1924], ser. II, LWVP.

2. *AI*, Nov. 1924, 7; J. Lewis Benton to JHH, 16 Aug. 1926, ser. II, LWVP; *NYT*, 24 Aug. 1924, sec. 2, p. 5; JHH, "Program of Department on Political Education, The NCF," 19 Nov. 1926, NCFR; Met Life, *An Adventure in Advertising*, n.p., [c. 1924], MLL; *Saturday Evening Post*, 25 Oct. 1924, 104, 27 Oct. 1928, 138; MWP, "The National League of Women Voters," [c. 1928], MWPP; "Opening Program—January 3," 1928, BSP; *WN*, 22 June 1928, ser. I, LWVP; *CW*, 18 Oct. 1924, 49.

3. The only extended discussion of the GOTV campaigns appears in Michael E. McGerr, *The Decline of Popular Politics: The American North, 1865–1928* (New York: Oxford University Press, 1986), 195–205. The GOTV campaigns are mentioned in Robert S. Lynd and Helen Merrell Lynd, *Middletown: A Study in American Culture* (New York: Harcourt, Brace and Company, 1925), 426; Evelyn Brooks Higginbotham, "Clubwomen and Electoral Politics in the 1920s," in Ann D. Gordon et al., eds., *African American Women and the Vote, 1837–1965* (Amherst: University of Massachusetts Press, 1997), 149; Marguerite Green, *The National Civic Federation and the American Labor Movement, 1900–1925* (Washington, D.C.: Catholic University of America Press, 1956), 476; Louise Young, *In the Public Interest: The League of Women Voters, 1920–1970* (Westport, Conn.: Greenwood Press, 1989), 74, 85, 91–94; Kate Kelly, *Election Day: An American Holiday, an American History* (New York: Facts on File, 1991), 193–94.

4. Joel H. Silbey, *The American Political Nation, 1838–1893* (Stanford: Stanford University Press, 1991); Richard L. McCormick, ed., *The Party Period and Public Policy: American Politics from the Age of Jackson to the Progressive Era* (New York: Oxford University Press, 1986); Paul Kleppner, *Continuity and Change in Electoral Politics, 1893–1928* (New York: Greenwood Press, 1987).

5. Elisabeth S. Clemens, *The People's Lobby: Organizational Innovation and the Rise of Interest Group Politics in the United States, 1890–1925* (Chicago: University of Chicago Press, 1997); Anna L. Harvey, *Votes Without Leverage: Women in Electoral Politics, 1920–1970* (Cam-

bridge: Cambridge University Press, 1998); Judith Shklar, *American Citizenship: The Quest for Inclusion* (Cambridge: Harvard University Press, 1991), 2.

6. Gary Cross, *An All-Consuming Century: Why Commercialism Won in Modern America* (New York: Columbia University Press, 2000), 1; Roland Marchand, *Advertising the American Dream: Making Way for Modernity, 1920–1940* (Berkeley: University of California Press, 1985), 7, 9.

7. *Saturday Evening Post,* 25 Oct. 1924, 104, 27 Oct. 1928, 138; *WN,* 3 Oct. 1924, ser. I, LWVP; Eleanore Raoul to Anne Williams Wheaton, 6 Oct. 1926, ibid.; *Woman Voter,* Nov. 1924, 8, ibid.; *WC,* 18 Oct. 1924, 21; *Ill. LWV Bulletin,* Dec. 1924, ser. II, LWVP; *WC,* 6 Sep. 1924, 21; Therese Loeb to BS, 20 June 1926, ser. II, LWVP; "Analysis of Entries for Award of Silver Cup[,] 1928[,] State League Pre-Election Activities," Feb. 1929, ibid.; GR LWV, *The First Fifty Years, 1921–1971* (GR: LWV of Grand Rapids, Michigan, 1972), 9; [N.J. LWV and N.J. State Federation of Women's Clubs] *Civic Pilot,* Oct. 1924, 14, ser. I, LWVP; *The Metropolitan,* 1924, 2, MLL.

8. McGerr, *Decline of Popular Politics,* 138–83.

9. Mary Fainsod Katzenstein, *Faithful and Fearless: Moving Feminist Protest Inside the Church and Military* (Princeton: Princeton University Press, 1998), 17.

10. Nancy Fraser, "Rethinking the Public Sphere: A Contribution to the Critique of Actually Existing Democracy," *Social Text* 25/26 (1991): 56–80 (quotes, 57, 70). My italics.

11. Guy Debord, *The Society of the Spectacle* (New York: Zone Books, 1994), 15.

12. *AI,* Nov. 1924, 5.

Chapter 1. "Civic Slackers" and "Poll Dodgers"

1. *Wilmington (Del.?) News,* 4 Jan. 1927, NCFR. These issues are explored in a different context in Liette Gidlow, "Delegitimizing Democracy: 'Civic Slackers,' the Cultural Turn, and the Possibilities of Politics," *Journal of American History* 89 (Dec. 2002): 922–57.

2. *Philadelphia Inquirer* quoted in *Literary Digest,* 23 Aug. 1924, 15.

3. *Los Angeles Express,* 19 Jan. 1920, Will H. Hays Papers, Indiana State Library, Indianapolis, Ind.; *CW,* 10 May 1924, 20; speech, Carrie Chapman Catt, 17 Oct. 1928, ser. II, LWVP; remarks of Charles Merriam, mtg., Department of Political Education, "Afternoon Session," 29 Jan. 1926, NCFR; Arthur M. Schlesinger and Erik McKinley Eriksson, "The Vanishing Voter," *The New Republic,* 15 Oct. 1924, 164; Lynd and Lynd, *Middletown,* 417, n. 5.

4. *NYT,* 11 May 1924, sec. I, pt. II, 5; *Nation's Business,* Oct. 1924, 90; Simon Michelet, "Voting a Civic Duty," [1927], Oliver Day Street Papers, State of Alabama Department of Archives and History, Montgomery, Ala.; F.H. Bartlett to JHH, 17 Nov. 1924, NCFR; untitled newsletter, Md. LWV, Nov. 1923, ser. I, LWVP; surveys by the Georgia, Montana, and California Leagues of Women Voters, 1925, ser. II, LWVP; speech, Eleanor Roosevelt, 2 Nov. 1927, Eleanor Roosevelt Papers, FDPL; Ida Koch Lane to BS, 14 Feb. 1928, *Ill. LWV Bulletin,* Dec. 1924, both in ser. II, LWVP; Eleanore Raoul to Anne Williams Wheaton, 6 Oct. 1926, ser. I, LWVP; political cartoon, Morris, "Are You A Vote Slacker?" *New Haven Journal-Courier* and 70 other newspapers, ibid.; political cartoon, Briggs, "Oh Man," *Richmond (Va.) Times-Dispatch,* 4 Nov. 1924, sports sec., 2; political cartoon, Smith, "There's Only One Way to Deal with This Gentleman," which appeared in six newspapers including the *Altoona (Penn.) Mirror* and *Lima (Ohio) News* on 15 Oct. 1924, and the *Bluefield (W.V.) Daily Telegraph* on 16 Oct. 1924, ser. II, LWVP; political cartoon, W.R. Loring, "No Vote—No Voice!" *Okla-*

homa City Times, 29 Oct. 1924, ibid.; political cartoon, Hammond, "Pigmy or Giant—Which Will You Be on Election Day," *Wichita (Kans.) Eagle,* 15 Oct. 1924, ibid.

5. Mtg., New York Committee on Active Citizenship, 11 May 1927, NCFR; *Current Opinion,* July 1924, 77; *ALM,* Nov. 1926, 34; *AI,* Oct. 1924, 11; *Literary Digest,* Aug. 1924, 15; *NYT,* 10 Oct. 1924, 5; Ralph Easley, "The Slacker Vote of 1924," [Nov. 1924], NCFR; *AI,* May 1924, 22; *Miles City (Mont.) American,* 22 Sep. 1924, MWPP; *Birmingham (Ala.) Reporter,* 25 Oct. 1924, 6.

6. U.S. Bureau of the Census, *Historical Statistics of the United States, Colonial Times to 1970,* Part I, Bicentennial Edition (Washington, D.C.: U.S. Government Printing Office, 1975), 231; *NYT,* 21 Oct. 1924, 7.

7. Gregg, "If Only Gulliver Would Wake Up!" *Atlanta Constitution,* 7 Sep. 1924, ser. I, LWVP.

8. *NYT,* 7 Oct. 1924, 22; *ALM,* Sep. 1926, 45; *(Minn.) Woman Voter,* 5 Sep. 1924, 3, ser. I, LWVP.

9. Thurlby, "Columbia Calls," *Seattle Daily Times,* 7 Oct. 1924, ser. II, LWVP; *Wilmington (Del.?) News,* 4 Jan. 1927, NCFR; clipping, probably from *WC,* n.d., BSP.

10. *CW,* 5 July 1924, 18.

11. Alexander Keyssar, *The Right to Vote: The Contested History of Democracy in the United States* (New York: Basic Books, 2000), 29–33; Michael Lewis Goldberg, *An Army of Women: Gender and Politics in Gilded Age Kansas* (Baltimore: Johns Hopkins University Press, 1997), 168–69; David R. Roediger, *The Wages of Whiteness: Race and the Making of the American Working Class* (London: Verso, 1999); Dana D. Nelson, *National Manhood: Capitalist Citizenship and the Imagined Fraternity of White Men* (Durham: Duke University Press, 1998). See Keyssar's Appendix A.4 and A.12 for lists of states that permitted alien suffrage.

12. Richard L. McCormick, *The Party Period and Public Policy.*

13. Silbey, *American Political Nation,* 46–71.

14. Paul Kleppner, *The Third Electoral System, 1853–1892* (Chapel Hill: University of North Carolina Press, 1979); Jean Baker, *Affairs of Party: The Political Culture of Northern Democrats in the Mid-Nineteenth Century* (Ithaca, N.Y.: Cornell University Press, 1983).

15. William Gienapp, "'Politics Seems to Enter Into Everything': Political Culture in the North, 1840–1860," in *Essays in American Antebellum Politics, 1840–1860,* eds. Stephen E. Maizlish and John J. Kushma (College Station: Texas A&M University Press, 1982), 14–69; Silbey, *American Political Nation,* 125–40; Jean H. Baker, "The Ceremonies of Politics: Nineteenth-Century Rituals of National Affirmation," in *A Master's Due: Essays in Honor of David Herbert Donald,* eds. William J. Cooper Jr., Michael Holt, and John McCardell (Baton Rouge: Louisiana State University Press), 161–78; Gil Troy, *See How They Ran: The Changing Role of the Presidential Candidate* (New York: The Free Press, 1991), 20–26; Kelly, *Election Day,* 82, 94; Elizabeth Varon, "Tippecanoe and the Ladies Too: White Women and Party Politics in Antebellum Virginia," *Journal of American History* 82 (Sept. 1995): 495.

16. Baker, "The Ceremonies of Politics," in *A Master's Due,* eds. William T. Cooper Jr. et al., 170; McGerr, *Decline of Popular Politics,* 5; Silbey, *American Political Nation,* 121–23.

17. Kelly, *Election Day,* 90–94; McGerr, *Decline of Popular Politics,* 12–41; Joel H. Silbey, "'The Salt of the Nation': Political Parties in Antebellum America," in *The Partisan Imperative: The Dynamics of American Politics Before the Civil War,* ed. Joel H. Silbey (New York: Oxford University Press, 1983), 50–68; Robert H. Wiebe, *Self-Rule: A Cultural History of Democracy* (Chicago: University of Chicago Press, 1995), 29–30, 61–85.

18. McGerr, *Decline of Popular Politics,* 40.

19. See "Note on Method and Sources."

20. J. Morgan Kousser, *The Shaping of Southern Politics: Suffrage Restriction and the Establishment of the One-Party South, 1880–1910* (New Haven: Yale University Press, 1974); Paul Kleppner, *Who Voted? The Dynamics of Electoral Turnout, 1870–1980* (New York: Praeger Publishers, 1982), 58–63; Jerrold G. Rusk and John J. Stucker, "The Effect of the Southern System of Election Laws on Voting Participation: A Reply to V.O. Key, Jr.," in *The History of American Electoral Behavior,* eds. Joel H. Silbey, Allan G. Bogue, and William H. Flanigan (Princeton: Princeton University Press, 1978), 223–47.

21. Kleppner, *Who Voted?* 8–10, 60–63; Kenneth J. Winkle, *The Politics of Community: Migration and Politics in Antebellum Ohio* (Cambridge: Cambridge University Press, 1988), 48–70.

22. Sara Alpern and Dale Baum, "Female Ballots: The Impact of the Nineteenth Amendment," *Journal of Interdisciplinary History* 16 (Summer 1985): 56; Walter Dean Burnham, "The Appearance and Disappearance of the American Voter," in *The Current Crisis in American Politics,* ed. Walter Dean Burnham (New York: Oxford University Press, 1982), 152; pamphlet, Ill. LWV, "A Reasonable Increase," Nov. 1923, ser. II, LWVP.

23. Paul Kleppner and Stephen C. Baker, "The Impact of Voter Registration Requirements on Electoral Turnout, 1900–1916," *Journal of Political and Military Sociology* 8 (Fall 1980): 209–13; Paul Kleppner, "Were Women to Blame? Female Suffrage and Voter Turnout, 1890–1930," *Journal of Interdisciplinary History* 12 (Spring 1982): 621–43; Walter Dean Burnham, "The System of 1896," in Paul Kleppner, Walter Dean Burnham, Ronald P. Formisano, Samuel P. Hays, Richard Jensen, and William G. Shade, *The Evolution of American Electoral Systems* (Westport, Conn.: Greenwood Press, 1981), 147–202; Paul Kleppner, *Continuity and Change,* 59–95; Richard Jensen, *The Winning of the Midwest: Social and Political Conflict, 1888–1896* (Chicago: University of Chicago Press, 1971); and Samuel T. McSeveney, *The Politics of Depression: Political Behavior in the Northeast, 1893–1896* (New York: Oxford University Press, 1972).

24. H.R. Campbell to JHH, 5 Dec. 1924, NCFR; Walter Dean Burnham, "The Changing Shape of the American Political Universe," in *The Current Crisis in American Politics,* ed. Walter Dean Burnham, 25–57; Kleppner, *Who Voted?* 73.

25. McGerr, *Decline of Popular Politics,* 69–106.

26. See "Note on Method and Sources."

27. Silbey, *American Political Nation,* 6–7.

28. Ben A. Arneson, "Non-Voting in a Typical Ohio Community," *American Political Science Review* 19 (Nov. 1925): 824; Kleppner, *Who Voted?* 63–70; Burnham, "The Changing Shape," 36; Stephen P. Erie, *Rainbow's End: Irish-Americans and the Dilemmas of Urban Machine Politics, 1840–1985* (Berkeley: University of California Press, 1988), 67–106.

29. Charles E. Merriam and Harold F. Gosnell, *Non-Voting: Causes and Methods of Control* (Chicago: University of Chicago Press, 1924); Barry D. Karl, *Charles E. Merriam and the Study of Politics* (Chicago: University of Chicago Press, 1974), 148; *The New Republic,* 21 Oct. 1925, 224–25; Harold F. Gosnell, *Getting Out the Vote: An Experiment in the Stimulation of Voting* (Chicago: University of Chicago Press, 1927); Arneson, "Non-Voting in a Typical Ohio Community," 824; *Scribner's Magazine,* Nov. 1924, 530–33.

30. Michelet's studies were published, reported, archived, or referenced by name in the *NYT,* 11 May 1924, sec. I, pt. II, 5; *Current Opinion,* July 1924, 77, Sep. 1924, 280–81; *GR*

Chronicle, 5 Sep. 1924, 2; *Nation's Business,* Oct. 1924, 90; *Washington Post,* 5 Oct. 1924, ser. II, LWVP; *BAH,* 12 Oct. 1924, Society, Club and Fashion section, 1; *Current History Magazine of the New York Times,* Nov. 1924, 247–49; *Minneapolis Sunday Tribune,* 5 Apr. 1925, 6; *American Review of Reviews,* Oct. 1924, 412; *ALW,* 31 Oct. 1924, 14; *NYT,* 2 Sep. 1924, 1, 9 Nov. 1924, 22; *NYT,* 27 July 1924, sec. 2, 1, ser. II, LWVP; Gladys Harrison to BS, 30 Aug. 1924, ser. II, LWVP; Adele Clark to Ann Webster, 30 July 1924, ibid.; newsletter to State LWVs, 23 Aug. 1924, ibid.; "The Get-Out-the-Vote Campaign as Reported by Mrs. Webster to the Board," [Nov. 1924?], ibid.; press release, 5 Oct. 1924, Robert M. La Follette Sr. Papers, La Follette Family Collection, LC; Simon Michelet, "Election Laws and Data," 17 Oct. 1932, "Stay-at-Home Vote and Absentee Voters," [1925?], "The Vote in 1924," [1925?], and "Absent Voter Laws[,] 1928," [1928], all in Papers of the National Committee of the Democratic Party, 1928–1948, FDRL; "Voting a Civic Duty," [1927], Street Papers.

31. Haley Fiske to ABP, 6 July 1925, NCFR; John Hays Hammond and Jeremiah W. Jenks, *Great American Issues: Political, Social, Economic* (New York: Charles Scribner's Sons, 1923), 33; *AI,* Oct. 1924, 15; *NYT,* 24 Oct. 1928, 18, 15 Aug. 1928, 10, 28 July 1928, 2; *CW,* 20 Sep. 1924, 12; *Nation's Business,* Apr. 1928, 14; *AI,* Oct. 1924, 16; *Birmingham (Ala.) News,* 3 Nov. 1924, 8; *AI,* June 1924, 16; NAM, *Proceedings of the Twenty-Ninth Annual Convention,* 1924, 109, NAMR; *Bulletin [of the] Michigan LWV,* July 1926, 3, ser. I, LWVP; *GR Spectator,* 3 Nov. 1928, GR Chamber of Commerce Records, BHL; newspaper clipping, Edward S. Van Zile, "Will H. Hays Sees G.O.P. Victory," Hays Papers.

32. *Ladies' Home Journal,* Oct. 1924, 155; *BAH,* 2 Nov. 1924, Society, Club and Fashion sec., 1; *NY Herald and Tribune,* 10 May 1925, ser. II, LWVP.

33. *CW,* 16 Aug. 1924, 13; *Current History Magazine of the NYT,* Nov. 1924, 247.

34. NAM, *Proceedings of the Twenty-Ninth Annual Convention,* 1924, 109, NAMR; *CW,* 21 June 1924, 20.

35. *Cleveland Plain Dealer,* 15 Apr. 1924, 1; *Current History Magazine of the New York Times,* Nov. 1924, 247; *CW,* 30 Aug. 1924, 6.

36. John Duffy to JHH, 13 Nov. 1924, F.H. Bartlett to JHH, 17 Nov. 1924, both in NCFR; *WN,* 17 Oct. 1924, ser. I, LWVP.

37. *Michigan Union,* Sep. 1924, ser. 2, Sligh Family Papers, BHL; *Open Shop Review,* Aug. 1924, 286; *NYT,* 11 May 1924, sec. I, pt. 2, 5; *Literary Digest,* 23 Aug. 1924, 15; political cartoon, Maurd, "It's Your Privilege—and Your Duty," *Syracuse (N.Y.) Journal,* 10 Oct. 1924, ser. II, LWVP; *GR Chronicle,* 5 Sep. 1924, 2.

38. *Richmond (Va.) Times-Dispatch,* 16 Apr. 1925, ser. I, LWVP; political cartoon, J.N. "Ding" Darling, "Always an Uncomfortable Season of the Year for the Men Folks," in Kristi Andersen, *After Suffrage: Women in Partisan and Electoral Politics before the New Deal* (Chicago: University of Chicago Press, 1996), 20.

39. Wiebe, *Self-Rule,* 176; William McDougall, *Is America Safe for Democracy?* (New York: Charles Scribner's Sons, 1921); H.L. Mencken, *Notes on Democracy* (New York: Alfred A. Knopf, 1926), 196; *CW,* 1 July 1922, 3–4; Walter Lippmann, *Public Opinion* (New York: Harcourt, Brace and Company, 1922), 273.

40. *AI,* Oct. 1924, 7–8, 10; *Atlanta Constitution,* 4 Nov. 1924, 5, 1, 3.

41. *CW,* 10 May 1924, 20; *Open Shop Review,* July 1924, 259.

42. Press release, NCF, 9 July 1927, NCFR; press release, LWV, Jan. 1924, ser. I, LWVP;

Rebecca Edwards, *Angels in the Machinery: Gender in American Party Politics from the Civil War to the Progressive Era* (New York: Oxford University Press, 1997); Samuel Gompers, "51 PERCENT DO NOT VOTE!" [c. 1924], NCFR.

43. *Birmingham Reporter,* 25 Oct. 1924, 6, 18 July 1925, n.p.

44. John Hope to ABP, 15 Jan. 1926, NCFR; *National Notes,* July 1926, 3; Evelyn Brooks Higginbotham, *Righteous Discontent: The Women's Movement in the Black Baptist Church, 1880–1920* (Cambridge: Harvard University Press, 1993), 185–229.

45. *(Birmingham) Labor Advocate,* 6 Jan. 1922, [1]; Merriam and Gosnell, *Non-Voting,* 198; Erie, *Rainbow's End,* 67–106.

46. Estelle Freedman, "Separatism as Strategy: Female Institution-Building and American Feminism, 1870–1930," *Feminist Studies* 5 (Fall 1979): 512–29; Sara Evans and Harry Boyte, *Free Spaces: The Sources of Democratic Change in America* (New York, 1986); Nancy F. Cott, *The Grounding of Modern Feminism* (New Haven: Yale University Press, 1987).

47. This is not to say that politics and culture are always the products of elites whose actions are unconstrained by less powerful groups. Far from it: the power of workers, racial and ethnic minorities, and women to shape political agendas and public culture is well documented. See, for example, Lizabeth Cohen, *Making a New Deal: Industrial Workers in Chicago, 1919–1939* (New York: Cambridge University Press, 1990); Clemens, *The People's Lobby;* and Michael Denning, *The Cultural Front: The Laboring of American Culture in the Twentieth Century* (London: Verso, 1998). On this issue, in these forums, in this period, however, politically marginalized groups exercised very little power.

48. *NYT,* 12 Nov. 1927, 18, 14 Nov. 1927, 20; Adele Clark to Ann Webster, 30 July 1924, ser. II, LWVP.

Chapter 2. "A Whole Fleet of Campaigns"

1. *NYT,* 12 Sept. 1924, 3; McGerr, *Decline of Popular Politics,* 195; NLWV, typescript of newsletter to state LWVs, 23 Aug. 1924, ser. II, LWVP.

2. *AI,* Nov. 1924, 7; Edna Fischel Gellhorn to ABP, 29 Aug. 1924, NCFR.

3. Coolidge quoted in Grace H. Brosseau, "Message of the President-General, National Society, Daughters of the American Revolution," July 1926, NCFR.

4. William J. McAuliffe to ABP, 25 Sept. 1924, NCFR; speech, MWP, 10 Apr. 1923, ser. I, LWVP; MWP, "A Record of Four Years in the National LWV, 1920–1924," MWPP.

5. Ill. LWV, "Prospectus for Citizenship Schools," [c. 1923], ser. I, LWVP.

6. Political cartoon, Halladay, "The Next Defence Day," 1924, *Providence (R.I.) Sunday Journal,* 15 Sep. 1924, ser. II, LWVP.

7. Press release, NCF, 21 May 1928, NCFR; Edith V. Alvord to presidents of the General Federation of Women's Clubs, 28 Feb. 1927, ibid.; RE to Grace Brosseau, 31 Jan. 1927, ibid.; "How to Get Out the Vote: Plans, Suggestions and Hints," 11 Sept. 1924, ibid.; "LWV Get Out the Vote Campaign," 1924, ser. II, LWVP; "Organizations Represented at 'Get Out the Vote' Conference," 1924, NCFR; Dorothy Dingham, "Through Two Wars—Part I" [1924], Advertising Women of New York, Inc. Papers, 1912–1970, Schlesinger Library; *Ill. LWV Bulletin,* Dec. 1924, ser. II, LWVP; *Michigan Women,* Oct. 1926, 22, ser. I, LWVP; *Montgomery (Ala.) Journal,* 27 Oct. [1924], ibid.; *(Minn.) Woman Voter,* 19 Sep. 1924, 2, ibid.; *WC,* 1 Nov. 1924, 21; Lora Harris Cook to ABP, 30 June 1924, NCFR; Grace Brosseau to RE, 10 July 1926, ibid.;

WC, 20 Sep. 1924, 21; Minnie Latham to ABP, 7 July 1924, NCFR; Grace Brosseau, "Message of the President-General, National Society, Daughters of the American Revolution," July 1926, ibid.; NLWV to "Friend of the League," 26 Oct. 1923, ser. I, LWVP; *Michigan Union,* Sep. 1924, ser. 2, Sligh Family Papers, BHL; *WC,* 28 June 1924, 21; *BAH,* 2 Nov. 1924, Society, Club and Fashion section, 5, 29 Oct. 1924, 3; Bina West to RE, 25 June 1924, NCFR.

8. John W. O'Leary to JHH, 10 July 1926, NCFR; minutes, Board of Directors Meetings 74 to 91 and Executive Committee Meetings, 26 to 30, [1923], pp. 5–6, 11, ser. I, Chamber of Commerce of the U.S.A. Records, Hagley Museum and Library, Wilmington, Del.; and the following, all of which are in the NCFR: ABP to Chambers of Commerce, 16 Aug. 1924; N.B. Kelly to ABP, Aug. 1924; C.W. Judd to JHH, 17 Nov. 1924; J.B. Hissong to JHH, 13 Nov. 1924; Sidney Detmers to ABP, 4 Sep. 1924; Harold O. Bosworth to ABP, 5 Sep. 1924; Jeannette Simmons to ABP, 9 Sep. 1924; J.A. Gawthrop to ABP, 21 Aug. 1924; M.R. Joseph to JHH, 18 Nov. 1924; F. Roger Miller to ABP, 18 Aug. 1924; Earl O. Stowitts to JHH, 17 Nov. 1924; Harry L. Ford to ABP, 22 Aug. 1924; J.A. Shoemaker to ABP, 22 Aug. 1924; John Lawrence Fox to ABP, 25 Aug. 1924; Edwin B. Lord to JHH, 13 Nov. 1924; Joseph H. Rayburn to ABP, 12 Sep. 1924.

9. Fred C.W. Parker to RE, 11 Jan. 1926, NCFR; RE to Parker, 23 Jan. 1926, ibid.; *NYT,* 4 Nov. 1924, 31, 10 Oct. 1924, 5; NCF, "Get Out the Vote Account," [1924], NCFR; H.E. Sharrer to ABP, 8 Sep. 1924, ibid.; remarks of Robert E. Condon, mtg., Department of Political Education, "Morning Session," 29 Jan. 1926, ibid.; T.A. Stevenson to NCF, 19 Nov. 1924, ibid.; *Santa Ana (Calif.) Register,* 3 Nov. 1924, 1; *AI,* Nov. 1924, 7; Everett W. Hill to JHH, 21 Nov. 1924, NCFR; Seymour N. Sears to JHH, 12 July 1926, ibid.; W.L. Saunders to JHH, 13 July 1926, ibid.; F. Robertson Johns to RE, 26 June 1924, ibid.

10. *NYT,* 24 Aug. 1924, sec. 2, 5; James West to ABP, 22 Aug. 1924, E.L. Harvey to RE, 17 Sep. 1924, J.C. Snyder to RE, 8 Dec. 1927, Stockton Broome to ABP, 2 July 1924, all in NCFR; *AI,* Nov. 1924, 7; Frank S. Land to JHH, 13 July 1926, NCFR.

11. *NYT,* 1 Aug. 1924, 13, 14 Sep. 1924, sec. I, 2; National Council of Jewish Women, *[Proceedings of the] Eleventh Triennial Convention,* 1927, Appendix B, n.p., AJHS; James A. Flaherty to JHH, 24 July 1926, Eugene M. Camp to NCF, 10 Sep. 1924, Ralph Easley, "The Slacker Vote of 1924," [1924], all in NCFR.

12. Frank Luther Mott, *A History of American Magazines, 1895–1905* (Cambridge: Belknap Press of Harvard University Press, 1957), 569; *WC,* 4 Oct. 1924, 20; *NYT,* 20 Aug. 1924, 3, 13 Sep. 1924, 12, 4 Feb. 1925, 4.

13. "Program of Department on Political Education," 19 Nov. 1926, NCFR.

14. "Get Out the Vote Account," [1924], "Organizations Represented at 'Get Out the Vote' Conference," 1924, George L. Darte to JHH, 19 July 1926, Darte to RE, 11 Aug. 1924, all in NCFR; "Resolution Adopted by the Service Star Legion," 1923, ser. II, LWVP; P.F. Harrington to JHH, 16 July 1926, William M. Galvin to JHH, 3 Aug. 1926, Reserve Officers Association to NCF, 1926, all in NCFR.

15. *NYT,* 10 Oct. 1924, 7; form letter, Committee on Increase of Registration to Vote, 30 Sep. 1926, NCFR.

16. Clipping, *NYT,* 27 July 1924, sec. II, 1, ser. II, LWVP; "Constitution of the National Get-Out-the-Vote Club," [1924], ibid.; *NYT,* 2 Sep. 1924, 1; Simon Michelet, "Absentee Voting in the 48 States in the Election of 1926," [c. 1927], "Voting a Civic Duty," [1927], Street Papers.

17. Hayward Kendall to BS, 28 Aug. 1924, ser. II, LWVP; *CW,* 3 Nov. 1928, 29; "The

Get-Out-the-Vote Campaign as Reported by Mrs. Webster to the Board," [Nov. 1924?], ser. II, LWVP; *AI,* Oct. 1924, 17–18; *NYT,* 29 Sep. 1925, 26; *AI,* Aug. 1924, 17–18.

18. RE to Thomas Dysart, 6 Aug. 1926, NCFR; "LWV Get Out the Vote Campaign," 1924, ser. II, LWVP; LWV to "Friend of the League," 26 Oct. 1923, ser. I, LWVP; M.J. Keough to JHH, 11 Aug. 1926, NCFR; Frank Feeney to JHH, 8 July 1926, ibid.

19. *WC,* 4 Oct. 1924, 20; and the following, all in NCFR: Samuel Gompers, "51 PER CENT DO NOT VOTE!" [c. 1924]; Thomas McMahon to JHH, 10 Aug. 1926; Edward J. McGivern to JHH, 28 July 1926; James Maloney to JHH, 5 Aug. 1926; *WC,* 6 Sep. 1924, 21.

20. John H.M. Laslett, "Samuel Gompers and the Rise of American Business Unionism," in *Labor Leaders in America,* eds. Melvyn Dubofsky and Warren Van Tine (Urbana: University of Illinois Press, 1987), 62–88 (quote, 75); *WC,* 1 Nov. 1924, 20; Mrs. Cooper King to Ann Webster, 5 July 1924, ser. II, LWVP.

21. William Green to JHH, 30 July 1926, NCFR; RE to Green, 2 Feb. 1927, ibid.; Green to RE, 10 Feb. 1927, ibid.; and the following, all in ser. II, LWVP: *Machinists Monthly Journal,* Jan. 1924, 35, Feb. 1924, 91; *Journal of Electrical Workers and Operators,* Mar. 1924, 235; *The Boilermakers Journal,* Mar. 1924, 134–35; *Brotherhood of Locomotive Firemen and Enginemen's Magazine,* Feb. 1924, 54; "Editors of the Magazines of the Association of Railroad Labor Organizations," [1924].

22. *AI,* Oct. 1924, 10.

23. *WC,* 1 Nov. 1924, 20; ibid., 4 Oct. 1924, 20; Milwaukee LWV, "Milwaukee Women Organize Drive to Increase Use of Ballot," [c. 1926], ser. II, LWVP; *(St. Louis) League Bulletin,* 22 Sep. 1924, ser. I, LWVP.

The LWV routinely supplied articles to the Foreign Language Information Service for translation and publication in eight hundred foreign-language newspapers. Because GOTV was such an important part of the League's overall agenda, it seems likely that GOTV materials were among these. I have not, however, been able to confirm this. See "Report of the First Vice President," 6 Oct. 1923, ser. I, LWVP.

24. "Analysis of Entries for Award of the Silver Cup[,] 1928," Feb. 1929, ser. II, LWVP; press release, NCF, 9 July 1927, NCFR.

25. Brown quoted in Glenda Gilmore, *Gender and Jim Crow: Women and the Politics of White Supremacy in North Carolina, 1896–1920* (Chapel Hill: University of North Carolina Press, 1996), 213.

26. Gilmore, *Gender and Jim Crow,* 219–24 (quotes, 224, 223); Rosalyn Terborg-Penn, *African American Women in the Struggle for the Vote, 1850–1920* (Bloomington: Indiana University Press, 1998), 151–57 (quote, 156).

27. RE to Haley Fiske, 19 Oct. 1926, NCFR.

28. *National Notes,* July 1926, 3; minutes, 31st Annual Session of the Alabama Federation of Colored Women's Clubs, June 1929, Mattie Rivers Trammell Papers, Savery Library, Talladega College, Talladega, Ala.

29. *Ill. LWV Bulletin,* Sep.–Oct. 1924, ser. I, LWVP; *National Notes,* July 1926, 25.

30. *WN,* 3 Oct. 1924, ser. I, LWVP; *[N.J. LWV] Civic Pilot,* Oct. 1928, 10, ibid.

31. *BAH,* 10 Oct. 1924, 7; *Birmingham Reporter,* 27 Feb. 1926, 1.

32. *The Crisis,* Oct. 1928, 336; *Birmingham Reporter,* 26 Jan. 1924, 4; *NY Amsterdam News,* 8 July 1925, 3.

33. James C. Scott, *Weapons of the Weak: Everyday Forms of Peasant Resistance* (New

Haven: Yale University Press, 1985); Higginbotham, *Righteous Discontent,* 185–88; Goldberg, *Army of Women,* 44. On a "deradicaliz[ed]" African American church and the bourgeois character of some African American middle-class politics in this period, see Robin D.G. Kelley, *Hammer and Hoe: Alabama Communists During the Great Depression* (Chapel Hill: University of North Carolina Press, 1990), 109–16.

34. Mtg., "Certain New York Members of Advisory Committee, Department on Political Education," 1925, NCFR; NCF to Robert Turnhill, [c. Jan. 1926], ibid.; typescript, Emily Newell Blair, [c. 1924], ser. II, LWVP; typescript, NLWV, [spring 1924], ibid.; "Delegates and Guests to the National Convention[,] Conference for Progressive Political Action," 1924, Robert M. La Follette Sr., Papers; *WN,* 9 Nov. 1928, ser. I, LWVP; press release, RNC, Papers of the Campaign and Transition Period, 1928–1929, Papers of Herbert Hoover, HHPL.

35. "Get Out the Vote Account," [1924], NCFR; Edna Fischel Gellhorn to ABP, 29 Aug. 1924, ibid.

A possible exception to the claim that the national parties did not engage in GOTV work can be found in the work of the Republican Service League (RSL), the Republican party's vehicle for bringing veterans of World War I into the Republican fold. In 1928 the RSL sent an American Legion GOTV "bulletin" to some of its officers. See Hanford MacNider to Albert S. Callan, 1 Oct. 1928 and MacNider to A.L. Burridge, 1 Oct. 1928.

Formally "independent of the National Republican organization," the RSL nonetheless "co-operate[d] with" the RNC, was "aided by it," mimicked the structure of the party at the state, county, and local levels, and was expected in time to merge with the party. See form letter [MacNider?], 26 Aug. 1924; stencil, "Our Organization," [1924]; and MacNider to Howard Baxter, 8 Oct. 1924. The RSL was the creation of Hanford MacNider, the National Commander of the American Legion in 1921 and 1922, an assistant secretary of war in the Coolidge administration, and a long-time Republican party activist. The RSL, which claimed to be organized in forty-three states, operated in presidential years between 1924 and 1936 to promote "a Republican Americanism." See "General Situation [of the] Republican Service League," Sep. 1924 and "The Republican Service League," [1924].

Through MacNider, the RSL enjoyed close ties to the Legion, and at least in New York and Michigan, the Republican group informed state RSL leaders of the Legion vote campaign. Despite this close connection between the Republican party and the Legion, MacNider wrote to a Michigan RSL leader that "the Service League has no intention of using nor perverting the Legion's [GOTV] campaign" but also added that "the fact remains . . . that if everybody votes, the Republican majority will be the greatest in history." See MacNider to Burridge, 1 Oct. 1928. Whether RSL leaders outside Michigan and New York received the same Legion materials, and whether any of them actually undertook GOTV work, is unclear. All this material can be found in the Hanford MacNider Papers, HHPL.

36. Gladys Harrison to MacPherson, [c. Nov. 1924], ser. II, LWVP; *Santa Ana (Calif.) Register,* 3 Nov. 1924, 11; VA LWV, "Get Out the Vote Committee and Campaign," [1924], ser. II, LWVP; "Details of Some State Plans," 18 Mar. 1924, ser. I, LWVP; *(Conn.) Woman Voter's Bulletin,* May 1926, ibid.; Mrs. James P. MacPherson to BS, 12 Sep. 1924, ibid.; BS to MacPherson, 19 Sep. 1924, ibid.; MacPherson to BS, 20 Nov. 1924, ibid.; *Bulletin [of the] Michigan LWV,* June 1929, ibid.

37. "Know Your Parties," [1923], ser. II, LWVP; *AI,* June 1924, 23, 26; *CW,* 24 July 1920, 12.

38. *CW,* 10 July 1920, 12; *ALM,* Nov. 1926, 34; *ALW,* 25 July 1919, 30.

39. Charles Evans Hughes to RE, 28 Aug. 1924, NCFR; RE to William Howard Taft, 13 July 1926, ibid.; RE to William Butler, 28 Nov. 1924, 8 July 1924, ibid.; John T. Adams to ABP, 1 Apr. 1924, ibid.; ABP to Chairmen of Republican and Democratic Committees, 10 Aug. 1925, ibid.; Peter Brady to Frank B. Kellogg, 6 Jan. 1927, ibid.; Peter Brady to Andrew W. Mellon, 6 Jan. 1926, ibid.; "Is One's Political Duty Fully Discharged by Voting at Elections and Primaries?" [c. 1926], Street Papers; Harriet Taylor Upton to Margaret H. Johnson, 6 Sep. 1923, ser. II, LWVP; Simon Michelet, "Stay-at-Home Vote and Absentee Voters," [1925?], "The Vote in 1924," [1925?], "Absent Voter Laws[,] 1928," [1928], Papers of the DNC, 1928–1948, FDRL; Michelet, "Voting A Civic Duty," [1927], Street Papers; C. Bascom Slemp to RE, 17 May 1924, NCFR. See "Note on Method and Sources" for a list of the political party records collections I examined, none of which indicate interest or involvement in the GOTV campaigns.

40. *CW,* 10 June 1922, 10, 2 Sep. 18; Young, *In the Public Interest,* 34.

41. RE to Jackson S. Elliott, 30 Dec. 1926, NCFR.

42. *Boston Globe,* 6 Nov. 1928, 7; *Santa Ana (Calif.) Daily Register,* 3 Nov. 1924, 4.

43. "American Legion and Major R.E. Condon/U.S. Junior Chamber of Commerce," [c. 1924], NCFR; *Bulletin [of] the Mo. LWV,* Sep. 1924, ser. I, LWVP; *NYT,* 10 Oct. 1924, 7; manuscript, Mrs. Stephen W. Collins, 14 May 1925, Papers of the GR Federation of Women's Clubs, 1896–1959, Michigan Family and History Department, GRPL; *Birmingham,* Apr. 1925, 5, Hill Ferguson Collection, Linn-Henley Research Library, BPL; Eleanore Raoul to Anne Williams Wheaton, 6 Oct. 1926, ser. II, LWVP.

44. Remarks of Mrs. Charles Tiffany, [1924], NCFR; *WC,* 9 Aug. 1924, 21, 20 Sep. 1924, 21; *(Minn.) Woman Voter,* 29 Oct. 1924, ser. I, LWVP.

45. George Creel, *How We Advertised America* (New York: Harper and Brothers, Publishers, 1920), 7–8, 137.

46. Typescript, [Ann Webster?], [c. 1924], ser. II, LWVP.

47. *[N.J. LWV] Civic Pilot,* Oct. 1928, 4, ser. I, LWVP; "Milwaukee Women Organize Drive to Increase Use of Ballot," [c. 1926], ser. II, LWVP.

48. *(St. Louis) League Bulletin,* 22 Sep. 1924, ser. I, LWVP; *St. Louis Post-Dispatch,* 7 Aug. 1924, 17, Edna Fischel Gellhorn Papers, Schlesinger Library.

49. Remarks of Mrs. J. Paul Goode, "Thursday Morning Session, Teaching to Teach," 1923, ser. I, LWVP; *WC,* 1 Nov. 1924, 21, 18 Oct. 1924, 21, 4 Oct. 1924, 21, 9 Nov. 1924, 21; *(Ind.) Woman Voter,* Oct. 1924, 13, ser. I, LWVP.

50. *WC,* 1 Nov. 1924, 20; Belle Glaser to [Florence] Whitney, 15 Mar. 1926, ser. II, LWVP; *WN,* 21 Sep. 1928, ser. I, LWVP.

51. *AI,* Oct. 1924, 6; Jeannette Simmons to ABP, 9 Sep. 1924, NCFR; Fred C.W. Parker to RE, 11 Jan. 1926, ibid.; RE to Fred C.W. Parker, 23 Jan. 1926, ibid.; J. Lewis Benton to JHH, 16 Aug. 1926, ser. II, LWVP; remarks of R.E. Condon, 11 Sep. 1924, NCFR.

52. "G.O.T.V. Activities," [c. 1925], ser. II, LWVP; J.A. Shoemaker to ABP, 22 Aug. 1924, NCFR; "Program of Department on Political Education," 19 Nov. 1926, ibid.; *WC,* 1 Nov. 1924, 21; Jesse S. Richard to ABP, 19 Aug. 1924, Joseph H. Rayburn to ABP, 12 Sep. 1924, Harold O. Bosworth to ABP, 5 Sep. 1924, and E.E. Jackson to JHH, 17 Feb. 1925, all in NCFR; *WC,* 6 Sep. 1924, 21. The "Program of Department on Political Education" erroneously locates Carson City in Arizona.

53. Ida Koch Lane to BS, 14 Feb. 1928, ser. II, LWVP; Roscoe Ady to JHH, 17 Nov. 1924, NCFR; National Council of Jewish Women, *[Proceedings of the] Eleventh Triennial Con-*

vention, 1927, Appendix B, n.p., AJHS; *Montgomery (Ala.) Journal,* 27 Oct. [1924], ser. I, LWVP; *WC,* 31 May 1924, 20–21; Adele Clark to Ann Webster, 30 July 1924, ser. II, LWVP; *AI,* Aug. 1924, 5; *[N.C. LWV] Monthly News,* Oct. 1924, ser. I, LWVP; *WC,* 1 Nov. 1924, 20; Dan S. Hollenga to ABP, 18 Aug. 1924, NCFR.

54. Ida Koch Lane to BS, 14 Feb. 1928, ser. II, LWVP; "News Bulletin," 6 Jan. 1923, Assorted Correspondence of the LWV of Birmingham, Ala., Department of Archives and Manuscripts, Linn-Henley Research Library, BPL; Dorothy Judd to BS, 29 Mar. 1929, ser. II, LWVP; *WN,* 30 Mar. 1928, ser. I, LWVP.

55. Amelia Fisk to "Presidents" [of Alabama organizations], 1 Sep. 1924, ser. II, LWVP; *BAH,* 19 Oct. 1924, Society, Club and Fashion section, 3; *[N.C. LWV] Monthly News,* Oct. 1924, ser. I, LWVP; Ruth Kimball Gardiner quoted in Ann Webster to Adele Clark, 26 July 1924, ser. II, LWVP; Adele Clark to Ann Webster, 30 July 1924, ibid.

56. On the conflicts between some of these groups, see J. Stanley Lemons, *The Woman Citizen: Social Feminism in the 1920s,* 2nd ed. (Charlottesville: University Press of Virginia, 1990), 209–23 and Cott, *The Grounding of Modern Feminism,* 247–61.

57. *WC,* 1 Nov. 1924, 20; *NYT,* 31 Oct. 1924, 3, 7 Oct. 1924, 4; J.M. Carson to RE, 23 Nov. 1924, NCFR; *CW,* 1 Nov. 1924, 24; political cartoon, John Baer, "Over the Top, Again," *Stars and Stripes,* 4 Oct. 1924, ser. I, LWVP.

58. *NYT,* 7 Oct. 1924, 4; *Current History Magazine of the NYT,* Nov. 1924, 248–49; *WC,* 28 June 1924, 21.

59. *AI,* Nov. 1924, 25–26; remarks of John B. Kennedy, "How to Get Out the Vote: Plans, Suggestions and Hints," 11 Sep. 1924, NCFR; *CW,* 1 Nov. 1924, 24.

60. "Summary of the Tabulations of the Voting Statistics of 1924–1928," Mar. 1929, ser. II, LWVP; "Report of Vote Cast for President in 1920 and 1924," [c. 1925], ibid.; U.S. Bureau of the Census, *Historical Statistics of the United States, Part II,* 1071; RE, "The Slacker Vote of 1924," [Nov. 1924], NCFR.

61. "Department on Political Education," n.d., Thomas G. Dignan to JHH, 14 Nov. 1924, RE to Jackson S. Elliott, 30 Dec. 1926, all in NCFR.

Chapter 3. *"Vote as You Please—But Vote!"*

1. "Plan of Work and Program for the National LWV, 1923–1924," [c. 1923], MWPP.

2. Ibid.

3. Speech, MWP, "The National LWV," [c. 1928], ibid.

4. "What Should the National LWV Do to Get Out the Vote in 1928," 15 Nov. 1927, ser. II, LWVP. All cites in this section come from the LWVP unless otherwise noted. In the 1920s the League was known as the National League of Women Voters (NLWV). Its name was shortened to the League of Women Voters in 1946. By "the National" I mean the League's leadership at headquarters in Washington, D.C.

5. Young, *In the Public Interest,* 49, 57, 60; Lemons, *The Woman Citizen,* 119.

6. Young, *In the Public Interest,* 1–2.

7. Ibid., 48; MWP, "A Record of Four Years in the National LWV, 1920–1924," [c. 1924], MWPP; speech, Carrie Chapman Catt, 17 Oct. 1928, ser. II.

8. Young, *In the Public Interest,* 41 n. 11; BS to [Caroline] Slade, 29 Apr. 1924, ser. II.

9. *Worcester (Mass.) Telegram,* 26 Apr. 1924, MWPP; Martin Schipper, comp., *Papers of the League of Women Voters, 1918–1974, Part III, Series A, National Office Subject Files,*

1920–1932 (Frederick, Md.: University Publications of America, 1986), xviii; [Minnie Fisher Cunningham] to BS, 24 Apr. 1923, ser. I; form letter from Minnie Fisher Cunningham, 14 July 1924, ser. II.

10. Mrs. Max Mayer, "Educated Citizenship Program Outlines," [c. 1924], ser. I; stencil, "Voters' Schools, Citizenship Schools and Other Educational Meetings," 1929, ser. II.

11. Minnie Fisher Cunningham, "Report of the Executive Secretary," [1923], "Report of Miss Hauser and Miss Sherwin on Mailing Lists," 28 Dec. 1923, and Elizabeth J. Hauser, "How to Get Out the Vote," [c. 1924], all in ser. I.

12. BS to Caroline Slade, 29 Apr. 1924, ser. II; *Bulletin [of the] Mich. LWV,* Oct. 1926, 1, ser. I; *(St. Louis) League Bulletin,* 28 June 1926, ibid.; Gladys Harrison to F. Perkins, 5 Nov. 1927, ser. II; BS to Amelia Fisk, 11 Sep. 1924, Assorted Correspondence; booklet, "Get Out the Vote," 1924, MWPP; "Proposed Program of Work for the National LWV, 1924–25," 1 Feb. 1924, ibid.; newspaper clipping, *Washington Post,* 5 June 1923, ibid.; circular letter, Minnie Fisher Cunningham to State LWV Presidents, 26 July 1923, ser. I; *[Wisc. LWV] Forward,* Sept. 1923, ser. I, cover; *[Kans. LWV] Progress,* June 1924, cover, ser. II; Illinois LWV, "A Reasonable Increase," Nov. 1923, back cover, ibid.; Alabama LWV, "Getting Out the Vote," 1924, ibid.; booklet, "Get Out the Vote," 1924, MWPP.

13. Gladys Harrison to BS, 30 Aug. 1924, *The ABC of Voting,* 1924, "Get-Out-The-Vote or Pre-Election Activities," 1928, "Status of the Get-Out-the-Vote Campaign as of Oct. 15, 1924," 1924, all in ser. II.

14. "Get-Out-the-Vote-Cartoon Contest," 1924, ser. II.

15. Copies of most of these cartoons are available in box 47, ser. II.

16. Press release, NLWV, 3 July [1924], ser. II; "The Get-Out-the-Vote Campaigns as Reported by Mrs. Webster to the Board," [Nov. 1924?], ibid.; *[N.J. LWV and N.J. State Federation of Women's Clubs] Civic Pilot,* Sep. 1928, 11, ser. I; *[Kans. LWV] Progress,* Sep. 1924, cover, ibid.; "Entry in Cup Contest," [1924], ser. II; *Richmond (Va.) News Leader,* 17 Apr. 1925, ser. I.

California was the home of the state League that produced the greatest percentage increase in turnout among entrants into the national League's contest. Wyoming showed the greatest percentage increase in turnout that year, but Wyoming also had almost no League and almost no GOTV campaign to speak of. This irony frustrated the League enormously and spurred it to change the rules for the silver cup contest in 1928. The National decided that the quantity and quality of work done by state and local Leagues was as important as the actual results, and under the new criteria awarded the 1928 trophy to Missouri. See "Comparative Report of Votes Cast for President in 1920, 1924, and 1928," Mar. 1929, ser. II; "Analysis of Entries for Award of the Silver Cup[,] 1928, State League Pre-Election Activities," Feb. 1929, ibid.; BS to Edna Gellhorn, 5 Apr. 1929, Edna Fischel Gellhorn Papers, Schlesinger Library.

17. Booklet, "Get Out the Vote," 1924, MWPP; "What Should the National LWV Do to Get Out the Vote in 1928," 15 Nov. 1927, ser. II; form letter from Minnie Fisher Cunningham, 14 July 1924, ibid.

18. Photograph, "Good Citizens Vote!" 1924, Dorothy Leonard Judd Papers, GRPL; *WC,* 20 Sep. 1924, 21; *NYT,* 17 Aug. 1924, sec. II, 2; Oregon LWV, "Getting Out the Vote," [1924], ser. II; Hilda R. Watrous, *In League with Eleanor: Eleanor Roosevelt and the League of Women Voters, 1921–1962* (New York: Foundation for Citizen Education, 1984), 18; *WC,* 1 Nov. 1924, 21; Mrs. O.A. Critchett, "El Paso LWV Get Out the Vote Campaign," [n.d.], ser.

II; *Bulletin [of the] Mich. LWV,* June 1929, ser. I; *[(Fond du Lac, Wisc.) Commonwealth?],* 3 Nov. 1924, ibid.; *BAH,* [21 Dec. 1924], ser. II; Amelia Fisk to BS, 20 Sep. 1924, ibid.

Abundant examples of local League GOTV activity can be found in the League pages of the *Woman Citizen,* usually pages 20 and 21, between 1923 and 1928.

19. Minneapolis LWV, "Daily Report," [c. 1924], ser. I; Gladys Harrison to Mrs. James MacPherson, [1924?], ser. II; map, Webster Grove, Mo., LWV, [c. 1924], ser. I; N.Y. LWV, "Getting Out the Vote," 1924, ser. II; *WC,* 1 Nov. 1924, 20–21; "Get-Out-the-Vote Report Presented to National Convention by Mrs. James Morrisson," 26 Apr. 1924, ser. II.

20. Young, *In the Public Interest,* 85; press release, LWV, [1924], MWPP; mtg. "Get Out the Vote Committee," 29 Mar. 1926, ser. II; "W-21 Report of the Get-Out-the-Vote Committee," [c. 1926], ibid.

21. "Report of the Vote Cast for President in 1920 and 1924 in All the States," [c. 1925], ser. II; "Find Your State!" [c. 1925], ibid.; surveys by the California, Georgia, and Montana Leagues, 1925, ibid.; "W-21 Report of the Get-Out-the-Vote Committee," [c. 1925], ibid.; "Conference on Voting and Non-Voting," 23 Apr. 1929, ibid.

22. "What Should the National LWV Do to Get Out the Vote in 1928," 15 Nov. 1927, ser. II; "Report of the Get-Out-the-Vote Activities Made to the Executive Committee," June 1926, ibid.; *Providence (R.I.?) Evening Bulletin,* 30 Oct. 1926, ibid.; *Bulletin [of the] Massachusetts LWV,* 2 Sep. 1926, ser. I; *Michigan Women,* Oct. 1926, 24, ibid.; *(St. Louis) League Bulletin,* 28 June 1926, ibid.; *Erie County (N.Y.) LWV Primary Bulletin,* Sep. 1926, ibid.; Gladys Harrison to Florence Whitney, 11 Mar. 1926, ser. II.

23. "What Should the National LWV Do to Get Out the Vote in 1928," 15 Nov. 1927, ser. II; Register and Vote Committee, "Citizens," [c. 1926], ibid.; *(Conn.) Women Voter's Bulletin,* May 1926, ser. I; *(Mich.) Women,* Oct. 1926, 22, ibid.; *(Minn.) Woman Voter,* Oct. 1926, 5, ibid.; Eleanore Raoul to Anne Williams Wheaton, 6 Oct. 1926, ser. II; *WC,* Dec. 1926, 13.

24. "1926 General Election Vote by States," [c. 1927], ser. II; press release, NLWV, 30 Apr. 1927, ibid.

25. "Extract from a letter from Miss Olive A. Colton," 4 Oct. 1927, *(St. Louis) League Bulletin,* 4 Apr. 1927, *Kentucky League Bulletin,* July 1927, back cover, program, S.Dak. LWV, 1927, all in ser. II; "A Guide to the Services of the National LWV," Apr. 1927, BSP.

26. Press release, LWV, 30 Apr. 1927, ser. II; "Data concerning Voting Statistics and the Voting Habit in the United States," Apr. 1927, MWPP; Gladys Harrison to Everett Sanders, 7 Feb. 1927, ser. II; Sanders to Harrison, 8 Feb. 1927, ibid.; typescript, "Voting Habit Surveys[,] Apr. 1927–Dec. 1927," [c. 1927], ibid.

27. "Get-Out-The-Vote or Pre-Election Activities," 1928, ser. II.

28. "Get Out the Vote[:] A Handbook of Pre-Election Activities," 1928, MWPP.

29. "Get-Out-The-Vote or Pre-Election Activities," 1928, ser. II; *(St. Louis) League Bulletin,* 15 Sep. 1928, [1], ser. I.

30. [Gladys Harrison] to "Regional Directors and Secretaries," 15 Sep. 1927, ser. II; "A Get-Out-the-Vote Film for Your Use," [1927], ibid.; Gladys Harrison to E.S. Bowles, 10 Sep. 1927, ibid.; Marion Neprud to Anne Wheaton, 11 Aug. 1927, ibid.

31. *WN,* 4 Sep. 1925, 2 Oct. 1925, 30 Oct. 1925, 1 Oct. 1926, 29 Oct. 1926, all in ser. I; "Get-Out-the-Vote Report Presented to National Convention by Mrs. James Morrisson," 26 Apr. 1924, ser. II; *Bulletin of the Ill. LWV,* Nov. 1926, ser. I; "Address by Miss Belle Sherwin," 1928, BSP.

32. Ibid.; "Opening Program—Jan. 3," 1928, ibid.

33. *[N.J. LWV] Civic Pilot*, Jan. 1928, 5, ser. I; *(St. Louis) League Bulletin*, 18 Feb. 1928, ibid.; "Address by Miss Belle Sherwin," 1928, BSP; *WN*, 20 July 1928, 20 Apr. 1928, ser. I.

34. *[N.J. LWV] Civic Pilot*, Jan. 1928, 5, ser. I; *WN*, 28 Dec. 1928, 22 June 1928, ibid.; Agnes Leach to Sherwin, 5 Jan. 1928, ser. II; Young, *In the Public Interest*, 100 n. 11.

35. *(St. Louis) League Bulletin*, 6 Oct. 1928, ser. I; *(Mo.) League News*, Oct. 1928, 6, ibid.; *(Conn.) Woman Voter's Bulletin*, Nov. 1928, ibid.; *[N.J. LWV] Civic Pilot*, Oct. 1928, 10, 4, ibid.; Ida Koch Lane to BS, 14 Feb. 1928, ser. II; Mich. LWV, "Political Highways," 1928, ibid.

36. "Summary of the Tabulation of the Voting Statistics of 1924–1928," Mar. 1929, ibid.; "Conference on Voting and Non-Voting," 23 Apr. 1929, ibid.

37. *Worcester (Mass.) Telegram*, 26 Apr. 1924, MWPP; "Get Out the Vote[:] A Handbook of Pre-Election Activities," 1928, ibid.

38. *NYT*, 7 July 1924, 4.

39. *AI*, June 1924, 8; NAM, *Proceedings of the Twenty-Ninth Annual Convention*, 1924, 14, NAMR.

40. NAM, *Proceedings of the Twenty-Fifth Annual Convention*, 1920, 292, 229-30, NAMR; *AI*, Oct. 1924, 16, 12.

41. *AI*, Oct. 1924, 7; *Open Shop Review*, Dec. 1924, 443; *NYT*, 21 Oct. 1924, 7.

42. *NYT*, 21 Oct. 1924, 7; *(N.Y.?) Evening Star*, 27 Sep. 1924, Papers Pertaining to the Campaign of 1924, FDRL; *AI*, Oct. 1924, 7, 14.

43. *Open Shop Review*, Aug. 1924, 286; *AI*, Oct. 1924, 15, 11, 24.

44. *NYT*, 7 July 1924, 4; *AI*, Oct. 1924, 6, Nov. 1924, 7–9, Oct. 1924, 17, Aug. 1924, 17–18. The NAM records that remain do not provide a basis for the claim of 3,000 GOTV organizations. I have identified about a thousand organizations, though my count is not exhaustive.

45. NAM, *Proceedings of the Thirtieth Annual Convention*, 1925, 49, NAMR; J. Lewis Benton to JHH, 16 Aug. 1926, ser. II, LWVP.

46. "Weekly Bulletin" [of the Associated Industries of Alabama], 6 Sep. 1924, ser. B, Robert M. La Follette Sr., Papers; Harold O. Bosworth to ABP, 5 Sep. 1924, NCFR; *Nation's Business*, Oct. 1924, 90; political cartoon, Maurd, "It's Your Privilege—and Your Duty," *Syracuse Journal*, 10 Oct. 1924, ser. II, LWVP; cartoon, W.R. Loring, "Vote As You Please, But Vote," *Oklahoma City Times*, 29 Oct. 1924, ibid.; cartoon, McDowell, "Vote As You Please, But—Vote!," *Los Angeles Record*, 3 Nov. 1924, ibid.; *WC*, 18 Oct. 1924, 4; *NYT*, 21 Sep. 1924, sec. II, 3; Charles H. Davis to ABP, 18 Aug. 1924, NCFR; remarks of Charles S. Morris, "How to Get Out the Vote: Plans, Suggestions and Hints," 11 Sep. 1924, ibid.; *Birmingham News*, 3 Nov. 1924, 8; paper tag, "Good Citizen," [1924], ser. II, LWVP; *Birmingham Reporter*, 25 Oct. 1924, 6; *(Birmingham) Labor Advocate*, 18 Oct. 1924, [n.p.]

47. *Santa Ana (Calif.) Register*, 3 Nov. 1924, 3; *Denver Post*, 4 Nov. 1924, 7; *St. Louis Post-Dispatch*, 4 Nov. 1924, 22; *Richmond Times-Dispatch*, 3 Nov. 1924, 12.

48. "Stockholders Meeting of the U.S.A.," [1924], ser. II, LWVP; *AI*, Sep. 1924, 22.

49. "Stockholders Meeting of the U.S.A.," [1924], ser. II, LWVP.

50. *AI*, Oct. 1924, 24; *(Ind.) Woman Voter*, Oct. 1924, cover, ser. I, LWVP; *Bulletin [of the] Saginaw County (Mich.) LWV*, 1 Nov. 1924, ibid.; political cartoon, John Baer, "Can't Afford to Pass This Meetin' Up," 1924, *Capper's Weekly*, 1 Nov. 1924, ser. II, LWVP.

51. *CW*, 21 June 1924, 20; *Nation's Business*, Oct. 1928, 9; *(Ga.) Voter*, Nov. 1928, 8, ser. I, LWVP; 100% Register and Vote League, "The Minority Govern When the Majority Fail," [1924], ser. II, ibid.; Kelly, *Election Day*, 194.

52. J. Lewis Benton to JHH, 16 Aug. 1926, ser. II, LWVP; NAM, *Proceedings of the Thirty-First Annual Convention,* 1926, 80, NAMR; NAM, *Proceedings of the Thirty-Second Annual Convention,* 1927, 46, ibid. A review of *American Industries/Pocket Bulletin* for 1927, 1928, and 1929 and of NAM convention proceedings for 1927, 1928, and 1929 shows no GOTV work by NAM in the 1928 election.

53. *AI,* Nov. 1924, 5; speech, James A. Emery, "Radicalism Repulsed but Not Defeated," 11 Dec. 1924, Vada Horsch Papers, NAMR; NAM, *Proceedings of the Thirtieth Annual Convention,* 1925, 49, NAMR.

54. *CW,* 1 Nov. 1924, 24.

55. Christopher P. Wilson, "The Rhetoric of Consumption: Mass-Market Magazines and the Demise of the Gentle Reader, 1880–1920," in *The Culture of Consumption: Critical Essays in American History, 1880–1980,* eds. Richard Wightman Fox and T.J. Jackson Lears (New York: Pantheon Books, 1993), 41–43, 47, 50; Lynd and Lynd, *Middletown,* 231–32, 239–40. Circulation figures come from *N.W. Ayer and Son's American Newspaper Annual and Directory* (Philadelphia: N.W. Ayer and Son, 1924).

Bruce Barton was hired at *Collier's* in 1912 as an assistant sales manager and advertising copywriter. Edward Anthony took a leave of absence from his position as Director of Publicity for Crowell-Collier magazines to serve as director of publicity for the Hoover presidential campaign in 1928. Goldsmith, once an associate editor at *Collier's,* served as director of the Bureau of Political Research at the Democratic National Committee in the early 1920s. See Donald L. Thompson, "Bruce Fairchild Barton," in *The Ad Men and Women: A Biographical Dictionary of Advertising,* ed. Edd Applegate (Westport, Conn.: Greenwood Press, 1994), 15; Raymond Henley, "Oral History Interview with Edward Anthony and Esther Anthony," 12 July 1970, HHPL; press release, DNC, 15 July 1921, Franklin D. Roosevelt Papers, 1920–1928, FDRL.

Crowell Publishing Company was a major magazine publishing house in the 1920s. *Collier's Weekly* was its flagship publication, but it also put out the *Woman's Home Companion* and *American Magazine,* each with a circulation of about two million. The company went through a series of mergers and acquisitions and was absorbed into Macmillan, Inc. in 1965. See the unpublished finding aid for the Records of the Crowell-Collier Publishing Company, 1931–1955, at the New York Public Library.

56. *CW,* 6 May 1922, 9, 7 July 1923, 6, 31 July 1920, 13, 4 Dec. 1926, 50, 17 Nov. 1923, 8, 28 July 1928, 50, 21 Oct. 1922, 5–6, 9 Oct. 1926, 8–9, 23 Aug. 1924, 18.

57. *CW,* 19 May 1923, 5, 1 Mar. 1924, 3, 18 Oct. 1924, 49.

58. *CW,* J.L. Herman to the editor, 2 May 1924, 38, 1 July 1922, 3, 21 Feb. 1925, 30; handwritten note, Ann Webster, [1924], ser. II, LWVP.

59. *CW,* 6 Aug. 1924, 12–13, 30 Aug. 1924, 6–7, 20 Sep. 1924, 11–12, 23 Aug. 1924, 10–11, 25 Oct. 1924, 14, 12 July 1924, 7, 10 May 1924, 20, 21 June 1924, 20, 5 July 1924, 18, 2 Aug. 1924, 18, 1 Nov. 1924, 24, 4 Oct. 1924, 47, 11 Oct. 1924, 18, 18 Oct. 1924, 49, 1 Nov. 1924, inside front cover, Mr. Schultz to the editor, 23 Aug. 1924, 34, Jack Brown to the editor, 9 Aug. 1924, 34; remarks of John B. Kennedy, "How to Get Out the Vote: Plans, Suggestions, and Hints," 11 Sep. 1924, NCFR.

60. *CW,* 4 Oct. 1924, 47, 12 July 1924, 7, 1 Mar. 1924, 18.

61. *NYT,* 8 Sep. 1924, 24; *CW,* 18 Oct. 1924, 49, 1 Nov. 1924, inside front cover.

62. *NYT,* 25 Aug. 1924, 3, 8 Sep. 1924, 24; *CW,* 18 Oct. 1924, 49, 1 Nov. 1924, inside front cover; Harris-Emery Company, "Will You Take This Pledge," [1924], ser. II, LWVP.

63. *CW,* 1 Nov. 1924, inside front cover; 24.

64. *CW,* 21 Feb. 1925, 30.

65. *CW,* 6 Oct. 1928, 54, 30 Oct. 1926, 50, 3 Nov. 1928, 50, 22 Sep. 1928, 54.

66. Green, *The National Civic Federation and the American Labor Movement,* ix; minutes, 21st Annual Meeting of the NCF, 15–16 Feb. 1921, NCFR; minutes, 27th Annual Meeting of the NCF, 14–15 Dec. 1927, ibid.

67. RE to Elihu Root, 19 Feb. 1924, NCFR; *CW,* 10 Nov. 1928, 21; Robert Livingston Schuyler, ed. *Dictionary of American Biography,* vol. 11, Part 2 (New York: Charles Scribner's Sons, 1958), 276.

68. *Dictionary of American Biography,* vol. 11, Part 2, 166; RE to Herbert Hoover, 14 May 1924, RE to Will Hays, 26 Feb. 1924, NCFR.

69. Green, *The National Civic Federation and the American Labor Movement,* 65–66, 78; RE to BS, 18 July 1924, NCFR.

70. Remarks, Mrs. Arthur L. Livermore, 18 Apr. 1923; "Resolutions Emphasizing the Citizens' Duty to Participate in Party Organization Work," Apr. 1924; "The Citizen's Civic Responsibilities," [c. 1924]; press release, NCF, 9 June 1924; Haley Fiske to ABP, 6 July 1925; RE to William G. Shepherd, 26 Feb. 1924; RE to Elihu Root, 4 Oct. 1924, all in NCFR.

71. Green, *The National Civic Federation and the American Labor Movement,* 476; RE to Elihu Root, 4 Oct. 1924, NCFR; "The Citizen's Civic Responsibilities," [c. 1924], ibid.

72. *NYT,* 12 Sep. 1924, 3; and RE to Elihu Root, 4 Oct. 1924, ABP to Chambers of Commerce, 16 Aug. 1924, "The Citizen's Civic Responsibilities," [c. 1924], all in NCFR.

73. Marjorie Say to ABP, 22 Sep. 1924; C.V. Shoup to JHH, 15 Nov. 1924; W.S. Whitten to ABP, 20 Aug. 1924; Haley Fiske to ABP, 6 July 1925, all in NCFP.

74. RE to BS, 31 July 1924; Lora Harris Cook to ABP, 30 June 1924; Everett W. Hill to JHH, 21 Nov. 1924; Stockton Broome to ABP, 2 July 1924; Eugene M. Camp to NCF, 10 Sep. 1924; George L. Darte to RE, 11 Aug. 1924; F. Robertson Johns to RE, 26 June 1924, all in NCFR.

75. *NYT,* 9 Nov. 1924, 22.

76. ABP to Pres. of the Cleveland Chamber of Commerce, 8 Aug. 1924; press release, NCF, 9 June 1924; RE to BS, 18 July 1924, all in NCFR.

77. RE, "The Slacker Vote of 1924," [Nov. 1924], NCFR; *BAH,* 9 Nov. 1924, 5; proceedings, NCF Executive Council of the Department on Political Education, 6 Jan. 1926, NCFR.

78. Simon Guggenheim to RE, 28 Feb. 1925; ABP to chairs of Republican and Democratic committees, 10 Aug. 1925; RE to Sam A. Baker, 27 Feb. 1925, all in NCFR.

79. NCF to Robert Turnhill, [c. Jan. 1926]; mtg., Department on Political Education, "Afternoon Session," 29 Jan. 1926; Frank C. Cross to Peter J. Brady, 11 Jan. 1926; [member of the Exec. Committee of the NCF Department on Political Education] to ABP, 12 Mar. 1926; [JHH] to William Mahon, 27 July 1926, all in NCFR.

80. RE to managing editor, *Detroit Free Press,* 31 Dec. 1926; telegram, E.M. Martin to NCF, [c. 16 July 1926]; F.G. Blair to RE, 11 Aug. 1926; William M. Galvin to JHH, 3 Aug. 1926; Thomas F. McMahon to JHH, 10 Aug. 1926; M.J. Keough to JHH, 11 Aug. 1926; Harold Fields to ABP, 19 Jan. 1926; L.J. Tabor to JHH, 4 Aug. 1926; Seymour N. Sears to JHH, 12 July 1926; Theodore Burton to Peter J. Brady, 13 Jan. 1926; Emanuel Celler to ABP, 25 Jan. 1926; Albert R. Hall to Peter J. Brady, 9 Jan. 1926; Edward I. Edwards to ABP, 12 Jan. 1926; Franklin S. Billings to ABP, 11 Jan. 1926, all in NCFR.

81. Mtg., Executive Committee of the Department on Political Education, 20 Apr. 1926;

remarks of Matthew Woll, mtg., Department on Political Education, "Afternoon Session," 29 Jan. 1926, both in NCFR.

82. Press release, NCF, 3 Jan. 1927, ibid.

83. "Program of Department on Political Education," 19 Nov. 1926; "What did you do in the 1926 election?" [c. Nov. 1926]; *Wilmington (Del.?) News,* 4 Jan. 1927; press release, NCF, 3 Jan. 1927, all in NCFR.

84. JHH to J. Irving Walsh, 12 July 1927, J. Irving Walsh to Real Estate Boards, 15 July 1927, "To the National Organizations Cooperating with the Department on Political Education," Nov. 1927, Edith V. Alvord to Presidents of the General Federation of Women's Clubs, 28 Feb. 1927, all in NCFR; Lola Clark Pearson to Edith Alvord, 6 Aug. 1928, 25 Aug. 1928, Edith Vosburg Alvord Papers, Burton Historical Collection, Detroit Public Library, Detroit, Mich.; press release, NCF, 21 May 1928, NCFR.

85. Dorothy Culp, "The American Legion: A Study in Pressure Politics" (Ph.D. diss., University of Chicago, 1939), 1; *ALW,* 22 Apr. 1921, 8; remarks of Arthur Proctor, mtg., Department on Political Education, "Morning Session," 29 Jan. 1926, NCFR; Raymond Moley Jr., *The American Legion Story* (New York: Duell, Sloan and Pearce, 1966), 75; *ALW,* 22 Jan. 1926, 7; typescript, [Hanford MacNider?], [1924], Hanford MacNider Papers, HHPL; Culp, "The American Legion," 237; *ALW,* 10 Nov. 1922, 36–37, 2 Mar. 1923, 30; *ALM,* Apr. 1928, 5.

A few qualifications are in order with respect to the gender, class, and racial makeup of the Legion. Women who had served in the Armed Services were in fact invited to join. See *ALW,* 26 Aug. 1921, 13, 2 Sep. 1921, 24–25. Nonetheless, the vast majority of women who had a Legion affiliation belonged to the American Legion Auxiliary, the organization for wives, mothers, sisters, and daughters of Legionnaires. See *ALW,* 16 Apr. 1920, 5. The Legion Auxiliary also took up GOTV work, though not nearly on the scale of the Legion.

The Legion's middle-class identity was enshrined even in its constitution, the preamble to which contained a pledge to fight "the autocracy of both the classes and the masses." See Ruth Evelyn Kern, "The Political Policy and Activities of the American Legion, 1919–1925" (master's thesis, University of California, 1934), n.p., chapter 1.

The racial composition of the Legion was not exclusively white. Included in the total of 11,000 posts was the "all-Indian" Chief Peo Post in Pendleton, Oregon, and African American posts in Detroit; Philadelphia; Pittsburgh; Harrisburg; Albany; Atlantic City; Brooklyn; Boston; Norfolk; Charlotte; East Providence, Rhode Island; and Orange, New Jersey. See *ALM,* Nov. 1927, 47, Sep. 1926, 57; *Birmingham Reporter,* 3 May 1924, 1.

86. Moley, *The American Legion Story,* 126; *ALW,* 6 June 1924, 30–31, 24 Sep. 1920, 29–30; Culp, "The American Legion," 212–14; *ALW,* 30 Jan. 1920, 10; *ALM,* Jan. 1927, 22; Kern, "The Political Policy," n.p., chapter 1; Clarence R. Smith, comp. and ed., *The American Legion in New York State: A History of the Department of New York for the Years 1919–1939* (New York: American Legion Department of New York, 1942), 473–75; "Report of the National Americanism Commission to the Eighth National Convention," Oct. 1926, ALR; *ALM,* May 1928, 35.

Virtually every definition of "Americanism" that appeared in Legion materials was tautological, suggesting that real Americanism was so self-evident to them as to make explicit definition unnecessary. See *ALW,* 13 Feb. 1920, 10, 3 June 1921, 20; Smith, *The American Legion in New York State,* 473.

87. *ALM,* Oct. 1928, 71, Nov. 1926, 20–21.

88. *WN,* 18 Jan. 1924, ser. I, LWVP; Kern, "The Political Policy," n.p., chapter 6; *ALW,* 10 Oct. 1924, 10; *NYT,* 2 Sep. 1924, 1; remarks of J.A. Hall, "How to Get Out the Vote: Plans, Suggestions and Hints," 1924, NCFR; *ALW,* 15 Feb. 1924, 10–11; *Santa Ana (Calif.) Register,* 3 Nov. 1924, sec. 2, 11, 9.

89. Proceedings, National Americanism Commission, 11 May 1926; "Report of the National Americanism Commission to the Eighth National Convention of the American Legion," Oct. 1926, both in ALR.

90. Ibid.; "Tentative Draft of Proposed Declaration and Resolutions to be Presented to Each Joint Meeting called by the National Americanism Commission of the American Legion on Sep. 21, 1926," [1926], NCFR; proceedings, National Americanism Commission, 11 May 1926, ALR.

91. RE to Thomas S. Dysart, 6 Aug. 1926; Frank S. Land to JHH, 13 July 1926; Grace Brosseau to RE, 10 July 1926; Brosseau, "Message of the President-General, National Society, Daughters of the American Revolution," July 1926; JHH, "Program of Department on Political Education," 19 Nov. 1926; R.L. Wilbur to JHH, 7 July 1926, all in NCFR; "Report of the National Americanism Commission to the Eighth National Convention of the American Legion," Oct. 1926, ALR.

92. "Program of the Department on Political Education," 19 Nov. 1926; RE to Haley Fiske, 19 Oct. 1926, both in NCFR.

93. *ALM,* Nov. 1926, 49; mtg., Americanism Commission, 11 Jan. 1928, ALR; *ALM,* Feb. 1927, 37. Legion sources provide no firm estimate of the number of conferences that took place on or around Sep. 21. The Americanism Commission reported in Oct. 1926 that "hundreds" of Legion posts sponsored meetings in their communities. See "Report of the National Americanism Commission to the Eighth National Convention of the American Legion," Oct. 1926, ALR. Americanism Commission Director Frank Cross estimated elsewhere the number of meetings at between 1500 and 2000. See "Program of Department on Political Education, The National Civic Federation, In Conjunction with National Americanism Commission, The American Legion," [1926], NCFR. A Legion editorial numbered them in the "thousands." See *ALM,* Nov. 1926, 34.

94. "Report of the National Americanism Committee to the National American Legion Convention," Sep. 1927, ALR.

95. *ALM,* Oct. 1928, 71; mtg., Americanism Commission, 11 Jan. 1928, ALR; *ALM,* Sep. 1928, 36.

96. *ALM,* Dec. 1930, 37, Jan. 1953, 31, Nov. 1954, 32; mtg., Americanism Commission, 14 May 1929, ALR.

97. John Edgerton to LWV, 4 July 1924, [BS] to State LWV Presidents, 22 July 1926, both in MWPP; O.H. Blackman to Ann Webster, 2 June 1924, "Plan for Co-Operation with *Collier's* on Get-Out-the-Vote Campaign," [c. 1924], "The Get-Out-the-Vote Campaign as Reported by Mrs. Webster to the Board," [1924?], all in ser. II, LWVP; RE to BS, 18 July 1924, BS to RE, 24 July 1924, RE to BS, 31 July 1924, BS to RE, 5 Aug. 1924, RE to BS, 7 Aug. 1924, RE to BS, 8 Aug. 1924, RE to BS, 25 Aug. 1924, all in NCFR.

Chapter 4. "Good for At Least 100 Votes"

1. *GR Herald,* 9 Sep. 1924, 3; photograph, "Good Citizens Vote!" 1924, Dorothy Judd Papers, GRPL; *GR Herald,* 10 Sep. 1924, 3.

2. Chris McNickle, *To Be Mayor of New York: Ethnic Politics in the City* (New York: Columbia University Press, 1993), 33; *NYT*, 21 June 1926, 7; Theodore Lowi, *At the Pleasure of the Mayor: Patronage and Power in New York City, 1898–1958* (London: The Free Press, 1964), 197.

3. *NYT*, 22 Sep. 1926, 12.

4. N.Y. LWV, "Training in Citizenship," [c. 1924], ser. I, LWVP.

5. Smith, *The American Legion in New York State*, 175, 177; *ALM*, Oct. 1927, 80–81; "Statement Regarding the 'Get Out the Vote' Campaign of the New York Chapter of the Council of Jewish Women," 11 Sep. 1924; William J. McAuliffe to ABP, 25 Sep. 1924, both in NCFR; *WN*, 3 Oct. 1924, 24 Oct. 1924, ser. I, LWVP; *[Met Life] Daily Bulletin*, 3 Oct. 1924, MLL; *WN*, 22 July 1927, ser. I, LWVP; *NYT*, 5 Oct. 1924, 7; *WN*, 26 Sep. 1924, [unknown] to BS, 4 June 1923, *WN*, 25 Feb. 1927, 20 July 1928, 18 Apr. 1924, 12 Sep. 1924, 1 Oct. 1926, 24 Oct. 1924, all in ser. I, LWVP; Charles A. Hale to RE, 6 Oct. 1924, NCFR; N.Y. LWV, "Information on Candidates," 1925, ser. I, LWVP; *WN*, 21 Sep. 1928, ibid.; N.Y. LWV, reply to questionnaire, 1930, ser. II, LWVP; *WN*, 2 Oct. 1925, ser. I, LWVP; N.Y. LWV, "Correspondence Course on Citizenship for Women," [c. 1928], ser. II, LWVP.

6. E.L. Harvey to RE, 17 Sep. 1924, NCFR; Seymour N. Sears to JHH, 12 July 1926, ibid.; announcement, NAM, 21 Sep. 1926, ser. II, LWVP.

7. U.S. Bureau of the Census, *Fourteenth Census of the United States Taken in the Year 1920*, vol. 1 (Washington, D.C.: U.S. Government Printing Office, 1921), 320–21; ibid., vol. 3 (Washington, D.C.: U.S. Government Printing Office, 1922), 691, 702, 704; *Atlanta Constitution*, 4 Nov. 1924, 2; *NY Amsterdam News*, 10 Oct. 1928, 10.

8. *NYT*, 6 Oct.1924, 6.

9. *WN*, 3 July 1925, ser. I, LWVP.

10. *NYT*, 12 Sep. 1924, 3; "Organizations and Representatives at the National Civic Federation's Political Conference," [1924], "Also Attended Political Conference," [1924], "Organizations Represented at 'Get Out the Vote' Conference at Hotel Astor," [1924], all in NCFR.

11. Remarks of [Ida] Slack and Mr. Brown, "How to Get Out the Vote: Plans, Suggestions and Hints," [1924], NCFR; *WN*, 19 Sep. 1924, ser. I, LWVP; Eveline W. Brainerd to Anne Williams, 23 Sep. 1924, ser. II, ibid.; *WN*, 26 Sep. 1924, 12 Sep. 1924, ser. I, ibid.; *NYT*, 10 Oct. 1924, 7; *N.Y. Daily News*, 4 Nov. 1924, 2; *NYT*, 6 Oct. 1924, 5; press release, N.Y. LWV, Aug., 1924, ser. II, LWVP.

12. RE, "The Slacker Vote of 1924," [Nov. 1924], NCFR; *WN*, 4 July 1924, N.Y. LWV, "Working Kit, Get Out the Vote Campaign," 1924, N.Y. LWV, "Training in Citizenship," [c. 1924], all in ser. I, LWVP.

13. Mrs. Taylor N. Phillips, "Statement regarding the 'Get Out the Vote' Campaign of the NY Chapter of the Council of Jewish Women," 11 Sep. 1924, NCFR; William McAuliffe to ABP, 25 Sep. 1924, ibid.; [unknown] to BS, 4 June 1923, ser. I, LWVP; *WN*, 25 Apr. 1924, 26 Sep. 1924, 24 Oct. 1924, ibid.; Non-Partisan Coordinating Committee to editor, *NYT*, 10 Oct. 1924, 7.

14. *NYT*, 7 Oct. 1925, 4, 15 Sep. 1925, 24, 19 Oct. 1925, 24, 31 May 1925, sec. 9, 8, 29 Sep. 1925, 26; N.Y. LWV, "Information on Candidates," 1925, "Have You Registered?" [c. 1925], "Election Information for New York City Voters," 1925, *WN*, 2 Oct. 1925, 30 Oct. 1925, all in ser. I, LWVP.

15. *NYT*, 4 Oct. 1926, 2, RE to editor, 19 Sep. 1926, sec. 10, 14; "O." to RE, 18 Sep. 1926, NCFR; "Program of Department on Political Education," 19 Nov. 1926, ibid.; *NYT*,

13 Feb. 1927, sec. 2, 1; "HMB," 19 Oct. 1926, NCFR; remarks of James J. Walker, 21 Sep. 1926, ibid.; *NYT*, 22 Sep. 1926, 12.

16. "Program of Department on Political Education," 19 Nov. 1926, NCFR; *WN*, 8 Oct. 1926, 1 Oct. 1926, 10 Dec. 1926, ser. I, LWVP; *NYT*, 4 Feb. 1926, 2; *WN*, 1 Oct. 1926, 29 Oct. 1926, ser. I, LWVP.

17. Mtg., NYC Committee on Active Citizenship, 11 May 1927, NCFR; "Action Taken at Meeting of NYC Committee on Active Citizenship," 11 May 1927, ibid.; *NYT*, 13 Feb. 1927, sec. 2, 1; *WN*, 7 Oct. 1927, ser. I, LWVP; *NYT*, 7 July 1927, 24, 13 May 1927, 6, 10 July 1927, sec. 2, 12; *WN*, 25 Feb. 1927, ser. I, LWVP; *NYT*, 4 July 1927, 4. Other estimates for awardees range as low as eight thousand. See *WN*, 22 July 1927, ser. I, LWVP.

18. *NYT*, 5 July 1928, 1; Peter J. Brady to Sir or Madam, 9 Mar. 1928, NCFR; *ALM*, Jan. 1929, 37; Niblick to editor, *NYT*, 20 Sep. 1928, 28; *NYT*, 28 July 1928, 2; N.Y. LWV, "Correspondence Course on Citizenship for Women," [c. 1928], ser. II, LWVP; *NYT*, 31 Oct. 1928, 18.

19. *WN*, 30 Sep. 1927, ser. II, LWVP; Smith, *The American Legion in New York State*, 174; W.A. Scully to editor, *NYT*, 3 June 1928, sec. 3, 5.

20. *WN*, 5 Sep. 1924, 24 Oct. 1924, 3 Oct. 1924, ser. I, LWVP; *NYT*, 10 Oct. 1924, 7; *WN*, 10 Dec. 1926, 22 July 1927, 21 Sep. 1928, ser. I, LWVP.

21. *Jewish Daily News*, 3 Oct. 1924, [8], 3 Nov. 1924, [8], 1 Nov. 1926, n.p.; *ALM*, Oct. 1927, 80–81; *Jewish Daily News*, 25 Sep. 1924, [8]; *NYT*, 11 July 1927, 5.

22. *Irish World and American Industrial Liberator*, 20 Sep. 1924, 11, 6 Sep. 1924, 4, 13 Sep. 1924, 4, 1 Nov. 1924, 4, 6 Sep. 1924, 4; "Democratic Candidate is a Thorough Reactionary," *The Nation*, reprinted in ibid., 25 Oct. 1924, 2; *Irish World and American Industrial Liberator*, 20 Sep. 1924, 4.

23. *NY Amsterdam News*, 10 Oct. 1922, 2, 4, 10 Oct. 1928, 1, 10 Oct. 1923, n.p., 7 Nov. 1923, n.p., 3 Oct. 1923, n.p.

24. RE, "The Slacker Vote of 1924," [Nov. 1924], NCFR; *NYT*, 26 Apr. 1926, 5. See "Note on Method and Sources" for turnout calculations.

25. *Birmingham Reporter*, 19 Jan. 1924, 3.

26. *BAH*, 28 Sep. 1924, State News and Society sec., 5.

27. The Democratic party was the dominant political force in Birmingham in this period, as it was in most of the rest of the South. The fact that Herbert Hoover carried Jefferson county in the 1928 presidential election revealed the fissures that the nomination of Al Smith caused within the "Solid South." The Birmingham Chamber of Commerce openly endorsed Hoover, as did several of the city's leading citizens, among them James Bowron, a member of a prominent local business family, and Dr. James E. Dillard, pastor of the Southside Baptist Church. See typescript, "National 'Who's Who' Poll[,] Hoover Advocates[,] Alabama," [1928], Papers of the Campaign and Transition Period, 1928–1929, Papers of Herbert Hoover, HHPL. The election of 1928 notwithstanding, Birmingham was no Republican town. Indeed, some locals maintained that it was Klan opposition to Smith that put Jefferson county in the Republican column. See Blaine A. Brownell, "Birmingham, Alabama: New South City in the 1920s," *Journal of Southern History* 38 (Feb. 1972): 45–46. The fact that in 1928 Jefferson county was neither safely Democratic nor safely Republican—a seemingly competitive political situation, in which turnout could be crucial—had little bearing on the GOTV campaigns. Neither the Republican nor the Democratic parties participated in GOTV

in Birmingham in any meaningful way, and, in any case, Birmingham put on a large GOTV campaign in 1924, and only a relatively small one in 1928.

28. Brownell, "Birmingham," 22–28 (quote, 28).

29. Ibid. 25, 48; Birmingham Semi-Centennial Scrapbooks, [1921], BPL.

30. O.L. Bunn to ABP, 19 Aug. 1924, NCFR; *BAH,* 28 Sep. 1924, 6, 19 Oct. 1924, 10; Stockton Broome to ABP, 2 July 1924, NCFR; mtg., Birmingham Civitan Club, 1 Aug. 1924, Records of the Birmingham Civitan Club, BPL; *Birmingham* [published by the Birmingham Chamber of Commerce], Aug. 1926, 14, Dec. 1927, 7, June 1928, n.p.; *BAH,* 3 Nov. 1924, 1–2; Amelia Fisk to "Co-Worker," 29 Nov. 1924, ser. II, LWVP.

31. "Stencil No. 38," [1923], ser. I, LWVP; Watrous, *In League with Eleanor,* 17; Jefferson County LWV to Mary Anderson, 15 Dec. 1924, "Official Records, Women's Bureau," BPL; [Jeannette] Adams to "Secretary," 1 May 1926, ser. II, LWVP; *Birmingham,* Apr. 1925, n.p.; Mollie Dowd to Anne [Williams] Wheaton, 31 Aug. 1926, ser. II, LWVP.

32. [Gladys Harrison?] to Mollie Dowd, 24 May 1927, Assorted Correspondence; Ala. LWV, "News Bulletin," 26 Feb. 1923, ibid.; Ala. LWV, "Election Day Is November 4, 1924," [1924], ser. II, LWVP; *BAH,* 23 Jan. 1928, 4, 2 Nov. 1924, Society, Club, and Fashion sec., 5; tag, "Be A Good Citizen," [1924], ser. II, LWVP; [Amelia] Fisk to "Co-Worker," 29 Nov. 1924, ibid.; Amelia Fisk to BS, 20 Sep. 1924, ibid.; Mollie Dowd to Gladys Harrison, 30 June 1928, Assorted Correspondence; news clipping labeled "*BAH,* 13 July 1928," ibid.; Catherine McReynolds to Mollie Dowd, 2 Mar. 1928, ibid.; questionnaire reply, Ala. LWV, 1930, ser. II, LWVP; Ala. LWV, "Getting Out the Vote," 1924, ibid.

33. Amelia Fisk to [Ala.] Statewide Non-Partisan Committee, 26 Sep. 1924, ser. II, LWVP; Amelia Fisk to Ann Webster, 29 Aug. 1924, ibid.; *BAH,* 3 Oct. 1924, 2; Ala. LWV, "Getting Out the Vote," 1924, ser. II, LWVP; Amelia Fisk to "Co-Worker," 29 Nov. 1924, ibid.; typescript, Birmingham Business and Professional Women's Club, 24 Apr. 1925, Records of the Ala. Federation of Business and Professional Women's Clubs, BPL; *BAH,* 1 Oct. 1924, 7, 15 Oct. 1924, 7.

34. *Birmingham News,* 3 Nov. 1924, 8; Amelia Fisk to "Co-Worker," 29 Nov. 1924, ser. II, LWVP; *(Ala.) Legionnaire,* 20 Oct. 1928, 3; *BAH,* 3 Nov. 1924, 1–2; unlabeled news clipping, [c. 1927], Assorted Correspondence; National Council of Jewish Women, *[Proceedings of the] Eleventh Triennial Convention,* 1927, Appendix B, n.p., AJHS; *WC,* 1 Nov. 1924, 20.

The Birmingham press also noted national GOTV efforts, including the League's GOTV cartoon contest and Met Life's GOTV advertising campaign. See *BAH,* 28 Sep. 1924, 7, 19 Oct. 1924, 16.

35. *Birmingham Reporter,* 25 Oct. 1924, 6, 26 Jan. 1924, 4.

36. Ibid., 26 Jan. 1924, 4, 27 Feb. 1926, 1, 6 Mar. 1926, 4, 14 Aug. 1926, 4, 15 Mar. 1924, 7.

37. Mtg., Ala. Federation of Colored Women's Clubs, June 1927, Trammell Papers; *National Notes,* July 1926, 40.

38. *BAH,* 1 Oct. 1924, 7; mtg., Ala. Federation of Colored Women's Clubs, June 1929, Trammell Papers; *National Notes,* July 1926, 38; mtg., Ala. Federation of Colored Women's Clubs, June 1927, Trammell Papers.

39. *Labor Advocate,* 28 Jan. 1922, [1], 18 Oct. 1924, n.p., 12 Jan. 1924, [1].

40. *Labor Advocate,* 12 Jan. 1924, n.p., 19 Jan. 1924, n.p., 23 Oct. 1926, n.p., 13 Oct. 1928, [1].

41. Ala. LWV, "Citizenship School," Oct. 1924, Assorted Correspondence; Mrs. Neil

Wallace to [Helen] Rocca, 21 Oct. 1924, ibid.; *BAH,* 5 Oct. 1924, Society, Club, and Fashion sec., 5; Ala. LWV, "Five Easy Lessons in Citizenship," 1924, Assorted Correspondence.

42. "Election Statistics in Ala. by Counties," [c. 1924], ser. I, LWVP; Amelia Fisk to "Presidents" [of Ala. organizations], 1 Sep. 1924, ser. II, LWVP; *BAH,* 19 Oct. 1924, Society, Club, and Fashion sec., 3; Mrs. Neil Wallace to Gladys Harrison, 27 Dec. 1924, Assorted Correspondence; *Birmingham,* Aug. 1926, 14; *Birmingham News,* 3 Nov. 1924, 8.

43. *Birmingham News,* 4 Nov. 1924, 7, 12; Ala. LWV, "Citizenship School," Oct. 1924, Assorted Correspondence; *BAH,* 4 Nov. 1924, 8, 4; *Birmingham News,* 2 Nov. 1924, 11.

44. Amelia Fisk to "Co-Worker," 29 Nov. 1924, ser. II, LWVP. Turnout increased in 1920 in part because Alabama, recognizing that the poll tax deadline had passed before the Nineteenth Amendment was ratified, permitted women to vote that year without paying the tax first. See "Note on Method and Sources" for turnout calculations.

45. Amelia Fisk to "Co-Worker," 29 Nov. 1924, ser. II, LWVP.

46. *[GR Civic League] Sentinel,* Mar. 1926, GRPL.

47. GR LWV, *The First Fifty Years, 1921–1971,* 8–9; BS to Mrs. Craig C. Miller, 31 Mar. 1924, ser. II, LWVP.

48. Frank E. Ransom, *The City Built on Wood: A History of the Furniture Industry in Grand Rapids, Michigan, 1850–1950* (Ann Arbor: Edwards Brothers, 1950), 53; *GR Spectator,* 23 Apr. 1927, 12, GR Chamber of Commerce Records, BHL; U.S. Bureau of the Census, *Fifteenth Census of the Population,* vol. 2, *General Report Statistics by Subjects* (Washington, D.C.: Government Printing Office, 1933), 248–50; Jeffrey Kleiman, "The Great Strike: Religion, Labor and Reform in Grand Rapids, Michigan, 1890–1916" (Ph.D. thesis, Michigan State University, 1985), 41; *GR [Association of Commerce] Progress,* 1921, 14, minutes, GR Association of Commerce Board of Directors, 14 Dec. 1920, 12 Oct. 1926, *GR Progress,* 1922, 27, all at BHL.

49. Frank L. Dykema, "A Record of the Development of the Grand Rapids Americanization Society's Plan of Citizenship Training Through the Ballot," *Michigan History* 6 (1922): 160–65 (quote, 160); mtg., GR Citizens' League, 9 Aug. 1918, Papers of the GR Citizens' League, GRPL; *GR Spectator,* 3 Nov. 1928, GR Chamber of Commerce Records, BHL; *Furniture Manufacturer and Artisan,* July 1924, 18.

50. GR LWV, *First Fifty Years,* 9–10; *GR Herald,* 3 Sep. 1924, 5, 9 Sep. 1924, 3, 10 Sep. 1924, 3; postcard, GR LWV, [1924], ser. I, LWVP; mss., Mrs. Stephen W. Collins, 14 May 1925, Papers of the GR Federation of Women's Clubs, GRPL.

51. *GR Herald,* 4 Nov. 1924, 2, 3, 9 Sep. 1924, 2.

52. Mss., Helen [Dean?], 14 May 1925, Papers of the GR Federation of Women's Clubs, GRPL; mss., Mrs. Stephen W. Collins, 14 May 1925, GRPL; *GR Progress,* Oct. 1924, GRPL; *GR Herald,* 3 Nov. 1924, 3, 28 Sep. 1924, 5, 9 Sep. 1924, 1; *GR Chronicle,* 5 Sep. 1924, 2; mtg., GR Woman's Club, 28 Oct. 1924, Records of the GR Woman's Club, GRPL; *Furniture Manufacturer and Artisan,* July 1924, 18; *GR Herald,* 9 Sep. 1924, 1.

53. *GR Observer,* 13 Oct. 1924, n.p.; *GR Labor News,* 2 Nov. 1928, 4. The above citation is the only reference to GOTV in the Sep., Oct., and Nov. 1924 issues of the *GR Observer.* That newspaper terminated publication in May 1926 and the *GR Labor News* began publication soon thereafter. The above citation is also the only reference in the *GR Labor News* to GOTV work in 1928. The records of the local printers' union, the Typographical Union #39, held at the GRPL, and the records of the Trades and Labor Council of GR and

the papers of Edward A. Kosten, both at the BHL, likewise show no evidence of labor involvement in the GOTV campaigns.

A survey of possible work in the GOTV campaigns in communities of ethnic and racial minorities in Grand Rapids is tricky due to problems of source availability, but all available records indicate that there was no involvement. A search for GOTV graphics or reports in *Echo Tygodnioew [Polish Echo]*, Sep.–Oct. 1924 and Sep.–Nov. 1928, and the records of the GR Study Club (a middle-class African American ladies club) and the Pierian Club (the Study Club's junior affiliate) also showed no evidence of GOTV activity.

Neither *The Michigan Citizen* (the newspaper of the Mich. Democratic State Central Committee), 1920–1928, nor the Records of the Mich. Republican Party State Central Committee, both at the BHL, show any political party involvement in the campaigns.

54. *GR Spectator,* 16 June 1928, GR Chamber of Commerce Records, BHL; mtg., GR Woman's Club, 23 Oct. 1928, GRPL; GR LWV, "YOU MUST REGISTER THIS YEAR," ser. II, LWVP; GR LWV, *First Fifty Years,* 10; mtg., GR Civic Round Table, 21 Mar. 1928, Records of the GR Chamber of Commerce, BHL; mtg., GR Woman's Club, 30 Oct. 1928, GRPL; *Bulletin [of the] Mich. LWV,* June 1929, ser. I, LWVP.

55. Lee Bierce to JHH, 14 Nov. 1924, NCFR. Bierce does not explain where the seventy-five percent figure comes from, nor do the Association's records indicate a basis for this claim. See "Note on Method and Sources" for turnout calculations.

Chapter 5. The Expert Citizen

1. "Immigration Service Bureau," 8 May 1928; photo, "Class in American Language," [1925]; photo, "Welfare Division, Immigrant Service and Citizenship Bureau[,] English and Citizenship Class at District Office," [n.d.]; photo, "Administering Oath, County Court House, Norristown, PA," 1922; "How to Take Out Your Second Papers: An Easy Book in Plain English for the Coming Citizen," [c. 1929], all in MLL.

2. McGerr, *Decline of Popular Politics,* 69–106; Richard D. Brown, *The Strength of a People: The Idea of an Informed Citizenry in America, 1650–1870* (Chapel Hill: University of North Carolina Press, 1996), 69; Bessie Louise Pierce, *Citizens' Organizations and the Civic Training of Youth* (Chicago: Charles Scribner's Sons, 1933), 174, 237, 8, 17; Wiebe, *Self-Rule,* 178.

3. Hammond and Jenks, *Great American Issues,* 33.

4. BS, "'Educate' is Slogan of LWV," 25 July 1920, BSP; National Council of Jewish Women, *Eleventh Triennial Convention,* [n.p.], 1926, 197, AJHS; *CW,* 23 Aug. 1924, 18; *[U.S. Chamber of Commerce] Board of Directors Meetings 74–91, Executive Committee Meetings 26–30, May 10, 1923 to May 12, 1926,* ser. I, Chamber of Commerce of the United States Records; *Bulletin of the N.H. LWV,* Mar. 1928, ser. I, LWVP; MWP, *A Record of Four Years in the National LWV, 1920–1924,* MWPP.

5. *ALW,* 5 Aug. 1921, 11; N.Y. LWV, "Correspondence Course on Citizenship for Women," [c. 1928], ser. II, LWVP; National Council of Jewish Women, *Eleventh Triennial Convention,* 1927, 197, AJHS; "Know Your Party," [1923], ser. II, LWVP; *AI,* Nov. 1924, 5; "Report of the Get-Out-the-Vote Committee," [1926], ser. II, LWVP.

6. Typescript, [Ann Webster?], [c. 1924], ser. II, LWVP; F.G. Blair to RE, 11 Aug. 1926, NCFR; R.L. Wilbur to JHH, 7 July 1926, ibid.; *Bulletin [of the] Mich. LWV,* May 1929, ser. I, LWVP; Charles Lory to JHH, 7 June 1927, NCFR.

7. Mrs. Max Mayer, "Educated Citizenship Program Outlines," [c. 1924], ser. I, LWVP; [Minnie Fisher Cunningham] to State LWV Presidents, 26 July 1923, ibid.; *Washington Post,* 5 June 1923, MWPP.

8. *NYT,* 5 Oct. 1924, 7; remarks of Mrs. Charles Tiffany, [1924], NCFR; *GR Herald,* 3 Nov. 1924, 3; Marion Neprud to Anne Wheaton, 11 Aug. 1927, ser. II, LWVP; University of Virginia Department of Extension, "Institute of Citizenship and Government," 1923, ser. I, LWVP.

9. NAM, *Proceedings of the Twenty-Fifth Annual Convention,* 1920, 292, NAMR; *AI,* Oct. 1924, 12; *Birmingham,* Mar. 1928, [n.p.]; *Nation's Business,* Nov. 1925, 52.

10. *AI,* Oct. 1924, 6, 10–11; O.L. Stone to ABP, 19 June 1924, B.W. Grills to ABP, 27 Aug. 1924, NCFR; *NYT,* 7 Sep. 1924, sec. 1, 29; "O." to RE, 8 Sep. 1924, NCFR; *Ill. LWV Bulletin,* Dec. 1924, ser. II, LWVP.

11. "How to Take Out Your First Papers: An Easy Book in Plain English for the Coming Citizen," [c. 1929]; "Immigration Service Bureau," 8 May 1928; "Home Sweet Home," *The Metropolitan,* [c. 1923], 5; "Vote!" *The Metropolitan,* 1924, 2, all in Met Life Records, MLL.

12. Smith, *The American Legion in New York State,* 473–75 (quote, 473); Culp, "The American Legion," 210–14.

13. *ALW,* 16 July 1920, 3–4, 22 Jan. 1926, 7.

14. Ibid., 26 Aug. 1921, 13, 16 Apr. 1920, 5–6.

15. Ibid., 24 Mar. 1922, 7–8, 2 Apr. 1920, 17.

16. Ibid., 24 Sep. 1920, 29–30, 28 Oct. 1921, 18, 3 Apr. 1925, 9, 23 Apr. 1926, 8.

17. Ibid., 28 Oct. 1921, 18.

18. Ibid., 15 Sep. 1922, 13; *ALM,* May 1928, 35, Oct. 1928, 28.

19. Wheeler P. Bloodgood to RE, 7 Apr. 1924, NCFR; *AI,* June 1924, 9–12; Fred B. Ryons to JHH, 12 July 1926, NCFR; *[Met Life] Daily Bulletin,* 15 Sep. 1928, MLL; *ALW,* 12 June 1925, 17.

20. Resolution of the LWV in convention in 1920, quoted in Young, *In the Public Interest,* 41, n. 11; "Voters' Schools, Citizenship Schools and Other Education Meetings Reported by State and Local Leagues during the year ending Apr. 1, 1929," ser. II, LWVP.

21. Gladys Harrison to F. Perkins, 5 Nov. 1927, ser. II, LWVP; "The National League of Women Voters: What It Is and How It Came to Be," [c. 1927], collection 5539, Prints and Photographs Division, LC; "Educational Methods, 1920–1930," 1930, ser. I, LWVP.

22. Young, *In the Public Interest,* 38.

23. LWV resolution passed at 1920 convention, quoted in Young, *In the Public Interest,* 41, n. 11; Mrs. J. Paul Goode, "Thursday Morning Session: Teaching to Teach," [1923], ser. I, LWVP; Woman's City Club of Chicago and Ill. LWV, "Pre-Election School of Citizenship," 1924, ibid.; "Report of the Conference of Standing Center Chairmen and Heads of Departments," 21 Sep. 1923, ibid.; *WC,* 1 Nov. 1924, 20–21; Marion Neprud to Anne Wheaton, 11 Aug. 1927, ser. II, LWVP; University of Virginia Division of Extension, "Institute of Citizenship and Government," 1923, ser. I, LWVP.

24. "Details of Some State Plans," 18 Mar. 1924, ser. I, LWVP; "Get-Out-The-Vote Report presented to National Convention by Mrs. James Morrisson," 26 Apr. 1924, ser. II, ibid.; Eleanore Raoul to Anne Williams Wheaton, 6 Oct. 1926, ibid.

25. *WN,* 26 Sep. 1924, 24 Oct. 1924, 2 Oct. 1925, 5 Sep. 1924, 30 Oct. 1925, 1 Oct. 1926, 29 Oct. 1926, all in ser. I, LWVP.

26. *WN,* 28 Dec. 1928, ser. I, LWVP; "Address by Miss Belle Sherwin[,] Radio Program," 3 Jan. 1928, BSP; Isabel Doughty to Franklin D. Roosevelt, 12 Jan. 1928, FDR Papers Pertaining to the Election of 1928, FDRL.

27. May Wood-Simons, "Prospectus for Citizenship Schools, 1923–24," [c. 1923], ser. I, LWVP.

28. Mrs. Max Mayer, "Educated Citizenship Program Outlines," [c. 1924]; Conn. LWV, "One Day Citizenship School on Machinery of Government," [c. 1925]; Calif. LWV, "An Institute of Government and Politics," [c. 1925]; Ga. LWV, "Woman's Place is in the Home—But, Madam, Who Keeps Your Home?" [c. 1925], all in ser. I, LWVP.

29. These arguments echoed the different strands of the arguments for woman suffrage. See Aileen Kraditor, *Ideas of the Woman Suffrage Movement* (New York: Columbia University Press, 1965).

30. *CW*, 1 July 1922, 3, 25 Mar. 1922, 15; remarks of Ruth Farnum, mtg., "Morning Session," Dept. of Political Education, 29 Jan. 1926, NCFR.

31. "To the National Organizations Cooperating with The Department on Political Education of The National Civic Federation," Nov. 1927, NCFR.

32. *Open Shop Review*, July 1924, 259; *[Met Life] Daily Bulletin*, 3 Oct. 1924, MLL.

33. Young, *In the Public Interest*, 73, 45–46, 84; *AI*, Apr. 1924, 16; Kern, "The Political Policy," n.p., chapters 2 and 6; *AI*, June 1924, 23, 26; *CW*, 24 July 1920, 12; "Address by the Honorable Elihu Root," 20 Apr. 1926, NCFR.

34. Speech by MWP, June 1920, MWPP; unlabeled newspaper clipping, 22 Feb. 1920, ibid.; RE to William G. Shepherd, 26 Feb. 1924, NCFR.

35. *CW*, 10 July 1920, 12, 10 May 1924, 20; *ALM*, Nov. 1926, 34; *ALW*, 25 July 1919, 30.

36. RE to Elihu Root, 19 Feb. 1924, NCFR; mtg., New York members of the Executive Council, Department on Political Education, 6 Jan. 1926, ibid.

37. *CW*, 9 Sep. 1922, 8; press release, 9 June 1924, NCFR; NAM, *Proceedings of the Twenty-Ninth Annual Convention*, 1924, 119, NAMR.

38. *ALW*, 9 May 1924, 6; "Tentative Draft of Proposed Declaration and Resolutions," [1926], NCFR; *ALM*, Nov. 1926, 34; Young, *In the Public Interest*, 36–37.

39. "Why I Am a Democrat," [1924?], *[N.Y. Democratic State Committee] News Bulletin*, Feb. 1925, both in the FDR Papers, 1920–1928, FDRL.

40. Justina L. Wilson to Franklin D. Roosevelt, 12 Mar. 1924, FDR Papers, 1920–1928, FDRL; "Program [for] Practical Politics," Hays Papers.

41. *CW*, 10 May 1924, 20.

42. *National Notes*, July 1926, 3; Samuel Gompers, "51 PER CENT DO NOT VOTE!" [c. 1924], NCFR.

43. Robert Wiebe argues suggestively that some progressives "tolerated" the exclusion of workers from civic life. See *Self-Rule*, 164.

44. Merriam and Gosnell, *Non-Voting*, 184, 223, 188, 193.

Chapter 6. The Methods of Wrigley and Barnum

1. McGerr, *Decline of Popular Politics*, 138–183.

2. T.J. Jackson Lears, "From Salvation to Self-Realization: Advertising and the Therapeutic Roots of the Consumer Culture, 1880–1930," in Fox and Lears, eds., *The Culture of Consumption*, 3–4; Warren I. Susman, *Culture as History: The Transformation of American Society in the Twentieth Century* (New York: Pantheon Books, 1984), xxii; Marchand, *Advertis-*

ing the American Dream, 9; Lizabeth Cohen, A Consumers' Republic: The Politics of Mass Consumption in Postwar America (New York: Alfred A. Knopf, 2003).

3. Marchand, Advertising the American Dream, 2, 269–74; Frederick Lewis Allen, Only Yesterday: An Informal History of the 1920s (New York: Harper and Row, 1964), 136; Kathy Reiss, Hope in a Jar: The Making of America's Beauty Culture (New York: Metropolitan Books, 1998).

4. Richard Koszarski, An Evening's Entertainment: The Age of the Silent Feature Picture, 1915–1928, History of American Cinema, vol. 3 (New York: Charles Scribner's Sons, 1990), 26; Lizabeth Cohen, Making a New Deal, 120–25.

5. Allen, Only Yesterday, 64–66, 137; Cohen, Making a New Deal, 139–40.

6. Lynd and Lynd, Middletown, 231–40; Allen, Only Yesterday, 83–84.

7. Marchand, Advertising the American Dream, 59; Allen, Only Yesterday, 157.

8. Marchand, Advertising the American Dream, 6–7.

9. George Leach to Minnie Fisher Cunningham, 15 Aug. 1923, ser. I, LWVP.

10. T.J. Jackson Lears, Fables of Abundance: A Cultural History of Advertising (New York: Basic Books, 1994), 137–39, 12.

11. Ronald R. Kline, Consumers in the Country: Technology and Social Change in Rural America (Baltimore: Johns Hopkins University Press, 2000), 281, 75, 53; Lizabeth Cohen, "The Class Experience of Mass Consumption: Workers as Consumers in Interwar America," in The Power of Culture: Critical Essays in American History, eds. Richard Wightman Fox and T.J. Jackson Lears (Chicago: University of Chicago Press, 1993), 139–40.

12. Susan Porter Benson, Counter Cultures: Saleswoman, Managers, and Customers in American Department Stores, 1890–1940 (Urbana: University of Illinois Press, 1986), 83.

13. Marchand, Advertising the American Dream, 80, 189, 193, 169.

14. WN, 20 Nov. 1925, ser. I, LWVP; WC, 28 June 1924, 21; remarks of J.A. Hall, "How to Get Out the Vote: Plans, Suggestions and Hints," 11 Sep. 1924, NCFR.

15. "All About Milk," [1910s], "Teeth, Tonsils, and Adenoids," [1910s], both in Lee Kaufer Frankel Papers, AJHS; "Every Resident a Citizen: Why Not?" 192[2], "Your Non-Citizen Neighbor: a Civic Opportunity," [192?], MLL; Met Life, An Adventure in Advertising, n.p., [c. 1924], ibid.

16. Ibid.; Saturday Evening Post, 25 Oct. 1924, 104; CW, 25 Oct. 1924, 3; remarks of Frederick H. Ecker, mtg., Coordinating Council on Getting Out the Vote, 22 Sep. 1924, NCFR.

17. CW, 27 Oct. 1928, 23; Saturday Evening Post, 27 Oct. 1928, 138; Home Office [Met Life in-house publication for employees], Oct. 1928, inside front cover, MLL.

18. CW, 2 Aug. 1924, 18, 1 Mar. 1924, 3, 12 July 1924, 7.

19. Ibid., 4 Oct. 1924, 47, 11 Oct. 1924, 18, 18 Oct. 1924, 49, 1 Nov. 1924, inside front cover.

20. Ibid., 11 Oct. 1924, 18, 18 Oct. 1924, 49.

21. Ibid.; NYT, 8 Sep. 1924, 24; CW, 11 Oct. 1924, 18.

22. Ibid., 18 Oct. 1924, 49.

23. Ibid.; CW, 1 Nov. 1924, inside front cover.

24. Ibid., 10 Sep. 1921, 17, 25 Aug. 1923, 18, 17 Nov. 1923, 8.

25. Ibid., 10 Sep. 1927, 39.

26. Ben Hapgood to JHH, 14 Nov. 1924, NCFR; Bulletin of the Ill. LWV, Nov. 1926, ser. I, LWVP; Winfield Clearwater to JHH, 19 Nov. 1924, Harry W. Luethi to ABP, 18

Aug. 1924, Roscoe Ady to JHH, 17 Nov. 1924, J.C. Richards to JHH, 14 Nov. 1924, all in NCFR.

27. *(St. Louis) League Bulletin,* 22 Sep. 1924, ser. I, LWVP; V.V. Mayer to Minnie Fisher Cunningham, 1 July 1924, ser. II, LWVP; Eleanore Raoul to Anne Williams Wheaton, 6 Oct. 1926, ibid.; *WC,* 20 Sep. 1924, 21; *WN,* 18 July 1924, 21 Sep. 1928, ser. I, LWVP; *Bulletin of the Ill. LWV,* Nov. 1926, ibid.; *Nation's Business,* Nov. 1924, 84; Mrs. O.A. Critchett, "El Paso LWV Get Out the Vote Campaign," n.d., ser. II, LWVP; "Details of Some State Plans," 18 Mar. 1924, ser. I, LWVP; Julia Lathrop, "The Game of 'Get Out The Vote,'" [c. 1924], ibid.

28. Eleanore Raoul to Anne Williams Wheaton, 6 Oct. 1926, ser. II, LWVP; *[Minn.] Woman Voter,* 29 Oct. 1924, 1, ser. I, LWVP; *WC,* 12 July 1924, 21.

29. "Suggested Plan for State Leagues in Efficient Citizenship Campaign," 18 Mar. 1924, ser. I, LWVP; *(St. Louis) League Bulletin,* 22 Sep. 1924, ibid.; *Bulletin of the Ill. LWV,* Nov. 1926, ibid.; *[N.J. LWV and N.J. State Federation of Women's Clubs] Civic Pilot,* Oct. 1924, 14, ibid.; Va. LWV, "Get out the Vote Committee and Campaign," [1924], ser. II, LWVP; *WC,* 1 Nov. 1924, 20, 6 Sep. 1924, 21, 9 Aug. 1924, 21, 20 Sep. 1924, 21.

30. Political cartoon, J.N. "Ding" Darling, "It's a Wonder There Aren't More Serious Accidents," *Des Moines Register,* 12 Oct. 1924, ser. II, LWVP.

31. *CW,* 6 Sep. 1924, 18.

32. *AI,* Nov. 1924, 7; *Indianapolis News,* 30 Oct. 1924, *Norwalk (Calif.) Call,* 24 Jan. 1924, *Lincoln (Neb.) Journal,* 23 Jan. 1924, *St. Paul (Minn.) Pioneer-Press,* 22 Jan. 1924, all in Hays Papers; Sidney Cohen to Ruth Kimball Gardiner, 5 Jan. 1924, ser. II, LWVP.

33. *AI,* Oct. 1924, 6; *(Conn.) Woman Voter's Bulletin,* May 1926, ser. I, LWVP; Eleanore Raoul to Anne Williams Wheaton, 6 Oct. 1926, ser. II, LWVP; [Gladys Harrison] to Regional Directors, 15 Sep. 1927, ibid.; Marion Neprud to Anne Wheaton, 11 Aug. 1927, ibid.; *WN,* 16 Sep. 1927, ser. I, LWVP; *WC,* 6 Sep. 1924, 21; *Bulletin of the Ill. LWV,* Nov. 1926, ser. I, LWVP; *WN,* 3 Oct. 1924, ibid.; *NYT,* 12 Sep. 1924, 3; *Bulletin of the Ill. LWV,* Dec. 1924, ser. II, LWVP; "Get-Out-The-Vote Report presented to National Convention by Mrs. James Morrisson," 26 Apr. 1924, ser. I, LWVP; *(St. Louis) League Bulletin,* 22 Sep. 1924, ibid.; "Analysis of Entries for Award of the Silver Cup[,] 1928," Feb. 1929, ser. II, LWVP.

34. *AI,* Oct. 1924, 6; *NYT,* 31 Oct. 1924, 3; "O." [secretary] to RE, 18 Sep. 1926, NCFR; remarks of John B. Kennedy, "How to Get Out the Vote: Plans, Suggestions and Hints," 11 Sep. 1924, ibid.

35. [Mo. LWV?], "LWV Radio School," [1928], ser. II, LWVP.

36. Milwaukee County LWV, "Milwaukee Women Organize Drive to Increase Use of Ballot," [c. 1926], ser. II, LWVP.

37. Va. LWV, "Get out the vote committee and Campaign," [1924], ser. II, LWVP; *Nation's Business,* Nov. 1924, 84; *[N.J. LWV and N.J. State Federation of Women's Clubs] Civic Pilot,* Oct. 1924, 14, ser. I, LWVP; *BAH,* 23 Jan. 1928, 4; remarks of John B. Kennedy, "How to Get Out the Vote: Plans, Suggestions and Hints," 11 Sep. 1924, NCFR; *WN,* 19 Sep. 1924, ser. I, LWVP; *[N.J. LWV] Civic Pilot,* Oct. 1928, 16, ibid.; *Nation's Business,* May 1928, 116.

38. *WN,* 3 Oct. 1924, 2 Oct. 1925, 2 Nov. 1928, ser. II, LWVP; questionnaire reply, N.Y. LWV, 1930, ibid.; *[N.J. LWV] Civic Pilot,* Oct. 1924, 15, 20, Oct. 1928, 16, ser. I, LWVP.

39. *WC,* 18 Oct. 1924, 21; Eleanore Raoul to Anne Williams Wheaton, 6 Oct. 1926, ser. II, LWVP; *WN,* 5 Sep. 1924, ibid.; *(Conn.) Woman Voters' Bulletin,* May 1926, ser. I, LWVP; *(Ind.) Woman Voter,* Nov. 1924, ibid.

40. William R. Leach, "Transformations in a Culture of Consumption: Women and Department Stores, 1890–1925," *Journal of American History* 71 (Sep. 1984): 325; *WC,* 6 Sep. 1924, 21; *NYT,* 10 Oct. 1924, 7.

41. McGerr, *Decline of Popular Politics,* 138–183; Richard Jensen, "Armies, Admen, and Crusaders: Types of Presidential Election Campaigns," *History Teacher* 2 (1969): 33–50; Robert J. Dinkin, *Campaigning in America: A History of Election Practices* (New York: Greenwood Press, 1989), 95–157.

42. Blair quoted in Edward L. Bernays, *Propaganda* (New York: Horace Liveright, 1928), 95; RNC, "How to Win a Vote for Hoover," [1928], Papers of the Campaign and Transition Period, HHPL; RNC, "Does He Think We Are a Nation of Fools?" [c. 1924], James Irving Clarke Papers, Department of Manuscripts and University Archives, Cornell University, Ithaca, N.Y.

43. Film, "Master of Emergencies," Will Irwin, arrangement and titles, 1928, HHPL; press release, Hoover-Curtis Campaign Committee, 2 Nov. 1928, Edward Anthony Collection, ibid.; press release, Young Republican Club Campaign Committee, 15 Oct. 1928, Papers of the Campaign and Transition Period, ibid.; press release, Emily Marx Campaign Committee, 27 May 1928, ibid.

44. Photo, Underwood and Underwood, "Elephant and Donkey in Luna Park, Coney Island," Prints and Photographs Division, LC; *The Star,* 17 Oct. 1924, Franklin D. Roosevelt Papers Pertaining to the Campaign of 1924, FDRL.

45. Leach, "Transformations in a Culture of Consumption," 338–39.

46. Creel, *How We Advertised America,* 7–8, quote on p. 4.

47. *St. Louis Post-Dispatch,* 4 Nov. 1924, 1; Kelly, *Election Day,* 195, 187–88.

48. *Emporia (Kans.) Daily Gazette,* 3 Nov. 1924, 10; *GR Press,* 6 Nov. 1928, 10; *Atlanta Constitution,* 5 Nov. 1928, 12; *St. Louis Post-Dispatch,* 4 Nov. 1924, 17; *Denver Post,* 4 Nov. 1924, 10; *BAH,* 3 Nov. 1924, 12, 6 Nov. 1928, 10; *Steuben (N.Y.) Courier,* 2 Nov. 1928, 19; *NY Herald Tribune,* 6 Nov. 1928, 18; *Boston Globe,* 6 Nov. 1928, 6; *San Francisco Chronicle,* 4 Nov. 1924, 9; *NY Daily News,* 4 Nov. 1924, 21; *Kansas City (Mo.) Star,* 4 Nov. 1924, 12.

49. *NY Daily News,* 4 Nov. 1924, 18, 21; *Kansas City (Mo.) Star,* 3 Nov. 1924, 13; *San Francisco Chronicle,* 4 Nov. 1924, 9.

50. *GR Herald,* 5 Nov. 1924, 3, 4 Nov. 1924, 1; *BAH,* 4 Nov. 1924, 18. See also "90-Year-Old Voter," *NYT,* 24 July 1927, 14; "Dies in Registration Place," *NYT,* 14 Oct. 1928, 4; "Crippled Girl Will Vote," *NYT,* 4 Nov. 1928, 26; "Oldest Voter," *Irish World and American Industrial Liberator,* 10 Nov. 1928, 1.

51. *Machinists Monthly Journal,* Feb. 1924, 91, ser. II, LWVP; Barton quoted in Marchand, *Advertising the American Dream,* 30.

52. Finnegan, *Selling Suffrage,* passim.

53. *Ill. LWV Bulletin,* Sep.–Oct. 1924, 41, ser. I, LWVP; [Ga. LWV] *Pilgrim,* Sep. 1926, 8, ibid.; [Kans. LWV] *Progress,* Sep. 1924, back cover, ibid.; program, NLWV Second Annual Convention, 1921, MWPP.

54. *Emporia (Kans.) Daily Gazette,* 3 Nov. 1924, 7; *Richmond (Va.) Times-Dispatch,* 6 Nov.

1924, 3, 4 Nov. 1924, 7; *NY Herald-Tribune,* 1 Nov. 1926, [page numbers not displayed on microfilm copy]; *Birmingham News,* 4 Nov. 1928, 8; *N.Y. Daily News,* 3 Nov. 1924, 11, 2 Nov. 1924, 5, 4 Nov. 1924, 5; *Kansas City (Mo.) Star,* 4 Nov. 1924, 8.

55. *NY Daily News,* 2. Nov. 1924, 46; *CW,* 30 Oct. 1920, 35.

56. Ibid., 19 May 1923, 5. Henry Ford won in a landslide. See *CW,* 14 July 1923, 5.

57. Marchand, *Advertising the American Dream,* 64; political cartoon, Dorman H. Smith, "A Thing of Beauty Should Be a Joy Forever," *Muncie (Ind.) Evening Press,* 29 Sep. 1924, 4.

58. Henry E. Jackson to editor, *NYT,* 13 Aug. 1924, 14; *Anaconda (Mont.) Standard* quoted in *AI,* Oct. 1924, 18; Conrad Shearer to JHH, 17 Nov. 1924, NCFR.

59. *GR Herald,* 9 Sep. 1924, 1.

A NOTE ON METHOD AND SOURCES

This bibliographic essay highlights the primary and secondary sources upon which I relied most heavily. It is intended to complement the endnotes, which are largely limited to primary sources.

Calculating Turnout

All turnout figures are for presidential elections. Turnout for other offices or for off-year elections was usually lower.

Voter turnout is the ratio between the number of ballots cast (numerator) and the number of eligible voters (denominator). Though the definition is straightforward, calculating voter turnout with precision is difficult, above all because it is difficult to ascertain accurately the number of eligible voters. Most elections do not coincide with federal census years, making population figures imprecise. Eligibility requirements varied from state to state, within states, and changed over time. Especially between 1840 and 1910, many states allowed immigrants to vote if they had begun the process of naturalization by taking out first papers. Women were enfranchised incrementally and acquired presidential suffrage in a number of states before the Nineteenth Amendment was ratified. Many states imposed different residency requirements on voters in urban and rural areas or exempted rural residents altogether. Literacy tests, applied at a registrar's discretion, disenfranchised by race and class as much as by the ability to read and write, rendering ineligible people who were constitutionally enfranchised. These complexities and others are amply documented in the appendix to Alexander Keyssar, *The Right to Vote: The Contested History of Democracy in the United States* (New York: Basic Books, 2000), 325–401.

Despite the difficulties, very careful estimates exist for the years through 1968 in the work of Walter Dean Burnham. See U.S. Bureau of the Census, *Historical Statistics of the United States,* Part II (Washington, D.C.: U.S. Government Printing Office, 1975), 1067–68, 1071–72, the figures for which were prepared by Burnham.

The best available figures for the period after 1968 were calculated on a different basis. For the years 1972 through 1992, I have used the U.S. Census Bureau's *Statistical Abstract Online,* table 458, which can be accessed at http://www.census.gov/prod/www/statistical-abstract-us.html. For the 1996 and 2000 elections, I have used figures prepared by Curtis Gans of the Committee for the Study of the American Electorate published in the *Washington Post,* 9 November 2000, A35. These sources define the number of eligible voters as the voting-age population and apparently do not take into account factors such as the millions of non-citizen immigrants living within U.S. borders, or policies of criminal disenfranchisement, which today render ineligible about fourteen percent of the nation's African American men and nearly a third of African American men in Florida and Alabama. See Keyssar, *The Right to Vote,* 308.

The turnout calculations for the case study cities reflect the availability of published census and election data. In each case, I used the 1920 population figures for the 1920 and 1924 calculations and the 1930 figures for the 1928 calculation. Since the population of all three case study areas grew between 1920 and 1930, this practice overestimates turnout in 1924 and underestimates it in 1928.

For New York City, the base figures were drawn from the U.S. Bureau of the Census, *Fourteenth Census of the United States Taken in the Year 1920,* vol. 3 (Washington, D.C.: Government Printing Office, 1922), 691; U.S. Bureau of the Census, *Fifteenth Census of the United States,* vol. 3 (Washington, D.C.: Government Printing Office, 1932), 290; James Malcolm, ed., *The New York Red Book* (Albany: J. B. Lyon Company, 1921), 530; the 1925 edition, 510; the 1929 edition, 365.

The numerator is the presidential vote in 1920, 1924, and 1928 for the five counties that comprise New York City. According to Keyssar, *The Right to Vote,* Table A12, the state of New York required voters to have been citizens for at least ninety days. To approximate that number, the denominator is the population of native-born whites, naturalized foreign-born whites, and "Negroes" in New York City 21 years of age and over for 1920 and 1930. Using these figures, turnout in New

York City was 52.5 percent in 1920, 57.6 percent in 1924, and 55.8 percent in 1928.

These data have certain biases. The use of 1930 population figures for the 1928 calculation helps to explain the absence of an increase in voter turnout in the city in 1928, a year in which national turnout increased, a fact that is attributed to Al Smith's candidacy and that likely boosted turnout in Smith's home city. Furthermore, the census tables separate whites but not "Negroes" into native-born, naturalized, and alien categories, so these calculations overestimate the number of African Americans eligible to vote by including, for example, significant numbers of non-naturalized immigrants from the Caribbean.

For the Birmingham case study, the base figures are drawn from the U.S. Bureau of the Census, *Fourteenth Census,* vol. 3, 62, 66 and *Fifteenth Census,* vol. 3, 101, 109. The number of ballots cast comes from Marie B. Owen, comp., *Alabama Official and Statistical Register* (Montgomery: Brown Printing Company, 1923), 355; the 1927 edition, 345; and the 1931 edition, 512.

The numerator in this case is the vote from Jefferson County for presidential electors in the general elections of 1920, 1924, and 1928. Birmingham constituted between 58 and 60 percent of the county population throughout this period. The denominator is the sum of native-born whites, foreign-born whites who were naturalized, and "Negro[es]" in Jefferson county 21 years of age and over for 1920 and 1930. Using these figures, turnout in Jefferson county was 19.0 percent in 1920, 13.7 percent in 1924, and 13.9 percent in 1928. Though presidential races and general elections in the South in this period did not necessarily draw the largest number of voters, I have retained the convention of using results from these races to keep the comparisons consistent.

The base figures for the Grand Rapids case study come from the U.S. Bureau of the Census, *Fourteenth Census,* vol. 3, 484; *Fifteenth Census,* vol. 3, 1137; Michigan Secretary of State, comp., *Michigan Official Directory and Legislative Manual* (Lansing: n.p., 1920, 318); the 1921 edition, 637; the 1925 edition, 386; the 1929 edition, 412; the 1931 edition, 154.

The numerator in this case is the presidential vote for Kent County in 1920, 1924, and 1928. The denominator is the number of native-born whites, naturalized whites, and "Negroes" in Kent County, 21 years of age and over. Between 1920 and 1930, the population of Grand Rapids constituted between 70 and 75 percent of the county population. Using these figures, turnout in Kent County was 58.6 percent in 1920, 59.4 percent in 1924, and 54.5 percent in 1928.

Primary Sources: National Get-Out-the-Vote Campaigns

The analysis of the GOTV campaigns rests upon group and individual correspondence; organizations' records and publications; large-circulation newspapers and magazines; and the records and correspondence of the major political parties. Both the presence and the absence of evidence in these sources is telling, for they indicate both who participated in the campaigns and who did not.

The GOTV activities of the League of Women Voters are extensively documented in the League of Women Voters Papers in the Manuscript Division at the Library of Congress. Many of the relevant records can be found in the files of the "Efficiency in Government" committee, but GOTV work permeated the League, and documentation of it is found throughout the collection. The extensive holdings here of reports and printed matter by state and local Leagues permitted an analysis of the ways the GOTV campaigns played out in local contexts. LWV correspondence files also documented extensive GOTV work by other groups.

League records can also be found in the Maud Wood Park Papers, the Belle Sherwin Papers, the Edna Lamprey Stantial Papers, and the Edna Fischel Gellhorn Papers at the Arthur and Elizabeth Schlesinger Library on the History of Women in America, Radcliffe Institute for Advanced Study, Harvard University, Cambridge, Mass. Portions of these collections duplicate the more extensive holdings of the Library of Congress.

The *Woman Citizen* likewise documents League activities in this period. This magazine once served as the official organ of the National American Woman Suffrage Association and its successor, the National League of Women Voters; in 1921, the League began simply to buy pages in each issue. The magazine was renamed the *Woman's Journal* in 1928.

The papers of the National Association of Manufacturers are held at the Hagley Museum and Library, Wilmington, Del. Organization records for the 1920s are thin, as many were destroyed in a fire. Convention proceedings, cataloged separately in the Imprints Collection, helped fill in the gaps. The NAM monthly magazine, which was entitled *American Industries* for most of the decade, with brief incarnations as *American Industries/Pocket Bulletin* and *Pocket Bulletin,* was a rich resource.

For information about *Collier's* GOTV campaign I relied upon *Collier's Weekly.* Though the Crowell-Collier Publishing Co. records at the New York Public Library do not contain materials relevant to this study, correspondence from *Collier's* editors and minutes from GOTV meetings attended by *Collier's* representatives can be found in the papers of other GOTV groups.

The records of the National Civic Federation at the New York Public Library contain extensive documentation of the GOTV campaigns. Information pertaining to GOTV can be found throughout the general correspondence files, but the richest cache of records is found in the files of the Department on Political Education. Also useful are the records of annual meetings, executive committee meetings, and the New York Committee on Active Citizenship. John Hays Hammond's *Autobiography* (New York: Farrar and Rinehart, Inc., 1935) contains pertinent discussions, as does Hammond's and Jeremiah W. Jenks, *Great American Issues: Political, Social, and Economic* (New York: Charles Scribner's Sons, 1923).

The records of the American Legion are held at the American Legion Library in Indianapolis, Ind. The report files, subject files, Americanism Commission minutes, Department (state) convention proceedings, and Department newspapers and bulletins all proved valuable. The American Legion also published reports of GOTV activity in the *American Legion Weekly* (1919–1926) and then the *American Legion Monthly*.

Primary Sources: Political Parties

An extensive review of political party records shows that GOTV groups made the parties aware of their activities but that the national parties did not participate in the campaigns. National political party records in this time period are scattered; the best concentrations can be found in the papers of the party's presidential nominees and party chairmen. David Burner notes in *The Politics of Provincialism: The Democratic Party in Transition, 1918–1932* (Cambridge: Harvard University Press, 1986), 143, n. 2, that many Democratic Party records from the 1920s were destroyed. I consulted much of what remains, in particular the Franklin D. Roosevelt (FDR) Papers, 1920–1928; the FDR Papers Pertaining to the Campaigns of 1924 and 1928; the Eleanor Roosevelt Papers, especially the speech and article file; and the Democratic National Committee (DNC) Papers, 1928–1948, all at the Franklin D. Roosevelt Presidential Library in Hyde Park, N.Y. Also pertinent were the papers of James Cox and of DNC chairman George White at the Ohio Historical Society. The Papers of Cordell Hull at the Library of Congress deal with his service as secretary of state rather than as DNC chair. Records from DNC Chair Clement Shaver are very limited and can be found in these other collections. The papers of DNC Chair John Raskob are located at the Hagley Museum.

For the Republican party, I examined several collections at the Herbert Hoover Presidential Library, in particular the Campaign and Transition Papers, 1928–1929; the Nathan MacChesney Papers; the Hanford MacNider Papers; and the Edward Anthony Collection and oral history. Also relevant were the Warren G. Harding Papers at the Ohio Historical Society; the papers of Calvin Coolidge at the Library of Congress; the papers of Will H. Hays at the Indiana State Library in Indianapolis, in particular the scrapbook collection; the microfilmed *Will Hays Papers* (Frederick, Md.: University Publications of America, 1986); the microfilmed *Papers of the Republican Party,* Part I, Meetings of the RNC, 1911–1980, Douglas D. Newman, comp. (Frederick, Md.: University Publications of America, 1986); and uncataloged papers of the Republican National Committee (RNC) at the National Archives, Washington, D.C.

The activities of Progressive candidate Robert M. La Follette Sr. are documented in the La Follette Family Collection in the Manuscript Division of the Library of Congress. Particularly useful were the special correspondence files and speeches and writings files of the Robert M. La Follette Sr. Papers and the papers of Alfred Thomas Rogers, a La Follette political advisor and RNC member.

Primary Sources: Case Study Cities

GOTV campaigns in the case study cities were richly documented not only in the files of national organizations, but also in the records and publications left by local groups, chapters, and organizers.

The New York City case study relied upon the files of the Non-Partisan Co-ordinating Committee, the main GOTV organizer in the city, which are housed in the NCF Records at the New York Public Library. Other useful collections include the records of the Advertising Women of New York at the Schlesinger Library and the run of *The Empire Legionnaire* at the American Legion Library in Indianapolis. The *New York Times,* the *New York Daily News,* the *New York Amsterdam News,* the *Irish World and Industrial Liberator,* and the *Jewish Daily News* all helped document the presence and absence of the GOTV campaigns in various communities in the city.

For the Birmingham case study, the Linn-Henley Research Library at the Birmingham Public Library is home to a host of collections relevant to this study. Most important were the papers of suffragist and League leader Pattie Ruffner Jacobs, the papers of community leader Rabbi Morris Newfield, the records of the League of Women Voters of Birmingham, the microfilmed Assorted Correspondence of the LWV of Birmingham, the records of the Birmingham Civitan Club, the City Commission Scrapbooks, the records of the Birmingham Unit #1 American Legion Auxiliary, the records of the Birmingham Rotary Club, the records of the Alabama Federation of Business and Professional Women's Clubs, and the Hill Ferguson collection. The papers of RNC member Oliver Day Street at the Alabama Department of Archives and History in Montgomery contain Street's correspondence with Republican leaders, including Will Hays and Herbert Hoover. The Mattie Rivers Trammell Papers at Savery Library, Talledega College, Talledega, Alabama, contain minutes and programs from annual meetings of the Alabama Federation of Colored Women's Clubs. The *Birmingham Age-Herald* and the *Birmingham News* were the city's largest-circulation daily newspapers. The *Birmingham Reporter* was published weekly and served the city's African American community; runs can be found at the Birmingham Public Library and the State of Alabama Department of Archives and History in Montgomery. *Birmingham* was published by the city's Chamber of Commerce and is available at the Birmingham Public Library. The *Labor Advocate,* which was published by the Birmingham Trades Council, can be found at the Birmingham Public Library and on microfilm. The *Alabama Legionnaire* is available at the American Legion Library in Indianapolis.

The Grand Rapids case study also relied on manuscript, newspaper, and published primary sources. The Michigan League of Women Voters Papers and the Ella Aldinger papers at the Bentley Historical Library in Ann Arbor and the Dorothy Judd Papers in the Michigan and Family History Department at the Grand Rapids Public Library effectively supplement the LWV holdings at the Library of Congress. The papers at the Bentley Library of the local furniture manufacturing Sligh Family were especially valuable, given that Grands Rapids' own Charles Sligh ran for governor in 1924.

The work of Grand Rapids businessmen is extensively documented. The papers of the Grand Rapids Chamber of Commerce are divided between the Bentley Library and the Grand Rapids Public Library. The Chamber records at the Bentley also include the records of the Grand Rapids Civic Roundtable and a run of the Chamber's biweekly newsletter, *The Spectator.* The Chamber records at the Grand Rapids Public Library also contain the holdings of the Grand Rapids Citizens League. Other sources included the Furniture Manufacturers Association Records at the Grand Rapids Public Library; the *Furniture Manufacturer and Artisan,* a manufacturers' trade magazine; and the *Grand Rapids Furniture*

Record, a retailers' industry magazine. The furniture industry was the topic of in-depth study in part 15 of the U.S. Senate Immigration Commission's *Reports of the Immigration Commission* (Washington, D.C.: U.S. Government Printing Office, 1911), also known as the Dillingham Commission report.

Activities of organized labor in Grand Rapids are documented in the *Grand Rapids Observer,* the *Grand Rapids Labor News,* and the papers of the Grand Rapids Typographical Union #39, all at the Grand Rapids Public Library, and the Edward A. Kosten papers and the minutes of the Grand Rapids Trades and Labor Council at the Bentley Library.

A number of community organizations left records relevant to this project at the Grand Rapids Public Library, among them the Grand Rapids Federation of Women's Clubs, the Grand Rapids Rotary Club, the Grand Rapids Woman's Club, and the (African American) Grand Rapids Study Club. Also relevant were the Arthur Vandenberg papers at the Bentley Library; the Russell family papers, the Black History Collection Exhibit, and the Woman's Suffrage Collection at the Grand Rapids Public Library; and the Edith Vosburg Alvord papers in the Burton Historical Collection at the Detroit Public Library in Detroit, Michigan. The *Michigan Bulletin* documents the activities of the Michigan Department of the American Legion and is available at the Legion Library in Indianapolis.

The *Grand Rapids Herald,* the *Grand Rapids Press,* the *Grand Rapids Chronicle,* and the *Echo Tygodniowe* (the *Weekly Echo,* in Polish and English) provide a record of activities in various Grand Rapids communities. Despite the entries in Winifred Gregory's *American Newspapers,* there are no holdings of the *Michigan State News* (an African American paper published in Grands Rapids in the 1920s) or the *Dutch Standard* (the city's Dutch weekly) at the Grands Rapids Public Library. Political party activities are documented in the Michigan Republican Party State Central Committee Records; the *Michigan Citizen,* published by the Michigan Democratic State Central Committee; and the papers of Frank Donald McKay, all at the Bentley Library.

Other Primary Sources

Because the business community was such an important player in the GOTV campaigns, I also found it helpful to examine runs of *Nation's Business,* which was published by the Chamber of Commerce of the United States; the *Open Shop Review,* which was published by the National Founders' Association and National Metal Trades Assocation and was intensely interested in GOTV; the records of the Metropolitan Life Insurance Company at the company library in Manhattan; and Metropolitan Life records in the papers of Lee Kaufer Frankel, a Met Life corporate officer in charge of educational and welfare activities, at the American Jewish Historical Society in Waltham, Mass.

To add breadth and to ascertain that the GOTV campaigns were well publicized and that the changes in political culture I identified were widespread, I examined a wide range of daily newspapers from September through November of the election years of 1924, 1926, and 1928, including the *Los Angeles Times*, the *Richmond Times-Dispatch*, the *Atlanta Constitution*, the *Boston Globe*, the *New York Herald Tribune*, the *Steuben (N.Y.) Courier*, the *Cleveland Plain Dealer*, the *St. Louis Post-Dispatch*, the *Kansas City Star*, the *Emporia (Kans.) Daily Gazette*, the *Denver Post*, the *Los Angeles Times*, and the *San Francisco Chronicle*.

Secondary Sources

Michael McGerr's *The Decline of Popular Politics: The American North, 1865–1928* (New York: Oxford University Press, 1986) served as a stimulating introduction to the Get-Out-the-Vote campaigns. His discussion of GOTV on pages 194–205, the only discussion of the campaigns in the secondary literature, offered important guidance for the early research.

The "new political history" provided essential underpinnings for this study: its analyses of nineteenth-century politics make clear how much in the twentieth century had changed. Crucial works include Joel H. Silbey, *The American Political Nation, 1838–1893* (Stanford: Stanford University Press, 1991); Paul Kleppner et al., eds., *The Evolution of American Electoral Systems* (Westport, Conn.: Greenwood Press, 1981); William Gienapp, *The Origins of the Republican Party, 1852–1856* (New York: Oxford University Press, 1987); Richard L. McCormick, ed., *The Party Period and Public Policy: American Politics from the Age of Jackson to the Progressive Era* (New York: Oxford University Press, 1986); William Chambers and Walter Dean Burnham, eds., *The American Party Systems*, 2nd. ed. (New York: Oxford University Press, 1975); Samuel P. Hays, *American Political History as Social Analysis* (Knoxville: University of Tennessee Press, 1980); Richard L. McCormick, *From Realignment to Reform: Political Change in New York State, 1890–1910* (Ithaca, N.Y.: Cornell University Press, 1981); Allan J. Lichtman, *Prejudice and the Old Politics: The Presidential Election of 1928* (Chapel Hill: University of North Carolina Press, 1979); William Gienapp, "'Politics Seems to Enter into Everything': Political Culture in the North, 1840–1860," in *Essays in American Antebellum Politics, 1840–1860,* eds. Stephen E. Maizlish and John J. Kushma (College Station: Texas A&M University Press, 1982), 14–69; Michael F. Holt, *Forging A Majority: The Formation of the Republican Party in Pittsburgh, 1848–1860* (New Haven: Yale University Press, 1969); and Kenneth J. Winkle, *The Politics of Community: Migration and Politics in Antebellum Ohio* (Cambridge: Cambridge University Press, 1988).

On the centrality of political participation by immigrants, ethnic Americans, and workers in the nineteenth century, see Lee Benson, *The Concept of Jacksonian Democracy: New York as a Test Case* (Princeton: Princeton University Press, 1961); Richard Jensen, *The Winning of the Midwest: Social and Political Conflict, 1888–1896* (Chicago: University of Chicago Press, 1971); Paul Kleppner, *The Third Electoral System, 1853–1892* (Chapel Hill: University of North Carolina Press, 1979); Jean Baker, *Affairs of Party: The Political Culture of Northern Democrats in the Mid-Nineteenth Century* (Ithaca, N.Y.: Cornell University Press, 1983); Joel H. Silbey, "'Let the People See': Reflections on Ethnoreligious Forces in American Politics," in *The Partisan Imperative: The Dynamics of American Politics Before the Civil War* (New York: Oxford University Press, 1985), 69–84; and Richard Oestreicher, "Urban Working-Class Political Behavior and Theories of American Electoral Politics, 1870–1940," *Journal of American History* 74 (May 1988): 1257–86.

Recent work on the history of women and political parties has firmly established that women played important roles in party politics before they were enfranchised. Key works include Rebecca Edwards, *Angels in the Machinery: Gender in American Party Politics from the Civil War to the Progressive Era* (New York: Oxford University Press, 1997); Elizabeth Varon, *We Mean to Be Counted: White Women and Politics in Antebellum Virginia* (Chapel Hill: University of North Carolina Press, 1998); Michael Lewis Goldberg, *An Army of Women: Gender and Politics in Gilded Age Kansas* (Baltimore: The Johns Hopkins University Press, 1997); Melanie Gustafson, *Women and the Republican Party, 1854–1924* (Urbana: University of Illinois Press, 2001), which has an extensive bibliography; Melanie Gustafson, Kristie Miller, and Elisabeth Perry, eds., *We Have Come to Stay: American Women and Political Parties, 1880–1960* (Albuquerque: University of New Mexico Press, 1999); and Jo Freeman, *A Room at a Time: How Women Entered Party Politics* (Lanham, N. Y.: Rowman and Littlefield, 2000). These recent works owe a great debt to earlier work on women in politics and public spaces, especially Paula Baker, *The Moral Frameworks of Public Life: Gender, Politics and the State in Rural*

New York, 1870–1930 (New York: Oxford University Press, 1991) and Mary P. Ryan, *Women in Public: Between Banners and Ballots, 1825–1880* (Baltimore: Johns Hopkins University Press, 1990).

The literature on voter behavior, including turnout, is vast. Peter H. Argersinger and John W. Jeffries provide a historically-minded overview in "American Electoral History: Party Systems and Voting Behavior," in *Structure, Process, and Party: Essays in American Political History,* ed. Peter Argersinger, (London: M. E. Sharpe, Inc., 1992), 3–33. Key works that cover the late nineteenth and early twentieth centuries include Charles E. Merriam and Harold F. Gosnell, *Non-Voting, Causes and Methods of Control* (Chicago: University of Chicago Press, 1924); Harold F. Gosnell, *Getting Out the Vote: An Experiment in the Stimulation of Voting* (Chicago: University of Chicago Press, 1927); Walter Dean Burnham, "The Changing Shape of the American Political Universe" and "The Appearance and Disappearance of the American Voter," in *The Current Crisis in American Politics,* ed. Burnham (New York: Oxford University Press, 1982), 25–57, 121–65; Paul Kleppner, *Who Voted? The Dynamics of Electoral Turnout, 1870–1980* (New York, Praeger Publishers, 1982); John F. Reynolds, *Testing Democracy: Electoral Behavior and Progressive Reform in New Jersey, 1880–1920* (Chapel Hill: University of North Carolina Press, 1988); Sara Alpern and Dale Baum, "Female Ballots: The Impact of the Nineteenth Amendment," *Journal of Interdisciplinary History* 16 (Summer 1985); 43–67; Paul Kleppner, "Were Women to Blame? Female Suffrage and Voter Turnout," *Journal of Interdisciplinary History* 12 (Spring 1982): 621–43; Frances Fox Piven and Richard A. Cloward, *Why Americans Don't Vote* (New York: Pantheon, 1988); Bill Winders, "The Roller Coaster of Class Conflict: Mass Mobilization and Voter Turnout in the U.S., 1840–1996," *Social Forces,* v. 77, no. 3 (1999): 833–60; and Mark Kornbluh, *Why America Stopped Voting: The Decline of Participatory Democracy and the Emergence of Modern American Politics* (New York: New York University Press, 1999).

A few scholars remain skeptical about the accuracy or meaning of the high turnout rates of the nineteenth century and argue either that the numbers reflect widespread fraud or that politics was not necessarily important to people even if they did vote in large numbers. See Philip E. Converse, "Change in the American Electorate" in Angus Campbell and Converse, eds., *The Human Meaning of Social Change* (Beverly Hills: Sage, 1972) and Glenn C. Altschuler and Stuart M. Blumin, *Rude Republic: Americans and Their Politics in the Nineteenth Century* (Princeton: Princeton University Press, 2000). These claims are persuasively refuted in

Walter Dean Burnham, "The Appearance and Disappearance of the American Voter," cited above; Burnham, "Theory and Voting Research," which is also found in *The Current Crisis in American Politics*, 58–91; and Sven Beckert, "Involved Disengagement? Reconsidering the Golden Age of Participatory Democracy," *Reviews in American History* 28 (December 2000): 560–68.

On the topics of enfranchisement and disenfranchisement, key works include Keyssar, *The Right to Vote*; J. Morgan Kousser, *The Shaping of Southern Politics: Suffrage Restriction and the Establishment of the One-Party South, 1880–1910* (New Haven: Yale University Press, 1974); James Kettner, *The Development of American Citizenship, 1608–1870* (Chapel Hill: University of North Carolina Press, 1978); Marchette Chute, *The First Liberty: A History of the Right to Vote in America, 1619–1850* (New York: E. P. Dutton and Company, 1969); Chilton Williamson, *American Suffrage from Property to Democracy, 1760–1860* (Princeton: Princeton University Press, 1960); and Kirk H. Porter, *A History of Suffrage in the United States* (New York: AMS Press, 1971).

The literature on political development makes clear that institutional arrangements are not neutral but encourage, privilege, discourage, or delegitimize particular political outcomes, behaviors, and ideas. Key works include Stephen Skowronek, *Building a New American State: The Expansion of National Administrative Capacities, 1877–1920* (Cambridge: Cambridge University Press, 1982); Peter B. Evans, Dietrich Rueschemeyer, and Theda Skocpol, *Bringing the State Back In* (Cambridge: Cambridge University Press, 1985); James G. March and Johan P. Olsen, *Rediscovering Institutions: The Organizational Basis of Politics* (New York: The Free Press, 1989); Mary Fainsod Katzenstein, *Faithful and Fearless: Moving Feminist Protest Inside the Church and Military* (Princeton: Princeton University Press, 1998); and Suzanne Mettler, *Dividing Citizens: Gender and Federalism in New Deal Public Policy* (Ithaca, N.Y.: Cornell University Press, 1998). On the importance of separate institutions or "free spaces" to the political development of disempowered groups, see Estelle Freedman, "Separatism as Strategy: Female Institution-Building and American Feminism, 1870–1930," *Feminist Studies* 5 (Fall 1979): 512–29; and Sara Evans and Harry Boyte, *Free Spaces: The Sources of Democratic Change in America* (New York, 1986).

The literature on woman suffrage has undergone substantial revision in recent years. Lively debates have emerged over its importance and accomplishments, and its significance for African Americans is just beginning to be recognized. See, for example, Sarah Hunter Graham, *Woman*

Suffrage and the New Democracy (New Haven: Yale University Press, 1996); Kristi Andersen, *After Suffrage: Women in Partisan and Electoral Politics Before the New Deal* (Chicago: University of Chicago Press, 1996); Eileen L. McDonough, "The Gendered American State and Women's Right to Vote: The Nexus of Power Politics and Republican Motherhood in the Progressive Era," in *Going Public: National Histories of Women's Enfranchisement and Women's Participation within State Institutions,* eds. Mary F. Katzenstein and Hege Skjeie (Oslo: Institute for Social Research, 1990), 45–78; Rosalyn Terborg-Penn, *African American Women in the Struggle for the Vote* (Bloomington: Indiana University Press, 1996); Anna L. Harvey, *Votes Without Leverage: Women in American Electoral Politics, 1920–1970* (Cambridge: Cambridge University Press, 1998); Marjorie Spruill Wheeler, *New Women of the New South: The Leaders of the Woman Suffrage Movement in the Southern States* (New York: Oxford University Press, 1993); Ellen Carol DuBois, *Harriot Stanton Blatch and the Winning of Woman Suffrage* (New Haven: Yale University Press, 1997); Ann D. Gordon, Bettye Collier-Thomas, John H. Bracey, and Joyce Avrech Berkman, eds., *African American Women and the Vote, 1837–1965* (Amherst: University of Massachusetts Press, 1997); and Jean H. Baker, ed., *Votes for Women: The Struggle for Suffrage Revisited* (New York: Oxford University Press, 2002). These works still build on the legacies left by Eleanor Flexner, *Century of Struggle: The Woman's Rights Movement in the United States* (New York: Atheneum, 1970) and Aileen Kraditor, *Ideas of the Woman Suffrage Movement* (New York: Columbia University Press, 1965).

Citizenship is likewise a vibrant field. This study was shaped by T. H. Marshall, *Class, Citizenship, and Social Development* (Garden City, N.J.: Doubleday and Company, Inc., 1964); Michael Walzer's discussion of "belongingness" in *Spheres of Justice: A Defense of Pluralism and Equality* (New York: Basic Books, 1983), 105–6; Robert H. Wiebe, *Self-Rule: A Cultural History of American Democracy* (Chicago: University of Chicago Press, 1995); Michael Schudson, *The Good Citizen: A History of American Civic Life* (New York: The Free Press, 1998); Robert D. Putnam, "Bowling Alone: America's Declining Social Capital," *Journal of Democracy* 6 (January 1995): 65–78; Theda Skocpol, *Diminished Democracy: From Membership to Management in American Civic Life* (Norman: University of Oklahoma Press, 2003); Judith Shklar, *American Citizenship: The Quest for Inclusion* (Cambridge: Harvard University Press, 1991); Rogers M. Smith, *Civic Ideals: Conflicting Visions of Citizenship in U.S. History* (New Haven: Yale University Press, 1997); Linda Kerber, *No Constitutional Right to Be Ladies: Women and the Obligations of Citizenship* (New York:

Hill and Wang, 1998); Bessie Louise Pierce, *Citizen's Organizations and the Civic Training of Youth* (Chicago: Charles Scribner's Sons, 1933); and Richard Brown, *The Strength of a People: The Notion of an Informed Citizenry in America, 1789–1850* (Chapel Hill: University of North Carolina Press, 1996). Gary Gerstle's *American Crucible: Race and Nation in the Twentieth Century* (Princeton: Princeton University Press, 2001), 81–127, offers a useful account of Americanization efforts in the 1920s. My "Delegitimizing Democracy: 'Civic Slackers,' the Cultural Turn, and the Possibilities of Politics," *Journal of American History* 89 (Dec. 2002): 922–57, explores representations of good and bad citizenship in the early twentieth-century U.S.

On increasing class stratification in the mid-nineteenth century, see Stuart M. Blumin, *The Emergence of the Middle Class: Social Experience in the American City, 1760–1900* (Cambridge: Cambridge University Press, 1989); Sam Bass Warner, *The Private City: Philadelphia in Three Periods of Its Growth* (Philadelphia: University of Pennsylvania Press, 1968) and *Streetcar Suburbs: The Process of Growth in Boston, 1870–1900* (Cambridge: Harvard University Press, 1962); and Lawrence W. Levine, *Highbrow/Lowbrow: The Emergence of Cultural Hierarchy in America* (Cambridge: Harvard University Press, 1988).

The literature on the 1910s and 1920s is immense. For an introduction to some of the key issues, see Nancy F. Cott, *The Grounding of Modern Feminism* (New Haven, Yale University Press, 1987); Elisabeth S. Clemens, *The People's Lobby: Organizational Innovation and the Rise of Interest Group Politics in the United States, 1890–1925* (Chicago: University of Chicago Press, 1997); Roland Marchand, *Advertising the American Dream: Making Way for Modernity, 1920–1940* (Berkeley: University of California Press, 1985); Robert S. Lynd and Helen Merrell Lynd, *Middletown: A Study in American Culture* (New York: Harcourt, Brace and Company, 1925); and Glenda Gilmore, *Gender and Jim Crow: Women and the Politics of White Supremacy in North Carolina, 1896–1920* (Chapel Hill: University of North Carolina Press, 1996). Still important are Richard Hofstadter, *The Age of Reform from Bryan to F.D.R.* (New York: Knopf, 1955); Robert H. Wiebe, *The Search for Order, 1877–1920* (New York: Hill and Wang, 1967); and John Higham, *Strangers in the Land: Patterns of American Nativism, 1860–1925* (New York: Atheneum, 1963), 194–330.

On the activities of clubwomen and businessmen in the late nineteenth and early twentieth centuries, see J. Stanley Lemons, *The Woman Citizen: Social Feminism in the 1920s* (1973; reprint, Charlottesville: University Press of Virginia, 1990); Robyn Muncy, *Creating a Female Do-*

minion in *American Reform, 1890–1935* (New York: Oxford University Press, 1991); Evelyn Brooks Higginbotham, *Righteous Discontent: The Women's Movement in the Black Baptist Church, 1880–1920* (Cambridge: Harvard University Press, 1993); Anne Firor Scott, *The Southern Lady: From Pedestal to Politics, 1830–1930* (Chicago: University of Chicago Press, 1970); Anne Firor Scott, *Natural Allies: Women's Associations in American History* (Urbana: University of Illinois Press, 1991); Robert H. Wiebe, *Businessmen and Reform: A Study of the Progressive Movement* (Cambridge: Harvard University Press, 1962); Paul W. Glad, "Progressivism and the Business Culture of the 1920s," *Journal of American History* 53 (June 1966): 75–89; Deborah Gray White, *Too Heavy a Load: Black Women in Defense of Themselves* (New York: W. W. Norton, 1999); Alan Trachtenburg, *The Incorporation of America: Culture and Society in the Gilded Age* (New York: Hill and Wang, 1982); and Cynthia Neverdon-Morton, *Afro-American Women of the South and the Advancement of the Race, 1895–1925* (Knoxville: University of Tennessee Press, 1989).

Among the wealth of works on the shift to a consumer economy and culture, see Richard Wightman Fox and T. J. Jackson Lears, eds., *The Culture of Consumption: Critical Essays in American History, 1880–1980* (New York: Pantheon Books, 1983) and *The Power of Culture: Critical Essays in American History* (Chicago: University of Chicago Press, 1993), especially Lizabeth Cohen's "The Class Experience of Mass Consumption: Workers as Consumers in Interwar America," 135–60. Also useful are John Brewer and Roy Porter, eds. *Consumption and the World of Goods* (London: Routledge, 1993), especially Jean-Christophe Agnew's essay, "Coming Up for Air: Consumer Culture in Historical Perspective," 19–39; Stuart W. Ewen, *All Consuming Images: The Politics of Style in Contemporary Culture* (New York: Basic Books, Inc., 1988); Gary Cross, *An All-Consuming Century: Why Commercialism Won in Modern America* (New York: Columbia University Press, 2000); Ronald R. Kline, *Consumers in the Country: Technology and Social Change in Rural America* (Baltimore: Johns Hopkins University Press, 2000); Warren I. Susman, *Culture as History: The Transformation of American Society in the Twentieth Century* (New York: Pantheon Books, 1984), 105–229; Susan Strasser, Charles McGovern, and Matthias Judt, eds., *Getting and Spending: European and American Consumer Societies in the Twentieth Century* (Cambridge: Cambridge University Press, 1998); Lary May, *Screening Out the Past: The Birth of Mass Culture and the Motion Picture Industry* (New York: Oxford University Press, 1980); Victoria de Grazia, ed., *The Sex of Things: Gender and Consumption in Historical Perspective* (Berkeley: University of

California Press, 1996); and Jennifer Scanlon, *Inarticulate Longings: The "Ladies' Home Journal," Gender, and the Promises of Consumer Culture* (London: Routledge, 1996). On the uneven prosperity of the decade, see Irving Bernstein, *The Lean Years: A History of the American Worker, 1920–1933* (Boston: Houghton Mifflin Company, 1960).

On advertisers and advertising, besides Marchand's *Advertising the American Dream*, see Jackson Lears, *Fables of Abundance: A Cultural History of Advertising in America* (New York: Basic Books, 1994); Stuart W. Ewen, *Captains of Consciousness: Advertising and the Social Roots of the Consumer Culture* (New York: McGraw-Hill Book Company, 1976); Otis Pease, *The Responsibilities of American Advertising: Private Control and Public Influence, 1920–1940* (New Haven: Yale University Press, 1958); and James D. Norris, *Advertising and the Transformation of American Society, 1865–1920* (New York: Greenwood Press, 1990). On department stores, see Susan Porter Benson, *Counter Cultures: Saleswomen, Managers, and Customers in American Department Stores, 1890–1940* (Urbana: University of Illinois Press, 1986); and William Leach, *Land of Desire: Merchants, Power and the Rise of a New American Culture* (New York: Pantheon Books, 1993).

Works that explore relationships between politics and consumer culture include Lizabeth Cohen, *Making a New Deal: Industrial Workers in Chicago, 1919–1939* (New York: Cambridge University Press, 1990) and *A Consumers' Republic: The Politics of Mass Consumption in Postwar America* (New York: Alfred A. Knopf, 2003); Ronald Edsforth, *Class Conflict and Cultural Consensus: The Making of a Mass Consumer Society in Flint, Michigan* (New Brunswick: Rutgers University Press, 1987); Robert Westbrook, "Politics as Consumption: Managing the Modern Election," in *The Culture of Consumption*, 143–73; Elisabeth Israels Perry, *Belle Moskowitz: Feminine Politics and the Exercise of Power in the Age of Alfred E. Smith* (New York: Oxford University Press, 1987); Margaret Finnegan, *Selling Suffrage: Consumer Culture and Votes for Women* (New York: Columbia University Press, 1999); John A. Morello, *Selling the President, 1920: Albert D. Lasker, Advertising, and the Election of Warren G. Harding* (Westport, Conn.: Praeger Publishers, 2001); Terry Hynes, "Media Manipulation and Political Campaigns: Bruce Barton and the Presidential Elections of the Jazz Age," *Journalism History* 4 (Autumn 1977): 93–98; Robert L. Bishop, "Bruce Barton: Presidential Stage Manager," *Journalism Quarterly* 42 (Spring 1966): 85–89; and Richard Jensen, "Armies, Admen, and Crusaders: Types of Presidential Election Campaigns," *History Teacher* 2 (1969): 33–50.

My understanding of political culture has been especially influenced by Michael McGerr, *The Decline of Popular Politics;* Ronald Formisano, *The Transformation of Political Culture: Massachusetts Parties, 1827–1861* (New York: Oxford University Press, 1983); Formisano, "The Concept of Political Culture," *Journal of Interdisciplinary History* 31 (Winter 2001): 393–426; Baker, *Affairs of Party;* Gabriel Almond and Sidney Verba, *The Civic Culture: Political Attitudes and Democracy in Five Nations* (Princeton: Princeton University Press, 1963); and Clifford Geertz, "Ideology as a Cultural System," in *The Interpretation of Cultures: Selected Essays* (New York: Basic Books, 1973).

GOTV groups wielded power in the public sphere in many ways. On the public sphere, see Nancy Fraser, "Rethinking the Public Sphere: A Contribution to the Critique of Actually Existing Democracy," *Social Text* 25/26 (1991): 56–80; Jürgen Habermas, *The Structural Transformation of the Public Sphere: An Inquiry into a Category of Bourgeois Society,* trans. Thomas Burger (Cambridge: MIT Press, 1991); Thomas Bender, "Wholes and Parts: The Need for Synthesis in American History," *Journal of American History* 73 (June 1986): 120–36, and reactions by Nell Irvin Painter, Richard Wightman Fox, and Roy Rosenzweig, *Journal of American History* 74 (June 1987): 109–30.

On power and dominance, see John Gaventa, *Power and Powerlessness: Quiescence and Rebellion in an Appalachian Valley* (Oxford: Clarendon Press, 1980); Elizabeth Kamarck Minnich, *Transforming Knowledge* (Philadelphia: Temple University Press, 1990); Guy Debord, *The Society of the Spectacle* (New York: Zone Books, 1994); James C. Scott, *Weapons of the Weak: Everyday Forms of Peasant Resistance* (New Haven: Yale University Press, 1985); James C. Scott, *Domination and the Arts of Resistance: Hidden Transcripts* (New Haven: Yale University Press, 1990); Michel Foucault, *The History of Sexuality,* trans. Robert Hurley, Vintage Books ed., vol. 1 (New York: Random House, 1980); Louis Althusser, "Ideology and Ideological State Apparatuses," in *Lenin and Philosophy and Other Essays,* trans. Ben Brewster (London: New Left Books, 1971), 121–73; Joseph Gusfield, *The Culture of Public Problems: Drinking-Driving and the Symbolic Order* (Chicago: University of Chicago Press, 1981); Michel de Certeau, *The Practice of Everyday Life,* trans. Steven Rendell (Berkeley: University of California Press, 1984); Quintin Hoare and Geoffrey Nowell, eds. and trans., *Selections from the Prison Notebooks of Antonio Gramsci* (New York: International Publishers, 1972); Aida Hurtado, "Relating to Privilege: Seduction and Rejection in the Subordination of White Women and Women of Color," in *Theorizing Feminism: Parallel Trends in* the Humanities and Social Sciences, eds. Anne C. Herrmann and Abigail J. Stewart (Boulder: Westview Press, 1994), 136–54; and Steven Lukes, ed., Power (Oxford: Basil Blackwell, 1986).

Crucial to the GOTV groups' project of creating civic hierarchy was the project of demarcating gender, class, ethnic, and racial difference. See Edward W. Said, Orientalism (New York: Pantheon Books, 1978); Joan Wallach Scott, "Gender: A Useful Category of Historical Analysis," American Historical Review 91 (December 1986): 1053–75; Seyla Benhabib, ed., Democracy and Difference: Contesting the Boundaries of the Political (Princeton: Princeton University Press, 1996); Martha Minow, Making All the Difference: Inclusion, Exclusion, and American Law (Ithaca, N.Y.: Cornell University Press, 1990); George Lipsitz, Time Passages: Collective Memory and American Popular Culture (Minneapolis: University of Minnesota Press, 1990); Evelyn Brooks Higginbotham, "African-American Women's History and the Metalanguage of Race," Signs 17 (Winter 1992): 251–74; Henry Louis Gates Jr., ed., "Race," Writing, and Difference (Chicago: University of Chicago Press, 1986); Michael Omi and Howard Winant, Racial Formation in the United States From the 1960s to the 1990s, 2nd ed. (New York: Routledge, 1994); and Lauren Berlant, The Queen of America Goes to Washington City: Essays on Sex and Citizenship (Durham: Duke University Press, 1997).

Institutional histories of GOTV groups include Louise Young, In the Public Interest: The League of Women Voters, 1920–1970 (Westport, Conn.: Greenwood Press, 1989); Marguerite Green, The National Civic Federation and the American Labor Movement, 1900–1925 (Washington, D.C.: Catholic University of America Press, 1956); Richard W. Gable, "A Political Analysis of an Employers' Association: The National Association of Manufacturers" (Ph.D. diss., University of Chicago, 1950); Raymond Moley Jr., The American Legion Story (New York: Duell, Sloan and Pearce, 1966); Dorothy Culp, "The American Legion: A Study in Pressure Politics" (Ph.D. diss., University of Chicago, 1939); Ruth Evelyn Kern, "The Political Policy and Activities of the American Legion, 1919–1925" (Master's thesis, University of California, Berkeley, 1934); William Pencak, For God and Country: The American Legion, 1919–1941 (Boston: Northeastern University Press, 1989); and Thomas A. Rumer, The American Legion: An Official History (New York: M. Evans and Company, 1990).

New York politics in the early twentieth century is explored in Roy V. Peel, The Political Clubs of New York City (New York: G. P. Putnam's Sons, 1935); Theodore Lowi, At the Pleasure of the Mayor: Patronage and Power in New York City, 1898–1953 (London: The Free Press, 1964); Jerome

Krase and Charles La Cerra, *Ethnicity and Machine Politics* (New York: University Press of America, 1991), which uses New York as a case study; Robert F. Wesser, *A Response to Progressivism: The Democratic Party and New York Politics, 1902–1918* (New York: New York University Press, 1986); Edwin R. Lewison, *Black Politics in New York City* (New York: Twayne, 1974); Stephen P. Erie, *Rainbow's End: Irish Americans and the Dilemmas of Urban Machine Politics, 1840–1985* (Berkeley: University of California Press, 1988); and Chris McNickle, *To Be Mayor of New York: Ethnic Politics in the City* (New York: Columbia University Press, 1993). On Legion activities in New York, see Clarence R. Smith, comp. and ed., *The American Legion in New York State: A History of the Department of New York for the Years 1919–1939* (New York: The American Legion, Department of New York, 1942). On LWV activities in New York, see Hilda G. Watrous, *In League with Eleanor: Eleanor Roosevelt and the League of Women Voters, 1921–1962* (New York: Foundation for Citizen Education, 1984).

On principals and organizations involved in GOTV in Birmingham, see Mark Cowett, *Birmingham's Rabbi: Morris Newfield and Alabama, 1895–1940* (Tuscaloosa: University of Alabama Press, 1986); Thomas M. Owen, comp., *The Alabama Department of the American Legion, 1919–1929* (Montgomery: Alabama Department of Archives and History, 1929); and Mary Swenson Miller, "Lobbyist for the People: The League of Women Voters of Alabama, 1920–1975," (M.A. thesis, Auburn University, 1978). On Alabama suffragists, many of whom became interested in GOTV, see Gillian Goodrich, "Romance and Reality: The Birmingham Suffragists, 1892–1920," *Journal of the Birmingham Historical Society* 5 (January 1978): 4–21.

On Birmingham workers, see Robin D. G. Kelley, *Hammer and Hoe: Alabama Communists During the Great Depression* (Chapel Hill: University of North Carolina Press, 1990). On one ethnic community in Birmingham, see Frank Joseph Fede, *Italians in the Deep South: Their Impact on Birmingham and the American Heritage* (Montgomery: The Black Belt Press, 1994). On Birmingham's African American community, see Wilson Fallin Jr., *The African-American Church in Birmingham, 1815–1963: A Shelter in the Storm* (New York: Garland Publishing, 1997).

For background on politics in Alabama, Birmingham, and the South, see Carl V. Harris, *Political Power in Birmingham, 1871–1921* (Knoxville: University of Tennessee Press, 1977); Blaine A. Brownell, "Birmingham, Alabama: New South City in the 1920s," *Journal of Southern History* 38 (February 1974): 21–48; Wyn Craig Wade, *The Fiery Cross: The Ku Klux Klan in America* (New York: Simon and Schuster, 1987); Sheldon Hackney, *Populism to Progressivism in Alabama* (Princeton: Princeton University Press, 1969); and William A. Link, *The Changing Face of Southern Progressivism: Social Policy and Localism, 1880–1930* (Chapel Hill: University of North Carolina Press, 1992).

Background on some of the GOTV groups in Grand Rapids can be found in Blanche Blynn Maw, comp. and Edith V. Alvord, ed., *A History of the Michigan State Federation of Women's Clubs, 1895–1953* (Ann Arbor, Mich.: Ann Arbor Press, 1953); the League of Women Voters of Grand Rapids, *The First Fifty Years, 1921–1971* (Grand Rapids: Grand Rapids League of Women Voters, 1972); and Frank L. Dykema, "A Record of the Development of the Grand Rapids Americanization Society's Plan of Citizenship Training Through the Ballot," *Michigan History Magazine,* vol. 6, no. 2 (1922): 160–74. On the woman suffragists of Grand Rapids, many of whom went on to become involved in GOTV, see Karolena M. Fox, "History of the Equal Suffrage Movement in Michigan," *Michigan History Magazine* 2 (January 1918): 90–109; and Ruth E. Hoogland's unpublished paper, "Petticoats, Politics, and Public Opinion: A Study of the Woman Suffrage Movement in Michigan, with Emphasis on Grand Rapids from 1910–1920," 1975, available at the Grand Rapids Public Library.

On the African American, ethnic, and working class communities in Grand Rapids, see Jeffrey Kleiman, "The Great Strike: Religion, Labor and Reform in Grand Rapids, Michigan, 1890–1916" (Ph.D. diss., Michigan State University, 1985); David G. Vanderstel, "The Dutch of Grand Rapids, Michigan 1848–1900: Immigrant Neighborhoods and Community Development in a Nineteenth-Century City" (Ph.D. thesis, Kent State University, 1983); and the very helpful unpublished paper by R. Maurice Moss, "Grand Rapids Social Survey of the Negro Population," [c. 1928], produced for the National Urban League and available at the Grand Rapids Public Library.

For background on Michigan politics, see Arthur Chester Millspaugh, *Party Organization and Machinery in Michigan Since 1890* (Baltimore: Johns Hopkins University Press, 1917), which also includes a good discussion of voter turnout; Samuel J. Eldersveld, "A Study of Urban Electoral Trends in Michigan, 1920–1940" (Ph.D. diss., University of Michigan, 1946); and Stephen B. Sarasohn and Vera H. Sarasohn, *Party Politics in Michigan* (Detroit: Wayne State University Press, 1957).

INDEX